THE
NEW CREATION
MODEL

A Paradigm for Discovering
God's Restoration Purposes from
Creation to New Creation

MICHAEL J. VLACH

Theological Studies Press
Cary, NC

Vlach, Michael, 1966 –

The New Creation Model / Michael J. Vlach

Paperback ISBN: 978-0-9798539-5-1
Hardcover ISBN: 978-0-9798539-6-8
Ebook ISBN: 978-0-9798539-7-5

Printed in the United States of America

All Scripture quotations, unless otherwise indicated, are taken from the New American Standard Bible®, Copyright © 1960, 1962, 1963, 1968, 1971, 1972, 1973, 1975, 1977, 1995 by the Lockman Foundation. Used by permission (www.Lockman.org).

Cover image: "View of the sea surf through a photographic lens lying on a sandy beach on a sunny day," by Alexey

Cover and text design: Amy Cole, JPL Design Solutions

Printed in the United States of America

◆

This is dedicated to my partners in working
through the specifics of the New Creation Model—
my wife Holly and my children Kyra, Colin, Colby, and Carlee.
This book summarizes the things we have
talked about for years.

◆

CONTENTS

◆

CHARTS

PREFACE

◆

Is our understanding of what God is accomplishing through Jesus big enough?

Daniel Block notes that "Christians often view the world and the Scriptures from an anthropocentric [man-centered] perspective—as if human beings are the center of the universe and everything exists for them." But in reality, "God has been engaged in a project that is vastly greater than the human population."[1]

Block seems to be on to something here. Christians often focus on personal redemption from sin and principles for living a godly life, which certainly are important and needed. But what if God's saving and restoring purposes are bigger than we thought? What if God's plans are more than individual and spiritual? What if they involve the restoration of earth, land, animals, nations, society, culture, friendships, homes, farms, agriculture, and many other areas? What if the coming "restoration of all things" in Jesus (Acts 3:21) actually extends to everything?[2] How would this change your perspective on life and the future if it were true?

To answer these questions, this book focuses on God's purposes through the lens of two models that believers have operated from in history—the New Creation Model and the Spiritual Vision Model. These two models represent contrasting paradigms concerning the nature of reality and eternal life. They address God's workings in history from Genesis 1 through Revelation 22. The ideas behind each model have influenced how Christians have understood the Bible's storyline and the nature of eternal

---

1   Daniel I. Block, *Covenant: The Framework of God's Grand Plan of Redemption* (Grand Rapids: Baker Academic, 2021), 13. He specifically refers to Genesis 1 here.

2   By "everything" we mean all aspects of creation, not the salvation of every individual.

1

life. The Spiritual Vision Model emphasizes individual and spiritual issues, and a spiritual existence in Heaven apart from earth and anything related to our current experiences.

But the New Creation Model asserts that in addition to the individual and spiritual, God is working to restore every area of creation. And eternal life is embodied existence on a restored earth where God's people live and thrive in His presence and experience vibrant social and cultural interactions with each other. This life is not a divorce from everything we experience now on earth. It is life in which our relationships and experiences are free from all taints of sin and the curse. This is the abundant life God created for us, not a transporting to a purely spiritual realm of existence. The destiny of God's people is related to how God structured them and the realm they were placed in at creation.

For over fifteen years I have addressed these two models and their implications in a seminary classroom context. But I now explain them in print for a broader audience. I also offer a robust argument for the New Creation Model as the proper perspective for viewing God's multi-dimensional purposes. The New Creation Model implores Christians to consider all of God's creation, kingdom, and covenant purposes, including the relevance of earth, land, nations, culture, economics, agriculture, natural resources, animal realm, inanimate creation (trees, fields), social-political realities, technology, and anything involving our environment.

These models are not just academic issues. They are practical. Not only do they address what God is doing in history, they help us understand our place in God's Story. And they relate to our hope in Jesus.

Grasping New Creation Model truths from Scripture is profitable and exciting. What God has planned for us and for all creation makes all our current sorrows pale in comparison. Paul stated, "For I consider that the sufferings of this present time are not worthy to be compared with the glory that is to be revealed to us" (Rom. 8:18). Much of what this "glory" is about has been revealed to us in the pages of Scripture—more than what often has been considered.

This book intends to be informative concerning how Christians have viewed God's creation and new creation purposes. It also is a challenge to examine our assumptions of Gods' plans to make sure they are consistently scriptural and free from unbiblical philosophies. We also should embrace and be encouraged by all God is accomplishing in Jesus and share this hope with others. But foremost, we should glorify God for the great things He is doing with His creation. As Revelation 4:11 states:

"You are worthy, our Lord and God,
   to receive glory and honor and power,
For you created all things,
   and by your will they were created
   and have their being" (NIV).

—Michael J. Vlach
St. Patrick's Day,
March 17, 2023

INTRODUCTION

"In the past couple of decades, many theologians have come to embrace what I call New Creation Eschatology. New Creation Eschatology believes that the eternal state is not a heavenly, timeless, non-material reality but a new heavens and new earth, such as in Isaiah 65, 2 Peter 3:13, and Revelation 21 and 22. The dwelling place of the redeemed in that new creation is not in heaven but on the new earth."

—Craig A. Blaising[1]

◆

What are God's creation purposes and what is the nature of eternal life? This book addresses these important issues through the lens of two theological models—the New Creation Model (NCM) and the Spiritual Vision Model (SVM). The wording of these models was coined by Craig Blaising in the book, *Three Views on the Millennium and Beyond.*[2] But the concepts behind them are well established in history. We will discuss these models in detail, but I first want to share a personal story about how these models have affected me.

I was born in Omaha, Nebraska in the late 1960s and was a child of the 70s. I was the youngest of six kids. Dad immigrated to the U.S. from Czechoslovakia and lived in Indiana. After serving in the Air Force he started his own photography business. Mom was from a big Irish family

---

1   Craig A. Blaising, "A Critique of Gentry and Wellum's, *Kingdom Through Covenant*: A Hermeneutical-Theological Response," *Master's Seminary Journal* 26.1 (Spring 2015): 122.

2   Craig A. Blaising, "Premillennialism," in *Three Views on the Millennium and Beyond: Three Views*, ed. Darrell L. Bock (Grand Rapids: Zondervan, 1999), 155–226.

in Chicago. Mom and Dad married and settled in Omaha, where the six of us kids grew up. We were a middle-class family living in the Midwest during what seemed to be simpler times. My early years were full of fun. There was little league baseball in the summer, watching Nebraska football games in the Fall, and mischievous exploring of the neighborhood with my friends. These were childhood wonder years for me. My father's sickness and death when I was 14–15 years old brought an end to this era, but I look back on that earlier time fondly.

As for my religious upbringing, both Mom and Dad came from generations of Roman Catholicism. I attended a Roman Catholic grade school where I was an altar boy, and then went to a Catholic high school. Consistent with Catholic theology, my religious views of eternity were very spiritual. I thought the purpose of life was to be a good person, follow what the church taught, and then someday live in Heaven forever, which would be a spiritual existence in another realm.

Around age 11, I was in the kitchen and asked Mom what she thought Heaven would be like. She said, "Heaven is where we will live in God's light forever and have great joy that is indescribable." What I picked up as a boy then was that Heaven would be a spiritual experience. Nothing of earth or anything tangible would be there. Activities like eating, playing, and working would be long gone. We would only think about spiritual things. Time would not exist. Heaven would be an out-of-this-world experience far removed from anything we encounter now. This was not something I longed for, but I figured I would be okay with it when that day arrived. And it certainly was better than being in hell.[3]

My ideas were not unique. Most people I knew thought like I did. And the surrounding culture affirmed these perceptions of Heaven.

---

3   Howard A. Snyder admits similar thinking: "Even as a young Christian, I felt vaguely dissatisfied with the promised afterlife we celebrated in church. Salvation was all about going to heaven. Heaven was the truly ultimate thing. Yet descriptions of 'heaven' seemed static, bland, and colorless compared to the beautiful world around me." Howard A. Snyder with Joel Scandrett, *Salvation Means Creation Healed: The Ecology of Sin and Grace: Overcoming the Divorce Between Earth and Heaven* (Eugene, OR: Cascade, 2011), ix. We also have heard many others with similar testimonies.

Television shows, commercials, movies, and cartoons all presented Heaven as a wispy spiritual experience in the sky. Movies like *Heaven Can Wait* pictured the afterlife as people walking around in the clouds. In the newspaper cartoons, Saint Peter was standing at the "pearly gates" of Heaven with clouds in the background letting people know if they could enter. With Saturday morning cartoons on television, characters who died were depicted as ghost-like figures on a cloud with wings and a halo. So it is no surprise that my concept of Heaven was only spiritual. It was part of the culture and my religious upbringing. Although not aware of the concept yet, a "Spiritual Vision Model" deeply permeated my thoughts. I may not have been aware of this model, but it dominated my thinking.

So even before studying the Bible I possessed a strong presupposition that God's purposes were spiritual and non-material. All things involving earth or physical matters were lesser and would disappear. Later, I learned that such assumptions were linked with ideas from the philosopher, Plato, and theologians like Thomas Aquinas. In fact, what my mother described about Heaven being a realm of light apart from earth was much like the empyrean (light-filled) heaven idea taught by Aquinas and presented in Dante's famous *Paradiso* (which we will discuss later).

During my father's illness and shortly before his death, I trusted in Jesus as my Savior (as did Dad, Mom, and my siblings). I attended an evangelical church and studied the Bible seriously. I learned much about God, Jesus, sin, salvation, and Christian living. These were exciting days and I learned much. Yet my Spiritual Vision Model assumptions about God's big-picture purposes and eternity largely remained the same. I still viewed God's plans as primarily individual and spiritual. Salvation was all about living in Heaven forever after this life was over. I heard much about being placed on God's heavenly trophy shelf. I also remember a church choir director state that someday we will join the heavenly choir in Heaven. I imagined myself in a long choir robe singing in a never-ending church service in the sky.

One of my favorite songs back then (and still is) was *The Old Rugged Cross*. One line says, "Then he'll call me someday to my home far away, Where his glory forever I'll share." Songs like this reaffirmed that our future home was forever "far away." At funerals I heard we would join our departed loved ones in Heaven forever. And those who died reached their final destination. Once in Heaven, no person would ever want to return to earth.

In short, I adopted an evangelical view of salvation, which was important, but my ideas concerning God's big-picture purposes and eternity remained the same. Talks about the future were vague. I was taught the earth must be annihilated. God's people in eternity would be a generic humanity with no distinctions. The idea of animals existing in Heaven was not even considered. I did not think much about God's plans for earth, land, animals, culture, society, or nature. I did not consider how God was moving in history with nations, Israel, and ethnic groups. I had no idea what the Day of the Lord was about. I thought the kingdom of God was only about salvation, or God's reign in my heart, or the church.

In my twenties I studied the Bible and theology more. I learned that God's plans included the earth, Israel, and nations. Jesus' second coming meant a return to earth where Jesus would reign over nations. I read *Things to Come* by J. Dwight Pentecost. This book introduced me to specific discussion of the biblical covenants—Noahic, Abrahamic, Mosaic, Davidic, and New. I discovered that these covenants addressed salvation from sin, but they also discussed the earth, Israel, land, geo-political nations, and other areas.

Also significant was Alva J. McClain's book, *The Greatness of the Kingdom*. McClain argued that a kingdom reign of the Messiah over all creation is the primary theme of Scripture. Salvation in Jesus involves redemption of individuals *and* restoration of the created order. Jesus will transform culture, society, and the political realm. And He will fulfill God's mandate for man to rule and subdue the earth (see Gen. 1:26–28). Also, McClain noted that the influence of Plato often directed Christians away from a holistic understanding of God's purposes. McClain addressed how Plato's influence on the church often suffocated the multi-dimensional hope of Jesus' coming kingdom that is presented in Scripture.

I attended seminary in Southern California in the mid-1990s. At that time, I read Robert Saucy's book, *The Case for Progressive Dispensationalism*.

Saucy promoted a holistic view of the kingdom and biblical covenants, noting their spiritual and material elements. He also addressed nations and the role of Israel to the nations. I also learned about God's multi-dimensional purposes in my Bible Survey and Theology classes. Theological dots were connecting in my mind.

Craig Blaising's chapter on "Premillennialism" in the 1999 book, *Three Views on the Millennium and Beyond* was particularly helpful. Blaising explicitly explained the New Creation and Spiritual Vision models and how these models influenced church history. Much of what I write attempts to build upon the two models Blaising discussed.[4]

Other works were also helpful. Anthony Hoekema's, *Created in God's Image*, addressed specifics of what society and culture could be like on the coming new earth. Randy Alcorn's popular book, *Heaven* (2004), described how the destiny of believers involves a tangible restored earth with nations, fellowship, and culture. While not using the designations, "New Creation Model" and "Spiritual Vision Model," Alcorn discussed the concepts of these models.[5] His approach is consistent with a New Creation Model view of eternity. And he critiqued "Christoplatonism," a form of the Spiritual Vision Model, which is the merger of Christianity with the highly spiritual ideas of Plato.

My journey from a Spiritual Vision Model perspective to the New Creation Model took time. It was a gradual paradigm shift. Yet I came far from my earlier understandings of God's purposes. What God was accomplishing through Jesus was much bigger than I originally thought. I went from viewing God's purposes as solely spiritual and individual to realizing they are holistic and multi-dimensional. For years I taught these ideas at the seminary level and now I put them in writing.

The reader should note I am not offering a new theological system. Nor am I saying every person must explicitly and only identify as a "new

---

4   I am not saying Blaising or anyone we quote will agree with everything said in this book.

5   We are not saying Alcorn uses the exact titles of these models or that he agrees with everything stated in our book.

creationist." But I do think studying these models can help sharpen our views of God's purposes no matter what system one identifies with. What matters is what is true and biblical. If a New Creation Model understanding of God's purposes is accurate, it must naturally arise from Scripture. The Bible presents an all-encompassing, comprehensive view of God's creation, kingdom, and covenant purposes. The more we understand these the better we can grasp what God is doing and our place in His story.

There are five parts of this book. The first three are the heart of the book. Part 1 is an Introduction to the two models and why they matter. Part 2 explains the New Creation and Spiritual Vision models in detail. Part 3 discusses the two models in church history. Parts 4 and 5 are more academic as they discuss how various millennial views and theological systems relate to the models. The Conclusion discusses what the New Creation Model should mean for Christians going forward.

PART ONE

INTRODUCTION TO THE MODELS

NEW CREATION
LANGUAGE
IN SCRIPTURE

"Behold, I will do something new."

—Isaiah 43:19

◆

Soon we will discuss specifics about the New Creation Model, but first we note specific "new creation" language in the Bible. This will be the basis for the ideas associated with the New Creation Model.

All creation has suffered greatly since the Fall of Genesis 3. Death, curse, disease, moral evil, natural catastrophes, and other negative realities are a regular part of our existence. The devastation and sorrow of a fallen world are pervasive and immense. Despair often results and one might wonder if this situation will ever change.

But hope abounds. Even with man's great failure in the garden, Genesis 3:15 foretold a coming seed of the woman who will defeat evil and reverse the curse. With Genesis 5:28–29, Lamech hoped for a descendant who would remove the curse over the ground. Genesis 49:8–12 declared that a coming messianic figure ("Shiloh") would rule the world and bring prosperity to earth. With Isaiah 43:19 the Lord declared, "Behold, I will do something new." This "something new" will transform the current fallen situation in every way. And it is at the heart of the New Creation Model.

"New Creation Model" wording comes from new creation language and terms in the Bible. Sometimes we see the specific designation "new creation" in Scripture, and other times we see words that express new creation ideas. "New creation" language is linked with three related areas where a transformation occurs:

1.   the new situation for a *person* in Jesus
2.   the new situation for the *community* in Jesus
3.   the new situation for *the created order* because of Jesus

Jesus eventually brings a new situation to all three realms. The first two have particular relevance for the present as a result of Jesus' first coming. Fulfillment with the third—the created order—awaits Jesus' second coming and kingdom, although concern and care for creation should occur now as well.

A NEW PERSON IN CHRIST

New creation wording applies to the individual person in union with Christ. Second Corinthians 5:17 states, "Therefore, if anyone is in Christ, the new creation has come: The old has gone, the new is here!" (NIV). The terms here are *kainos* (new) and *ktisis* (creation). *Kainos* emphasizes a fresh situation that replaces the old. For the person in union with Christ a "new creation has come." The "old" situation is past; the "new" has arrived.

Colossians 3:9–10 expresses this idea. Paul said, "you laid aside the old self [lit. "old man"] with its evil practices and have put on the new self [lit. "new man"]." The "new self" or "new man" Paul mentioned involves a new creation situation. Thus, for the Jesus-follower, the "old man" has given way to the "new man." The "old-man" represents everything a person was in Adam, and the "new man" concerns everything a person now is in Christ. Romans 5:12–21 reveals that Adam brought sin, death, and condemnation for all people. But Jesus brings life and justification to those in Him.

The outworking of this transition from old man to new self and new creation is found in Ephesians 4:22–24 where Paul stated, that, in reference to your former manner of life, you lay aside the old self, which is being corrupted in accordance with the lusts of deceit, and that you be renewed in the spirit of your mind, and put on the *new self*, which in the likeness of God has been created in righteousness and holiness of the truth.[1]

Paul's words for "new self [man]" in 4:24 are *kainos* [new] *anthropos* [man]. Again, "new" language is applied to the Christian. For the person who is now a new creation or new man in Christ, he is commanded to live in light of this reality. Thus, act like you are! In sum, the idea of "new creation" applies to the individual in Jesus.

A NEW COMMUNITY IN CHRIST

New creation language also extends to corporate and community entities. The arrival of Jesus and the New Covenant ministry of the Holy Spirit means messianic salvation now extends equally to both believing Jews and believing Gentiles. Ephesians 2:11–3:6 explains this. No barrier remains between Jews and Gentiles when it comes to salvation. Gentiles who formerly were "far off" have been "brought near" because of Jesus (Eph. 2:13). Ephesians 2:14–15 explains this new situation:

> For He [Jesus] Himself is our peace, who made both groups [believing Jews and Gentiles] into one and broke down the barrier of the dividing wall, by abolishing in His flesh the enmity, which is the Law of commandments contained in ordinances, so that in Himself He might make the two into *one new man*, thus establishing peace.[2]

The Greek terms for "one new man" are *heis* [one] *kainos* [new] *anthropos* [man]. Thus, new creation language is used explicitly of the new community in Jesus.

---

1   Emphases added.

2   Emphases added.

Galatians 6:15 also uses "new creation" language for the new community of Jews and Gentiles: "For neither is circumcision anything, nor uncircumcision, but a *new creation*."[3] Again, Paul's point here is that entrance into Jesus' community is not based on circumcision. Salvation in Jesus applies to both believing Jews (the circumcised) and believing Gentiles (the uncircumcised). Colossians 3:10–11, too, uses new creation language for the new community in Jesus regardless of ethnicity or social status:

> and have put on the *new self* who is being renewed to a true knowledge according to the image of the One who created him—a renewal in which there is no distinction between Greek and Jew, circumcised and uncircumcised, barbarian, Scythian, slave and freeman, but Christ is all, and in all.[4]

The passages above reveal that Jesus brought messianic salvation and unity to believing Gentiles and Jews. Thus, the "new creation" concept applies not only to individuals who trust in Christ, it involves the new community of believing Jews and Gentiles. This, too, reveals a present and already aspect of the new creation idea.

Passages like Isaiah 19:16–25 and Zechariah 14 also foretell that geo-political nations will become God's people alongside Israel. Egypt, for example, will be called God's people (Isa. 19:25). So the new community in Jesus has implications today with the church and the future with nations in the kingdom of God. The "peoples" and "nations" in Revelation 21–22 will reside on a "new earth" in connection with a "new Jerusalem" because of what Jesus has done (Rev. 21:1–3; 24, 26).

But as will be shown, the "new creation" concept does not stop with individual and corporate salvation. It has cosmic implications. As Snyder notes,

> In all these passages, Paul begins with the fact of individual and corporate personal salvation through Christ. But he places personal

---

3   Emphases added.

4   Emphases added.

salvation within a picture of cosmic transformation. The redemption of persons is thus the *center* of God's plan, but not the *circumference* of that plan.[5]

A TRANSFORMATION OF NATURE/CREATION

New creation language also applies to the coming transformation of nature and creation. When the Lord declared, "Behold, I will do something new" (Isa. 43:19), this "something new" includes a roadway in the wilderness (43:19d); rivers in the desert (19e); the restoration of animals (20a); and aid to Israel (20b). These coming wonderful blessings bring a restoration of creation.

Isaiah 65:17–25 also is a major new creation passage. Verse 17 states: "For behold, I create new heavens and a new earth; And the former things will not be remembered or come to mind." This verse mentions "heavens" and "earth," first referred to in Genesis 1:1. Here the "new heavens and a new earth" refers to a fresh, restored universe. What does this new situation bring? It means gladness for Jerusalem (18–19); eradication of infant/child death (20a, 23); long life (20b); the building of houses and eating from vineyards (21–22); and harmony in the animal kingdom (25). This new condition reverses human and cosmic consequences of the Fall. Other Old Testament passages describe the new creation aspect of the restoration of nature such as Jeremiah 30–33 and Ezekiel 36–37.

Moreover, the new heaven and new earth language of Isaiah 65:17 is also found in the New Testament. Second Peter 3:13 states: "But according to His promise we are looking for *new heavens* and a *new earth*, in which righteousness dwells." Revelation 21:1 says, "Then I saw a *new heaven* and a *new earth*; for the first heaven and the first earth passed away, and there is no longer any sea." Revelation 21:5 reads: "And He who sits on the throne said, 'Behold, I am making *all things new*.'" This new earth situation involves

---

5   Snyder, *Salvation Means Creation Healed*, 99.

nations and kings who travel to bring their cultural contributions into the New Jerusalem (see Rev. 21:24, 26).

With Matthew 19:28–30 Jesus uses the term "regeneration" to describe the coming new creation situation that brings the restoration of the tribes of Israel and rewards concerning relationships, houses, and farms:

> And Jesus said to them, "Truly I say to you, that you who have fol-
> lowed Me, in the *regeneration* when the Son of Man will sit on His
> glorious throne, you also shall sit upon twelve thrones, judging the
> twelve tribes of Israel. And everyone who has left houses or brothers
> or sisters or father or mother or children or farms for My name's sake,
> will receive many times as much, and will inherit eternal life. But many
> who are first will be last; and the last, first."

The Greek word for "regeneration" is *paliggenesia* which literally means "genesis again" and refers to renewal and restoration. Acts 3:21 speaks of the coming "restoration of all things." Romans 8:19–23 also presents a new creation situation concerning nature/creation which will be transformed when God's people receive glorified bodies:

> For the anxious longing of the creation waits eagerly for the revealing
> of the sons of God. For the creation was subjected to futility, not will-
> ingly, but because of Him who subjected it, in hope that the creation
> itself also will be set free from its slavery to corruption into the free-
> dom of the glory of the children of God. For we know that the whole
> creation groans and suffers the pains of childbirth together until now.
> And not only this, but also we ourselves, having the first fruits of the
> Spirit, even we ourselves groan within ourselves, waiting eagerly for
> our adoption as sons, the redemption of our body.

Moo notes that the creation that suffered from human sin "will also enjoy the fruits of human deliverance":

> If creation has suffered the consequences of human sin, it will also
> enjoy the fruits of human deliverance. When believers are glorified,
> creation's "bondage to decay" will be ended, and it will participate in

the "freedom that belongs to the glory" for which Christians are destined. Nature, Paul affirms, has a future within the plan of God. It is destined not simply for destruction but for transformation.[6]

Colossians 1:20 links the death of Jesus with the reconciliation of the universe: "and through Him [Jesus] to reconcile all things to Himself, having made peace through the blood of His cross; through Him, I say, whether things on earth or things in heaven." Since sin impacted all creation, Snyder notes that "salvation must be as deep and wide, as high and broad, as creation itself."[7]

To sum up, new creation language is used in the Bible for (1) individual persons in Christ; (2) the new community in Christ; and (3) nature/creation because of Christ. The first two have been inaugurated with the first coming of Jesus and the third will happen with Jesus' second advent. Moo rightly notes, "Paul's phrase 'new creation' therefore appears to be his way of summarizing the new state of affairs that has been inaugurated at Christ's first coming and is to be consummated at his second."[8]

This new creation language is the basis for the New Creation Model we will be discussing.

---

6   Douglas J. Moo, "Nature in the New Creation: New Testament Eschatology and the Environment," *Journal of the Evangelical Theological Society* 49.3 (September 2006): 462.

7   Snyder, 146. In Colossians this cosmic reconciliation is linked with the reconciliation of people to God and the defeat of evil.

8   Moo, 476.

2

INTRODUCING
THE MODELS

◆

A model summarizes the beliefs of a complex view or perspective for the purpose of better understanding. Models can apply to various areas. There are economic and political models. Models also can apply to doctrine or theology. As Craig Blaising notes, "An interpretive model is a heuristic device for comprehending complex views. Models are used to categorize theological views on a number of doctrinal issues."[1]

The models we are studying represent two paradigms concerning God's purposes and eternal life. We now turn to introductory definitions of the New Creation and Spiritual Vision models. Later chapters will dive into even more detail on them, but we now offer an introduction to these models.

THE NEW CREATION MODEL IN BRIEF

The New Creation Model is a paradigm or framework that attempts to account for and summarize: (1) all dimensions of God's creation purposes and (2) the nature of eternal life. It addresses the creation realities of Genesis 1–2 and the New Creation realities of Revelation 20–22.

First, the New Creation Model tries to detect God's multi-dimensional creation purposes, particularly as found in Genesis 1–2. This

---

1   Blaising, "Premillennialism," in *Three Views on the Millennium and Beyond*, 160, n. 2.

includes His plans for the universe, earth, and all living creatures. It also involves His plans for the inanimate creation such as land, trees, seas, rocks, hills, etc. The New Creation Model tries to capture the central role of man, including man's mandate to rule and subdue the earth and its creatures for the glory of God (see Genesis 1:26–28 and Psalm 8). This model also includes the importance of human relationships and institutions such as marriage and family. It accounts for societies, culture, houses, farms, agriculture, architecture, food, music, education, work, art, technology, science, and government. The New Creation Model also detects God's purposes for nations, ethnic groups, and the lands in which these nations and peoples live. In short, the New Creation Model addresses all aspects of God's creation, kingdom, and covenantal purposes—spiritual or material, individual or corporate. As Snyder puts it:

> This vision…sees *all* elements of culture—food, art, technology, music, language, literature, economics, political structures, clothing, soil, minerals, architecture, agriculture, energy, climate, communications, symbols, education, customs, sexuality, entertainment, science, plant and animal life, ethics, and moral values—as all *inextricably* interrelated.[2]

Moore also notes:

> The picture then is not of an eschatological flight from creation but the restoration and redemption of creation with all that entails: table fellowship, community, culture, economics, agriculture and animal husbandry, art, architecture, worship—in short, *life* and that abundantly.[3]

Second, the New Creation Model addresses the nature of eternal life and God's new creation purposes. It asserts that eternal life and the coming

---

2   Snyder, *Salvation Means Creation Healed*, 140. Emphases in original. Snyder was specifically addressing the concept that salvation means all creation is healed. We are not saying Snyder explicitly uses the title "New Creation Model."

3   Russell D. Moore, "Personal and Cosmic Eschatology," in *A Theology for the Church*, ed. Daniel L. Akin (Nashville: B&H, 2007), 859. Emphases in original.

kingdom of God bring the restoration of all creation in all its dimensions from the negative effects of the Fall. This includes both the resurrection of saved humanity and the restoration of all creation (see Acts 3:21). Eternal life is associated with embodied life on a restored earth with nature and the animal kingdom functioning in harmony. This also involves a functional reign of man in Jesus' messianic/millennial kingdom (see Rev. 20:4) and the new earth after the Millennium (see Rev. 22:5) with nations and real cultural and societal activities (see Rev. 21:24, 26). These all occur because of Jesus, the Last Adam and Messiah, who restores and reconciles all things (Acts 3:21; Col. 1:20) and fulfills the rule and subdue mandate of Genesis 1:26–28.

This model also believes eternal life on a new earth will have *continuity with our current life experiences on the present earth, minus the effects of sin, death, and the curse.* Eternal life is not a mystical, wispy experience in a foreign spiritual realm. The experience of God's people and creation will be greater than the original pre-fall situation of Genesis 1–2, but it will be connected to it. The new heaven and new earth of Revelation 21–22 will be a restoration of the original heaven and earth of Genesis 1–2. How that all occurs with the intense fiery purging discussed in 2 Peter 3 is challenging to know, but in the end there will be a tangible earth in eternity where real people with real bodies will exist and do real things.

The "vision of God" (or beatific vision) believers will experience in eternity is social, cultural, and real. It happens on earth. It is not a bodiless existence in a purely spiritual state with only mental contemplation occurring. Redeemed people will operate according to the structure and design God made for them. They will exist in the presence of God on a new earth in the context of relationships with God and other people along with real societal activities and cultural pursuits. Man was created to rule and subdue the earth and all it contains (see Gen. 1:26–28). And man's final destiny involves living and reigning on the earth (see Rev. 22:5). This model also seeks to grasp all dimensions of God's new creation purposes as explained in passages like Isaiah 11, 65, Romans 8, and Revelation 20–22 which depict a restoration of the previously fallen creation.

The New Creation Model also affirms the great importance of spiritual realities and individual human salvation. Make no mistake, spiritual realities are vital to the New Creation Model. So too is individual salvation. God is Spirit (see John 4:24). A relationship with God is spiritual. But both spiritual and material realities are part of God's purposes. And both must be taken seriously. The New Creation Model also opposes the spiritualization of tangible, material, and national entities. It rejects spiritualizing things God did not intend to be spiritualized.

Also, asserting the importance of the New Creation Model does not mean we can know everything about eternity. Studying passages about Messiah's coming kingdom and the Eternal State is like looking through a keyhole. What we see is real information that can give us a good idea and framework of what is there. But we do not have full knowledge and all the answers this side of the kingdom. There still is much we do not know. Yet for much of its history, the church and Christians have erred greatly on the other side. The strong tendency has been to say we cannot know anything at all or we make eternity so "other than" and spiritual that we have a hard time grasping what we can understand. Or we make it so weird and contrary to how God made us, that we struggle with looking forward to the future at all. And then we feel guilty when we do not. For a long time we have been told something like, "Heaven will be much greater than we can think so there's no use in even trying to think about it." While showing humility about what we can know about eternity is important, we still should strive to understand what the Bible says about the future. When we do, I think we will see there is a lot we can grasp and understand, much more than what often has been thought.

Other titles and designations for the New Creation Model include New Creationism, New Creation Eschatology, Holistic Redemption, Holistic Eschatology, etc. The exact wording is not important. What matters are the concepts behind this model. Many have promoted New Creation Model ideas without using this title. Much more will be said about the New Creation Model as we move forward. But next we summarize the Spiritual Vision Model.

THE SPIRITUAL VISION
MODEL IN BRIEF

The Spiritual Vision Model also addresses the nature of reality and eternal life. Concerning the nature of reality, this model recognizes material and spiritual realities in the universe. But a cosmic dualism exists in which spiritual things are viewed as good or better while physical things are perceived as bad or lesser. There also is an emphasis on spiritual things over material realities. The earthly and tangible are viewed as distractions or hindrances to more important spiritual things. With the eastern religions like Hinduism and Buddhism the material realm and perceptions about the physical world are viewed very negatively. These must be overcome for true enlightenment to occur. The purpose of meditation, yoga, and other disciplines is to get one's mind off of the material so that one's soul can unify or merge into an impersonal absolute. Interaction with the material realm is a problem with the eastern religions. Escape from it is the solution. The Greek philosopher, Plato, also held to a very strong distinction between spirit and matter with the former being much greater.

Christian versions of the Spiritual Vision Model are less severe and less dualistic than those of the eastern religions. Even Christians with strong Spiritual Vision Model tendencies affirm the material realm has a purpose in God's plan. There also is belief in the resurrection of the body. But a strong distinction still exists between the value of the spiritual and material realms. In a "Christian" context, a Spiritual Vision Model approach focuses exclusively on individual spiritual salvation and spiritual blessings. Little to no emphasis is devoted to the earth and its creatures. These are merely the backdrop or temporary background for the accomplishing of God's greater spiritual purposes. And these will be destroyed or go out of existence someday. Entities such as national Israel, Israel's land, and physical blessings are viewed as inferior things surpassed by spiritual New Testament entities. Tangible Old Testament realities often are perceived as inferior types and shadows that lose significance with the coming of greater spiritual realities in the New Testament.

Next, a Spiritual Vision Model perspective also impacts how eternal life is viewed. The nature of eternal life primarily is a spiritual existence in a spiritual realm. For Hinduism and Buddhism this means an impersonal merger into an impersonal absolute in which one loses all personhood and consciousness. The image of a drop of water into an ocean has been used to describe this *nirvana* experience. Time also ceases to exist for those who reach the ultimate state.

The Christian Spiritual Model view of eternal life is not as extreme as that of the eastern religions or Platonism, but it is still very spiritual and anti-material. The ultimate experience is leaving earth for Heaven forever. Space and time no longer exist. There will be no social or cultural interactions in this state since these would detract from one's focus on and worship of God. Or if there is social interaction it is mostly to come together to sing to and worship God.[4] The believer might have a resurrected body, but this body is not significant since the person is now in God's presence apart from earth and engaged in mental contemplation and worship of God. The eternal state of the believer is existence in a spiritual realm. The emphasis is on the soul's experience in Heaven apart from anything physical or social.

With this model, the kingdom of God is no longer the earthly kingdom that the Old Testament prophets predicted. It is salvation or Heaven. It is the reign of departed saints now in Heaven or it is God's reign in the heart of believers and/or the church. Gary Burge promoted a spiritual vision view when he stated that earth is not our homeland: "But Hebrews says that our 'homeland' has changed. It is not on the earth."[5] Leon Morris denied that the New Jerusalem of Revelation 21 will be a material reality: "When John speaks of streets paved with gold, of a city whose gates are made of single pearls and the like, we must not understand that the heavenly city will be as material as present earthly cities."[6] He then said,

---

4   We believe singing to and worshipping God will be wonderful happenings in eternity. We also think other activities will be part of the eternal experience too.

5   Gary M. Burge, *Jesus and the Land: The New Testament Challenge to "Holy Land" Theology* (Grand Rapids: Baker, 2010), 101.

6   Leon Morris, *Revelation* in Tyndale New Testament Commentaries (Downers Grove, IL: InterVarsity Press, 1987), 231.

"He [John] is concerned with spiritual states, not with physical realities."[7] David Engelsma insists that the kingdom of God is spiritual:

> There is a truth about the kingdom of God that is basic to the confession that the kingdom of God is the church. This is the truth that the kingdom of God is spiritual. Spirituality is an essential quality of the kingdom of God. Knowledge of the spiritual nature of the kingdom is essential to the right belief about the kingdom.[8]

He then scolds the idea that the kingdom could be earthly, political, and physical: "The great errors about the kingdom that are afoot today have this in common, that they view the kingdom as earthly, as political, as carnal."[9] And for Engelsma, the kingdom of God is "unearthly" and outside the realm of the physical senses: "In keeping with its unearthly nature, the kingdom of God cannot be known by man's physical senses."[10] These statements coincide with the Spiritual Vision Model.

In sum, the Spiritual Vision Model presents a cosmic dualism and value distinction between the spiritual and material. And eternity is spent in an entirely spiritual realm. Whereas the New Creation Model is holistic, accounting for all areas of reality, the Spiritual Vision Model emphasizes the spiritual over the material and the individual over the corporate. Spiritual Vision Model ideas stem from non-Christian philosophies like Platonism and Neo-Platonism, and eastern religions like Hinduism and Buddhism. The non-Christian religions and philosophies offer the strongest forms of the Spiritual Vision Model, but there also are "Christian" forms of this model. More will be said about the Spiritual Vision Model later.

---

7   Ibid.

8   David J. Engelsma, *The Kingdom of God* (Grandville, MI: Evangelism Committee of Southwest Protestant Reformed Church, 2002; reprint 2012), 14–15.

9   Ibid., 15.

10   Ibid., 16. He uses John 3:3 and Luke 17:20 to support this.

A SPECTRUM

Are these two models mutually exclusive? Or can one affirm elements of both? The answer is complex but, in short, one can affirm elements of both models. The Spiritual Vision and New Creation models are not entirely mutually exclusive. As Steven James notes, "Though the two conceptions have their respective emphases, one should not think of the two conceptions as necessarily exclusive."[11] While the Spiritual Vision Model emphasizes spiritual matters to the exclusion of material realities, the New Creation Model does not only emphasize material issues. It accounts for and affirms the importance of both material *and* spiritual things. The New Creation Model, though, opposes the spiritualization of material realities.

Also, most Christians hold to elements of both models. For example, many Christians have affirmed resurrection of the body but then believe that eternity occurs in a spiritual realm apart from earth. This combines a new creation reality (resurrection of the body) with a Spiritual Vision Model idea (eternity in non-earthy Heaven). Also, many will spiritualize Jesus' millennial kingdom but then believe the Eternal Kingdom takes place on a new earth. Some do the opposite, believing the Millennium is tangible and earthly, while making the Eternal Kingdom only a spiritual existence in a spiritual realm.

Thus, when it comes to evaluating theologians and theological systems with the two models, it is best to think in terms of a spectrum. When all beliefs of a person or system are considered, most fall on a spectrum between a full Spiritual Vision Model and a full New Creation Model. One could even use a scale of 1 to 10 with "1" being a full Spiritual Vision Model and "10" being a full New Creation Model. Platonism, Neo-Platonism, Gnosticism, and the eastern religions like Hinduism and Buddhism would be in the 1–2 range on the spectrum. Theologians like Augustine and Thomas Aquinas are probably a 4 and a 3, respectively.

---

11   Steven L. James, "Recent New Creation Conceptions and the Christian Mission," *Canadian Theological Review* 4.1 (2015): 25.

Most Christian thinkers and systems today would fall between a 5 and an 8. Even people and systems linked with Spiritual Vision Model ideas will at times espouse New Creation thinking. In fact, no true Christian could affirm a full Spiritual Vision Model since this would mean denying the goodness of God's original creation, the humanity of Jesus, and the resurrection of the body. The third-century theologian, Origen (AD 185–254), came close to being unclear on the resurrection of the body.[12] Fortunately, though, Christians throughout history have affirmed resurrection, even if at times they adopted elements of the Spiritual Vision Model. Most Christians and theological systems will fall on a spectrum between the Spiritual Vision and New Creation models.

SIMILAR MODELS

Has anyone else discussed the models presented in this book? As this book unfolds we will see others who have used the language of the New Creation and Spiritual Vision models.

Plus, others have addressed these models while calling them something else. In their book, *Heaven: A History*, Colleen McDannell and Bernhard Lang present two models concerning how Christians have understood eternal life. First, they speak of a "Theocentric Model of Heaven," which coincides with the Spiritual Vision Model. The title, "Theocentric," emphasizes that Heaven is God-centered with no social interactions among people. God is viewed as sitting on His throne in Heaven and man passively stares into God's presence in a static, timeless, spiritual state. With this model there are no activities or social interactions among people in Heaven. Time, culture, and anything associated with earth are gone forever. The following quotations from McDannell and Lang summarize this Theocentric Model of Heaven:

---

12   For a fuller discussion of Origen's views on the body see J. Richard Middleton, *A New Heaven and a New Earth: Reclaiming Biblical Eschatology* (Grand Rapids: Baker Academic, 2014), 284–85. See Origen, *On First Principles* 2.2.2; 2.10.3.

According to this model, heaven is for God, and the eternal life of the saints revolves around a divine center.

The saints may be involved in an everlasting liturgy of praise, they may meditate in solitude, or they may be caught up in an intimate relation with the divine.

Worldly activities earn no place in heaven.

At the end of time the earth either is destroyed or plays a minor role in everlasting life.

Heaven is fundamentally a religious place—a center of worship, of divine revelation, and pious conversations with sacred characters.

The theocentric model presents heaven as the opposite of earth.

Death marks a radical difference between this life and the next.

At one's personal death or at the death of history at the end of the world, a radically new life commences.

Heavenly life is not a perfected version of life on earth.

The theocentric model asserts that eternal life has little in common with everyday earthly activities.

Heavenly existence means a life free not only from the pains of earth but from everything earthly.

Not only do sorrow, illness, death, and labor cease, but friends, family, change, and human creativity are utterly unimportant.

Since only the perfect exists in heaven, there is no need for change.

McDannell and Lang then offer a succinct summary of this Theocentric Model: "By subscribing to a theocentric model, the question of what the saints *do* for eternity falls by the wayside. The saints do not have to *do* anything, they merely experience the fullness of their being by existing with God."[13] In sum, the Theocentric Model views Heaven as a non-material state where the focus is only on God.

The second model McDannell and Lang discuss is the "Anthropocentric Model." The word "*anthropos*" refers to "man." But "Anthropocentric" in this context does not mean salvation is man-centered or the focus of Heaven is mostly on man. It means that the final Heaven involves social interactions among people. Saved people relate with other saved people, doing real activities, including culture, on a tangible new earth. Redeemed people will worship and serve God while also loving and knowing each other. God does not view social interactions among His people as a threat to their love for Him.

Thus, with the Anthropocentric Model, the final state includes people. It also involves time, space, activities, culture, and human fellowship. These are not viewed as detractors from God's glory, but as good gifts God wants His people to enjoy. God is glorified as man enjoys the new earth in all its dimensions, including human fellowship. With this model man's destiny remains tied to earth, an earth fully restored and purged of sin's affects. This model is closely related to the New Creation Model.

Later chapters of this book will examine the two models in history in more detail. But it should be noted that the dominance of one model over the other has switched at times in history. As McDannell and Lang observe: "Although the two models often co-exist, one of them can generally be considered the dominant view for a given time and place."[14] Neither model has been "established in the long run."[15] When one model becomes prominent a pendulum swing will occur to the other model.

---

13   Colleen McDannell and Bernhard Lang, *Heaven: A History* (Yale University Press, 2001). These quotations come from pages 178–180. Emphases are in the original.

14   Ibid., 357.

15   Ibid.

THE NEW CREATION MODEL ACCOUNTS FOR

Kingdom Mandate

Earthly Kingdom of God

All physical, spiritual, individual, national, and international elements of the biblical covenants

Ethnicities

Geo-Political Nations

National Israel

Earth

Land

Animals, Birds, Fish

Inanimate creation (rocks, trees, grass, etc.)

Physical Blessings

Societies and social interactions

Cultural activities

3

PRACTICAL IMPLICATIONS OF THE MODELS

◆

Do the New Creation and Spiritual Vision models really matter? We think they do. These models summarize two paradigms for understanding God's creation purposes and the nature of eternal life. Much discussion of God's plans is done at the micro-level, focusing on individual salvation and Christian living. This is good and essential. But we also should look at God's purposes from a big-picture perspective. Examining the New Creation and Spiritual Vision models helps us do that. And contemplating these models challenges our own thinking. What model do we hold? Are we basing our views on Christian assumptions or on other worldviews or philosophies? Even a mostly Christian worldview can have taints of unbiblical thinking.

We believe the Spiritual Vision Model detracts from the glory of God because it is too narrow. By focusing exclusively on the spiritual and the individual it misses or ignores the full scope of what God is doing. It does not sufficiently detect God's multi-dimensional purposes for humanity and all creation. Genesis 1 details the glories of God's universe. And the first statements given to man involve a kingdom reign over all the earth and its creatures (see Gen. 1:26–28). The Fall of Genesis 3 brought death and a curse that impacts man and all creation. Yet God is pursuing the restoration of people and nature. A right model aids us in perceiving the fullness of the biblical worldview in all its dimensions. We can grasp the beauty of God's creation, the tragic nature of the Fall, God's interactions throughout the Old Testament, the central importance of Jesus and the cross, and the glorious restoration of all things in Jesus as He comes again, judges His enemies, and establishes His kingdom on earth. A new creationist approach connects the theological dots between Genesis 1 and Revelation 22.

Also, a New Creation Model hope can make our hearts long for the Lord's return and kingdom where God's will and righteousness always prevail. It helps us pray, "Your kingdom come. Your will be done, on earth as it is in heaven" (Matt. 6:10). This fallen world will not remain forever. God will take back planet earth and make everything right. The hope God offers is not a ghostly existence in a spiritual realm. It includes tangible, glorified bodies and abundant life on a renewed earth. It involves being in the presence of God and seeing the Father and Jesus face to face. It also includes believers from all ethnicities and nations who relate and interact with each other at social and cultural levels. Knowing these things affects how we think of and worship God whether in church, at work, at the beach, in the mountains, in our neighborhoods, or in our living rooms at home. And it impacts how we view tragedies in this age. Paul said the creation currently subjected to futility has "hope" (Rom. 8:20) and will be "set free from its slavery" (Rom. 8:21). When God's people receive new bodies, creation will be restored as well.

New Creationism brings perspective. This present evil age will not last forever. The Fall will be reversed. Every tear will be wiped away (Rev. 21:4). God will make all things new (Rev. 21:5). Every negative thing will be swept away in victory. Even death and the grave are defeated (see 1 Cor. 15:50–58). God is reconciling all things in Jesus (Col. 1:20). Vibrant life on a new earth in God's presence awaits. Knowing these truths should influence how we deal with personal loss, offer hope to the depressed, minister to a dying person, and speak at a funeral. Truly, momentary light affliction cannot be compared with the glory to come (see 2 Cor. 4:17).

Any loss for Jesus in this age will be exponentially rewarded and multiplied back. Jesus promised ruling positions on the new earth, relationships, houses, and farms to those who follow Him (see Matt. 19:28–30).

His resurrection from the dead guarantees all this will happen. The coming kingdom will be a glorious celebration banquet and reunion with real food and drink (see Isa. 25:6–8; Matt. 8:11; Luke 22:15–18; Rev. 19:9). The most joyous celebration in history awaits God's people. These truths should encourage us in tough times and make the negative things we face pale in comparison. A biblical New Creation Model gives us hope and perspective. As Paul stated, "If we endure, we will also reign with Him" (2 Tim. 2:12).

IMPORTANCE OF THE MODELS IN CHURCH HISTORY

The New Testament and early church history reveal the importance of the two models. On several occasions erroneous Spiritual Vision Model ideas were confronted. In 1 Corinthians 4:8 Paul sarcastically chided the Corinthians for thinking they were ruling in some already spiritual kingdom: "You are already filled, you have already become rich, you have become kings without us; and indeed, I wish that you had become kings so that we also might reign with you."

Paul also addressed the heresy that the resurrection already happened. With 2 Timothy 2:8 he referred to "men who have gone astray from the truth, claiming that the resurrection has already taken place; and they are jeopardizing the faith of some." In 1 John 4:2–3, the apostle John said there were people who denied that Jesus came in the flesh (i.e., a physical body). Such people were not of God. This refuted the Docetic idea that possessing a human body was not worthy of Jesus. Allegedly, Jesus just "appeared" to be human. These examples show that Spiritual Vision Model views were threats to the Christian faith in the apostolic era.

The post-apostolic church also faced serious threats from Spiritual Vision Model ideas. Gnosticism denied the goodness of creation and the human body. Marcion removed the Hebrew Scriptures and Jewish elements from the Bible. Fortunately, New Creation ideals such as the goodness of God's creation, the goodness of the human body, and the importance of the Hebrew Scriptures, were used by orthodox Christians to refute false beliefs. While the titles of New Creation and Spiritual Vision models were not explicit in the early church, the ideas of these models were evident.

God is not honored when false beliefs prevail. And wrong ideas have consequences. When Christians adopt Spiritual Vision Model ideas they stray from the Bible's storyline and can fall into doctrinal error. It can also lead to missing the dynamic hope Scripture offers.

A CASE STUDY

In the early stages of writing this book, a doctoral student, who also is a pastor and former student of mine, contacted me. He wanted to link his doctoral project with the New Creation Model.[1] This involved teaching a ten-part series called "Glimpses of Glory" to his church. The purpose was to teach the biblical view of Heaven from a New Creation Model perspective and contrast this with the Spiritual Vision Model view. He also wanted to show how this issue mattered in the present:

> The goals for the sermon series were to instill a greater understanding of the nature of heaven from the Scriptures, to help the congregation differentiate between a spiritual-vision model and a new creation model of eschatology as well as to help them to see the ethical implications this doctrine has in the present.

To monitor the effectiveness of this series he used surveys along with a focus group. How did the people respond to this? The results were encouraging, as he explains:

> One respondent said, "I became more aware of how the doctrines and truth of the final heaven affects my life in the here and now."

---

1   My thanks to Robert Wauhop for allowing us to use information from his doctoral project in this chapter. See Robert Charles Wauhop, "Glimpses of Glory: Preaching the Doctrine of Heaven at Faith Bible Church, Sharpsburg, Georgia," Doctor of Ministry Project, The Master's Seminary, 2021.

Another said, "I didn't realize that even the little things I do now, like praying for a brother or sister, could have an impact once I'm in heaven and meet that brother or sister."

Someone else said, "The series was a shift from seeing heaven as a boring place where we sing and play harps all day, to one that takes all the good things of this life and has that grow from there no longer tainted by sin and with God and the saints forever."

As these quotations show, this project revealed the practical nature of a new creationist perspective in a local church.

In his proposal, this pastor explained why he did this project. Years earlier, his father, a Christian, was dying from cancer. In the weeks leading up to his father's death he longed to share Scriptures about the reality of Heaven. While he did mention Scriptures such as Romans 8 and Revelation 21, he still felt frustrated with his explanations:

> But I found myself wanting to be able to articulate a clear picture of Heaven for my dad in his last days. Yet, I felt that while I had a biblical concept of Heaven and the final new earth, I had difficultly organizing my thoughts in a clear and comprehensive way.

His experience motivated him to study the Bible's hope so he could explain it better to others. Also, as a pastor, he sensed that many Christians share a similar frustration. They know Heaven is real but have a difficult time explaining the biblical hope. He rightly noted that a person's view of Heaven impacts "choices and conduct in the present." This pastor truly understands the practical nature and importance of the New Creation Model as expressed in Scripture. And the church benefited as a result.

BENEFITS OF THE RIGHT MODEL

Transitioning to an accurate model of God's purposes is like taking off poor prescription eyeglasses and putting on a correct prescription. A person with a faulty eye prescription might see the general shape and colors of an object like a painting. But with the right glasses, blurriness changes to sharpness. Details and depth emerge. The Spiritual Vision Model causes blurry vision concerning God's purposes. Or even worse Spiritual Vision Model assumptions can function as blinders so the Christian cannot see creation realities and what the restoration of all things looks like. He or she can only see the "spiritual" things but cannot see the importance of the created material realm and the glories of the new earth they will inhabit.[2] The New Creation Model, though, brings clarity. The Bible's storyline from beginning to end comes into focus.

We need to think accurately about all of the Bible's truths. There is more in Scripture than what often is taught in Christian settings. Much Christian teaching, including in churches, is individualistic. It focuses on how to live a better life now. Of course, some of that is fine. But much of the Bible also concerns what God is doing in history with the world, nations, and matters such as the Day of the Lord and the Kingdom of God. Sections addressing these issues are important too, and they can have practical impact in the here and now. Knowing the "big picture" coincides with how we as individuals and the church fit into it. A new creationist approach also involves teaching the whole counsel of God, including the Old Testament, the Gospels (including Matthew and Luke), and Revelation.

A Spiritual Vision view muddies what God is doing. But we can see correctly with right assumptions and interpretations. Let us heed Paul's hope in Ephesians 1:18 that we will properly grasp what God is doing in Jesus:

> I pray that the eyes of your heart may be enlightened, so that you will
> know what is the hope of His calling, what are the riches of the glory
> of His inheritance in the saints.

---

2   See Randy A. Alcorn, *Heaven* (Sandy, OR: Eternal Perspective Ministries, 2004), 482. Alcorn uses the analogy of "blinders" that hinders Christians from understanding the richness of God's revelation about the coming new earth.

WHAT WE WILL ARGUE

The Spiritual Vision Model has been dominant in church history since the third century. But we believe the New Creation Model best represents God's purposes and the Bible's storyline from Genesis 1 through Revelation 22. This model rightly grasps that God's purposes are holistic and multi-dimensional. It helps us detect all God is doing in history and enables us to know our place in God's story. On the other hand, adopting Spiritual Vision Model ideas leads to a lesser, incomplete, and even myopic understanding of God's purposes. It mistakenly makes God's purposes mostly spiritual and individual, and does not detect the fullness of the "restoration of all things" God is accomplishing through Jesus (Acts 3:21). The Spiritual Vision Model is too narrow. It puts blinders on people, hindering them from seeing the glory of God and Christ in all they are doing.

THE MODELS AND PREUNDERSTANDINGS

*"A spiritualized understanding of the material world has
become the reigning worldview of popular
American Evangelicalism."*

—Howard Snyder[1]

◆

No one approaches the world from a blank slate. We all are influenced by our families, friends, neighbors, experiences, education, the era we live in, the surrounding culture, and other things. These impact how we view and interpret the world. This leads us to a discussion of preunderstandings and how these relate to the New Creation and Spiritual Vision models. In short, we will argue that faulty preunderstandings often have led to Christians in history not seeing the fullness of all God is accomplishing in Jesus. Christians have often tended towards a Spiritual Vision Model understanding of God's purposes that leaves out key elements of what God is doing when a New Creation Model perspective is better.

But to start, what is "preunderstanding"? Blaising describes preunderstanding as "the understanding one has about a subject before researching it."[2] It involves *a priori* assumptions about the world and how it works.

---

1   Snyder, *Salvation Means Creation Healed*, 45.

2   Blaising, "Premillennialism," in *Three Views on the Millennium and Beyond*, 164.

Concerning Scripture, preunderstanding is "the understanding one has about what a text is probably saying before one begins to study it."[3] Duvall and Hays define preunderstanding as "all our preconceived notions and understanding that we bring to the text, which have been formulated, both consciously and subconsciously, *before* we actually study the text in detail."[4] In short, preunderstanding concerns assumptions about something apart from study or evidence. Concerning the Bible, preunderstanding relates to assumptions we have about Scripture and God's plans that we take into our study of the Bible.

Preunderstanding closely relates to presuppositions and worldview. People often have presuppositions about topics or issues before they study them. Preunderstandings are unavoidable and they are not all necessarily bad. At times our assumptions are correct. For example, we assume our own existence. That is accurate. We also assume that other people exist. That too is right. Those are correct presuppositions because they correspond to reality. Most people intuitively know God exists and that murder is wrong. Those are good assumptions. But sometimes assumptions are not accurate and need to be changed. This can involve assumptions about God's purposes. Presuppositions should be measured by Scripture. Biblical assumptions should be maintained while unbiblical presuppositions should be rejected. Erroneous preunderstandings can be changed. But doing so often is hard.

Discussion of "preunderstandings" can make some nervous. Sometimes postmodernists use the concept of preunderstanding to conclude there are no objective truths and that everyone's assumptions are equally valid. Postmodernist conclusions about preunderstanding are in error. Because God exists there are objective realities. There is absolute truth. We should strive to make sure that our understanding of reality matches God's reality, which ultimately is what matters. Preunderstandings

---

3   Ibid.

4   J. Scott Duvall and J. Daniel Hays, *Grasping God's Word: A Hands-On Approach to Reading, Interpreting, and Applying the Bible* (Grand Rapids: Zondervan, 2012), 139. Emphases in original.

that deviate from God's reality are wrong. But preunderstandings that correspond to God's reality are true.

If unchecked, faulty preunderstandings can result in believing things without sufficient reason. We can ignore or overlook clues to the contrary and dismiss what does not fit our assumptions. We might not use proper critical thinking. For example, this can happen with political views or theological positions. Have you ever held to a political or theological view of which you were very sure, but when challenged you struggled to defend your view? What you thought was obvious was not obvious to someone else. Or perhaps you were surprised when the other person brought up information contrary to your view. You might have been flustered that the other person did not "see things" like you did. If you have ever felt this way your preunderstandings were challenged.

So how do preunderstandings relate to the Spiritual Vision and New Creation models? As true for everyone, Christians often have preunderstandings and assumptions about the nature of reality and eternal life that are incomplete or wrong. Throughout history, many have assumed significant Spiritual Vision Model ideas about reality and eternal life. The influence of Plato and Platonism often have tainted how Christians view God's purposes. This was especially true in the twelve hundred years leading up to the Protestant Reformation when most people assumed over-spiritualized views of God's purposes.

Spiritual Vision Model thinking hinders Christians from seeing what God is doing with His creation. This can occur by not seeing what is there or spiritualizing matters that were not meant to be spiritualized. Texts in the Bible that address earth, land, animals, Israel, nations, physical blessings, etc., often are ignored or not taken literally. Why? Because these matters are assumed as irrelevant. And when this occurs for decades or centuries, wrong presuppositions can become deeply entrenched and hard to spot and remove. As Blaising notes:

> One must not underestimate the power of longstanding tradition in shaping the hermeneutical preunderstanding by which individual texts as well as whole portions of biblical literature are read—preunderstandings which are reinforced by the expositional commentary

traditions in evangelical preaching and by traditional forms of theological catechesis in evangelical teaching.[5]

For example, the church's longstanding belief that national Israel no
longer is significant in God's purposes because the church in Jesus is the
new/true Israel has been very hard to overcome. It took about one hundred years after the Reformation for this erroneous view to be seriously
challenged, and even today supersessionism is believed by many. Also, the
idea that the eternal Heaven is a spiritual existence in another dimension
apart from earth has been hard to displace. Defeating centuries of Spiritual
Vision Model tradition is difficult. Blaising rightly notes that "The spiritual vision model functions as the preunderstanding with which many
Christians begin to study or investigate biblical teaching about our future
hope."[6] He also rightly states, "The long dominance of the spiritual vision
model has conditioned the way Christians traditionally and habitually
think and converse about eternal life."[7]

On the other hand, preunderstandings also relate to the New Creation
Model. If people understand that God's purposes are holistic and multi-
dimensional then they can see the full dimensions of what God is accomplishing. They will grasp the complete panorama of God's purposes. Their
preunderstanding allows them to soak in and embrace all God is saying
and doing. They do not ignore or spiritualize key biblical evidence. Those
with a New Creation Model worldview will understand earthly, physical, and national matters in the Bible more literally. When Isaiah 11:6–9
predicts harmony in the animal kingdom, that will happen literally one
day. The animal world will exist and be restored in the kingdom of God.
When Isaiah 2:2–4 predicts international harmony among nations when
the Lord reigns from Jerusalem, a new creation adherent expects that to
happen just as stated. Literal geo-political nations will exist and peacefully

5   Craig A. Blaising, "The Future of Israel as a Theological Question," in *Journal of the Evangelical Theological Society* 44.3 (September 2001): 443.

6   Blaising, "Premillennialism," 164.

7   Ibid.

interact with each other. When Jesus told the apostles they will judge the twelve tribes of Israel on a regenerated earth, that is what He meant (see Matt. 19:28). No reason exists to spiritualize these texts.

The key here is whether we have a worldview that allows us to see the full range of God's purposes or whether our worldview excludes what God has planned. Concerning confusion on the kingdom of God, McClain notes the influence of Platonic philosophy:

> A great deal of this confusion, in my opinion, has been due to the influence of Platonic philosophy in the field of Christian theology. Many a preacher, who may have never read a single sentence from Plato, has been more or less, perhaps unconsciously, under the sway of the rigid metaphysical dualism of this philosopher. To such men, the premillennial doctrine of a divine Kingdom established on earth, having political and physical aspects, seems to be sheer materialism.[8]

In reference to the influences of Platonism and Gnosticism, Bavinck notes that these views "have for centuries impacted theology."[9]

Unlike myself, who was raised under strong Spiritual Vision Model views, my children grew up with a new creationist understanding of God's purposes. So they have more accurate ideas than I did at their ages. They believe earth, land, Israel, nations, science, technology, etc. are part of God's purposes. They know Jesus is returning to rule the earth and nations. They believe music, art, and culture will exist and be restored in the kingdom of God. They affirm that birds, animals, and fish will exist in eternity. Their love for nature and God's creation is strong and they give God glory for these. Thus, when I mention that some believe our destiny is all about absorbing light rays in another dimension forever, they laugh and ask, "Who believes that?" I tell them, "I did when I was your age." I explained to

---

8 Alva J. McClain, *The Greatness of the Kingdom: An Inductive Study of the Kingdom of God* (Winona Lake, IN: BMH Books, 1959, 1987), 519. Later we discuss that Premillennialism is the view that Jesus will return before or "pre-" His millennial kingdom on earth. Premillennialism is consistent with the New Creation Model.

9 Herman Bavinck, *Reformed Dogmatics: God and Creation*, (Grand Rapids: Baker, 2004), vol. 2, 103. Bavinck mostly refers to the "dualism" between spirit and matter that these views have promoted.

one of my sons that I once believed Heaven was about escaping the body and the world to live in a spiritual realm forever. He said, "That sounds like Hinduism!" He was right!

The models also are related to interpretation and hermeneutical issues. The Spiritual Vision Model promotes Bible interpretation principles that promote the spiritualization of physical and national entities. The New Creation Model, though, takes passages about physical and national matters seriously and literally.

AN EXAMPLE: THE INTERMEDIATE STATE AND THE SPIRITUAL VISION MODEL

One example of common Spiritual Vision Model thinking involves beliefs about the intermediate Heaven. The current Heaven is real. It is the place where the Father, the resurrected Jesus, angels, and the souls of departed believers in God reside. When a Christian dies in this age before the resurrection, his or her soul goes to Heaven. We should not miss the importance of Heaven as it now exists. A new creationist approach affirms this.

Some, though, assume that the current, intermediate Heaven is our ultimate goal and destination, not earth. When some think of the future destiny of the saved, they think of the current Heaven. For instance, when a Christian dies in this age we often assume that person has reached his or her final home. And the departed saint is so happy in Heaven he or she would not return to earth if he or she could. Not much discussion is given to the deceased longing for Jesus' return to earth. Nor is there much talk of a return to earth for a kingdom reign (see Rev. 5:10).[10] The emphasis often is placed on the person reaching his or her final destiny in Heaven. And one day we will join him or her in Heaven forever. As the song, "I'll Fly Away" puts it:

---

10   We are making a general statement here. We understand there are solid Bible teaching churches that teach sound doctrine at funerals.

Just a few more weary days and then
I'll fly away
To that land where joy will never end
I'll fly away.

But the Bible does not present the current Heaven as man's final destiny or the end of God's purposes. Paul said that being bodiless is like being naked (2 Cor. 5:3). Peter said we are looking for "a new heaven and a new earth" (2 Pet. 3:13). Earth is the destiny of man. Psalm 115:16 states, "The heavens are the heavens of the Lord, But the earth He has given to the sons of men." The destiny of Jesus the Messiah is earth. Jesus will return to earth to rule the nations (see Matt. 25:31–46; Rev. 19:15). Jesus' saints will reign on earth (see Rev. 5:10). Those who are now with the Lord in Heaven are anticipating a return to earth.

Revelation 6:9–11 presents an intermediate state situation in which the souls of believers who were killed on earth arrive in Heaven. They desire justice on the earth, but they are told to wait awhile. Their desire will not be satisfied until the second coming of Jesus when they are raised from the dead and reign with Jesus on the earth (see Rev. 20:4). Thus, in one of the rare depictions of the intermediate state in the Bible, God's people are not pictured in their final ultimate state. They await something even more glorious on earth.

A Spiritual Vision Model perspective can lead to projecting the current Heaven as the final destiny of the saints when it is not. A new creationist perspective, though, sees the final Heaven as life on a restored earth with resurrected bodies. It also affirms the reality of a current intermediate state in which souls of believers go to Heaven at death, but this is not the final and ultimate experience the Bible presents. Resurrection of the body and life on a new earth in God's presence is the ultimate experience. Concerning the New Creation Model view of eternal life, Blaising states, "Whereas the believing dead are in the presence of Christ now, this model expects that their vision of and fellowship with God will be enriched within the fullness of life in a new creation."[11]

---

11   Blaising, "Premillennialism," 163.

In sum, a new creation approach affirms personal relationship and fellowship with the Creator as the highest experience. But this also occurs within a tangible new creation. This is a biblical Beatific Vision, not one created with Spiritual Vision Model assumptions.

PART TWO

THE NEW CREATION AND SPIRITUAL VISION MODELS EXPLAINED

THE NEW CREATION MODEL FURTHER EXPLAINED

*"It is clear that New Creation Eschatology envisions not
a nonmaterial eternity nor an alternate material reality
but the redemption of this earth and heavens fit for an
everlasting glorious manifestation of the presence of God."*

—Craig A. Blaising[1]

◆

Earlier, we offered introductory definitions for the New Creation and
Spiritual Vision models. Now we look at these models in more depth.
We start first in this chapter with the New Creation Model.

NEW CREATION LANGUAGE

We mentioned previously that "new creation" language is found in various Bible texts such as 2 Corinthians 5:17 ("new creature") and Galatians
6:15 ("new creation"). Both verses refer to the new situation believers
have in Jesus. For our purposes, though, we use "new creation" in the context of God's creation realities as explained in Genesis 1–2 and the new

---

1   Craig A. Blaising, "A Critique of Gentry and Wellum's, *Kingdom Through Covenant*: A Hermeneutical-Theological Response," *Master's Seminary Journal* 26.1 (Spring 2015): 122.

creation situation described in passages like Isaiah 2, Isaiah 65, Romans 8, and Revelation 20–22. Thus, the "New Creation Model" addresses creation and new creation realities from Genesis 1 through Revelation 22. The original "very good" creation of Genesis 1, that suffered from the Fall of man, is headed for restoration and the new creation situation of Revelation 20–22.[2]

The New Creation Model accounts for the nature of creation realities and the coming restored creation. But to understand the latter one must grasp the former. Protology (first things) helps with understanding eschatology (last things). As Snyder notes, "Biblically speaking, the doctrine of new creation depends upon a clear understanding of the original creation."[3]

The New Creation Model also intersects with the doctrine of man (anthropology) and how man interacts with time, even into eternity. Blaising notes that this model involves both a "holistic anthropology" and a "redeemed creation" within the time-sequence of history. Thus, eternal life:

> will be an embodied life on earth … set within a cosmic structure such as we have presently. It is not a timeless, static existence but rather an unending sequence of life and lived experiences. It does not reject physicality or materiality, but affirms them as essential both to a holistic anthropology and to the biblical idea of a redeemed creation. This is what is meant by the 'creation' part of the label for this model.[4]

Blaising observes that the New Creation Model title is linked with "creation." The originally "very good" creation of Genesis 1, that experienced the Fall, is *en route* to becoming a "redeemed creation."

---

2   Galatians 6:15 is the only specific mention of "new creation." Here the designation refers to the fact that the community of Jesus is not determined by being circumcised or uncircumcised. Second Corinthians 5:17 says those in Christ are a "new creature."

3   Snyder, *Salvation Means Creation Healed*, 55.

4   Ibid.

THE NEW CREATION MODEL, CREATION, AND ETERNAL LIFE

Most of the focus on the New Creation Model has been on the nature of eternal life. And this emphasis is well-deserved. Eternal life has been too spiritualized for too long. The corrective that the New Creation Model brings to the eternal life issue is overdue and welcome. Yet, the New Creation Model also addresses the nature of creation.

THE NATURE OF REALITY

Genesis 1–2 reveals a vast, spectacular creation involving cosmic bodies (sun, moon, stars), the earth, seas, animal kingdom, vegetation, sky, planets, humans, etc. God's plans also include culture (see Genesis 4) and various nations and ethnicities (see Genesis 10–11). Colossians 1:16 states that through Jesus "all things were created, both in the heavens and on earth, visible and invisible." Thus, creation is multi-dimensional, involving spiritual matters and material things. There is no cosmic dualism between spirit and matter. As Alva McClain states, "there is no unbridgeable chasm between that which is physical and that which is spiritual."[5]

Understanding this must impact our worldview. *In short, the New Creation Model accounts for all dimensions of God's creation and new creation purposes—material and immaterial.* The "restoration of all things" God is pursuing in Jesus (see Acts 3:21; Col. 1:20) concerns the entire array of creation realities.

Also, while man is the high point of God's creation, the creation has value in itself and is more than just the background of salvation history. As Snyder states, "Creation has intrinsic value, not just instrumental value."[6] God desires the creation to thrive for His glory and He has tasked man with responsibly governing it. Thus, a major part of the New Creation Model is grasping the full array of God's creation realities. These are part

---

5   McClain, *The Greatness of the Kingdom*, 523.

6   Snyder, 61.

of God's purposes before sin arrives in Genesis 3, and they will be part of God's purposes after all effects of sin and death are vanquished (see Revelation 21–22).

THE NATURE OF ETERNAL LIFE

The New Creation Model also addresses the nature of eternal life. Eternal life entails resurrected bodily existence for God's people on a tangible, restored earth where the saints will enjoy the direct presence of God, interact with others, and experience cultural and social activities. As Blaising explains:

> The *new creation model* of eternal life draws on biblical texts that speak of a future everlasting kingdom, of a new earth and the renewal of life on it, of bodily resurrection (especially of the physical nature of Christ's resurrection body), of social and even political concourse among the redeemed.[7]

This model follows the language of passages like Isaiah 25; 65; 66; Romans 8; and Revelation 21 which speak of a regenerated and transformed earth.[8]

The New Creation Model affirms that the greatest part of eternal life is seeing God and being in His presence. So, there is a real "vision of God" or Beatific Vision. Yet, this experience, by God's design, involves a restored earth with relationships, activities, and social-political-cultural interactions. Relationships are key to the Eternal Kingdom—with God and others—but these relationships will occur in the context of a beautiful, restored creation.

The New Creation Model also accounts for *ethnic and national diversity* among God's people. This includes the nation Israel, Gentile nations, and the lands Israel and the nations live on. God's people, or even better— "peoples" (see Isa. 25:6), is more than a generic collection of individuals

---

7   Blaising, "Premillennialism," in *Three Views on the Millennium and Beyond*, 162. Emphases in original.

8   Other relevant passages include Genesis 49:8–12; Isaiah 2; 11; Ezekiel 36–37; Micah 4; Amos 9:11–15, Matthew 19:28–30, etc.

with no diversity. God's people do not become a generic humanity. Ethnic and national diversity will be part of the new earth conditions. God brings glory to himself through both unity and diversity. The redeemed are all saved the same way in Jesus—unity. Yet there are distinctions in ethnicity and nationhood—diversity. These distinctions are beautiful and harmonize with the unity all believers have in Christ (see Eph. 2:11–3:6). So salvation and restoration involve unity and diversity in perfect harmony.

CONTINUITY WITH PRESENT EXPERIENCES

World religions often present a great difference between our current experiences on earth and our coming experiences in eternity. Hinduism and Buddhism, for instance, offer an impersonal eschatology in which the ultimate goal for man is to merge into an impersonal absolute where no self-consciousness or anything tangible exists. A person will be like a drop of water dropped into a vast ocean of mystical, impersonal reality. Surprisingly, Christian traditions, too, often have presented Heaven as a purely spiritual existence—the soul dazzled by light in an immaterial realm forever.

But that is not the picture the Bible presents. The New Creation Model asserts that eternal life is dynamic, colorful, tangible, and relational. It affirms real experiences and activities like those in the present world. The main difference is that sin, the curse, and death do not taint these coming real-world experiences. As Blaising notes, "The new creation model expects that the ontological order and scope of eternal life is essentially continuous with that of present earthly life except for the absence of sin and death."[9] Thus, eternal life is not spirits floating in an immaterial realm. That is not how God created man to be and function. Instead, it is more accurate to think of eternal life in terms of healthy social, cultural, and relational activities in the context of love and righteousness with no taint of anything negative.

---

9   Blaising, "Premillennialism," 162.

This continuity of experience involves space and time. Steven James notes, "the new creation model emphasizes an earthly, material, time-sequenced and embodied existence in a new heavens and new earth."[10] He also says, "Redemption as a biblical theme certainly includes the spiritual realm but it also includes the physical realm, specifically the promise of a new heaven and a new earth."[11]

In sum, the New Creation Model affirms the following:

+ The goodness of all God's creation—spiritual and material

+ A coming new earth

+ Renewal of life on the new earth/redeemed creation

+ Bodily resurrection/embodied existence

+ Social, cultural, and political discourse among God's people

+ Experiences on the new earth similar to the present earth but without sin, decay and death

+ Holistic anthropology (humanity)

+ Time-sequenced history

MORE THAN INDIVIDUAL SALVATION

Nothing is more immediately urgent for a person than repenting and trusting in Jesus for salvation. Personal godliness and Christian living also are important. This involves the spiritual disciplines of prayer, self-denial, and Bible study. A New Creation Model approach affirms the importance of all this. Yet a new creationist perspective also addresses God's "big-picture" purposes beyond individual human salvation and daily Christian living. It detects what God is doing in history with the earth, nations, Israel,

---

10   Steven James, *New Creation Eschatology and the Land: A Survey of Contemporary Perspectives* (Eugene, OR: Wipf and Stock, 2017), 1.

11   Ibid., 12.

the Day of the Lord, and the kingdom of God. When it comes to God's purposes we are dealing with a "both/and" situation. We can focus on our own personal relationship with God and grasp what God is doing at a big-picture level.

Michael Williams notes that the influential theologian, Augustine (AD 354–430), taught "verticalism," which is a view of the future solely focused on the soul going to Heaven.[12] Steven James claims that such a heavy focus on the individual often has led to a "devaluing" of other aspects of God's creation that has "dominated the history of the church":

> According to Snyder, the tendency to focus solely on individual sin and salvation and the tendency toward dualism have led to the devaluing of the non-human creation. These tendencies have dominated the history of the church and made predominant the view that has made the salvation of souls not merely the center of God's redemption plan, but the circumference of that plan.[13]

A New Creation Model perspective, though, is *creation* and *kingdom-oriented*. It includes serious contemplation of individual human salvation *and* the whole scope of God's creation. Noting the work of Donald Gowan, James observes that "there is promised a threefold transformation of creation—that of the human person, human society, and nature."[14] Thus, the transformation of creation involves:

1. The Human person

2. Human society (social, cultural, political structures)

---

12   Michael Williams, "A Restorational Alternative to Augustinian Verticalist Eschatology," *Pro Rege* 20 (1992): 11.

13   James, 11–12. See Snyder, *Salvation Means Creation Healed*, 99.

14   James, xv. Gowan stated, "God must transform the human person; give a new heart and a new spirit....God must transform human society; restore Israel to the promised land, rebuild cities, and make Israel's new status as a witness to the nations....And God must transform nature itself." Donald E. Gowan, Eschatology in the Old Testament (Philadelphia: Fortress, 1986), 2. See Robert L. Saucy, *The Case for Progressive Dispensationalism: The Interface between Dispensational and Non-Dispensational Theology* (Grand Rapids: Zondervan, 1993), 221–22.

3.   Nature (creation, land, sea, vegetation, animals, birds, fish,
      aquatic creatures, etc.)

A New Creation Model approach affirms the importance of all three areas,
not just the first. As Snyder states, "…Jesus is the renewer of the whole creation, the whole face of the earth, and all the dimensions of life. Salvation
is that big."[15]

JESUS' ROLES

Theologians have rightly noted that Jesus fulfills the roles of Prophet,
Priest, and King. He is the ultimate Prophet, the One greater than Moses,
who reveals God's perfect will. Jesus also is the Priest who offered one perfect sacrifice for sins forever. He continually intercedes for us in Heaven.
Jesus, too, is King. We will discuss what this means in more depth below.

In our estimation the Bible particularly emphasizes Jesus' roles as
Savior and King. Jesus as Savior emphasizes Jesus' sacrificial atonement
for sin. He came "to give His life as a ransom for many" (Mark 10:45). His
Savior role means man can be forgiven and reconciled to God.

Jesus' role as King needs explanation because this dimension of Jesus'
role often has been understated in church history. With the dominance of
Amillennialism since the late fourth century onward, Jesus' role as King in
His messianic kingdom often has been understood in a spiritual way. Jesus
is King over a spiritual kingdom. Jesus' kingdom mostly involves salvation
from sin.

Yet while there is a spiritual dimension to Jesus' kingdom, Jesus' role
as King is much deeper than individual salvation from sin, as important as
that it. This is where the New Creation Model grasps the multiple dimensions of "Jesus as King."

Jesus' role as King also includes being (1) Ruler over geo-political nations; and (2) Restorer of all creation. Concerning Jesus as *Ruler*

---

15   Snyder, 129.

over nations, God promised the Messiah the nations as His inheritance (Ps. 2:8). He also said the Messiah will rule the nations with a rod of iron (Ps. 2:9; cf. Rev. 19:15). Zechariah 14 states that the Messiah (Jesus) will be "King over all the earth" (14:9) and the nations, including Egypt, must obey Him or experience negative consequences (14:16–19). In Daniel 2, the kingdom of God, the "stone made without hands," comes to earth and smashes the geo-political nations represented in the statue (Babylon, Medo-Persia, Greece, Rome).

Importantly, Jesus' reign as King must not be restricted to only spiritual salvation or saving individuals who come from nations. Jesus also will function as King over geo-political nations and over the lands they live in with a political rule that encompasses the entire earth (see Isa. 2:2–4; Zech. 9:10).

Jesus' role as King also means He is *Restorer of creation.* He will restore the earth and its creatures and bring harmony to all nature. This role is emphasized in passages like Isaiah 11; Hosea 2:18; and Romans 8:19–22. The intertextual connection of Hosea 2:18 with Genesis 1:26, 28 reveals that the Messiah will restore the animal realm that suffered from the Fall in Genesis 3. This results in animal-animal harmony and animal-human peace. He also brings agricultural prosperity to the earth (see Gen. 49:8–12; Ps. 72:16).

Thus, a New Creation Model view affirms the depth of Jesus' role as King, including the functions of ruling nations and restoring creation.

JESUS' ATONEMENT AND THE NEW CREATION

Jesus' atonement on the cross is central for the restoration and reconciliation of all things. Without it there is no salvation of persons or restoration of anything. Jesus came to give His life as a ransom for many (see Mark 10:45). He reconciles people to God with His death (see Col. 1:22). He also died for both Gentiles and Israel (see Isaiah 52–53). Thus, dying for the sins of humans is a central part of Jesus' death and atonement. Also, Jesus' atonement affects the whole person, including the body. In reference to Jesus and what His death means for resurrected saints, Richard Baxter declared, "As Christ bought the whole man, so shall the whole partake of the everlasting benefits of the purchase."[16]

Yet in addition to atonement for human sin and the whole person, the cross has implications for all creation. Colossians 1:15–20 teaches the reconciliation of "all things" in Christ "through the blood of His cross" (v. 20). This refers to everything God created, including all things visible and invisible (Col. 1:16). Jesus' atonement reconciles and restores both people and creation.[17] Thus, a New Creation Model approach calls for accepting all dimensions and implications of Jesus' atonement. As Steven James notes, "the work of Christ includes not only the salvation of the individual, but also the redemption of the entire creation from the effects of sin."[18] Howard Snyder aptly explains the cosmic aspects of Jesus' reconciliation:

> The reconciliation won by Christ reaches to all the alienations that result from our sin—alienation from God, from ourselves, between persons, and between us and our physical environment. The biblical picture therefore is at once personal, ecological, and cosmic. As mind-boggling as the thought is, Scripture teaches that this reconciliation even includes the redemption of the physical universe from the effects of sin as everything is brought under its proper headship in Jesus (Rom. 8:19–21).[19]

That all creation, which suffered from the Fall, would be transformed by the salvation Christ brings makes sense on a symmetrical level. As Saucy observes, "If we regard the negative affects of the fall of mankind as materially evident, then it is perfectly sound to regard the positive transformation wrought by messianic salvation as empirical as well."[20]

The resurrection of Jesus also relates to the earth. The resurrected Jesus walked on the earth, held conversations on the earth. He even ate

---

16   Richard Baxter, *The Saint's Everlasting Rest*, (Glasgow: Khull, Blackie, & Co. 1822), 11.

17   The reconciliation of all things does not mean the salvation of all people who have ever lived.

18   James, 3.

19   Snyder, 99.

20   Saucy, 237.

meals. This seems to have implications for the coming new earth: "If Jesus' body was recognizably the same after his resurrection, so also the earth will be recognizably the same after its renewal. To the degree that Jesus' resurrected body was and is physical, so also will be the earth and our bodies."[21]

The New Creation Model asks us to consider everything the cross of Jesus accomplishes. God is pursuing the "restoration of all things" in Jesus (see Acts 3:21) and this involves creation.

SPIRITUAL REALITIES AND THE NEW CREATION MODEL

Some think a New Creation Model perspective is too focused on material things and is not spiritual enough.[22] But the New Creation Model is *not* opposed to spiritual realities. It affirms them and their importance. This model does not demote spiritual matters to a secondary status. God is spirit. Man has a spirit. Loving God and loving people are the two greatest commands and the two most important things a person can do. The kingdom of God involves justice, righteousness, peace, joy, and love. Yet these "spiritual" realities exist alongside material realities. Passages like Isaiah 11 and Psalm 72 reveal that Messiah's kingdom will be an earthly kingdom that is characterized by the spiritual qualities of justice, fairness, and righteousness. A New Creation approach asks that both material and spiritual aspects of God's purposes be properly considered. And material and national entities should not be spiritualized.

While the Spiritual Vision Model presents a cosmic dualism between spirit and matter by elevating the former and denigrating the latter, the New Creation Model has no such dualism. It affirms the importance of both the spiritual and the physical.

---

21 Snyder, 107.

22 See Michael Allen, *Grounded in Heaven: Recentering Christian Hope and Life in God* (Grand Rapids: Eerdmans, 2018). Allen calls the New Creationist approach "eschatological naturalism."

THE NEW CREATION MODEL AND SIN

The New Creation Model focuses on positive issues such as God's creation purposes and the vibrant, multi-dimensional nature of eternal life. Yet this model also addresses the impact of sin on every level. Sin is a spiritual issue, but it also is anti-creational. It affects all creation. No aspect of creation is left untouched by sin. We should consider the multi-dimensional nature of sin so that the multi-faceted nature of salvation and restoration in Christ can be appreciated.

First, and most importantly, sin is an offense against *God*. God is worthy of worship and obedience from man, but man does not do this. Man is under the wrath of a holy God who cannot tolerate sin and sinners. Sin, therefore, is an offense against God—"Against You, You only, have I sinned" (Ps. 51:4).

Second, sin brings devastating turmoil to the *individual human person*. Adam's sin brought guilt, shame, and fear to himself. The same is true for all of Adam's descendants. The inner anguish for people, including depression, in a fallen world is great. This is evident by the many addictions, destructive behaviors, and suicides in our society. Snyder observes, "Because of sin, people are not at home within themselves. They experience uneasiness, disquiet, inner conflicts, and fears. Sin brings that whole range of maladies and symptoms that psychology and psychiatry deal with."[23] Sin wreaks havoc internally on the sinner.

Sin also impacts the two genders specifically. For men, sin brings frustration in the realm of work, including thorns and thistles to frustrate him. In the realm where man was to rule and subdue, he will be frustrated. Sin also brings increased pain in childbirth for the woman. Sin brings devastation to all people, and it affects men and women in their respective roles.

Third, at the *community* level, sin introduced tension and hatred amongst people. Cain's murder of Abel is one early example. Sin affects nations and ethnicities through constant wars, hatred, genocide, and persecution. The political, societal, and cultural realms are also polluted with

---

23   Snyder, 73.

sin. Thus, sin devastates man at the community and societal levels. God instituted government to regulate evil in society (see Romans 13), but in a fallen world sin occurs on a community and societal level.

Fourth, sin affects creation. *Earth and land* also are affected by sin. "Cursed is the ground because of you" (Gen. 3:17). As Snyder observes, "The land suffers from human sin in three ways: it suffers directly from human ill treatment of the land; indirectly it suffers the consequences of human violence; finally, it languishes from the lack of proper stewardship care that was entrusted to humankind."[24] The animal kingdom also suffers in a fallen world.

EXTENT OF JESUS' SALVATION

The bad news from sin is extensive but so too is the solution. Salvation in Jesus is multi-faceted. Jesus reverses, restores, and heals all the negative effects of sin at every level.

First, salvation in Jesus means reconciliation and restored relationship with God for the individual person.

Second, salvation in Jesus replaces the inner turmoil of guilt, shame, and fear with joy and peace.

Third, Jesus brings healing to human relationships. Christians are now able to love their neighbor as they should.

And fourth, Jesus will bring healing and peace to all creation including the earth, land, and all creatures.

In every area where sin mars and destroys, Jesus fixes and renews—"I am making all things new" (Rev. 21:5). Through His two comings, Jesus forgives sins and reconciles man to God. Jesus replaces hate with love so His people can love their neighbor. Yet, the benefits of salvation continue even further. Jesus will wipe out all disease and resurrect the body. He will reverse the curse on the ground and bring restoration to the entire creation, including the animal kingdom (see Hos. 2:18; Romans 8; Isaiah 11). He will bring healing to the nations and people groups of the world

---

24   Snyder, 76.

(see Rev. 5:9). He restores society and culture. Snyder is right that, "The reconciliation won by Christ reaches to all the alienations that result from our sin—alienation from God, from ourselves, between persons, and between us and our physical environment. The biblical picture therefore is at once personal, ecological, and cosmic."[25] Thus, the New Creation Model relates to sin in that sin affects man and creation holistically, but the restoration Jesus brings is holistic as well.

PARTICULARS AS MEANS TO BLESS THE UNIVERSAL

A new creationist approach also affirms the importance of both particulars and universals in God's purposes. God sometimes uses particulars to bless the universal. Or as Gerald McDermott puts it, "God reaches the universal through the particular."[26] But as this occurs the particular remains relevant.

How does this apply to God's purposes? It concerns the important relationship between Israel and the nations. In short, God uses the particulars of Israel and Israel's land to one day bless the nations of the world in their lands (universals). Genesis 12:2–3 revealed that Abraham and the "great nation" from him—Israel—would be the means for blessing all the families and nations of the earth (see Gen. 18:18). This involves the role of the land of Israel (see Gen. 12:6–7) which is the geographical locale for world blessings. God uses the particulars of Israel and Israel's land to bless Gentile nations in their lands.

Particulars and universals both matter. One does not cancel the relevance of the other. For example, God's plans are not all about the particular of Israel. Nor are they all about the universal of peoples other than Israel. God's purposes concern both Israel and the nations. Isaiah 27:6 states, "In the days to come Jacob will take root, Israel will blossom and sprout, and they will fill the whole world with fruit." Israel exists to bless the whole

---

25   Snyder, 99.

26   Gerald R. McDermott, *Israel Matters: Why Christians Must Think Differently about the People and the Land* (Grand Rapids: Brazos Press, 2017), 114.

world. With Isaiah 49:3–6, God says His Servant will restore Israel and bring light to all nations. So as God blesses Israel, He also will bless other nations (Amos 9:11–15). Likewise, when God fulfills His land promises with Israel (Gen. 15:18–21) He will bless other nations in their lands (Isaiah 19:16–25).

As we have seen, universal blessings to the nations do not remove particular promises to Israel. Nor do God's plans to bless the nations mean Israel as a nation no longer is significant. Yet many theologians believe the significance of national Israel has been removed because God is now blessing the world. As McDermott aptly notes:

> Whereas the pattern of both Testaments is that God saves the world (the universal) through Israel (the particular), most theologians say that the pattern changes in the New Testament. There the particular drops out. That is, most theologians today say that the particular people of the Jews and their particular land are no longer of importance to God.[27]

The correct view is that fulfillment with the *particular* (Israel) leads to the fulfillment of the *universal* (the world). This is a both/and situation. Since Israel and Israel's land are microcosms of what God will do for all people groups, these particulars do not need to be denied or universalized. Blaising summarizes this point:

> It is not necessary to eliminate the particular in order to institute the universal nor is it necessary to expand the particular to become the universal, rather the particular is both the means to the blessing of the universal as well as a central constitutive part of it.[28]

---

27 Ibid., 113. He also states, "But for all too many theologians today, the particular is missing." Ibid., 114.

28 Craig A. Blaising, "Israel and Hermeneutics," in *The People, The Land, and the Future of Israel: Israel and the Jewish People in the Plan of God*, eds. Darrell L. Bock and Mitch Glaser (Grand Rapids: Kregel, 2014), 162.

INDIVIDUALS, NATIONS, AND ISRAEL

While a Spiritual Vision Model perspective focuses exclusively on the salvation of individuals or the elect, a new creationist perspective affirms the importance of individuals, Israel, and all ethnicities and nations in God's plans. First, God saves individuals (Matt. 11:28–29). Second, He uses the nation Israel as a vehicle for His plans (Gen. 12:2; Rom. 11:12). And third, God works with nations and ethnicities. God will bless all people groups and nations (Gen. 12:3; 22:18; Rev. 5:9). Isaiah 19:16–25 promises that in the coming kingdom the nations of Egypt, Assyria, and Israel will exist and function harmoniously as geo-political entities. Revelation 21:24, 26 tells of multiple nations and kings bringing their glory into the New Jerusalem. The gospel is going to all nations in this present age, but a future era is coming when national entities will serve the Lord (see Isa. 2:2–4).

McDermott notes that, "We all will be renewed, both as individuals and as nations."[29] Why is this issue so important to get right? It is because "Today's theologies...tend to accent the individual at the expense of the social." And "ethnic, national, and linguistic identities have been erased from most Christian portrayals of the world to come...."[30] But a New Creation Model approach captures the richness and dimensions of all people groups in God's purposes.

---

29   McDermott, 116.
30   Ibid., 115.

SPIRITUAL VISION MODEL AND NEW CREATION MODEL VIEWS ON ETERNITY COMPARISON

	Spiritual Vision Model	New Creation Model
The present earth's destiny	The present earth is annihilated	The present earth is restored and renewed
The "new earth" in eternity	An entirely different planet exists; or the new earth is spiritual Heaven	The present earth is restored
Destiny of the saved	Spiritual Heaven	A tangible new earth
Time	Time does not exist	Time exists
Motion	Motion does not exist	Motion exists
Relationship of this present age to eternity	No relationship. Eternity takes place in another realm with different experiences	The experiences on the new earth are similar to the experiences on the present earth, minus the effects of sin, the fall, and the curse
Focus of the saved	God alone is the focus of the saved	God is primary focus, but love of other saved persons exists, and interaction with the new earth exists

	Spiritual Vision Model	**New Creation Model**
Culture (art, music, technology, etc.)	Culture does not exist	Culture exists
Social-Political interactions	Social-political interactions do not exist	Social and Political interactions exist
Geo-Political Nations	Geo-political nations do not exist; only saved individuals	Geo-political nations with leaders exist
Ethnicities	Ethnicity no longer matters	Diverse ethnicities exist in harmony and are celebrated
Awareness of other saved persons	No awareness of other people, or only aware of others as they join in worshipping God	Awareness and social interactions with the saved
Food and Celebrations	Does not exist	Food and celebrations exist
Knowledge	No need to learn anything	Learning about God and His creation continues
Resurrected body	Resurrected body exists but has little use as Heaven is mostly about mental contemplation of God	People use their resurrected bodies to move and interact with other people and the new earth
Physical senses	Saved persons will see and perceive God but no need exists for senses like taste, smell, or hearing	The senses of sight, smell, taste, hearing, and touch will exist and work better than they do now

	Spiritual Vision Model	**New Creation Model**
Houses	Houses do not exist	Houses exist on the new earth
Farms, Agriculture	Farms and agriculture do not exist	Farms and agriculture exist
Animals	Animals do not exist; they have instrumental value now but have no place in eternity	Animals exist on the new earth; they have inherent value to God and remain important in eternity
Talking/ Communication	Talking and communication do not exist	Saved people talk and communicate with each other
Knowledge of the present earth and age	No memory exists of the present earth or age	People remember other people and experiences from the present age; what does not carry over are negative memories and experiences from the present earth and age
Oceans, bodies of water	Oceans and bodies of water do not exist; aquatic creatures do not exist	Salt water oceans that are dangerous and separate people by large distances are removed; but large bodies of water and aquatic creatures exist

KEY ELEMENTS OF THE NEW CREATION MODEL (PART 1)

"Christians often talk about living with God 'in heaven' forever. But in fact the biblical teaching is richer than that: it tells us that there will be new heavens and a new earth—an entirely renewed creation—and we will live with God there."

—Wayne Grudem[1]

◆

The last chapter defined the New Creation Model paradigm and offered strategic beliefs associated with it. This chapter and the next now offer sixteen important elements of God's creation and new creation purposes associated with the New Creation Model.

MAN'S DESTINY TIED TO EARTH

Man and earth are inseparable in God's purposes. While a Spiritual Vision Model approach views man as needing to escape planet earth, the New Creation Model affirms that man's destiny is tied to the earth. God "formed man of dust from the ground" (Gen. 2:7). And God tasked man to "rule" and "subdue" the earth and its creatures (see Gen. 1:26, 28; Psalm 8). Man

---

1   Wayne, Grudem, *Systematic Theology* (Grand Rapids: Zondervan, 1994), 1158.

was not created to flee earth for a spiritual realm. He was made to rule from and over the earth. Psalm 115:16 states, "The heavens are the heavens of the LORD, but the earth He has given to the sons of men." Commenting on this verse, Middleton notes, "Whereas God reigns from heaven, earth is the distinctively human realm."[2]

The relationship of man to the earth is affirmed after the Fall. According to Genesis 3 the ground was cursed and now works against man. Full of thorns and thistles, the ground frustrates man at every step. Death, decay, and destruction are now man's experience. But God has not given up on man or the earth. With Genesis 3:15 God promised that a coming "seed" of the woman would defeat the power behind the serpent. And with Genesis 5:28–29, Lamech hoped for a descendant who "will give us rest from our work and from the toil of our hands arising from the ground which the LORD has cursed." Genesis 49:8–12 declares that a messianic figure ("Shiloh" or "Him to whom it belongs") will rule the nations and bring prosperity to the earth. Thus, three early messianic passages present hope for man on the earth.

Because of sin, man cannot fulfill his God-given destiny to rule the earth successfully. But this destiny will be fulfilled through the ultimate man—Jesus, the Last Adam, who will succeed where Adam failed and reign successfully from and over the earth. In a second coming passage, Zechariah 14:9 states: "And the LORD will be king over all the earth." Concerning the destiny of Jesus' saints, Revelation 5:10 states: "You have made them to be a kingdom and priests to our God; and they will reign upon the earth." This is fulfilled in Revelation 20 when Jesus reigns with His saints on the earth. In the Eternal Kingdom, the saints will reign from a new Jerusalem and a new earth (see Rev. 21:1–2; 22:5). Man and earth are inseparably linked from Genesis 1 through Revelation 22.

---

2   J. Richard Middleton, "A New Earth Perspective," in *Four Views on Heaven*, ed. Michael E. Wittmer (Grand Rapids: Zondervan, 2022), 72.

RESURRECTION OF THE BODY

Extreme forms of the Spiritual Vision Model view the human body as a hindrance to existence and enlightenment. The eastern religions, for example, have no room for a resurrected body in their eschatology. Neither do philosophies stemming from Plato. The heretical Docetics believed Jesus did not have a human body since the body is bad. But the New Creation Model affirms that the human body is good and is destined for physical resurrection. A one-to-one correspondence exists between the body a person has now and the body a person will experience on the new earth. The you of today will be the same you in eternity. But with no imperfections!

In fact, the connection between now and then applies to both believers and unbelievers (see Dan. 12:1–2; John 5:28–29). Both will be called from the grave and have a physical body fit for their destinies. Most emphasis in Scripture, though, is on the resurrection of believers. Paul said we are "waiting eagerly for … the redemption of our body" (Rom. 8:23b). Isaiah 26:19a: "Your dead will live; Their corpses will rise. You who lie in the dust, awake and shout for joy."

Resurrection is based on Jesus, who is the first fruits of the resurrection (1 Cor. 15:20). The Jesus who was placed in a tomb is the same Jesus who came out. Jesus could talk, walk, be touched, and eat meals. He talked with those whom He knew before He died. Fortunately, belief in resurrection of the body has been held by Christians throughout church history. This is one element of the New Creation Model that has been most consistently held throughout church history.

Also, in connection with the resurrection of the body is the perfecting of our physical senses. Our bodies were created to see, hear, smell, taste, and touch. These senses will work in the future even better than they do now. As Richard Baxter stated: "… so far shall our senses exceed those we now possess. Doubtless as God advanceth our senses, and enlargeth our capacity, so will he advance the happiness of those senses, and fill up with himself all that capacity."[3]

---

3   Richard Baxter, *The Saint's Everlasting Rest*, 11.

The resurrection of the body also is linked with the transformation of creation. Paul makes this point in Romans 8:21: "that the creation itself also will be set free from its slavery to corruption into the freedom of the glory of the children of God." Thus, the resurrection affects not only humans but also the entire created order. As one author notes, "It is *absurd* to think that Jesus died and rose again to save our souls—not our bodies and the whole creation. Why should Jesus rise *physically* to save us only *spiritually?*"[4]

Sometimes Paul's discussion of the "spiritual body" in 1 Corinthians 15:44 is taken to mean that our future bodies will not be physical. But this is not Paul's meaning. As we just saw, in Romans 8:23 Paul referred to the coming "redemption of our body" which must mean a resurrected physical body. Paul's reference to a "spiritual body" concerns the *source* of our future resurrection body, not its *substance*. The source and power of our future resurrection body is the Holy Spirit. As Ian Smith explains:

> Care should be taken to understand what is meant by a "spiritual body." Greek can differentiate the substance from which a body is made from that which empowers a body. Paul refers to "spiritual" as that which empowers the body, not as its substance. A steam train is not made of steam, nor is an electric kettle made of electricity, and a gas oven is not made of gas.[5]

Blaising also notes, "the 'spirituality' of eternal life in the new creation model" is "not the absence of materiality but the full effect of the Holy Spirit's indwelling the resurrected physical bodies of the redeemed."[6] In sum, the "spiritual body" that Paul explains concerns the spiritual source of our coming resurrected physical bodies.

---

4   Snyder, *Salvation Means Creation Healed*, 226. Emphases in original.

5   Ian K. Smith, *Not Home Yet: How the Renewal of the Earth Fits into God's Plan for the World* (Wheaton, IL: Crossway, 2019), 127.

6   Blaising, "Premillennialism," 163.

RENEWAL/RESTORATION
OF THE EARTH

I once thought the earth was so corrupt and irredeemable that it had to be exploded out of existence and replaced with an entirely new realm. This is referred to as the "annihilation view." Later I learned this idea was related to Spiritual Vision Model-thinking. As Craig Blaising notes, "The idea of cosmic annihilation properly belongs to gnostic eschatology, which generally held that materiality as such would be annihilated to make way for a purely spiritual order."[7]

While the transition from the old to the new is dramatic, God will not annihilate His "very good" creation (Gen. 1:31)—He will restore it. Jesus called the coming new earth "the regeneration" (see Matt. 19:28). The Greek term, *paliggenesia*, means "genesis again" or "renewal." Also, Paul said Jesus is reconciling all things "through the blood of His cross" (see Col. 1:20). This refers to the reconciliation of all things created. With Acts 3:21 Peter referred to the coming "restoration of all things" in connection with the return of Jesus. Restoration is the plan, not annihilation. Paul said the current corrupted creation longs eagerly for freedom: "... the creation itself also will be set free from its slavery to corruption into the freedom of the glory of the children of God" (see Rom. 8:21). The current creation exists in a state of "hope" (Rom. 8:20). If creation were headed for annihilation "hope" would not apply. Annihilation from existence is no reason for hope.

The New Creation Model affirms a coming renewal/restoration of earth and its elements. This earth that was cursed and plunged into futility because of man's sin (see Rom. 8:20; cf. Genesis 3) will be renewed. It will be purged and purified and found better than before. The fiery purging of 2 Peter 3:10–13 results in the earth being "found" or "manifested." Much like precious metals go through fire to be purged, the earth will be purged but remain. The fiery destruction connected with the new heavens and earth is linked to purification. As Blaising notes, "What will be eliminated in the

---

7   Craig A. Blaising, "The Day of the Lord Will Come: An Exposition of 2 Peter 3:1–18," *Bibliotheca Sacra* 169.676 (October-December 2012): 398.

Day of the Lord is not the cosmos or materiality as such, but sin and evil. And this is where the language of refinement by fire finds its proper place."[8]

God does not give up on His creation. Poythress rightly notes that when it comes to "the renewal of the world ... [t]he solution is redemption and transfiguration, not vaporization."[9] This gives God the victory with His originally "very good" creation (see Gen. 1:31). Anthony Hoekema states, "If God would have to annihilate the present cosmos, Satan would have won a great victory."[10] Snyder argues, "The new creation is not a second creation *ex nihilo*; it is the restoration and enhanced flourishing of the original creation."[11]

Language concerning new heavens and new earth is found explicitly in Isaiah 65:17; 66:22; 2 Peter 3:13; and Revelation 21:1. Transformation of the earth/land is discussed in Isaiah 35:1–2a where the wilderness and desert will be changed:

> The wilderness and the desert will be glad,
> And the Arabah will rejoice and blossom;
> Like the crocus
> It will blossom profusely
> And rejoice with rejoicing and shout of joy.

Lush conditions are described in Isaiah 35:6b–7:

> For waters will break forth in the wilderness
> And streams in the Arabah.
> The scorched land will become a pool
> And the thirsty ground springs of water;
> In the haunt of jackals, its resting place,
> Grass becomes reeds and rushes.

---

8   Ibid.

9   Vern Sheridan Poythress, "Currents within Amillennialism," *Presbyterion* 26.1 (2000): 23.

10   Anthony A. Hoekema, *The Bible and the Future* (Grand Rapids: Eerdmans, 1979), 280.

11   Snyder, 121.

Restoration of the land is linked with a return to Eden-like conditions in Ezekiel 36:34–35:

> The desolate land will be cultivated instead of being a desolation in the sight of everyone who passes by. They will say, "This desolate land has become like the garden of Eden; and the waste, desolate and ruined cities are fortified and inhabited."

Note how biblical language reveals the glorious destiny of creation:

"the *regeneration*" –Matt. 19:28
"the *restoration* of all things" –Acts 3:21
"to *reconcile* all things" –Col. 1:20
"a *new* heaven and a *new* earth" –Rev. 21:1
"I am making all things *new*" –Rev. 21:5

While not using the title, "New Creation Model," Michael Williams speaks of a "restorational perspective" that is consistent with the New Creation Model: "The restorational perspective can be summed up in a single declaration: Redemption reverses the fall."[12]

Knowing that God will restore creation is a thrilling truth. The creation that has been subjected to futility will also see the benefits of Jesus' redemptive reach. As Eduard Thurneysen puts it:

> The world into which we shall enter in the Parousia of Jesus Christ is therefore not another world; it is this world, this heaven, this earth; both, however, passed away and renewed. It is these forests, these fields, these cities, these streets, these people, that will be the scene of redemption. At present they are battlefields, full of the strife and sorrow of the not yet accomplished consummation; then they will be fields of victory, fields of harvest, where out of seed that was sown with tears the everlasting sheaves will be reaped and brought home.[13]

---

12   Michael Williams, "A Restorational Alternative to Augustinian Verticalist Eschatology," 14.

13   Eduard Thurneysen, *Eternal Hope*, trans. Harold Knight (London: Lutterworth, 1954), 204.

NATIONS AND ETHNICITIES

Some think eternity will mean we join a generic heavenly community with no ethnic, national, or functional identities or distinctions. Ethnicities and nations will be no more. Some also think that since Jesus arrived, God's plan for nations are only about saving certain individuals from various ethnicities and nations in this age. But God's purposes do not stop there. God's plans also include corporate entities, not only for the church in this age, but for nations in the coming kingdom. As Andrew Kim puts it, "kingdom consummation" involves "a multinational reality, composed not just of individuals, but of individuals with distinct ethnic and territorial affiliations."[14]

But before we look more at what the Bible says about nations we want to discuss God's plans for both unity and diversity. We are one race—the human race. And all people are made in the image of God. Believers are saved the same way in Jesus (see Gal. 3:28; Eph. 2:11–3:6). And in the church there are no functional distinctions based on ethnicity. All of these truths reveal unity of God's people.

Yet there also are elements of diversity. Ethnic and national diversity are major parts of God's plans. From Adam various people groups comprise the human family. Acts 17:26 declares: "He [God] made from one man *every nation* of mankind to live on all the face of the earth, having determined their appointed times and the boundaries of their habitation."[15] God cares for the nations. He determines when they exist and where they live and function.

Genesis 10–11, with its table of nations, reveals the diversity of nations and peoples stemming from Noah's three sons. These nations, carefully mentioned one by one, set the scene for Abraham and the Abrahamic Covenant of Genesis 12. God chose Abraham and the "great nation" Israel (see Gen. 12:2) to bless all the "families" and "nations" of the earth (see

---

14   Andrew H. Kim, "The Eschatological Kingdom as a Multinational Reality in Isaiah," Ph.D. diss. Southwestern Baptist Theological Seminary, 2019: 170.

15   Emphases mine.

Gen. 12:3; 18:18; 22:18). Thus, early in the Bible we learn God has a plan for all nations to be blessed via one nation. Nations matter. God could have let mankind remain a collection of individuals, but He determined that nations would be part of His purposes.

The major prophets contain sections devoted specifically to Gentile nations and groups—Isaiah 13–23; Jeremiah 43–51; Ezekiel 25–32. Daniel 2 and 7 describe the importance of various successive empires in history—Babylon, Medo-Persia, Greece, Rome, and what appears to be a final form of the Roman Empire. These are geo-political nations with kings who live in specific geographical areas. They are related to God's plans for the past, present, and future.

Various Bible passages describe warfare and battles involving geo-political nations that still await future fulfillment. Ezekiel 38 mentions Russia, Turkey, Iran, Ethiopia, Libya, and Turkey as all engaged with an attempted invasion of Israel. Daniel 11 speaks of "the king of the South" and "the king of the North" (40) coming against an evil king who blasphemes God (36). Nations and peoples mentioned in this chapter include Edom, Moab, Ammon, Egypt, Libya, Ethiopia, and Israel ["the Beautiful Land"] (41, 43). Revelation 16:12–16 refers to "the kings from the east" and "the kings of the whole world" that gather for battle at Armageddon. Revelation 19:19 mentions "the kings of the earth and their armies assembled to make war against Him who sat on the horse [Jesus] and against His army." Jesus said the last days would be characterized by nations at war with each other (see Matt. 24:6–7). The point here is not to speculate on all the details of these battles. But they reveal that geo-political nations and their rulers are involved in God's plans for history.

Also concerning the future, Isaiah 2:2–4 and Micah 4 picture representatives from geo-political nations traveling to Jerusalem to learn God's ways. The Lord also will make decisions for these nations. Isaiah 19:24 mentions three specific territorial nations in the coming kingdom—Israel, Egypt, and Assyria: "In that day Israel will be the third party with Egypt and Assyria, a blessing in the midst of the earth." Egypt will make a monument to the Lord in the land of Egypt (see Isa. 19:19). Isaiah 19:23 speaks of Egypt coming into Assyria, and Assyria into Egypt, to worship the Lord:

In that day there will be a highway from Egypt to Assyria, and the
Assyrians will come into Egypt and the Egyptians into Assyria, and
the Egyptians will worship with the Assyrians.

Zechariah 14 states that the Lord [Jesus] will rescue Jerusalem from
the nations (1–5). And when Jesus reigns as King over the entire earth (9),
the nations will be required to send a delegation to Jerusalem to worship
Him. If they refuse a plague will occur (see 14:16–19).

The passages above are just samples of what the Bible says about
nations in God's plans. Discerning God's historical purposes means grap-
pling with His plans for nations and people groups. God is not seeking
the disintegration of ethnicities and nations—He will rule over them with
a righteous kingdom reign (see Psalm 2; 110). Jesus' second coming will
bring His rule over "the nations" with "a rod of iron" (see Rev. 19:15). God
will save and enable nations, with their leaders, to make contributions to
the new earth (see Rev. 21:24). Alcorn notes, "Tribes, peoples, and nations
will all make their own particular contribution to the enrichment of life in
the New Jerusalem."[16]

This truth of multiple people groups and nations in God's plans coincides with salvific equality for all in Jesus (see Gal. 3:28). Yet there also is
diversity of people groups. There is one people of God salvifically in Jesus,
yet there are also peoples of God since God's people come from various ethnicities and nations. In this age, individuals from various people groups
and nations are being saved into Jesus' church. Yet in the future when Jesus
comes to reign on the earth, corporate nations will be there. Nations also
will experience salvation. Romans 11:26 predicts the national salvation
of Israel: "All Israel will be saved." Romans 11:26–27 then quotes Isaiah
59:20–21 (and perhaps Jer. 31:34), which also predicts a national salvation of Israel. Coming back to Isaiah 19, this chapter speaks of the coming salvation of Egypt. Verse 20 says God will send "Egypt a Savior and a
Champion." Verse 21 then declares—"Thus the Lord will make Himself
known to Egypt, and the Egyptians will know the Lord in that day."

---

16   Alcorn, Heaven, 380.

In the last three chapters of Scripture, Revelation 20–22, the "nations" are referred to five times, revealing their importance. Revelation 21:3 says, "And they shall be His peoples (*laoi*)." And these "peoples" are "the nations" mentioned in Revelation 21:24, 26; 22:2:

> The *nations* will walk by its light, and the *kings of the earth* will bring their glory into it (Rev. 21:24).

> and they will bring the glory and the honor of the *nations* into it (Rev. 21:26).

> and the leaves of the tree were for the healing of the *nations* (Rev. 22:2b).[17]

Genetics matter. Randy Alcorn notes that, "Racial identities will continue (Revelation 5:9; 7:9), and this involves a genetic carryover from the old body to the new."[18] Just as people do not lose their gender or individual identities when they become believers, neither do people lose their ethnicity or the significance of it. It is part of who they are. Jesus himself always will be an Israelite, a descendant of David. So both unity and diversity exist with the people(s) of God. Part of the beauty of the coming kingdom is the diversity among God's people(s). As Herman Bavinck states, "diversity is not destroyed in eternity but cleansed from sin and made serviceable to fellowship with God and others."[19] Isaiah 25:6 refers to a beautiful kingdom meal involving the peoples: "The Lord of hosts will prepare a lavish banquet for all peoples on this mountain; a banquet of aged wine, choice pieces with marrow, and refined, aged wine."

The significance and place of nations in the Bible's storyline is often missed or understated. Much of this is related to the Spiritual Vision Model assumption that God is only working with individuals. Yet English

---

17   Emphases mine in these quotations.

18   Alcorn, *Heaven*, 290.

19   Herman Bavinck, *Reformed Dogmatics: Holy Spirit, Church, and New Creation*, Volume 4, ed. John Bolt, trans. John Vriend (Grand Rapids: Baker Academic, 2008), 715. We are not claiming Bavinck would agree with everything we assert in this section.

Bible translations might also contribute to the problem. The word "nations" in the New Testament comes from the Greek term, *ethnos*. Forms of *ethnos* occur 162 times in the New Testament. And while this term is sometimes rightly translated as "nation" or "nations," Bible translations mostly use "Gentile" or "Gentiles." This is not always wrong, but it can present a slightly different understanding for the term and contribute to a disconnect with the Old Testament understanding of nations.

"Gentile" seems to imply "non-Jew" in a generic way. Whereas "nation" carries the broader and richer idea of people groups with different cultures in different lands outside of Israel. O. Palmer Robertson rightly notes, "In many passages of the New Testament," *ethnos* "simply cannot be translated 'Gentiles' and do justice to the point of the text."[20] He then references Matthew 24:14; Mark 11:17; Acts 10:34, 35; and Revelation 15:3 as examples. Robertson also states that *ethnos* "might be better rendered consistently as 'nation' or 'people.'"[21] Why? "The translation 'nation' provides a positive dimension when all the various peoples of the world are being considered."[22] We agree with his assessment. Timothy Whitaker notes that when "Gentiles" is the translation English readers lose the connection with the Old Testament meaning of "nations": "When *ethne* in the New Testament is translated as *the Gentiles* rather than *the nations*, the connection between the account of the nations in the Old Testament and the new prominent concern for the nations in the New Testament is obscured for English-speaking readers."[23]

In short, the Bible's storyline includes the importance of nations and people groups. The New Creation Model detects their significance. Next, we look at one of the key nations in God's plans—Israel.

---

20   O. Palmer Robertson, "Israel and the Nations in God's Covenants," in *Covenant Theology: Biblical, Theological, and Historical Perspectives*, eds. Guy Prentiss Waters, J. Nicholas Reid, and John R. Muether (Wheaton, IL: Crossway, 2020), 515.

21   Ibid., 514.

22   Ibid.

23   Timothy W. Whitaker, "The Nations in the Bible," https://providencemag.com/2021/02/ the-nations-bible/ (February 18, 2021), accessed March 4, 2023. Emphases in original.

ISRAEL

Since geo-political nations are important in God's plans it should be no surprise that Israel as a nation is important as well. As Barry Horner noted, "the mention of distinctive national contributions [in the Bible] ... would surely have to include the cultural benefactions of Israel!"[24] Horner's point is well taken. If nations exist on the new earth, engaging in real culture and activities, then Israel will do so as well. The land of Israel also is important. Blaising asserts, "Now, given that the new earth has geographical particularity and that it is essentially this earth redeemed for an everlasting glory, is it not important to ask about the territorial promises to Israel?"[25]

In both testaments Israel is depicted as an ethnic, national, territorial entity stemming from Abraham, Isaac, and Jacob. The significance of Israel is affirmed in sections such as Jeremiah 30–33 and Ezekiel 36–48 which foretell the coming restoration of national Israel, including the land. On His ascension day, Jesus and the apostles discussed the coming restoration of the kingdom to Israel (Acts 1:6–7). In Romans 11:11–32 Paul explained the coming salvation of "all Israel" (11:26) and the increased blessings this would bring the world (11:12, 15). The restoration of the twelve tribes of Israel is mentioned in Matthew 19:28; Luke 22:30 and Revelation 7:4–8. Israel remains significant as a corporate national entity. Horton is not accurate when he claims, "Israel no longer is identified with a nation or an ethnic people ...."[26] This is a Spiritual Vision Model statement. No ethnic people or nation, not even Israel, loses its identity. Christ brings salvific unity between Israel and Gentiles, but identities are not lost.

---

24 Barry E. Horner, *Future Israel: Why Christian Anti-Judaism Must Be Challenged* (Nashville, TN: B&H Academic, 2007), 217.

25 Craig A. Blaising, "Israel and Hermeneutics," in *The People, The Land, and the Future of Israel*, 163.

26 Michael S. Horton, "Covenant Theology," in *Covenantal and Dispensational Theologies: Four Views on the Continuity of Scripture*, eds. Brent E. Parker and Richard J. Lucas (Downers Grove, IL: IVP Academic, 2022), 71. Horton's comment ends with "but with Christ as the head with his body— 'one new man,' ending even the distinction between Jew and Gentile in his kingdom (Eph 2:14–16; cf. Gal 3:28)." Yes, Christ ends the "distinction between Jew and Gentile" when it comes to salvation, but this does not mean all distinctions no longer exist. Jews are still Jews and Gentiles are still Gentiles ethnically.

Yet Israel's significance is not an end in itself. Universal blessings to other nations and peoples will occur because of the particulars of Israel and Israel's land.[27] Genesis 12:2–3 reveals that through Abraham and the great nation, Israel, blessings will come to the families of the earth. Psalm 67:7 states, "God blesses us [Israel] that all the ends of the earth may fear Him."

A Spiritual Vision approach is supersessionist since it views the church in Jesus as superseding, replacing, or fulfilling Israel in a way that makes the nation Israel nonsignificant theologically. But a consistent new creationist perspective is non-supersessionist. National Israel remains significant in God's purposes and the Bible's storyline because Israel and other nations matter. When Jesus rules from David's throne over a regenerated earth the apostles will rule over the restored tribes of Israel (see Matt. 19:28; Luke 1:31–33). This will coincide with blessings to other nations (see Isa. 2:2–4). God is concerned about each distinct nation and the contributions each nation, including Israel, will make. As Bavinck notes:

> all the nations, Israel included, maintain their distinct place and calling (Matt. 8:11; Rom. 11:25; Rev. 21:24; 22:2). And all those nations— each in accordance with its own distinct national character—bring into the New Jerusalem all they have received from God in the way of glory and honor (Rev. 21:24, 26).[28]

LAND

The issue of "land," and the land of Israel in particular, is much debated in Christian circles. On this topic Spiritual Vision Model assumptions often prevail. In 2007, I spoke at a church during the middle of the week on the topic of Israel and Israel's land with an audience that was not in agreement with what I believed. To their credit they wanted to hear an

---

27 And this occurs because of Jesus the ultimate Israelite.

28 Bavinck, 720.

opposing view. I argued that ethnic/national Israel remains significant in God's purposes and that Israel would be saved and restored to their land. This would coincide with blessings to other nations in their lands in an earthly kingdom under Jesus (see Isa. 19:23–25). My presentation and the ensuing questions went well and the setting was professional and polite. But soon after a woman hastily approached me with hands raised in the air crying out, "Land! Why are we talking about land? Do you think God cares about land?" For her, land was not important to God, and we should be focused on more spiritual things. Her reaction remained with me. Was she right? She and I had different presuppositions concerning the importance of land in God's plans. So is land important to God? It seems to be—and in a major way.

Land is one of the most discussed topics and themes in the Bible. There are 2,504 references to *eretz* in the Old Testament, a word often interpreted as "land" (1,581 times) and "earth" (651 times). The New Testament word for "land" or "earth"—*gē*—shows up approximately 250 times. There are about 1,700 references to "land" and 685 references to "earth" in the New American Standard Bible.

Many passages detail the importance of land promises. Land was central to the Abrahamic Covenant in Genesis 12:6–7, and the boundaries of Israel's promised land are stated in Genesis 15:18–21. In Deuteronomy 30 God predicted that Israel would be dispersed from their land for disobedience, but then restored to it: "The Lord your God will bring you into the land which your fathers possessed, and you shall possess it; and He will prosper you and multiply you more than your fathers" (Deut. 30:5). Leviticus 26:40–45 says God will restore Israel to the land connected to the Abrahamic Covenant after a period of dispersion to the nations: "If they confess their iniquity and the iniquity of their forefathers...then I will remember My covenant with Jacob, and I will remember also My covenant with Isaac, and My covenant with Abraham as well, and I will remember the land" (Lev. 26:40–42).

The Book of Joshua is dominated by the issue of land. The word for land—*eretz*—occurs 102 times. Thomas Schreiner notes, "The importance of land in Joshua can scarcely be overestimated."[29] Joshua is a book "consumed with the place where Yahweh rules over his people."[30]

Land is not just an Old Testament issue. Jesus began His ministry in the northern part of Israel where the first tribes of Israel were conquered with the Assyrian Captivity (Matt. 4:12–16). From here He would preach the nearness of the kingdom (see Matt. 4:17). Jesus said the humble will "inherit the land/earth" (Matt. 5:5). In Acts 7, Stephen mentioned "land" six times (3, 4, 6, 29, 36, 40). With Acts 13:19 Paul said that God "distributed their [Israel's] land as an inheritance."

While the importance of land promises in the Bible often is downplayed or the land is spiritualized or universalized, the land God promised to Abraham's descendants is important to God's creational purposes and His plans to save humanity. After the Fall and the global flood, the world was a dark place. Israel's land was to function like a beachhead and point of light for God's plans to save and restore the world. According to Deuteronomy 4:1, 5–8, if Israel obeyed God in the promised land, other nations would notice and be drawn to God. Thus, land is a major part of the Bible's storyline, and its significance is often emphasized in prophetic passages about the future. Several passages reveal that when Israel possesses the land in the coming kingdom, other nations will benefit greatly as well (see Isaiah 2; 19; Zechariah 14).

So the correct answer to the question, "Who cares about land?" is God and the Bible! Land and earth are major parts of the Bible's storyline.

Surprisingly, some who promote New Creationism resist the significance of Israel and Israel's land. This issue was directly addressed by Steven James in his book, *New Creation Eschatology and the Land: A Survey of Contemporary Perspectives.* James discussed various theologians who hold to New Creationism on many areas yet resist the significance of Israel and Israel's land.[31] Some of these theologians we often quote favorably

---

29   Thomas Schreiner, *The King in His Beauty: A Biblical Theology of the Old and New Testaments* (Grand Rapids: Baker, 2013), 107.

30   Ibid., 108. We are not claiming Schreiner agrees with our theology of land.

31   These include N. T. Wright, Richard Middleton, Russell Moore, and Howard A. Snyder.

in this book. But James notes that such an approach is inconsistent since it takes "earth" passages at face value but not passages about Israel. And sometimes this occurs when earth and Israel are mentioned together in the same contexts like in Isaiah 2 and Ezekiel 36–37. James observes the "logical inconsistency" here:

> ...a logical inconsistency arises between the new creation conceptions and a metaphorical fulfillment of the promise of the particular territory of Israel. The inconsistency involves the practice of new creationists affirming a new earth that corresponds in identity to the present earth while denying an enduring role for the particular portion of territorial Israel as a part of that earth.[32]

Blaising also detects an inconsistency on this issue. James states, "As Blaising argues, there is inconsistency and incoherence in new creation conceptions that affirm a restored or regenerated earth while neglecting the particular territory of Israel."[33] We agree with James and Blaising. We have yet to see a compelling argument for taking "earth" passages literally in the Bible while not doing so for "Israel" texts. A controlling theological presupposition against the significance of Israel must be present to come to this conclusion. Later we will identify this presupposition against Israel and Israel's land as "structural supersessionism."

Thus, *a consistent New Creation Model approach affirms the significance of the particulars of Israel and Israel's land in God's plans.* These are emphasized in Scripture. And these are particulars God uses for universal purposes—to save and bless all nations in their lands.

GOVERNMENTS

In this fallen world it is hard to think positively of human governments, and rightfully so. Governments are often characterized by corruption and injustice. They often abuse the people they govern. Psalm 2 presents the

---

32   James, *New Creation Eschatology and the Land*, 95.

33   Ibid., 97.

nations as being in rebellion against God. Knowing this, how can governments exist in the kingdom of God?

Human government was established by God and is part of His
plan for an orderly society. The foundation for government is the Noahic
Covenant when God granted man the right to administer justice to those
who murdered a human being (see Gen. 9:6).[34] With Romans 13:1 Paul
said that "governing authorities" are "established by God." He also said that
government is a "minister of God" (Rom. 13:4). Governments, in general,
reward those who do good and punish evildoers.

Egypt operated under the rule of Pharaoh. Israel functioned under
the mediatorial leaders of Moses, Joshua, the judges, and then Saul, David,
and Solomon. The divided kingdoms of Israel and Judah operated under
various kings. The Gentile nations of Babylon, Medo-Persia, Greece, and
Rome exercised governmental rule as predicted in Daniel 2 and 7.

But the governments of nations will give way to the ultimate government of the Messiah. In Genesis 49:8–12, Jacob predicted a messianic person known as "Shiloh" who would possess a
"ruler's staff" and to Him would be "the obedience of the peoples."
Isaiah 9:6a predicted that the Messiah would have a governmental rule: "For a child will be born to us, a son will be given to us;
And the *government* will rest on His shoulders."[35] Isaiah 9:7 reveals that
this governmental rule of the Messiah will involve a reign from David's
throne with peace, justice, and righteousness forever:

> There will be no end to the increase of His *government* or
> of peace, On the throne of David and over his kingdom, To
> establish it and to uphold it with justice and righteousness
> From then on and forevermore. The zeal of the LORD of hosts will
> accomplish this.[36]

---

34 For more on governmental implications stemming from the Noahic covenant see David VanDrunen,
    Politics after Christendom: Political Theology in a Fractured World (Grand Rapids: Zondervan
    Academic, 2020), 79–123.

35 Emphases mine.

36 Emphases mine.

The angel, Gabriel, affirmed a coming governmental rule when he predicted that Jesus would rule Israel forever from the throne of David:

> He will be great and will be called the Son of the Most High; and the Lord God will give Him the throne of His father David; and He will reign over the house of Jacob forever, and His kingdom will have no end (Luke 1:32–33).

Revelation 19:15 states that at Jesus' second coming, He will rule the nations: "From His mouth comes a sharp sword, so that with it He may strike down the nations, and He will rule them with a rod of iron."

Messiah's coming reign brings a tangible governmental rule on earth that replaces Gentile powers. The dream statue of Nebuchadnezzar in Daniel 2 depicted four geo-political earthly kingdoms—Babylon, Medo-Persia, Greece, and Rome. The metals mentioned with each empire—gold, silver, bronze, and iron—represent the quality of these empires. But a fifth and final empire is a divine kingdom that replaces the other kingdoms. It is a stone cut without hands that represents God's kingdom from Heaven (see Dan. 2:44–45). This stone (God's kingdom) comes dramatically and crushes the previous earthly empires and itself becomes a great kingdom upon the earth. Significantly, God's kingdom crushes and displaces Gentile kingdoms on earth. Just as Babylon, Medo-Persia, Greece, and Rome were geo-political governments that exercised reigns upon the earth, so too God's kingdom will be a geo-political government that reigns upon the entire earth.[37]

With Isaiah 2, the Lord's coming reign from Jerusalem includes Him making executive decisions on behalf of the nations:

> For the law will go forth from Zion
> And the word of the Lord from Jerusalem.
> And He will judge between the nations,
> And will render decisions for many peoples (Isa. 2:3b–4a).

---

37   The truths of Daniel 2 are repeated in Daniel 7 with the vision of the four beasts, which refers to the four Gentile empires mentioned in Daniel 2. And with Daniel 7, the kingdom of the Messiah replaces the earthly kingdoms and the kingdom of the "little horn" who appears to be an antichrist figure who persecutes God's people on the earth.

This reign of the Lord from Jerusalem involves international peace and the use of material resources for peace and not for war:

> And they will hammer their swords into plowshares and their spears into pruning hooks. Nation will not lift up sword against nation, and never again will they learn war (Isa. 2:4b).

When the Lord returns to earth according to Zechariah 14:9, He will reign over the nations and instruct them concerning what to do. He also punishes nations and governments that do not act as they should. This is explained in Zechariah 14:16–19:

> Then it will come about that any who are left of all the nations that went against Jerusalem will go up from year to year to worship the King, the LORD of hosts, and to celebrate the Feast of Booths. And it will be that whichever of the families of the earth does not go up to Jerusalem to worship the King, the LORD of hosts, there will be no rain on them. If the family of Egypt does not go up or enter, then no rain will fall on them; it will be the plague with which the LORD smites the nations who do not go up to celebrate the Feast of Booths. This will be the punishment of Egypt, and the punishment of all the nations who do not go up to celebrate the Feast of Booths.

In sum, government is important, and its significance is manifest in the future kingdom of God when government will operate righteously under the Messiah.

SOCIETY

Man is a social creature. And the presence of nations includes society. "Society" refers to the aggregate of people living together within an orderly community. The coming kingdom of God will have real societies and social activities. People will build houses and cultivate agriculture. Yet, unlike this present era, these will be done in the contexts of fairness, justice, and righteousness. For example, Isaiah 65:21–22b states that on the new earth people will build real houses and plant real vineyards. Yet as they do so they personally benefit from their labors:

They will build houses and inhabit them;
They will also plant vineyards and eat their fruit.
They will not build and another inhabit,
They will not plant and another eat (21–22b).

Psalm 72:12–14 reveals that those with lesser means will be treated fairly:

For he will deliver the needy when he cries for help,
The afflicted also, and him who has no helper.
He will have compassion on the poor and needy,
And the lives of the needy he will save.
He will rescue their life from oppression and violence,
And their blood will be precious in his sight.

The Messiah will reign over a world in which society functions with righteousness and justice.

CULTURE

Culture is linked with the ways of life for a society. It includes laws, morality religious beliefs, customs, language, dress, art, music, agriculture, architecture, technology and many other areas. Culture involves human ingenuity and creativity. It is an inherent part of people groups who reside together. Culture emerged early in the Bible's storyline. God commanded man to "rule" and "subdue" the earth, and "cultivate" and "keep" the garden (Gen. 1:26, 28; 2:15). This sometimes has been called the "cultural mandate" since man was to have dominion over the earth and its resources. Although the ground was cursed culture developed with the events of Genesis 4. Jabal, Enoch's descendant through Lamech, became the first cattle rancher or dweller with herds (4:20). Jabal's brother, Jubal, became the first to compose and play music (Gen. 4:21). Tubal-cain specialized in metals. He "was the forger of all instruments of bronze and iron" (Gen. 4:22).[38]

---

38   See John MacArthur and Richard Mayhue, eds. *Biblical Doctrine: A Systematic Summary of Bible Truth* (Wheaton, IL: Crossway, 2017), 447.

The Fall negatively impacted human culture which often is tainted with sin. For instance, the attempt to build a tower to Heaven in Genesis 11:1–9 was an act of culture that God did not approve. We should heed John's instruction, "Do not love the world nor the things in the world" (1 John 2:15). But there is another side. Culture itself is not bad. Building things, making music, creating art, working a trade, and advancing in technology and science can be very good. The tabernacle and temple in Israel's history were beautiful works of art. Messiah's coming kingdom will redeem culture for the glory of God. Multiple Bible passages speak of culture in the kingdom. Isaiah 19:18 states that cities in Egypt will learn the Hebrew language.[39] Zechariah 14:20–21 shows that objects such as bells and cooking pots will exist and be holy in the kingdom:

> In that day there will be inscribed on the bells of the horses, "HOLY TO THE LORD." And the cooking pots in the LORD's house will be like the bowls before the altar. Every cooking pot in Jerusalem and in Judah will be holy to the LORD of hosts; and all who sacrifice will come and take of them and boil in them.

Concerning conditions on the new earth Revelation 21:24 states, "The nations will walk by its light, and the kings of the earth will bring their glory into it." This "glory" most probably refers to cultural contributions. Revelation 21:26 repeats this truth, "and they [the nations] will bring the glory and the honor of the nations into it." Commenting on these two verses Anthony Hoekema states, "Is it too much to say that, according to these verses, the unique contributions of each nation to the life of the present earth will enrich the life of the new earth?"[40] These contributions include "the best products of culture and art which this earth has produced."[41] The message of Revelation 21:24, 26 is similar to Isaiah 60:11 which also speaks of wealth:

---

39   "In that day five cities in the land of Egypt will be speaking the language of Canaan" (Isa. 19:18).

40   Hoekema, The Bible and the Future, 286.

41   Ibid.

Your gates will be open continually;
They will not be closed day or night,
So that men may bring to you the wealth of the nations,
With their kings led in procession.

Micah 4:3b says in the "last days" (4:1) nations, under the rule of the Lord, "will hammer their swords into plowshares and their spears into pruning hooks." Resources devoted to military weapons will then be redirected to peaceful instruments. Much wealth has been spent on military weapons throughout history. Ponder what it will be like when nations use their wealth solely for peaceful and constructive things.

Prosperity concerning metals is seen with Micah 4:13a:

Arise and thresh, daughter of Zion,
For your horn I will make iron
And your hoofs I will make bronze.

Micah 4:13b then states that unjust wealth will be used correctly:

That you may pulverize many peoples,
That you may devote to the LORD their unjust gain
And their wealth to the Lord of all the earth.

Isaiah 60:5b–7a foretells the presence of wealth from the sea, livestock, and precious metals:

Because the abundance of the sea will be turned to you,
The wealth of the nations will come to you.
A multitude of camels will cover you,
The young camels of Midian and Ephah;
All those from Sheba will come;
They will bring gold and frankincense,
And will bear good news of the praises of the LORD.
All the flocks of Kedar will be gathered together to you,
The rams of Nebaioth will minister to you.

Isaiah 60:9b also speaks of wealth during this time:

And the ships of Tarshish will come first,

To bring your sons from afar,

Their silver and their gold with them.

The transformation of culture is an exciting reality of the coming kingdom of God. Concerning culture on the new earth Anthony Hoekema noted that, "The possibilities that now arise before us boggle the mind."[42] He then asks some interesting questions: "Will there be 'better Beethoven in heaven,'" and "Shall we see better Rembrandts, better Raphaels, better Constables?" Also, "Shall we read better poetry, better drama, and better prose? Will scientists continue to advance in technological achievement, will geologists continue to explore the treasures of the new earth, and will architects continue to build imposing and attractive structures?"[43] Hoekema notes that we do not know the answers to these questions, but thinking of the possibilities is exciting.

---

42   Anthony A. Hoekema, *Created in God's Image* (Grand Rapids: Eerdmans, 1994), 95.

43   Ibid.

5 VIEWS ON THE FUTURE OF THE EARTH IN ETERNITY

1. The new earth in eternity will be **this present earth** purified, refined, and renewed. God's people will live on this new earth, which has connections with the present earth, forever. (Many today hold this view)

2. The new earth in eternity will be **a tangible replacement of this current earth.** God will annihilate the present earth and replace it with a physical new earth where God's people will live forever. (Many today hold this view)

3. The present earth will be **vacated in eternity** but it still exists as a memorial of God's workings in history. It will be frozen in light. God's people will live in Heaven forever and not on the earth in any way. (The view of Thomas Aquinas)

4. This present earth will not be renewed. It will **become a fiery hell forever** for the wicked. The saints will live in Heaven forever, while the earth functions as hell for unbelievers. (The view of Jonathan Edwards)

5. The present earth **ceases to exist** as God's people live in Heaven forever. (Popular throughout church history after the fourth century AD)

7

KEY ELEMENTS OF
THE NEW CREATION
MODEL (PART 2)

◆

FOOD/DRINK/CELEBRATION

Eating and drinking are essential to man's existence. At creation Adam was told to eat from the trees in the garden (see Gen. 2:16). Even in a fallen world food, drink, and celebration are considered good gifts from God. When speaking to Gentiles at Lystra, Paul said: "and yet He [God] did not leave Himself without witness, in that He did good and gave you rains from heaven and fruitful seasons, satisfying your hearts with food and gladness" (Acts 14:17). Paul appealed to "food and gladness" as evidence for God.

Both testaments speak often of celebrations involving food and drink. And banquet activity is linked with the coming kingdom of God. Isaiah 25:6 speaks of a "lavish banquet" for "all peoples" involving "aged wine" and "choice pieces with marrow." With Matthew 8:11 Jesus said, "I say to you that many will come from east and west, and recline at the table with Abraham, Isaac and Jacob in the kingdom of heaven." This is not figurative language. The kingdom will involve celebration with food. Revelation 19:9 refers to people "who are invited to the marriage supper of the Lamb." At the Last Supper Jesus promised that He would eat the Passover meal again with His followers in the kingdom of God:

> And He said to them, "I have earnestly desired to eat this Passover with you before I suffer; for I say to you, I shall never again eat it until

it is fulfilled in the kingdom of God." And when He had taken a cup and given thanks, He said, "Take this and share it among yourselves; for I say to you, I will not drink of the fruit of the vine from now on until the kingdom of God comes" (Luke 22:15–18).

Just as the Passover on that solemn day was a tangible meal, the Passover celebration in the kingdom of God will be a real meal.

Shortly after His resurrection Jesus appeared to His disciples. They were startled and afraid, thinking they might be seeing a spirit. After showing them His hands and feet Jesus asked, "Do you have anything here to eat?" (Luke 24:41). At that point, "They gave Him a piece of a broiled fish; and He took it and ate it before them" (Luke 24:42–43). After defeating Satan and death, the resurrected Jesus took time to eat a piece of fish before His disciples.

Eating and drinking are important and will exist in the kingdom. With Romans 14:17, Paul said the kingdom is not just about food and drink. Love and relationships are always most important. But food and drink matter. They are linked with human relationships and celebrations in this age, and they will do so in the future. Randy Alcorn observes, "When I'm eating with people here, enjoying food and friendship, it's a bridge to when I'll be eating there, enjoying food and friendship at the banquet table God prepared for us (Revelation 19:9). This isn't making a blind leap into a shadowy afterlife, it's just taking a few natural steps in the light Scripture has given us."[1]

HOUSES AND FARMS

The kingdom of God will have houses and farms. Jesus affirmed this in Matthew 19:28–30 when He discussed future rewards for those who follow Him:

---

1   Randy Alcorn, *Eternal Perspectives: A Collection of Quotations on Heaven, The New Earth, and Life after Death* (Carol Stream, IL: Tyndale House Publishers, 2012), 177.

"And everyone who has left *houses* or brothers or sisters or father or mother or children or *farms* for My name's sake, will receive many times as much, and will inherit eternal life."[2]

Following Jesus in this present age often means leaving possessions we have and people we know. But whatever is lost or given up in this age is multiplied back exponentially—this includes living places. Real people will inhabit real houses. If we have resurrected bodies on a renewed earth, it follows that houses and farms would be part of our experience as well. Isaiah 65 reveals that the coming "new heavens and new earth" will involve "houses" and "vineyards." In John 14:2–3 Jesus spoke of dwelling places for His followers:

"In My Father's house are many dwelling places; if it were not so, I would have told you; for I go to prepare a place for you. If I go and prepare a place for you, I will come again and receive you to Myself, that where I am, there you may be also."

While not mentioning houses specifically, Zechariah 8:4–5 notes the existence of streets with playful activity occurring:

Thus says the LORD of hosts, "Old men and old women will again sit in the streets of Jerusalem, each man with his staff in his hand because of age. And the streets of the city will be filled with boys and girls playing in its streets."

A New Creation Model affirms that the kingdom will see the presence of houses, farms and activities associated with these. This makes sense since people will live on a restored earth with physical bodies.

---

2   Emphases mine.

ECONOMIC AND AGRICULTURAL PROSPERITY

The coming kingdom will have economic and agricultural prosperity. Such prosperity in the Bible is often associated with grain, oil, wine, and flocks. According to Genesis 49:10–12 the messianic figure known as "Shiloh" (49:10) will bring great prosperity:

> "He ties his foal to the vine,
> And his donkey's colt to the choice vine;
> He washes his garments in wine,
> And his robes in the blood of grapes.
> His eyes are dull from wine,
> And his teeth white from milk" (Gen. 49:11–12).

Although this language is strange to modern readers, the mention of "choice vine," "garments in wine," "blood of grapes," "eyes dull from wine," and "teeth white from milk," indicate luxurious agricultural conditions.

Psalm 72:16 reveals that the ultimate Davidic King will bring an "abundance of grain": "May there be abundance of grain in the earth on top of the mountains; Its fruit will wave like the cedars of Lebanon." Amos 9:13–14 declares that the future kingdom will contain abundant agricultural prosperity on earth:

> "Behold, days are coming," declares the Lord,
> "When the plowman will overtake the reaper
> And the treader of grapes him who sows seed;
> When the mountains will drip sweet wine
> And all the hills will be dissolved.
> Also I will restore the captivity of My people Israel,
> And they will rebuild the ruined cities and live in them;
> They will also plant vineyards and drink their wine,
> And make gardens and eat their fruit."

With the New Covenant chapter of Jeremiah 31, God promises that there will be blessings of "grain," "new wine," "oil, and "flocks":

They will come and shout for joy on the height of Zion, and they will be radiant over the bounty of the Lord—Over the grain and the new wine and the oil, and over the young of the flock and the herd; and their life will be like a watered garden, and they will never languish again (Jer. 31:12).

Joel 2:24 states this as well: "The threshing floors will be full of grain, and the vats will overflow with the new wine and oil." According to Ezekiel 36:29 the future kingdom on earth will involve the multiplying of grain and the removal of famine: "Moreover, I will save you from all your uncleanness; and I will call for the grain and multiply it, and I will not bring a famine on you." With Micah 4:13b, the prophet indicates that unjust wealth from the nations will be returned to the Lord: "That you may devote to the Lord their unjust gain and their wealth to the Lord of all the earth." Zechariah 8:12 notes:

For there will be peace for the seed: the vine will yield its fruit, the land will yield its produce and the heavens will give their dew; and I will cause the remnant of this people to inherit all these things.

Closely associated with agricultural prosperity in the coming kingdom is abundant rainfall:

For He has given you the early rain for your vindication.
And He has poured down for you the rain,
The early and latter rain as before (Joel 2:23).

And I will cause showers to come down in their season; they will be showers of blessing (Ezek. 34:26).

On every lofty mountain and on every high hill there will be streams running with water (Isa. 30:25).

In the kingdom, rain could be withheld from any nation refusing to come to Jerusalem to worship: "And it will be that whichever of the families of the earth does not go up to Jerusalem to worship the King, the Lord of hosts, there will be no rain on them. If the family of Egypt does not go up or enter, then no rain will fall on them" (Zech. 14:17–18a).

Many other passages could be cited. But the main point is that a New Creation Model accounts for economic and agricultural prosperity on the coming new earth. It also accounts for the significance of rainfall.

In his article, "The Fertility of the Land in the Messianic Prophecies," Antonine DeGuglielmo argues persuasively that fertility and prosperity of land in Old Testament prophecies should be taken seriously and literally, and not metaphorically. This is consistent with the coming new earth:

> Of course, a metaphorical interpretation in the sense indicated removes all grounds for the objection expressed above. But it may well be that the sacred writers also intended to describe the actual condition of the earth in the messianic age. In fact, the messianic doctrine of the OT points in that direction, since a feature of the messianic age is the renovation of heaven and earth. If we think along these lines, the fertility of the land passages would retain their proper sense, and an abundant fertility would be a characteristic of the new earth.[3]

RELATIONSHIPS AND FRIENDSHIPS

I once chatted with a friend who said he was sad because in Heaven he would no longer remember his family and friends. But that is not true. There is no evidence that we forget people we knew in this age. While a person's relationship with God is most important, healthy social relationships are part of God's design for us. Nowhere in the Bible is love of others viewed as a threat to a relationship with God. In fact, love of neighbor is evidence one knows and loves God (see 1 John 4:7–8).

In the coming kingdom, relationships exist and are considered good. In Matthew 19:28–29 Jesus said the "regeneration" of the cosmos would involve "father," "mother," and "children." These indicate close human relationships in the kingdom. With Luke 22:15–16, Jesus said He would eat again with His disciples in the kingdom of God: "And He said to them, 'I

---

3   Antonine DeGuglielmo, "The Fertility of the Land in the Messianic Prophecies," *Catholic Biblical Quarterly* 19:3 (July 1957): 311. He also points out the fertility in the land is "a necessary feature of the messianic kingdom" (309).

have earnestly desired to eat this Passover with you before I suffer; for I say to you, I shall never again eat it until it is fulfilled in the kingdom of God." The people Jesus ate with before His death are the same people He will dine with in the kingdom. So on the night before His death Jesus looked forward to a reunion meal with His beloved disciples.

Relationships also were on Paul's mind in 1 Thessalonians 4. The Thessalonians were worried deceased loved ones would miss the return of Jesus. But Paul said they should not worry:

> But we do not want you to be uninformed, brethren, about those who are asleep, so that you will not grieve as do the rest who have no hope (1 Thess. 4:13).

Paul then says that "God will bring with Him those who have fallen asleep in Jesus" (4:14b). Departed loved ones will return when Jesus does. Verses 15–17 then discuss the coming great reunion that will occur:

> For this we say to you by the word of the Lord, that we who are alive and remain until the coming of the Lord, will not precede those who have fallen asleep. For the Lord Himself will descend from heaven with a shout, with the voice of the archangel and with the trumpet of God, and the dead in Christ will rise first. Then we who are alive and remain will be caught up together with them in the clouds to meet the Lord in the air, and so we shall always be with the Lord.

The return of Jesus brings restored relationships and reunion—"together with them."

A holistic eschatology affirms the presence of friendships and relationships, even in the future. We will remember and fellowship with others who love God. Human relationships were part of God's intentions for man before the Fall (see Gen. 1:27) and they are part of His plans into eternity.

THE ANIMAL KINGDOM

The Bible affirms the special status and role of man in God's purposes. Yet the Bible also affirms the importance of animals. The animal realm of beasts, birds, fish, reptiles, etc. matters to God. Jesus said, "Are not five sparrows sold for two cents? Yet not one of them is forgotten before God" (Luke 12:6). The last verse of Jonah reveals God's desire to show compassion to the people of Nineveh. But God also was concerned for the animals there. Jonah 4:11 states: "Should I not have compassion on Nineveh, the great city in which there are more than 120,000 persons who do not know the difference between their right and left hand, *as well as many animals?*"[4]

Animals are a part of God's creation and new creation plans. The creation account of Genesis 1 involved beasts, birds, and fish (see Gen. 1:20–25). And the Noahic Covenant was made with all living creatures:

> "Now behold, I Myself do establish My covenant with you, and with your descendants after you; and with every living creature that is with you, the birds, the cattle, and every beast of the earth with you; of all that comes out of the ark, even every beast of the earth" (Gen. 9:9–10).

Thus, creation and the Noahic Covenant highlight the importance of the animal realm in God's purposes.

Psalm 104 reveals God's delight in His wonderful and diverse creation. Nearly every aspect of nature is discussed—birds, animals, fish, mountains, oceans, trees, sun, moon, skies, etc. Much is stated about God's provision for animals and birds: "All creatures look to you to give them their food at the proper time. When you give it to them, they gather it up; when you open your hand, they are satisfied with good things" (Ps. 104:27–28, NIV). Significantly, the animal world has inherent value to God, not just instrumental value for human beings. God's care for animals in Psalm 104 applies to animals, birds, and fish that are outside the realm of human communities. As Douglas and Jonathan Moo note, "What is most striking in Psalm 104 is the breadth of God's concern with and delight in creation, which extends beyond the neat boundaries of settled human life and civilization."[5]

---

4 Emphases mine.

5 Douglas J. Moo and Jonathan A. Moo, *Creation Care: A Biblical Theology of the Natural World* (Grand Rapids: Zondervan, 2018), 56.

And man has an important role in stewarding this realm that God delights in. Snyder notes: "In the biblical view, earth's creatures and species are to be 'stewarded' for four key reasons: God created them; God delights in them; we depend on them; they are part of God's larger plan."[6]

The animal realm is mysterious. Much about it is beautiful. We enjoy and even take many animals into our homes. And yet much about it is dangerous and tragic. As Snyder notes, "The animal kingdom is full of violence, predation, and death—billions of creatures great and small devouring and being devoured. Scripture is very frank about this. The biblical worldview is not romantic. It recognizes the fallenness and transitoriness of nature."[7]

It should be no surprise, therefore, that animals will be a significant part of the coming kingdom of God. Animals are headed for restoration. Isaiah 11:6–8 predicts not only the presence of animals in the kingdom, but also animal-animal harmony and animal-human harmony:

> And the wolf will dwell with the lamb,
> And the leopard will lie down with the young goat,
> And the calf and the young lion and the fatling together;
> And a little boy will lead them.
> Also the cow and the bear will graze,
> Their young will lie down together,
> And the lion will eat straw like the ox.
> The nursing child will play by the hole of the cobra,
> And the weaned child will put his hand on the viper's den.

Concerning the new earth Isaiah 65:25 states: "'The wolf and the lamb will graze together, and the lion will eat straw like the ox; and dust will be the serpent's food. They will do no evil or harm in all My holy mountain,' says the LORD."

The restoration of Israel is linked with animals who give glory to God:

---

6   Snyder, *Salvation Means Creation Healed*, 123.

7   Ibid., 43.

"The beasts of the field will glorify Me,
The jackals and the ostriches,
Because I have given waters in the wilderness
And rivers in the desert,
To give drink to My chosen people" (Isa. 43:20).

Ezekiel 47:9 speaks of the abundance of fish during kingdom conditions:

It will come about that every living creature which swarms in every
place where the river goes, will live. And there will be very many fish,
for these waters go there and the others become fresh; so everything
will live where the river goes.

The belief that animals will not exist in eternity is a common Spiritual
Vision Model idea. And the importance of the animal realm often is
ignored. But New Creationism accounts for animals. Not only are they
important parts of God's creation now, but they will also exist in the future.

Hosea 2:18 foretells the restoration of animals, birds, and creeping things:

"In that day I will also make a covenant for them
With the beasts of the field,
The birds of the sky
And the creeping things of the ground."

Note that the threefold animal categories of Hosea 2:18 were mentioned
in Genesis 1:24–28:

"beasts of the earth" (Gen. 1:24, 25)
"birds of the sky" (Gen. 1:26, 28)
"creeping things" (Gen. 1:24) and "creeping thing that creeps on the
earth" (Gen. 1:26)

The connection between Genesis 1:24–28 and Hosea 2:18 is explicit.
Thus, the kingdom conditions of Hosea 2:18 involve the restoration of
animals, as mentioned in the creation text of Genesis 1. The creatures
that suffered the consequences of man's sin and the Fall will be restored
in the kingdom of God. And in the context of Hosea 2 this has positive

implications for God's people who also benefit from the restoration of creation. The animal realm will no longer be a threat to God's people in any way. John K. Goodrich observes, "In the messianic kingdom, Israel would be at peace with the entire creation: animals and humanity."[8]

NATURAL RESOURCES AND
THE ENVIRONMENT

Psalm 24:1 declares, "The earth is the Lord's, and all it contains" (cf. 1 Cor. 10:26). Not only does earth in general belong to God but everything in it does as well. God receives glory for creating all things as Revelation 4:11 states, "Worthy are You, our Lord and our God, to receive glory and honor and power; for You created all things, and because of Your will they existed, and were created." This has big ramifications for man's responsibility to creation, including its natural resources.

Genesis 1:26, 28 speaks of man being tasked to rule and subdue the earth and its creatures. Also, Genesis 2:15 tells of Adam needing to cultivate and keep the garden of Eden. God is concerned about the welfare of the earth, earth's creatures, land, and the environment. And man has a stewardship to manage these areas well.

Various texts discuss man's relationship to nature. According to Deuteronomy 20:19–20, during warfare Israel could cut down trees but they were not to cut down fruit-bearing trees. With Deuteronomy 22:6–7, if anyone came across a bird nest the eggs could be gathered but the mother bird was to be left alone—"you shall certainly let the mother go." Also, every seventh year, with the law of the sabbatical year, Israel was to let the land rest so it could refresh and be fertile in the future (see Leviticus 25).[9]

Anthony Hoekema fleshes out details of what man's stewardship over the earth involves: "This includes holding property, tilling the soil, growing fruit trees, mining coal, and drilling for oil not for personal aggrandizement

---

8   John K. Goodrich, "Hosea," in *The Moody Bible Commentary*, eds. Michael Rydelnik and Michael Vanlaningham (Chicago: Moody Publishers, 2014), 1318.

9   The order of verses used here is similar to Alva J. McClain, *The Greatness of the Kingdom*, 83.

but in a responsible way, for the benefit and welfare of one's fellowmen."[10] He then says,

> In our present world this also includes concern for the conservation of natural resources, and opposition to all wasteful or thoughtless exploitation of these resources. It includes concern for the preservation of the environment and for the prevention of whatever hurts that environment: erosion, wanton destruction of animal species, pollution of air and water. It includes concern for adequate distribution of food, the prevention of famine, and the improvement of sanitation. It also embraces the advancement of scientific investigation, research and experimentation, including the continuing conquest of space, in such a way to honor God's commands and to give him the praise.[11]

In a fallen world responsible stewardship of natural resources and the environment does not occur. But this does not mean man is unaccountable to God for not doing this. The mandate for man to rule the earth well has never been revoked and is affirmed in texts like Psalm 8 and Hebrews 2:5–8. When man is in rebellion against God the earth suffers. Snyder rightly notes, "Humans have dominion over the earth—constructively or destructively."[12] Unfortunately, we see too much "destructively." Hosea 4:1–3 states that because of the sinfulness of man, nature suffers:

> Therefore the land mourns,
> And everyone who lives in it languishes
> Along with the beasts of the field and the birds of the sky,
> And also the fish of the sea disappear (v. 3).

But as Hebrews 2:5 indicates, the successful reign of man over the earth will happen in "the world to come." Paul also states that the restoration of creation will occur in the future when the saints receive their glorified bodies (see Rom. 8:19–23). Thus, a New Creation Model approach

---

10   Hoekema, *Created in God's Image*, 88.

11   Ibid.

12   Snyder, 106.

properly accounts for the importance of natural resources and how these fit into God's purposes. These will not be properly managed until Jesus and the saints reign on the earth, but their importance always remains. And it is a realm that we should be concerned about and impact positively when we can.

TIME

Another area where the New Creation and Spiritual Vision models differ is time. With eastern religions like Hinduism and Buddhism time will cease for the one who becomes liberated from the cycle of births and rebirths associated with the physical universe. This liberation or *moksha* means release from the confines of space and time. This view of an eternity beyond time also finds expression in some Christian versions of the Spiritual Vision Model. For instance, the empyrean heaven of Thomas Aquinas and some medieval theologians involved an existence for God's people in eternity that transcends time. A well-known hymn, "When the Roll is Called up Yonder," states: "When the trumpet of the Lord shall sound and time shall be no more." Other hymns make similar statements.

I once remember a worship leader calling us to stand and sing in church so we could get used to worshiping God when "time will be no more." This type of thinking might be furthered by a wrong translation of Revelation 10:6 in the King James Version which states, "that there should be time no longer." The correct translation is "that there will be delay no longer" (NASB) concerning God's plans to judge the earth and set up His kingdom. Revelation 10:6 is not a statement time will not exist in eternity.

The traditional Christian Spiritual Vision Model view of time is that time is linked with a fallen world and imperfection. So when the perfect state comes in eternity, time no longer exists. But the New Creation Model differs with this understanding. Time is not inherently connected with a fallen world or with imperfection. Time existed at creation before sin and the Fall according to Genesis 1–2. The successive six days of creation in Genesis 1 reveal sequence and time. And Adam and Eve were acting in time before the Fall.

Also, we know there is time in the current Heaven. Revelation 8:1 states, "When the Lamb broke the seventh seal, there was silence in heaven for about half an hour." This "about half an hour" is a specific time reference. With a heavenly scene in Revelation 6:9–11, the souls of martyrs who arrived in Heaven were "told that they should rest for a little while longer" (Rev. 6:11) concerning their desire for God to avenge their deaths. Waiting implies time.

Jesus' millennial kingdom also is related to time. Six times we are told it lasts for "a thousand years" in Revelation 20. And this kingdom is placed sequentially after the second coming of Jesus in Revelation 19 and the Eternal Kingdom of Revelation 21–22.

Time also will exist in the Eternal Kingdom after the Millennium. With two "new earth" passages time is present. Isaiah 66:22a states, "For just as the new heavens and the new earth" which is followed by "And it shall be from new moon to new moon and from sabbath to sabbath, All mankind will come to bow down before Me,' says the Lord" (66:23). Alcorn rightly notes, "New Moons and Sabbaths required moon, sun, and time."[13]

Second the "new earth" passage of Revelation 21:1–22:5 mentions months. Revelation 22:2a states, "On either side of the river was the tree of life, bearing twelve kinds of fruit, yielding its fruit *every month*."[14] Fruit is produced "every month." "Every month" implies time. There are multiple months with one following another, and so on. The concept of "months" involves days since it takes days to make a month. Months also are linked to years. The mention of months also implies seasons and cycles.

So even in the Eternal Kingdom time will exist and we will have lived experiences that play out in time. As the nations and kings go in and out of the New Jerusalem (see Rev. 21:24, 26) they will do so in time. The claim that time will become no more is false. As Randy Alcorn says, "For too long we've allowed an unbiblical assumption ("there will be no time in Heaven") to obscure overwhelming biblical revelation to the contrary."[15]

---

13   Alcorn, *Heaven*, 267.

14   Emphases added.

15   Alcorn, 269.

Wayne Grudem also notes, "The New Creation Will Not Be 'Timeless' but Will Include an Unending Succession of Moments."[16]

But is it not the case that all good things must come to an end? Will we become bored or exhausted in eternity? Won't we weary of things after a while, like losing interest in an overplayed favorite song? A detailed answer for these questions goes beyond our purposes here. But living with and loving our infinite God could never become boring. And we will never tire of loving people in the Eternal Kingdom. Plus, we will never cease to enjoy the beauty of the new earth and the endless good gifts from God. Also, on the new earth we will have glorified bodies that are in perfect health and are able to enjoy love, relationships, and discoveries of the new earth to a degree we cannot fathom now. People who are in perfect health, who are loving and being loved, and who love what they do, are not wanting these conditions to end. Why would they?

Time is a cruel enemy in a fallen and sinful world. In our current non-glorified state our lives are like a vapor (see James 4:14). We live only about 70–80 years as Moses stated in Psalm 90. Each tick of the clock brings us closer to death and separation from loved ones and what we love to do. But in the Eternal Kingdom time will never be an enemy. Time will be a friend of God's people.

CONCLUSION

God's plans include but also concern more than individual human salvation. They involve a wide variety of areas. We mentioned sixteen of these but there are many more that can be discussed. Our glorious and infinite God has created a beautiful and multi-dimensional universe that reveals His glory. The New Creation Model attempts to detect all God is doing from creation to new creation to see God's glory manifested in all realms.

---

16   Wayne Grudem, *Systematic Theology* (Grand Rapids: Zondervan, 1994), 1162. The capital letters are for the title of a section about "The New Heavens and New Earth."

KEY ELEMENTS OF THE NEW CREATION MODEL

1. Earth as Man's Destiny

2. Resurrection of the Body

3. Restoration of Earth

4. Nations and Ethnicities

5. Israel

6. Land

7. Governments

8. Society

9. Culture

10. Eating/Drinking/Celebration

11. Houses and Farms

12. Economic and Agricultural Prosperity

13. Relationships and Friendships

14. Animals, Birds, Fish

15. Natural Resources

16. Time

THE NEW CREATION
MODEL IN THE
OLD TESTAMENT

*"The cosmic vision of the redemption of 'all things' through
Christ is grounded in the ecological vision of the early
chapters of Genesis, where humans and their earthly
environment are intrinsically intertwined—so that human
salvation is unthinkable without the renewal of the world."*

—J. Richard Middleton[1]

◆

The last two chapters examined key elements of the New Creation
Model from a topical perspective. Here we highlight key passages
that affirm the significance of areas like earth, land, physical matters, and
nations in God's purposes. The passages mentioned are not exhaustive,
nor is our discussion of each passage deep. And we have introduced some
of these in previous chapters. But the purpose here is to offer a sampling
of Bible passages showing how holistic and multi-dimensional God's purposes are. They also reveal that the New Creation Model arises from an
inductive study of Scripture.

---

1   J. Richard Middleton, "A New Earth Perspective," in *Four Views on Heaven*, 85.

GENESIS 1

Genesis 1 highlights the six days of creation. "In the beginning God created the heavens and the earth." The rest of the chapter highlights the details of God's creative activity for these six days. God creates the universe, the earth, light, seas, vegetation, animals, birds, fish, and eventually man. "Earth" (*eretz*) is mentioned twenty times. Six times the creation is described as "good" (4, 10, 12, 18, 21, 25). Then with 1:31 the created order is described as "very good"— "God saw all that He had made, and behold, it was very good." This makes a value statement on the physical creation. It is "very good," not lesser or bad as believed with the eastern religions and philosophies linked to Plato. Nor is there any indication that this "very good" universe is something man must flee to enter a higher state of existence.

GENESIS 1:26–28; 2:15

Genesis 1:26–28 is foundational for understanding the Bible's storyline and the functional purpose for man's existence. Not only is it significant on its own but other passages also will rely on its truths (see Psalm 8; Hos. 2:18; 1 Cor. 15:27; Heb. 2:5–8).

God created man in His image and likeness to represent God and rule over the earth and its creatures for His glory. God created a beautiful and wonderful world and then tasks man as mediator to rule and subdue it. This text says:

> Then God said, "Let Us make man in Our image, according to Our likeness; and let them rule over the fish of the sea and over the birds of the sky and over the cattle and over all the earth, and over every creeping thing that creeps on the earth." God created man in His own image, in the image of God He created him; male and female He created them. God blessed them; and God said to them, "Be fruitful and multiply, and fill the earth, and subdue it; and rule over the fish of the sea and over the birds of the sky and over every living thing that moves on the earth."

As God's "image" (*tselem*) man was made to represent God on the earth. And as God's "likeness" (*demuth*) man was created as a son in relationship with God. Together man's creation is regal and relational. Man was created in relationship with God. And as God's representative and mediator man is responsible to rule over creation.

The word "rule" (*radah*) is a strong term. It can refer to the oppression of foreign invaders (see Neh. 9:28), the authority exercised by a king (see 1 Kings 4:24; Ps. 72:8), and even the Messiah's rule (see Ps. 110:2).[2] The term "subdue" (*kabash*) also is a forceful term, used thirteen times in the Old Testament. It means to force, bring into bondage, and make subservient. It is used of subduing a land (Num. 32:22, 29) or nation (Josh. 18:1). While the term can be used of a violation in a negative sense (see Est. 7:8) the term does not imply anything negative.[3] But it involves force and action.

In Genesis 1:26–28, the ruling and subduing of earth and its creatures by man concerns all fish, birds, cattle, and everything that walks on the earth. The implications of this are vast. As Anthony Hoekema observes, the word "subdue" means "man is to explore the resources of the earth, to cultivate its land, to mine its buried treasures."[4] And even more, "Man is called by God to develop all the potentialities found in nature and in humankind as a whole. He must seek to develop not only agriculture, horticulture, and animal husbandry, but also science, technology, and art."[5]

Note how earth-focused this text is. Man is to rule *from* and *over* the earth with what Middleton calls "an earthly vocation."[6] In addition to his relationship with God, Adam possessed physical and social/political authority. This was to manifest itself in every area—agriculture, architecture, domestication of animals, harnessing of energy and natural resources,

---

2   Moo, "Nature in the New Creation: New Testament Eschatology and the Environment," 478, n. 108.

3   Ibid.

4   Hoekema, *Created in God's Image*, 79.

5   Ibid.

6   Middleton, *A New Heaven and a New Earth*, 39.

and other areas.[7] As Middleton notes, "the human creature is made to worship God in a distinctive way: by interacting with the earth, using our God-given power to transform our earthly environment into a complex world (a sociocultural world) that glorifies our creator."[8]

The significance of this passage should not be missed or underemphasized. This is God's original intent and mandate for humankind. The Creator made a beautiful world full of wonderful things and creatures. He then makes and tasks man to rule over it on His behalf. Man is given the keys to a wonderful creation and God blesses him with the opportunity and responsibility to care for it and make it flourish. As Daniel Block states:

> As the climax of his "very good" creative week, God had created *Adam* to serve as his representative and deputy in governing this creation. For this reason, we may refer to *Adam's* role as administrative; humankind's primary task was to promote the well-being of the physical environment and all living things (creatures and plants) so that the universe might glorify its Creator in a majestic and harmonious symphony of sound and sight. In short, *Adam's* role was to keep the triangular relationship involving God, the physical world, and living things well oiled and running smoothly.[9]

With Genesis 2:15 man was tasked with managing the garden of Eden: "Then the Lord God took the man and put him into the garden of Eden to cultivate it and keep it." The terms "cultivate" and "keep" add more dimensions to man's responsibility over the earth. In addition to ruling and subduing, there was to be cultivation, caring, and guarding of the

---

7   See Wayne Grudem, *Politics According to the Bible: A Comprehensive Resource for Understanding Modern Political Issues in Light of Scripture* (Grand Rapids: Zondervan, 2010), 325. Grudem says, "God expected Adam and Eve and their descendants to explore and develop the earth's resources in such a way that they would bring benefit to themselves and other human beings."

8   Middleton, 41.

9   Daniel Block, *Covenant*, 44. Emphases in original.

land where Adam was placed.[10] Man was not called to recklessly or selfishly consume the earth's resources; he was to care and keep them as a good steward.

The more we grasp man's role as God's appointed mediator and king over the earth, the more we will grasp what God is accomplishing with His creation—including His plans for a new creation! And we will be better able to detect when some wrongly claim that the kingdom God is pursuing is only a spiritual kingdom.

The Bible's storyline starts with God's regal and relational intent for creation. It involves the earth and its creatures and man's kingly role in governing the world on God's behalf. As will be seen below, sin and the Fall will disrupt man's ability to fulfill the vocation God gave to him. Yet the kingdom mandate of Genesis 1:26–28 and 2:15 is foundational for understanding God's purposes for man.

GENESIS 3:17–19

Genesis 3 describes the fall of man and the devastating consequences sin brings for man and all creation. When Adam and Eve sinned a curse was pronounced upon the ground with consequences for man's relationship to the ground. This is evidenced in Genesis 3:17b–19a:

> "Cursed is the ground because of you;
> In toil you will eat of it
> All the days of your life.
> Both thorns and thistles it shall grow for you;
> And you will eat the plants of the field;
> By the sweat of your face
> You will eat bread,
> Till you return to the ground."

---

10   Hoekema says, "Adam, in other words, was not only told to rule over nature; he was also told to cultivate and care for that portion of the earth in which he had been placed." *Created in God's Image*, 80.

Man was made to successfully rule and subdue the earth for God, but as man rebelled against His Creator a dramatic negative turn occurs. God cursed the ground that man was created to rule over. With tragic irony, because of sin man will be thwarted in the realm where he is supposed to rule. And the ground will eventually cover him in death. Thus, among other things, sin is anti-creational. It affects not only man, but the whole created order, something Paul explains in Romans 8:19–22 when he says creation was unwillingly subjected to futility.

GENESIS 5:28–29

But there is hope. In Genesis 3:15, God stated that the seed of the woman would crush the seed of the serpent. And a specific seed from this seedline would accomplish this task. Someone from mankind would defeat evil and reverse the curse. This "messianic hope" for restoration is then seen with Genesis 5:28–29. Here Lamech hoped that his son Noah would be the one to reverse the curse upon the ground:

> Now he called his name Noah, saying, "This one will give us rest from our work and from the toil of our hands arising from the ground which the LORD has cursed."

Note that this early messianic hope text is tangible. With man's failure in Genesis 3 the ground was cursed and work was hard. Lamech's expectation is that these negative consequences will be removed someday, and he hopes Noah will be the one to do it. We now know that Noah was not the man who would reverse the curse. But this hope was real. In sum, Genesis 5:28–29 reveals both a messianic hope for a Deliverer and an expectation that this Deliverer will reverse the curse upon the earth. After the Fall an expectation existed that the curse upon the ground would be removed. A messianic hope is tied with a restored earth.

GENESIS 8:20–9:17

The Noahic Covenant of Genesis 8:20–9:17 is the first covenant mentioned in Scripture. It also is a creational covenant that is foundational for God's purposes going forth from this time. God's kingdom purposes and all other biblical covenants—Abrahamic, Mosaic, Davidic, and New—can only happen because of this covenant. The flood of Noah's day destroyed most life on the earth and creation was in dismay. Yet the Noahic Covenant will function as a platform for stability of nature so that God's kingdom, covenant, and salvation purposes can play out in history. Genesis 8:22 states:

> "While the earth remains,
> Seedtime and harvest,
> And cold and heat,
> And summer and winter,
> And day and night
> Shall not cease."

This verse conveys a stability that will exist. There will be seasons and cycles. This will set the scene for the coming Abrahamic Covenant and God's plans to save the world through Abraham.

While this covenant is pronounced to Noah it is really a covenant with all creation. It concerns Noah as representative of mankind, every living creature, and the earth. As Genesis 9:12–13 states:

> God said, "This is the sign of the covenant which I am making between Me and you and every living creature that is with you, for all successive generations; I set My bow in the cloud, and it shall be for a sign of a covenant between Me and the earth."

This affirms that God's purposes in history are creational. The Noahic Covenant is not just a "human salvation" covenant. The word "earth" is used twenty-three times in Genesis 8–9, highlighting how significant the earth is in God's plans. "Every living creature" is mentioned four times. In a fallen, post-flood world, all creation remains important in God's purposes. And to understand what God is doing in history, all creation must be considered.

GENESIS 10–11

Genesis 10–11 describes the origin of people groups and nations, and where they are placed, as they spread from the Tower of Babel event via the three sons of Noah. An attempt was made by evil men to stay in one area and make a great name for themselves. But God forced a spreading out on the earth, something that was part of God's original creation intent. This sets the scene for Genesis 12 in which Abraham and the great nation to come from him (Israel) will be a means for blessing the people groups of the world (see Gen. 12:2–3) that were mentioned in Genesis 10–11. Thus, Genesis 10–11 reveals the importance of nations. Throughout Scripture the nations of the earth are presented as important to God's plans. They often will be presented as sinful and opposing God's purposes. But nations also are a positive part of God's saving plans. Their existence remains even into the Eternal State where they are pictured as making cultural contributions to the new earth (see Rev. 21:24, 26).

GENESIS 12:6–7; 15:18–21

The earth is important to God and specific land also is significant in God's purposes. Genesis 12:6–7 reveals that a specific area of land was promised to Abraham's descendants:

> Abram passed through the land as far as the site of Shechem, to the oak of Moreh. Now the Canaanite was then in the land. The LORD appeared to Abram and said, "To your descendants I will give this land."

The dimensions of the promised land are given in Genesis 15:18–21:

> On that day the Lord made a covenant with Abram, saying, "To your descendants I have given this land, From the river of Egypt as far as the great river, the river Euphrates: the Kenite and the Kenizzite and the Kadmonite and the Hittite and the Perizzite and the Rephaim and the Amorite and the Canaanite and the Girgashite and the Jebusite."

As mentioned earlier in our discussion of "Land," the particular land of Israel will have importance in God's historical purposes. The land of Israel was to function as a light in a dark world and a beachhead for the takeback of planet earth for God's kingdom purposes. Israel's history with the land will be one of ups and downs and eventually up permanently, but the significance of land for God's universal purposes is great and must be considered.

GENESIS 49:8–12

With Genesis 49:8–10 the elderly Jacob predicted that a messianic figure ("Shiloh") will come from the line of his son, Judah. Verse 10 explains that the "peoples" will obey Him:

> "The scepter shall not depart from Judah,
> Nor the ruler's staff from between his feet,
> Until Shiloh comes,
> And to him shall be the obedience of the peoples."

His kingdom will lead to great earthly prosperity:

> "He ties his foal to the vine,
> And his donkey's colt to the choice vine;
> He washes his garments in wine,
> And his robes in the blood of grapes.
> His eyes are dull from wine,
> And his teeth white from milk" (Gen. 49:11–12).

These words indicate luxurious abundance and show that Messiah's reign will bring incredibly prosperous conditions upon the earth. As Snyder notes, "It is creation *flourishing* unendingly to God's glory. God's work is not just restorative; it is creative, generative, beautifully bountiful."[11] Thus, Genesis 49:8–12 shows that this messianic person from Judah will rule the world during a time of great prosperity on earth.

---

11   Snyder, *Salvation Means Creation Healed*, 108. Emphases added.

PSALM 2

Psalm 2 explains how the coming Messiah relates to God's plans for an earthly kingdom. It presents the nations on earth, with their leaders, as defiantly rebelling against God and His anointed Messiah. But God, from Heaven, laughs at these foolish leaders and announces that He will install the Messiah as King on earth, in the very realm where the rebellion is now occurring: "But as for Me, I have installed My King upon Zion, My holy mountain" (Ps. 2:6). Then Psalm 2:8–9 states that God will give the nations to the Messiah as an inheritance and the Messiah will rule them with a rod of iron:

> "Ask of Me, and I will surely give the ⌊nations as Your inheritance,
> And the very ends of the earth as Your possession.
> You shall break them with a rod of iron,
> You shall shatter them like earthenware."

So this foundational psalm reveals that God's Messiah will rule the nations when He comes to earth. This psalm will be used in Revelation 19:15 to describe Jesus' return to earth to rule the nations.

PSALM 8

Psalm 8 affirms that even in a fallen world man still possesses the right to rule the earth and its creatures. The language of verses 6–8 relies upon the wording of Genesis 1:26–28 concerning man's destiny to rule the earth:

> You [God] make him [man] to rule over the works of Your hands;
> You have put all things under his feet,
> All sheep and oxen,
> And also the beasts of the field,
> The birds of the heavens and the fish of the sea,
> Whatever passes through the paths of the seas.

So even in a fallen world, man's God-given task to successfully rule the world still exists. This psalm will be used several times in the New Testament to describe the coming reign of man on the earth, and how this will happen through Jesus, the ultimate Man (see Heb. 2:5–8; 1 Cor. 15:27).

PSALM 72

Psalm 72 describes the coming reign of the ideal Davidic King, the Messiah. In addition to ruling with "righteousness" and "justice" (v. 2) this King will rule the earth. He will vindicate and save people who are afflicted and needy (v. 4). His reign will extend throughout the globe as He will "rule from sea to sea and from the River to the ends of the earth" (v. 8). All kings and nations will serve Him (v. 11). There will be agricultural prosperity: "May there be abundance of grain in the earth on top of the mountains" (v. 16a).

This kingdom contains spiritual elements such as righteousness and justice, but it is also an earthly kingdom. This psalm shows the multi-dimensional nature of the Messiah's kingdom. It is an earthly kingdom that covers the entire earth. It is characterized by prosperity. Yet it also has spiritual qualities of fairness, righteousness, and justice. David and Solomon never experienced the reign that is described here, but Jesus the Messiah will.

ISAIAH 2:2-4

Isaiah 2 describes a coming reign of the Lord from Jerusalem that will involve the Lord making decisions for nations during a time of peace. When God's kingdom is established from Jerusalem the nations will stream to this city to learn God's ways (2–3). The Lord will make executive decisions for the nations (4a). This will be a time of international harmony as nations discard their weapons of war and use their resources for peaceful purposes.

ISAIAH 11

Few passages describe the impact of Messiahs' kingdom to so many areas as much as Isaiah 11 does. Isaiah 11 describes a coming earthly kingdom under the Messiah who is called "the stem of Jesse" (1). This kingdom will have spiritual characteristics of "righteousness" and "fairness" (4). And it brings the healing of nature which currently suffers because of the Fall. There will be harmony in the animal world as "the wolf will dwell with the lamb" (6), "the cow and the bear will graze" together (7a), and the lion will eat straw (7b). In addition, animals and humans will live in harmony: "The nursing child will play by the hole of the cobra, and the weaned child will put his hand on the viper's den" (8). The mention of animals here naturally draws us to the importance of animals in Genesis 1 and looks forward to their restoration.

Isaiah 11 reveals other great truths. "The earth will be full of the knowledge of the Lord" (9). At this time the nations of the earth will serve the Lord (10) and the nation Israel will be gathered from the corners of the earth (12). The conditions of this chapter have not been fulfilled in history yet, but they will be in Messiah's coming kingdom.

ISAIAH 19

Isaiah 19 predicts the presence of geo-political nations during an earthly kingdom of God. Three nations are highlighted here—Egypt, Assyria, and Israel. The kingdom certainly will involve more than these three countries, but these highlight the importance of Israel among other nations, even traditional enemies of Israel.

With Isaiah 19:16–25 all three nations are portrayed as existing in harmony and enjoying the blessings of God's kingdom. At that time, five cities in Egypt will learn the Hebrew language. A monument to God will be built near the border of Egypt. Egypt and Assyria will construct a highway that allows them to worship the Lord together.

Significantly, terms once used of Israel will also apply to Gentile nations. Egypt will be called God's people ("My people") and Assyria will be called "the work of My hands." And the nation of Israel is also here. They are still God's "inheritance" (see Isa. 19:24–25). This shows that as Gentiles and Gentile nations become "God's people" they do not become "Israel." The concept of the people of God expands to include Gentiles, yet at the same time, national Israel remains significant. Gentiles become God's people without becoming incorporated into Israel.

The importance of this exciting text is great. A time is coming when there will be an earthly kingdom of God with geo-political nations existing and acting in harmony with each other. These nations will have independent identities, but they are all unified as God's people. This evidences a beautiful "unity-diversity" theme we often see in Scripture.

There also is the presence of culture as evidenced by language and the building of a highway. Chapters like these are foundational to the New Creation Model idea of a beautiful, multi-dimensional kingdom of God.

ISAIAH 25

Isaiah 25 is part of Isaiah 24–27, a section often referred to as "Isaiah's Little Apocalypse" because it describes much that is found in the Book of Revelation. It describes a global Day of the Lord, which brings judgment upon the entire earth and its people. Then this is followed by a glorious earthly kingdom with nations experiencing its glory. Verses 6–8 describe a glorious celebration banquet for the peoples of the earth, a banquet with great food and drink. This is done in honor of God's salvation and the removal of death on a global scale:

> The Lord of hosts will prepare a lavish banquet for all peoples on
> this mountain;
> A banquet of aged wine, choice pieces with marrow,
> And refined, aged wine.
> And on this mountain He will swallow up the covering which is over
> all peoples,
> Even the veil which is stretched over all nations.
> He will swallow up death for all time,
> And the Lord God will wipe tears away from all faces,
> And He will remove the reproach of His people from all the earth;
> For the Lord has spoken.

Note the tangible nature of this prophecy. It involves the peoples of the earth, a banquet with food and drink, and the removal of physical death. This is a party/celebration like none other in history. This kingdom banquet scenario is also found in New Testament passages like Matthew 8:11 where Jesus said: "I say to you that many will come from east and west, and recline at the table with Abraham, Isaac and Jacob in the kingdom of heaven."

ISAIAH 35

Isaiah 35 is a kingdom passage that foretells the restoration of nature to Eden-like conditions. It also discusses physical healing. The wilderness and desert will prosper (1–2). "The scorched land will become a pool" (7). No animals will harm anyone (v. 9). The blind, deaf, and lame will be healed (5–6). Jesus referred to this chapter in Matthew 11:2–5 to let John the Baptist's disciples know that Jesus was who He claimed to be. Jesus did the kingdom miracles that Isaiah 35 predicted. Jesus' physical miracles were previews of restoration and healing that will take place on a permanent and global scale in the future.

ISAIAH 65:17–25

The coming new heavens and new earth (v. 17) involve real-life conditions. This includes situations that are much like our current experiences in this age, but with much better results. It has people both young and old (v. 20). People will build houses and live in them (21a). They will plant vineyards and eat their fruit (21b). All of these are done in the context of fairness as people get to live in the houses they build and eat the fruit they produced. Also, childbearing will go well for both mothers and their children: "They will not labor in vain, Or bear children for calamity" (23a). This shows a reversal of conditions from the present age in which both mothers and their children are often in danger during pregnancy and childbirth. While filling the earth via procreation has been occurring since Genesis 4, for the first time it will happen without the negative consequences of a fallen world. (This condition most probably occurs in Messiah's millennial kingdom since procreation probably does not occur in the Eternal State after the Millennium.)

Harmony in the animal kingdom also will exist: "The wolf and the lamb will graze together, and the lion will eat straw like the ox; and dust will be the serpent's food" (v. 25). This repeats the truth concerning animals found previously in Isaiah 11.

With Isaiah 65, creation is restored and people live in harmony with each other and with animals in ideal conditions never seen before. The new earth will involve conditions similar to what we experience now but without the negative effects of the fall.[12]

EZEKIEL 36

The nation Israel was dispersed to the nations for disobedience but it will be saved and restored to the land of promise. The tribes of Israel will be unified. When this occurs God will rebuild cities that had been ruined, and He will make the land "become like the garden of Eden":

> Thus says the Lord God, "On the day that I cleanse you from all your iniquities, I will cause the cities to be inhabited, and the waste places will be rebuilt. The desolate land will be cultivated instead of being a desolation in the sight of everyone who passes by." They will say, "This desolate land has become like the garden of Eden; and the waste, desolate and ruined cities are fortified and inhabited" (Ezek. 36:33–35).

Note the mix of spiritual and physical blessings. Being cleansed from iniquities is linked with physical blessings in the land and cities. The same land and cities that underwent decay are headed for restoration. They will be like "Eden" again.

JEREMIAH 30–33

Jeremiah 30–33 is known as the Book of Consolation describing Israel's restoration after a time of captivity. These four chapters describe many spiritual and physical blessings, more than we can cover here. Nevertheless, consider the physical blessings—"the bounty of the LORD"—that awaits Israel:

> They will come and shout for joy on the height of Zion,
> And they will be radiant over the bounty of the Lord—

---

12   Whether this passage speaks of a coming millennial kingdom or the Eternal State or both is a discussion for another time. The key point is that the future kingdom of God involves real activities on a tangible earth.

> Over the grain and the new wine and the oil,
> And over the young of the flock and the herd;
> And their life will be like a watered garden,
> And they will never languish again (31:12).

Coming kingdom conditions will involve "grain," "new wine," "oil," and "flock of the herd." These reveal the blessings of prosperity in the land. Later in the chapter Jeremiah will discuss the spiritual blessings of the New Covenant (see Jer. 31:31–34), the perpetuity of Israel as a nation (31:35–37), and the rebuilding of the city of Jerusalem (Jer. 31:38–40). So physical, national, and spiritual blessings are part of the New Covenant.

HOSEA 2:14-23

The Book of Hosea has much to say about Israel's disobedience. Yet like the other prophets Hosea also promises salvation and restoration. God will grant Israel vineyards (2:15) and permanent peace—"And I will abolish the bow, the sword and war from the land, and will make them lie down in safety" (2:18b). Agricultural prosperity will occur—"And the earth will respond to the grain, to the new wine and to the oil" (2:22). Using the language and concepts from Genesis 1:20–24, Hosea 2:18a foretells positive conditions for the creatures of the earth:

> "In that day I will also make a covenant for them
> With the beasts of the field,
> The birds of the sky
> And the creeping things of the ground."

Thus, the restoration of Israel will involve a return to pre-fall conditions on the earth and a healing of the living creatures mentioned in Genesis 1:20–25.

MICAH 4

Micah 4 contains much of the information found in Isaiah 2:2–4. The prophet also reveals that people will live in peace in the context of what they do: "Each of them will sit under his vine and under his fig tree, with no one to make them afraid" (4:4). The Lord will also make sure the wealth of the nations is used properly: "That you may devote to the LORD their unjust gain and their wealth to the Lord of all the earth" (4:13b). Not only does this passage affirm the earth and earthly conditions, but it also addresses the issue of wealth on the earth. Justice applies to economic wealth.

AMOS 9:13–15

Amos 9:13–15 describes coming kingdom conditions involving plowing of fields, treading of grapes, prosperous mountains, vineyards, wine, gardens, fruit, land, and a restored Israel:

> "Behold, days are coming," declares the LORD,
> "When the plowman will overtake the reaper
> And the treader of grapes him who sows seed;
> When the mountains will drip sweet wine
> And all the hills will be dissolved.
> "Also I will restore the captivity of My people Israel,
> And they will rebuild the ruined cities and live in them;
> They will also plant vineyards and drink their wine,
> And make gardens and eat their fruit.
> "I will also plant them on their land,
> And they will not again be rooted out from their land
> Which I have given them,"
> Says the LORD your God."

The restoration of Israel in the future is linked with prosperity on the earth.

ZECHARIAH 8

Zechariah 8 reveals that neighborhoods and children playing safely in streets will be part of the kingdom. This involves a sweet scene involving older men and women, along with boys and girls:

> Thus says the LORD of hosts, "Old men and old women will again sit
> in the streets of Jerusalem, each man with his staff in his hand because

of age. And the streets of the city will be filled with boys and girls playing in its streets" (Zech. 8:4–5).

The New Creation Model depiction here is noted by Alva McClain: "This is no kingdom of asceticism where the normal impulses of humanity, implanted by divine creation, will be rigorously suppressed." This is a time of "glad release" and "joyous and safe recreation."[13]

ZECHARIAH 14

Zechariah 14 offers many specific details about Messiah's coming earthly kingdom. The Lord physically comes to deliver Jerusalem from hostile nations. His return to the Mount of Olives brings major changes to the geography of the region (1–4). He will establish a global earthly kingdom: "the LORD will be king over all the earth; in that day the LORD will be the only one, and His name the only one" (9).

Thus, when this kingdom occurs, it will be the Lord's on earth, it involves the defeat of nations, and it brings the rescue of Jerusalem. And it will be a time when everyone on earth knows the Lord is King and there will be no rivals. His name is the only name! These conditions have not been fulfilled yet in history, but they will be. We believe they await the second coming and kingdom of Jesus as described in Revelation 19–20. Here Jesus returns to earth, defeats His enemies and then reigns for a thousand years.

With Zechariah 14, the Lord will exercise His reign over the nations of the earth who must pay tribute to Him by coming to Jerusalem. Those who resist this command will experience punishment (16–19). This appears connected with Revelation 19:15 which states that Jesus will come to rule the nations with a rod of iron.

This chapter shows that the Lord will reign over the entire earth and the nations. Nations must serve Him and will face consequences if they do not. Also, every item, including common ones, will be considered holy in the kingdom:

---

13   McClain, *The Greatness of the Kingdom*, 28.

> In that day there will be inscribed on the bells of the horses, "HOLY
> TO THE LORD." And the cooking pots in the LORD's house will be
> like the bowls before the altar. Every cooking pot in Jerusalem and in
> Judah will be holy to the LORD of hosts (Zech. 14:20–21a).

The kingdom of God will make all objects holy, even those considered
common previously.

Zechariah 14 shows that Jerusalem, Israel, nations, the earth, common objects, and other tangible realities are associated with the return of
the Messiah, we now know as Jesus.

MALACHI 4:6

I once read a theology book that asserted that "land" is prominent
in Genesis, but it loses its significance gradually throughout the Old
Testament. Not only is that false, but the last verse of the Old Testament
mentions "land." In discussing the coming day of the Lord, Malachi noted
that Elijah would appear and restore Israel so that "the land" would not be
stricken with a curse:

> "Behold, I am going to send you Elijah the prophet before the coming
> of the great and terrible day of the Lord. He will restore the hearts
> of the fathers to their children and the hearts of the children to
> their fathers, so that I will not come and smite the land with a curse"
> (Mal. 4:4–6).

So, the last verse of the Old Testament ends with a promise that God
plans to restore Israel, and this involves the land. The Old Testament ends
with the expectation that both Israel and the land of Israel are significant
in God's plans. As we will see, this truth, along with other New Creation
realities, are reaffirmed in the New Testament to which we now turn.

As we now turn to New Testament passages, Saucy offers a helpful summary of the New Creation Model hope of the Old Testament—a
hope that is "comprehensive and holistic":

> The Old Testament prophetic picture reveals a hope that is com-
> prehensive and holistic. Its themes provide for the restoration of all

things spiritual and material. Humankind, the focus of the original creation, is also the center of the redemptive purpose. All aspects of human life—the personal, inward, and individualistic as well as the social, communal, and international—are part of the total prophetic picture.[14]

---

14   Saucy, *The Case for Progressive Dispensationalism*, 241–42.

THE NEW CREATION MODEL IN THE NEW TESTAMENT

◆

The New Testament introduces the arrival of Jesus the Messiah. And while many theological areas are addressed in the New Testament, it is fair to say that Jesus' saving work is heavily emphasized. But do we see New Testament passages express the New Creation Model hope so often expressed in the Old Testament? The answer is a resounding Yes! We see much continuity between Old Testament and New Testament expectations on tangible matters related to earth, land, nations, Israel, physical blessings, the Day of the Lord, and Messiah's kingdom. Below are some New Testament verses and passages that express the New Creation Model expectations.

LUKE 1–2

Luke 1–2 reveals several expectations concerning the arrival of Jesus that are consistent with the Old Testament New Creation Model hope. The angel Gabriel told Mary that her son Jesus would reign from David's throne over Israel forever—"the Lord God will give Him the throne of His father David; and He will reign over the house of Jacob forever, and His kingdom will have no end" (see Luke 1:32–33). No spiritualization of Israel or David's throne is mentioned. Here, the Old Testament hope of a kingdom reign of the Messiah over Israel from David's throne is affirmed.

The Holy Spirit-filled, Zacharias, expected a coming national deliverance for Israel from enemies that was promised in the Abrahamic and Davidic covenants:

> As He spoke by the mouth of His holy prophets from of old—
> Salvation from our enemies,
> And from the hand of all who hate us (Luke 1:71).

The prophetess, Anna, and others were "those who were looking for the redemption of Jerusalem" (Luke 2:38). Thus, tangible Old Testament expectations are reaffirmed early in the New Testament.

MATTHEW 4:17

In Matthew 4:17 Jesus began His public ministry by stating: "Repent, for the kingdom of heaven is at hand." That Jesus offered no definition or redefinition of this kingdom is significant. This shows He probably expected His Jewish audience to know about this kingdom He was now proclaiming as "at hand." How would they know what it was like? From the Hebrew Scriptures. J. Ramsey Michaels notes that Jesus' expectation of the kingdom is "well within the framework of contemporary Jewish messianic and apocalyptic expectations. This is a kingdom that is "*both* spiritual and national, *both* universal and ethnic."[1]

MATTHEW 5:5

The Old Testament often talked about land and the earth. Psalm 37:11, for example, declared that prosperity in the land would occur for those who were humble:

> But the humble will inherit the land
> And will delight themselves in abundant prosperity.

---

1   J. Ramsey Michaels, "The Kingdom of God and the Historical Jesus," in *The Kingdom of God in 20th Century Interpretation*, ed. Wendell Willis (Peabody, MA: Hendrickson, 1987), 114, 116. Emphases in original.

This verse mentions both "land" and "abundant prosperity." In His Sermon on the Mount Jesus referred to the earth/land as a future inheritance: "Blessed are the gentle, for they shall inherit the earth [or "land"]" (Matt. 5:5). The term here for "earth" also can refer to land. Whether He refers specifically to the earth in general or the land of Israel specifically, or both, is difficult to discern. Blessings to the land of Israel will also mean blessings for all nations in their lands.

Jesus views earth and/or land as the destiny of those characterized by gentleness. As Jesus offers New Covenant instruction, He states that His followers will inherit the earth/land.

MATTHEW 6:10

When Jesus taught His disciples to pray the first thing He directed them to ask for was the coming of God's kingdom to earth where God's will would be done perfectly:

> "Your kingdom come.
> Your will be done,
> On earth as it is in heaven" (Matt. 6:10).

Jesus mentions many things to pray for in this "Lord's Prayer" but the first concerns the coming of the kingdom to earth. We are to ask for its coming so God's will can be done on earth just like it is done in Heaven. This shows the kingdom had not arrived yet when Jesus offered these words since we are to pray for its coming.

And this verse reveals that when the kingdom comes it will be on earth. Only then will God's will be done on earth as it is in heaven. When we combine Matthew 5:5 and Matthew 6:10, we see the importance Jesus gives to inheriting the land/earth and God's kingdom coming to earth. These verses also show that the Old Testament expectations of land/earth and an earthly kingdom remain. Jesus does not transcend these expectations but expects their literal fulfillment.

MATTHEW 8–9

Jesus brings salvation from sin. Yet, Matthew 8–9 also shows that Jesus' kingdom power applies to all aspects of human existence. Jesus demonstrated mastery over physical diseases, death, nature, and demons. He heals the body, restores creation, defeats the enemy, and brings resurrection.[2]

Note the tangible nature of Jesus' ministry in these chapters. When it comes to healing, Jesus healed a leper (8:1–4), a paralyzed servant of a centurion (8:5–13), Peter's mother-in-law who had a fever (8:14–17), and a paralytic (9:1–8). He raised a girl from the dead and healed a woman who had a hemorrhage issue for twelve years (9:18–26). Jesus healed two blind men (9:27–31) and a mute man who was demon possessed (9:32–33). Jesus also calmed a great storm (8:23–27) and cast out demons (8:28–34). Matthew 9:35 summarizes the great magnitude of Jesus' healing ministry: "Jesus was going through all the cities and villages, teaching in their synagogues and proclaiming the gospel of the kingdom, and healing every kind of disease and every kind of sickness."

Jesus cared about physical needs and spent much of His time bringing physical wholeness. The "gospel of the kingdom" is linked with physical healing, resurrection, and mastery of nature. When Jesus chose the twelve apostles to proclaim the kingdom to Israel, He gave them authority to do the same things: "Jesus summoned His twelve disciples and gave them authority over unclean spirits, to cast them out, and to heal every kind of disease and every kind of sickness" (Matt. 10:1).

Jesus' ministry included acts of physical restoration, resurrection, authority over demons, and authority over nature. These were more than just individual acts of kindness to people (which they were). They were displays of kingdom power. The kingdom of God involves not only spiritual salvation but also acts of physical restoration. This will fully occur when Jesus returns and establishes His reign upon the earth.

---

2   We are not saying physical healing and resurrection occur in this age, but when the two comings of Jesus are accomplished, these will be the result for all believers.

MATTHEW 19:28–30

With Matthew 19:28–30 Jesus discussed rewards for those who follow Him. Significantly, these rewards are not just spiritual rewards. They include tangible benefits. Jesus refers to a coming "regeneration" when at that time He sits upon His glorious [Davidic] throne and His twelve apostles judge the twelve tribes of Israel (v. 28).

The "regeneration" is the Greek term *paliggenesia* which means "renewal" or "rebirth." Here it refers to the restoration of earth/creation. The created order will experience transformation when Jesus comes to reign. At that time houses, relationships, and farms will be multiplied to those who gave up everything to follow Jesus in this present age (v. 29). The mention of "houses" and "farms" reveals that land and dwelling places are part of God's future purposes for His people. Their destiny is not sitting on a cloud, like many cultural depictions of eternity show.

Rewards in the coming kingdom relate to real-life experiences we now have. Just as relationships, houses, and farms are part of our current experience, so too, they will be in the future. But then they will be permanent and not affected by sin and the curse.

LUKE 22

At the Last Supper Jesus discussed several details that have implications for a New Creation Model understanding. The first involves Jesus eating a tangible meal with His disciples in the coming kingdom of God. As Luke 22:15–16 states:

> And He said to them, "I have earnestly desired to eat this Passover with you before I suffer; for I say to you, I shall never again eat it until it is fulfilled in the kingdom of God."

The Passover meal Jesus was eating with His disciples was a real meal. And they will eat a Passover meal again when the kingdom of God arrives. A tangible meal will occur in the kingdom. This is consistent with other passages that describe celebration banquets in the kingdom of God (see Isa. 25:6–8; Matt. 8:10–12).

Then, in Luke 22:28–30, Jesus again brings up eating and drinking at His table in the kingdom, but then adds the detail of His disciples sitting on real thrones judging the twelve tribes of a restored national Israel:

> "You are those who have stood by Me in My trials; and just as My Father has granted Me a kingdom, I grant you that you may eat and drink at My table in My kingdom, and you will sit on thrones judging the twelve tribes of Israel."

In sum, Luke 22 reveals the importance of a coming tangible kingdom of God in which eating and drinking, and the judging of the restored tribes of Israel by the apostles will occur.

ACTS 1:6; 3:21

If you could have asked Jesus anything before He ascended to Heaven, what would you have brought up? The apostles had this chance. After forty days of instruction concerning the kingdom of God (see Acts 1:3), the disciples asked Jesus, "Lord, is it at this time You are restoring the kingdom to Israel?" (1:6). This question revealed the expectation of the disciples on Jesus' ascension day. They believed the kingdom would be restored to national Israel. They were not asking *if* the kingdom would be restored to Israel. That was assumed. Instead, they asked a *when* question. Note that Jesus does not say they were wrong with this expectation. He assumes the correctness of their assumption but then tells them that only the Father knows *when* the restoration of the kingdom to Israel will occur (see Acts 1:7). Both the apostles and Jesus assumed what the Old Testament revealed on many occasions—a coming restored kingdom for Israel.

With Acts 3:19–21, Peter told Israel to repent and return. Doing this would lead to forgiveness of sins, times of refreshing, the return of Jesus, and the restoration of all things. The "restoration of all things" is closely related to the "regeneration" of Matthew 19:28 and the reconciliation of all things of Colossians 1:20, and thus is an expectation of cosmic renewal. The word for "restoration" in Acts 3:21 is the same word concerning the *restoration* of the kingdom to Israel in Acts 1:6. The coming "restoration of all things" involves the restoring of the kingdom to national Israel and all things the Old Testament prophets predicted.

ROMANS 8:19–22

Much of Romans concerns how sinners can be right with God. But with chapter 8 Paul noted that creation is headed for restoration. This makes sense since man's condition impacts creation:

> For the anxious longing of the creation waits eagerly for the revealing of the sons of God. For the creation was subjected to futility, not willingly, but because of Him who subjected it, in hope that the creation itself also will be set free from its slavery to corruption into the freedom of the glory of the children of God. For we know that the whole creation groans and suffers the pains of childbirth together until now (Rom. 8:19–22).

Creation will transition from "slavery" to "freedom." This coincides with the glorification of God's people (see Rom. 8:23). Creation follows man's destiny. When the Fall occurred the ground was cursed. Man's sin led to creation's downfall. But not forever. When saved people are glorified in the future the creation will become free and restored. Thus, Romans 8 reveals that the fallen creation will give way to a renewed earth.

COLOSSIANS 1:15–20

The cross of Jesus clearly involves atonement for sins (see Isaiah 53). But it also has cosmic implications. Jesus' cross not only brings atonement for human sin, but it also results in the reconciliation of all things. Colossians 1:16–17 states that Jesus created and sustains all things both visible and invisible:

> For by Him all things were created, both in the heavens and on earth, visible and invisible, whether thrones or dominions or rulers or authorities—all things have been created through Him and for Him. He is before all things, and in Him all things hold together.

Yet note that this same Jesus who created and sustained all things also reconciles all things through His cross:

> and through Him to reconcile all things to Himself, having made peace through the blood of His cross; through Him, I say, whether things on earth or things in heaven (Col. 1:20).

Here the benefits of Jesus' cross connect with the cosmic reconciliation of "all things," which refers to the whole realm of creation. Just as man's sin brought curse and devastation to all creation, Jesus' atonement and salvation bring restoration to all creation. Richard Middleton rightly notes:

> Colossians 1 does not myopically limit the efficacy of Christ's atonement to the individual or even to humanity. Without denying that the atonement suffices for individual people, the text applies the reconciliation effected by Christ's shed blood as comprehensively as possible, to "all things, whether on earth or in heaven."[3]

Snyder also catches the cosmic aspects of Jesus' atonement too: "Jesus' atonement through his death and triumphant resurrection is a cosmic-historical act through which all creation is redeemed—potentially and partially now, and fully when the kingdom comes in fullness."[4]

HEBREWS 2:5–8

Hebrews 2:5–8 is strategic for understanding God's purposes. The intertextual connections for this passage are Genesis 1:26, 28 and Psalm 8. Both of these earlier passages state the importance of man someday having a successful mediatorial reign over all earth and earth's creatures. With Hebrews 2:5, the writer speaks of the "world to come" and declares that man, not angels, are destined to rule in this period. With Hebrews 2:5b–8a, the writer quotes Psalm 8:4–6 and its expectation for man to rule the earth and its creatures. This shows that even after Jesus' first coming and

---

3   Middleton, *A New Heaven and a New Earth*, 158.

4   Snyder, *Salvation Means Creation Healed*, 103.

the beginning of the church, God still expects man to subdue creation in the "world to come." And with Hebrews 2:8b, the writer states that this expectation still needs to occur: "For in subjecting all things to him [man], He left nothing that is not subject to him. But now we do not yet see all things subjected to him."

Thus, Hebrews 2:5–8 reveals that man is still destined to rule and subdue the earth and its creatures, but this rule awaits the "world to come" since it is not happening in this age. Hebrews 2:9 introduces Jesus as the One who will make this happen. Thus, Jesus will be the one who fulfills man's destiny to subdue the earth for the glory of God. This passage also shows great continuity between Old Testament expectations for a coming earthly kingdom of God and what the New Testament believed about this kingdom.

REVELATION 5:10

Revelation 4–5 describes the most glorious heavenly throne room scene in Scripture. It pictures the Father on His heavenly universal kingdom throne being worshipped. It also presents the Son (Jesus the Lamb) as the One worthy to take the book from the Father's right hand. This Jesus is the Lamb who purchased people from every ethnic group (5:9). Because of this there will be a kingdom reign of the saints upon the earth: "You [the Lamb] have made them to be a kingdom and priests to our God; and they will reign upon the earth" (Rev. 5:10).

Significantly, even with this glorious heavenly scene, the focus shifts to a coming reign of the saints with Jesus *on earth*. Heaven is not the final destiny of Jesus and the saints. Their destiny is an earthly kingdom. Even the martyred saints of Revelation 6:9–11 in Heaven look forward to the vengeance of God on earth: "How long O Lord, holy and true, will you refrain from judging and avenging our blood on those who dwell on the earth?"

Earlier we mentioned how in Matthew 6:10 Jesus told His disciples to pray for God's will to be done on earth. Noting the connection between Matthew 6:10 and the Book of Revelation, Christopher Rowland observes, "In Revelation we find how the petition of the Lord's Prayer is fulfilled, how God's kingdom comes on earth as it is in heaven. Here, heaven is not an escape from the things of earth."[5]

REVELATION 20

Revelation 20 describes a thousand-year reign of Jesus and His saints on earth after His second coming to earth, but before the Eternal Kingdom of Revelation 20–22. This is the messianic/millennial reign of Jesus and His people over the nations. This also involves resurrection of the body for martyrs before this kingdom began (20:4). More is discussed about Revelation 20 in other parts of this book.

REVELATION 21:3, 24, 26

God intends a wonderful diversity of people groups in eternity. This includes ethnicities and nations. Nations were the main theme in Genesis 10–11 as God spread the descendants of Noah and his sons across the earth. In Acts 17:16 Paul stated that God has appointed the time and boundaries of each nation. Revelation 5:9 says Jesus purchased persons from every tribe, tongue, people, and nation.

Multiple people groups and ethnicities will exist on the new earth. Revelation 21:3 states, "and they shall be His people(s)." The term here, *laoi*, is plural and literally means "peoples." This is reminiscent of Isaiah 25:6: "The Lord of hosts will prepare a lavish banquet for *all peoples* on this mountain."[6]

Revelation 21:24, 26 specifically mentions nations on the new earth:

The nations will walk by its light, and the kings of the earth will bring their glory into it (21:24).

and they [the nations] will bring the glory and the honor of the nations into it (21:26).

---

5   Christopher Rowland, "The Eschatology of the New Testament Church," in *The Oxford Handbook of Eschatology*, ed. Jerry L. Walls (New York: Oxford University Press, 2008), 69.

6   Emphases added.

This mention of "nations" is significant as Middleton observes, "The reference to nations in the new creation is a telling signal that cultural, even national, diversity is not abrogated by redemption. Salvation does not erase cultural differences; rather, the human race, still distinguished by nationality, now walks by the glory or light of the holy city.... (Rev. 21:24)."[7] The reference to "kings" also implies leaders associated with nations.

These nations and kings "bring their glory" into the New Jerusalem. This "glory" refers to cultural contributions. The nations outside the city bring the best of their culture into the city, all for the glory of God. Revelation 22:2 also notes that the nations will live in harmony with each other. The leaves of the tree of life will be for "the healing of the nations." Harmony among nations will be the norm on the new earth.

This refutes the Spiritual Vision Model understanding that eternity is only about the individual's static contemplation of God. Nations, kings, and culture reveal interactions among the peoples of God. Eternity is not about a generic group with no distinctions whatsoever holding hands in the clouds. It involves nations and peoples serving and working for God on a restored new earth.

CONCLUSION

The texts mentioned above are only a few that reveal the importance of earth, land, Israel, nations, society, culture, and many other tangible things both now and in the future. The Christian worldview properly accounts for these matters. Man's place in God's plans is multi-dimensional, involving the full array of God's creation.

---

7   J. Richard Middleton, "A New Earth Perspective," in *Four Views on Heaven*, 87.

THE SPIRITUAL
VISION MODEL
FURTHER EXPLAINED

*"Many of us have unconsciously accepted a worldview that
inverts the direction of salvation. We think salvation means
going up to heaven rather than heaven coming to earth, as
the Bible teaches. We have been taught that Jesus ascended to
heaven so that our spirits could join there eternally!—rather
than what the Bible says: Jesus will come to earth to redeem all
creation, including our own physical bodies. To a surprising
degree, contemporary Christians are modern-day Gnostics."*

—Howard Snyder[1]

◆

We now shift attention to the Spiritual Vision Model. The Spiritual
Vision Model is a paradigm that focuses on spiritual and individual realities to the exclusion or downplaying of material, physical, cosmic, national, and international matters. A strong cosmic dualism exists
between spirit and matter. Spiritual things are viewed as good and better while physical-material entities are perceived as bad or lesser. Also, the
nature of eternal life is perceived as predominately spiritual. Eternal life is
a spiritual existence apart from earth and societal interactions with a sole

---

1   Snyder, *Salvation Means Creation Healed*, 61.

focus on the absolute or God. A spiritual existence and/or heaven is the highest level of ontological reality—the realm of spirit as opposed to matter. As Blaising explains concerning this model, "This is the destiny of the saved, who will exist in that nonearthly, spiritual place as spiritual beings engaged eternally in spiritual activity."[2]

The Spiritual Vision Model also focuses on individual human salvation. Little or no attention is given to corporate entities such as Israel or Gentile nations. And little attention is given to future prophetic events involving the Day of the Lord, an earthly kingdom, the new earth, Israel, nations, and other tangible matters.

The strongest forms of the Spiritual Vision Model exist with non-Christian worldviews and religions such as Platonism, Neo-Platonism, Gnosticism, Hinduism, and Buddhism. Since orthodox Christianity affirms the goodness of God's creation and resurrection of the body, Christianity cannot be a full Spiritual Vision Model religion.

Within Christendom the Spiritual Vision Model has been most present in the Roman Catholic tradition, particularly in the Middle Ages. It also exists in the Eastern Orthodox Church and liberal Protestant mainline denominations. Evangelical theological traditions are less in line with this model but still often contain elements of the Spiritual Vision Model.

While many elements are associated with a Spiritual Vision approach in Christianity, the following are key parts of this model:

1. Earth and physical things are a lesser form of reality.

2. Salvation is only about forgiveness of sins.

3. Jesus' role is only that of Savior from sin, not reigning King over the earth and all creation.

4. The kingdom of God is salvation or living in Heaven.

5. Societal, cultural, ethnic, and national distinctions need to be removed.

---

2   Blaising, "Premillennialism," in *Three Views on the Millennium and Beyond*, 161.

6. This present earth will be annihilated.

7. Heaven, not earth, is man's final destiny.

8. Eternal Heaven involves only mental contemplation of God.

Blaising notes that the Spiritual Vision Model is linked with certain biblical themes:

1. The promise that believers will see God

2. The promise that believers will receive full knowledge

3. The description of Heaven as the dwelling place of God

4. The description of Heaven as the destiny of the believing dead prior to the resurrection[3]

While none of these themes above are inaccurate when understood correctly, they often are emphasized or taught in a way that excludes other tangible realities the Bible speaks about.

In addition to the biblical themes just mentioned, the Spiritual Vision Model also draws upon cultural ideas common to the classical philosophical tradition:

1. A basic contrast between spirit and matter

2. An identification of spirit with mind or intellect

3. A belief that eternal perfection entails the absence of change[4]

The Spiritual Vision Model presents a strong dualism between spirit and matter with spirit being most important: "Central to all three of these is

---

3   Ibid.

4   Ibid.

the classical tradition's notion of an ontological hierarchy in which spirit is located at the top of a descending order of being. Elemental matter occupies the lowest place."[5] Heaven is a realm of spirit as opposed to matter and is a nonearthly, spiritual place for spiritual beings who are engaged only in spiritual activity. This Heaven is also free from all change. Eternal life, therefore, is viewed primarily as "cognitive, meditative, or contemplative."[6] Blaising notes that this Spiritual Vision Model thinking caused many Christians to view eternal life "as the *beatific vision* of God—an unbroken, unchanging contemplation of the infinite reality of God."[7]

Another result of the Spiritual Vision approach concerns viewing the current intermediate state in Heaven as the goal and final destiny of believers, instead of the new earth. Poythress notes, "In many circles people looked forward primarily to death and the intermediate state rather than to the Second Coming, the resurrection of the body, and the new heavens and the new earth, which are the primary focus of New Testament hope."[8] This is significant since Christians often view the intermediate Heaven as a person's final destiny instead of a future tangible new earth.

In his book, *Models of the Kingdom*, Howard A. Snyder points out that a purely spiritual view of the kingdom, which he calls "the kingdom as inner spiritual experience model," "may be traced to the influence of Platonist and Neoplatonist ideas on Christian thinking...."[9] This model "draws to some degree on Greek philosophical roots."[10] He states that, "One can sense the Platonism lying behind this model."[11] Snyder says this Platonism was linked with a disdain for material things:

---

5   Ibid.

6   Ibid., 162.

7   Ibid.

8   Vern Poythress, "Currents within Amillennialism," 21.

9   Howard A. Snyder, *Models of the Kingdom* (Eugene, OR: Wipf and Stock, 1991), 42.

10   Ibid., 52.

11   Ibid.

Historically this model has often been tainted with a sort of Platonic disdain for things material, perhaps seeing the body or matter as evil or at least imperfect and imperfectible. It is thus dualistic, viewing the 'higher' spiritual world as essentially separate from the material world.[12]

Historically, the Spiritual Vision Model is linked to allegorical and spiritual methods of Bible interpretation. Blaising notes that this model "was intimately connected with practices of 'spiritual interpretation' that were openly acknowledged to be contrary to the literal meaning of the words being interpreted."[13] This had a huge impact on how people viewed what God is doing: "The long term practice of reading Scripture in this way so conditioned the Christian mind that by the late Middle Ages, the spiritual vision model had become an accepted fact of the Christian worldview."[14]

CHRISTOPLATONISM

Spiritual Vision Model ideas in the church are connected with Greek philosophy, particularly ideas stemming from Plato. Randy Alcorn addressed the impact of Greek philosophy on Christianity in his book, *Heaven*. While not using the designation, "New Creation Model," Alcorn's book is a strong case for a new creationist approach against a Spiritual Vision paradigm. Alcorn affirms that eternal life involves a restored earth, nations, culture, society, and a host of other issues associated with a New Creation Model. And he opposes the spiritualization of material realities.

Alcorn notes the significance of the philosopher Plato (c. 429–347 BC) and how Plato's ideas were merged with those of Christianity. He calls this merger *Christoplatonism*, which "has blended elements of Platonism with Christianity."[15] But this joining of Platonism with Christianity "has

---

12   Ibid., 54.

13   Blaising, 165.

14   Ibid.

15   Alcorn, *Heaven*, 475.

poisoned Christianity and blunted its distinct differences from Eastern religions."[16]

Eastern religions have presented physical experiences on earth as *maya* or "illusion." Thus, man's pursuit of ultimate reality involves escaping the illusion of the physical world to merge with a transcendent, impersonal absolute like Brahman. This thinking will be similar to many Christians who believe Heaven concerns fleeing earth to live in a spiritual heaven forever.

According to Alcorn, Christoplatonism's pervasive influence causes many Christians to resist the following biblical truths when it comes to eternity: life on the New Earth; eating and drinking; walking and talking; living in dwelling places; traveling down streets; going through gates from one place to another; ruling; working; playing; and engaging in earthly culture.[17] As a result, Christoplatonism has had "a devastating effect on our ability to understand what Scripture says about Heaven, particularly about the eternal Heaven, the new earth."[18] Alcorn cites a statistic from *Time* showing that two-thirds of Americans who believe in the afterlife do not believe they will have resurrected bodies.[19] Prevailing ideas of Platonism imposed on eschatology rob Christians of their hope: "The human heart cries out for answers about the afterlife," but the answers are not being given.[20]

Alcorn notes that hope is part of Christianity, but a Christoplatonism hope is not a biblical hope. Humans were not created to long for a purely spiritual existence: "Trying to develop an appetite for a disembodied existence in a non-physical Heaven is like trying to develop an appetite for gravel. No matter how sincere we are, and no matter how hard we try, it's not going to work. Nor should it."[21] Alcorn is correct since *God did not*

---

16   Ibid.

17   Ibid., 476.

18   Ibid., 52.

19   Ibid., 112.

20   Ibid., xiii.

21   Ibid., 7.

create human beings to desire things contrary to their nature. Humans were created with a physical body to dwell on a physical earth. God does not make humans with a body on earth and then expect them to long for a bodiless existence in a purely spiritual realm. If a true Christian struggles with longing for eternity, it might be because he or she has bought into Plato's version of eternal life more so than the Bible's depiction.

Alcorn claims that misunderstandings about the nature of Heaven have nefarious roots. "Satan need not convince us that Heaven doesn't exist. He need only convince us that Heaven is a place of boring, unearthly existence. If we believe that lie, we'll be robbed of our joy and anticipation."[22] He researched more than 150 books on Heaven, both old and new. But a common theme emerged: "One thing I've found is that books about Heaven are notorious for saying we can't know what Heaven is like, but it will be more wonderful than we can imagine," he says.[23] "However, the moment we say that we can't imagine Heaven, we dump cold water on all that God has revealed to us about our eternal home. If we can't envision it, we can't look forward to it. If Heaven is unimaginable, why even try?"[24]

This "Christoplatonism" that Alcorn explains and critiques is consistent with the Spiritual Vision Model paradigm we are examining.[25]

SPIRITUAL VISION MODEL IN SUMMARY

The Spiritual Vision Model focuses on spiritual and individual realities to the exclusion of material and corporate entities. Examples of Spiritual Vision thinking can be seen with the following:

+ Spiritual entities are of higher value and are more important than material things.

---

22   Ibid., 11.

23   Ibid., 17.

24   Ibid.

25   To be clear, Alcorn disagrees with Christoplatonism and the Spiritual Vision Model.

+ God's purposes only involve the salvation of individuals.

+ Man's goal is to escape earth and physical things which are obstacles to knowing and worshiping God.

+ The earth and the non-human creatures only have instrumental value as the backdrop for God's plans to save humans.

+ God will annihilate the current earth and replace it with a new realm of existence.

+ Jesus' primary role is Savior of people from sin and His kingdom reign is human salvation.

+ Ethnicities and nations do not exist in eternity.

+ Israel is now only a spiritual community.

+ Jesus' messianic/millennial kingdom is a spiritual kingdom.

+ Rest in eternity means no activity.

+ All human desires will cease to exist except for the desire for God.

+ Eternal life only involves direct worship of God, not social, cultural, or political interactions with people.

+ Our experiences in eternity will be entirely different than our experiences on earth now.

+ In eternity, believers will know everything with no need to learn new things.

+ Singing and mental contemplation of God is all people will do in eternity.

+ There is no time or linear progression of events in eternity.

+ There will be no eating or drinking in eternity.

- God's people will have no memory of anything with their previous life on earth.

- We will not know or have relationships with the people we know and love in this age.

ISRAEL, STRUCTURAL SUPERSESSIONISM, AND THE SPIRITUAL VISION MODEL

◆

Discussion of the New Creation Model must address the controversial issue of Israel. From Genesis 12 through the last verse of Malachi, corporate, national Israel is a major factor in God's plans. Malachi 4 ends with the promise of a coming Day of the Lord that will lead to the salvation and prospering of Israel in the land. No indication exists in the Old Testament that the importance of national Israel would change or end.

Yet many Christians believe Israel underwent a transformation with the arrival of Jesus and the New Testament era. A change in the story occurred. Allegedly, Israel transitioned from a corporate national, territorial entity to a spiritual community—the church. A redefinition of Israel occurred with the result that Old Testament promises of a restoration of national Israel will not happen. Because of Jesus, the true Israel, the church in Jesus becomes a spiritual Israel that inherits the promises first made with national Israel. The result is that national Israel will not see the fulfillment of the covenants and promises made with her in the Old Testament.

This view often is called replacement theology, supersessionism, or more recently, fulfillment theology.[1] The title does not matter as much as the idea behind the title. With it, Jesus is viewed as the true Israel and thus everyone in Him, whether Jew or Gentile, becomes part of a spiritualized, redefined Israel. Yet there is subtraction since corporate national Israel no longer is theologically significant and will not experience the restoration predicted for it in the Old Testament. Curses and dispersion for Israel, yes! Blessings and restoration for Israel, no!

This leads us to supersessionism's relationship to the Spiritual Vision Model. Various forms of supersessionism exist. First, punitive supersessionism asserts that God permanently rejected Israel and replaced it with the church. This form of supersessionism was quite common in the church until the last hundred years. Second, there is economic supersessionism, which asserts that it was God's plan all along to eventually transition from national Israel to a spiritual Israel (the church). The national entity was an inferior type that allegedly gave way to the superior antitype—Jesus and the church. This is a softer form of replacement theology or supersessionism. In my book, *Has the Church Replaced Israel?* I discuss these two forms of supersessionism in detail.[2]

STRUCTURAL SUPERSESSIONISM

Our focus here, though, is on a third type of supersessionism— "structural supersessionism." This designation was coined by R. Kendall Soulen in his book, *The God of Israel and Christian Theology*.[3] This is deeper than the other two forms of supersessionism. Structural supersessionism

---

1   Ligon Duncan states, "Covenant theology isn't replacement theology, it's fulfillment theology. There's promise and fulfillment. The promises of God to Israel are fulfilled in both the Jews and the Gentiles being part of the one people of God in the purposes of God's redemption." Ligon Duncan, "What Are Some Misconceptions about Covenant Theology," https://rts.edu/resources/what-are-some-misconceptions-about-covenant-theology/ October, 13, 2020 (accessed February 5, 2023).

2   Michael J. Vlach, *Has the Church Replaced Israel?: A Theological Evaluation* (Nashville, TN: B&H Academic, 2010).

3   R. Kendall Soulen, *The God of Israel and Christian Theology* (Minneapolis, MN: Augsburg Fortress, 1996). Soulen also coined the titles "punitive supersessionism" and "economic supersessionism."

contains assumptions and presuppositions about the Old Testament's ability (or non-ability) to speak to the issues it addresses. According to Soulen, "Structural supersessionism refers to the narrative logic of the standard model whereby it renders the Hebrew Scriptures largely indecisive for shaping Christian convictions about how God's works as Consummator and as Redeemer engage humankind in universal and enduring ways."[4]

In short, structural supersessionism involves the assumption that the Hebrew Scriptures, in their own contexts, do not contribute to the Bible's storyline. Their messages should not be understood literally. Instead, the New Testament supersedes the message of the Old Testament. So, on their own, the Hebrew Scriptures do not have a voice concerning God's purposes.

Structural supersessionism involves beliefs and assumptions that do not allow the Old Testament to speak to the issues it addresses, particularly concerning Israel. This occurs through concepts like "reinterpretation," "redefinition," "transforming," "transcending," or other similar language that allegedly shows that Old Testament prophecies about Israel should not be understood literally. As Blaising observes, "The usual choice ... is to see the Israel of the Tanak [i.e., Jewish scriptures] *redefined, spiritualized,* or *transcendentalized as,* or sometimes simply *replaced as,* the church of the New Testament."[5]

STRUCTURAL SUPERSESSIONISM'S INCOMPLETE STORYLINE

Soulen notes that structural supersessionism is linked with the standard canonical narrative model that the church has accepted since the second century. This standard model turns on four key episodes:

1. God's intention to create the first parents

---

4   See Ibid., 181, n. 6.

5   Craig Blaising, "Biblical Hermeneutics," in *The New Christian Zionism: Fresh Perspectives on Israel and the Land,* ed. Gerald R. McDermott (Downers Grove, IL: InterVarsity Press, 2016), 80. Emphases in original.

2. The Fall

3. Christ's incarnation and the inauguration of the church

4. The final consummation[6]

Few Christians, including us, would dispute the importance of these four parts of the story. But the large gap between points 2 and 3 (the Fall and Christ) is a problem. It means a huge leap over the Hebrew Scriptures from the Fall until Christ. Thus, the problem of supersessionism goes beyond explicit claims that the church has replaced or fulfilled Israel. It assumes the Old Testament cannot have a voice on God's plans for Israel. Soulen notes:

> The problem of supersessionism in Christian theology goes beyond the explicit teaching that the church has displaced Israel as God's people in the economy of salvation. At a deeper level, the problem of supersessionism coincides with the way in which Christians have traditionally understood the theological and narrative unity of the Christian canon as a whole.[7]

The Hebrew Scriptures and the role of national Israel are neglected! Soulen notes that this approach "completely neglects the Hebrew Scriptures with the exception of Genesis 1–3!"[8] God's purposes as Consummator and Redeemer "engage human creation in a manner that simply outflanks the greater part of the Hebrew Scriptures and, above all, their witness to God's history with the people of Israel."[9] What is the result of this leap over the Hebrew Scriptures? God's identity as the God of Israel and His history with the Jewish people "become largely indecisive for the Christian conception of God."[10] Thus, many Christians have adopted a framework

----

6   Soulen, 31.

7   Ibid., 33.

8   Ibid., 31.

9   Ibid., 32.

10   Ibid., 33.

that removes the Hebrew Scriptures from having a voice in God's purposes. Blaising states that the "structural nature of supersessionism" has established "the deep set tradition of excluding ethnic, national Israel from the theological reading of Scripture."[11]

Gerald McDermott also believes structural supersessionism has altered the Bible's storyline. After observing that "the people and land of Israel are central to the story of the Bible," he then says, "But Israel has not been central to the church's traditional way of telling the story of salvation. Typically, the story has moved from creation and fall to Christ's death and resurrection, with Israel as an illustration of false paths."[12] This contrasts with the better view that "the people of Israel and their land continue to have theological significance."[13]

NEW TESTAMENT PRIORITY AND STRUCTURAL SUPERSESSIONISM

Structural supersessionism is closely linked with the concept of New Testament priority over the Old Testament. New Testament priority involves the belief that the Old Testament can only be understood through New Testament interpretations or reinterpretations. Thus, the Old must be interpreted through the grid of the New. For example, concerning Old Testament prophecies about a future earthly kingdom, Robert Strimple asserts, "[T]he crucial question the Christian must ask, of course, is this: How does the *New Testament* teach us to interpret such passages?"[14] Richard Gaffin states that, "...hermeneutical priority belongs to New Testament statements, especially overall generalizations, about the Old."[15]

---

11   Blaising, "The Future of Israel as a Theological Question," 442.

12   Gerald R. McDermott, "Introduction," in *The New Christian Zionism: Fresh Perspectives on Israel & the Land*, ed. Gerald R. McDermott (Downers Grove, IL: InterVarsity Press, 2016), 11–12.

13   Ibid.

14   Robert B. Strimple, "Amillennialism," in *Three Views on the Millennium and Beyond*, ed. Darrell L. Bock (Grand Rapids: Zondervan, 1999), 84.

15   Richard B. Gaffin, Jr., "The Redemptive-Historical View," in *Biblical Hermeneutics: Five Views*, eds. Stanley E. Porter and Beth M. Stovell (Downers Grove, IL: IVP Academic, 2012), 98.

In a similar way Merkle says, "Rather, we must learn from how the New Testament writers themselves interpreted the Old Testament. When we do this, we will see that the Old Testament prophecies concerning the nation of Israel are fulfilled in Christ and in the gospel."[16] These quotations are consistent with the idea of New Testament priority.

EXAMPLES OF STRUCTURAL SUPERSESSIONISM

An example of structural supersessionism is found with Louis Berkhof when he comments on Old Testament restoration prophecies about Israel:

> It is very doubtful, however, whether Scripture warrants the expecta-tion that Israel will finally be re-established as a nation, and will as a nation turn to the Lord. Some Old Testament prophecies seem to predict this, but these should be read in light of the New Testament.[17]

Berkhof admits that Old Testament prophecies on their own "seem to pre-dict" the re-establishment and salvation of Israel as a nation. But instead of accepting this testimony he appeals to the New Testament for a different meaning. He says, "these [Old Testament prophecies] should be read in light of the New Testament." So, for Berkhof, Old Testament prophetic passages should not be understood on their own. One must seek the New Testament for the true meaning. This is an example of structural superses-sionism. The Old Testament states something, but the presupposition is not to accept what it says. The New Testament is appealed to for a differ-ent meaning. Old Testament texts do not have a voice on their own.

Structural supersessionism occurs with Bruce Waltke's response to Bruce Ware in the book, *Dispensationalism, Israel and the Church: The Search for Definition*. Waltke criticized Ware's article, "The New Covenant and the People(s) of God." Why? Ware started his discussion of the New

---

16   Benjamin L. Merkle, "Old Testament Restoration Prophecies Regarding the Nation of Israel: Literal or Symbolic?" *The Southern Baptist Journal of Theology* 14.1 (2010): 21.

17   Louis Berkhof, *Systematic Theology* (Grand Rapids: Eerdmans, 1941; reprint 1991), 699.

Covenant with Jeremiah 31:31–34, the first Bible text to explicitly mention the New Covenant. Ware also discussed New Covenant texts in the New Testament. But according to Waltke this was not good enough. Waltke said, "Ware begs the issue by starting with the Old and uses the book of Hebrews selectively to substantiate his interpretation."[18] Waltke criticized Ware for starting his discussion of the New Covenant with the first passage to explicitly refer to the "New Covenant." But for Waltke, Ware should have begun in the New Testament, not Jeremiah 31:31–34. In criticizing Ware, though, Waltke took a structural supersessionist approach against Jeremiah 31:31–34 by not allowing this passage to contribute to an understanding of the New Covenant in its own context.

STRUCTURAL SUPERSESSIONISM APPLIED TO THE NEW TESTAMENT

Structural supersessionism usually involves muting the voice of the Old Testament in its own context—particularly prophetic texts about Israel. But structural supersessionism is not limited to the Old Testament. *It can even apply to New Testament texts.* Sometimes New Testament passages are downplayed or not taken literally because they sound too much like the Old Testament. Robert Strimple, for example, does this with Luke 1. The songs of Mary (Luke 1:46–55) and Zechariah (Luke 1:67–79) contain several Israelite themes. Mary spoke of God's mercy to Israel because of the Abrahamic Covenant (Luke 1:46–55). With Luke 1:70–74, the Spirit-inspired Zechariah appealed to the Abrahamic Covenant concerning national deliverance for Israel, including deliverance from enemies:

> "As He spoke by the mouth of His holy prophets from of old—
> Salvation from our enemies, and from the hand of all who hate us; To
> show mercy toward our fathers, and to remember His holy covenant,

---

18   Bruce K. Waltke, "A Response," in *Dispensationalism, Israel and the Church: The Search for Definition*, eds. Craig A. Blaising and Darrell L. Bock (Grand Rapids: Zondervan, 1992), 351. For Ware's article see Bruce A. Ware, "The New Covenant and the People(s) of God," in *Dispensationalism, Israel and the Church*, 68–97.

The oath which He swore to Abraham our father, To grant us that we, being rescued from the hand of our enemies, Might serve Him without fear."

But Strimple thinks Mary's and Zechariah's words in Luke 1 "sound like passages from the Psalms or from one of the Old Testament prophets,"[19] as if that were wrong. Instead of accepting their messages at face value, Strimple says Mary and Zechariah spoke like Old covenant saints, but not like Paul, or even John the Baptist:

> Mary and Zechariah speak as they do here because they are old covenant saints, and this is the Spirit-inspired language of their old covenant piety. They are like the prophets before John the Baptist, and we would not expect them to speak in the language of the apostle Paul. Although there are, of course, similarities in the imagery of the later apostles, there is an unmistakable Old Testament tinge to the songs of Luke.[20]

The structural supersessionism here is evident. Strimple says Mary and Zechariah spoke like Old Testament saints and we must note the "Old Testament tinge" of their words. Old Testament tinge? This reveals how Strimple views the Old Testament and these New Testament persons who rely on the Old Testament. He does not want us to be literal with what Mary and Zechariah stated because they sound too much like the Old Testament.[21] This is structural supersessionism applied to the Old Testament, and in the case of Mary and Zechariah, the New Testament, too.

A New Creation Model perspective, though, asserts that all Bible passages, including those in the Old Testament, should be allowed to speak. It also believes Israel and promises to Israel are important parts

---

19   Strimple, 95.

20   Ibid.

21   Strimple asserts that Acts 2, 13, and 15 will show a different understanding than what Mary and Zechariah communicated. The evidence Strimple gives for this is minimal. Plus, there are passages in Acts that seem to support a literal understanding of Mary and Zechariah's understandings about Israel (see Acts 1:6, 3:19–21).

of God's purposes. On the other hand, structural supersessionism contributes to a Spiritual Vision Model understanding. It removes the voice of the Old Testament, and even the New Testament at times, when they comment on Israel. And it removes the place of Israel and Israel's land in the grand narrative.

Darrell Bock rightly notes, "The holistic program of the kingdom of God means Israel cannot be lost in the telling of Christ's story."[22] Losing Israel means losing a major part of God's purposes. Since the New Creation Model affirms the Old Testament's voice and the significance of Israel, one cannot be a consistent adherent of this model while embracing structural supersessionism.

---

22 Darrell Bock, "A Progressive Dispensational Response," in *Covenantal and Dispensational Theologies: Four Views on the Continuity of Scripture*, eds. Brent E. Parker and Richard J. Lucas (Downers Grove, IL: IVP Academic), 222.

THE MODELS
SIDE BY SIDE

◆

T his chapter presents the key beliefs of the New Creation and Spiritual Vision models in a brief, side-by-side format so the reader can see the main ideas of the models. The points in this chapter concern the models within the context of Christianity. They do not address the models in relation to non-Christian philosophies and religions which would present even stronger forms of the Spiritual Vision Model. Note that the New Creation Model is referred to as "NCM" and the Spiritual Vision Model as "SVM."

REALITY/CREATION

SVM: Spiritual and material realities are created by God, but the spiritual entities are of higher value than the material and should be emphasized and elevated over the material (cosmic dualism).

NCM: Both spiritual and material realities are created by God, and both are essential parts of God's "very good" creation purposes; no cosmic dualism exists.

SCOPE OF GOD'S PURPOSES

SVM: God's purposes primarily concern salvation—saving man from his sin.

NCM: God's purposes involve human salvation from sin and the restoration of all aspects of creation.

GOD'S ULTIMATE PURPOSE

SVM: God's ultimate purpose is the salvation of some individual human beings so they can worship and enjoy Him forever in Heaven.

NCM: God's ultimate purpose is to establish a multi-ethnic, multinational, righteous kingdom of God on earth, in His presence, that lasts forever.

MAN'S RELATIONSHIP TO EARTH

SVM: Man's goal is to escape earth and physical things which are obstacles to knowing and worshiping God.

NCM: Man and the earth are inseparably tied from creation to new creation; man is created to live upon and rule the earth as God's mediator.

VALUE OF NON-HUMAN CREATION

SVM: Animals and the inanimate creation have instrumental value as the backdrop for God's plans to save humans; once man is perfected they have no existence in eternity.

NCM: Animals and the inanimate creation have inherent value to God, not just instrumental value; they will be restored and exist throughout eternity.

THE FATE OF EARTH

SVM: God will annihilate the current earth and replace it with an entirely new one. Or God will annihilate the current earth and not replace it.

NCM: God is working to bring the restoration and renewal of the present earth and all creation.

THE PURPOSE OF DAY OF THE LORD FIRE

SVM: The purpose of the fire of the Day of the Lord is to annihilate the present earth.

NCM: The purpose of the fire of the Day of the Lord is to purge and refine the present earth.

EXTENT OF SALVATION

SVM: Jesus' salvation extends primarily to individuals so they can be in a right relationship with God.

NCM: Jesus' salvation extends to individuals, Israel, Nations, and creation. Jesus' salvation reverses the multi-dimensional nature of sin by: (1) healing the enmity between man and God; (2) bringing love and healing to human relationships; (3) bringing a clean conscience and inner healing to the individual person; (4) removing the curse and bringing harmony between man and creation.

JESUS' ROLE

SVM: Jesus' primary role is Savior from sin.

NCM: Jesus' role involves being: (1) Savior from sin; (2) Ruler of geopolitical nations; and (3) Restorer of all creation.

GOD'S PURPOSES FOR ETHNICITIES AND NATIONS

SVM: God saves individuals who come from ethnic groups and nations as they become a spiritual community that transcends ethnicity or nation.

NCM: God saves people from all ethnic groups and nations equally and in the same way, and ethnic and national identities continue into eternity; God's people evidence salvific unity and ethnic/national diversity.

IMPORTANCE OF CORPORATE, NATIONAL ISRAEL

SVM: Corporate national Israel is a type of Jesus and the church that loses theological significance once Jesus and the church arrive; Israel transitions from a national entity to a spiritual community of all believers in Jesus, regardless of ethnicity.

NCM: Corporate, national Israel is elect and an object of God's eternal covenants of promise, thus corporate, national Israel remains significant in God's purposes now and into eternity.

JESUS' MESSIANIC/MILLENNIAL KINGDOM

SVM: Jesus' messianic/millennial kingdom is a spiritual kingdom in this age over saved individuals.

NCM: Jesus' messianic/millennial kingdom takes place on earth with spiritual qualifications (being born again) and characteristics such as righteousness, justice, and fairness; it involves saved individuals, nations, and the transformation of all creation.

NATURE OF THE ETERNAL STATE

SVM: The Eternal State primarily is a spiritual existence in Heaven apart from earth where the saints focus solely on God.

NCM: The Eternal State takes place on a restored earth where believers in resurrected bodies live, worship God, and interact socially and culturally with other believers.

REST AND ACTIVITY IN ETERNITY

SVM: Rest in eternity means no activity and only mental contemplation and worship of God.

NCM: In eternity, there will be rest from negative experiences of a fallen world, but God's people(s) will be active with their gifts and talents; nations and their kings will bring their work into the New Jerusalem.

HUMAN DESIRES IN ETERNITY

SVM: All human desires will cease except for the desire to be in God's presence and worship Him.

NCM: Wholesome human longings will exist; this includes the desire for relationships with God and human beings. The desires to eat, learn, and work will still exist. All negative or selfish desires will be absent.

SOCIAL, POLITICAL, CULTURAL INTERACTIONS IN ETERNITY

SVM: Eternal life only involves direct worship of God; no social, cultural, or political interactions will happen since those would detract from worshipping God.

NCM: Eternal life includes social, political, and cultural interactions among God's people.

UNITY-DIVERSITY AMONG GOD'S PEOPLE IN ETERNITY

SVM: Salvation means unity in the one people of God, the church, which is a trans-ethnic, trans-national entity of all believers of all ages.

NCM: Concerning salvation there is one people of God (unity), but since salvation extends to various ethnicities and nations there are also "peoples of God" (diversity).

CONNECTION OF PRESENT AND FUTURE EXPERIENCES

SVM: The Eternal State experiences are radically different from the experiences we have in this age.

NCM: Eternal State experiences are comparable to our current experiences in this age (except for marriage), but without the negative effects of sin, the curse, decay, and death; this includes living, breathing, walking, talking, living in houses, music, art, technology, etc.

KNOWLEDGE AND LEARNING IN ETERNITY

SVM: Knowledge is complete in eternity; no need exists for learning new things.

NCM: In eternity, God's people grow in knowledge and learn more about God, His ways, and the universe.

PART THREE

THE MODELS
IN HISTORY

13

HISTORICAL ROOTS OF THE SPIRITUAL VISION MODEL

◆

How did so many adopt over-spiritualized views of God's purposes? To understand the Spiritual Vision Model and its impact on Christianity in history, three areas need to be surveyed: (1) Non-Christian influences—eastern religions, Platonism, and Neo-Platonism; (2) Gnosticism and Marcion; and (3) Augustine. The first explains the non-Christian roots of the Spiritual Vision worldview. The second explains how Spiritual Vision ideas infiltrated Christianity. The third highlights the significant Spiritual Vision influence of Augustine on traditional Christianity. This chapter will focus on the first two, while an upcoming chapter will look at Augustine's influence.

NON-CHRISTIAN ROOTS OF THE SPIRITUAL VISION MODEL

EASTERN RELIGIONS

The eastern religions of Hinduism and Buddhism present a strong, undiluted Spiritual Vision approach to reality. The ancient religion of Hinduism has been doing so for thousands of years. So, too, has Buddhism, a sixth-century BC offshoot of Hinduism. A spirit-matter dualism is at the heart of these eastern religions.

The eastern religions view the material world as *maya*, which means "illusion." The *Encyclopedia Britannica* explains how *maya* denies the reality of the phenomenal or physical world:

> Maya originally denoted the magic power with which a god can make human beings believe in what turns out to be an illusion. By extension, it later came to mean the powerful force that creates the cosmic illusion that the phenomenal world is real.[1]

With Hinduism and Buddhism, the main problem for people is entanglements with the illusion of the material world. Cravings and desires that are linked with the body and the world trap people in a cycle of rebirths (*samsara*). The way to escape this cycle is for one's soul or real self (*atman*) to become united with the ultimate impersonal reality—Brahman.

With Hinduism and Buddhism, a spiritual escape from the phenomenal/physical realm to an impersonal spiritual existence is the ultimate goal. This is referred to as *nirvana*, which is the highest state a person can attain. This escape to *nirvana* is linked with *moksha*, which means "liberation" or "freedom." *Moksha* occurs when the real self breaks free from the illusion and entanglements of the physical world and merges with the eternal absolute. Some liken *moksha* to a drop of water meeting the ocean. One's personhood is dissolved into an infinite impersonal reality. Horton refers to this idea as "Ontological monism" and states that it "destroys personal existence."[2]

The major eastern religions assert that one must become enlightened and flee from the illusions of the tangible universe to union with an impersonal, non-physical existence. This perspective is the strongest form of the Spiritual Vision Model.

---

1   See Matt Stefon, "Maya," https://www.britannica.com/topic/maya-Indian-philosophy (accessed September 10, 2019).

2   Michael Horton, *The Christian Faith: A Systematic Theology for Pilgrims On the Way* (Grand Rapids: Zondervan, 2011), 907.

PLATO AND PLATONISM

The most significant Spiritual Vision Model influence on Christianity came from the Greek philosopher, Plato (c. 429–347 BC). His ideas greatly influenced Western civilization and the Christian church. Middleton notes, "The idea of a transcendent nonearthly realm as the goal of salvation can be traced back to the innovative teaching of Plato in the late fifth and early fourth centuries."[3]

Two key beliefs of Plato influenced the Christian church towards a Spiritual Vision perspective: (1) a strong cosmic dualism between the material and immaterial realms with the latter being more valued; and (2) an anthropological dualism between the body and the soul.

COSMIC DUALISM

First, Plato believed a dualism exists between the material and immaterial realms.[4] There is the earthly-material realm that people live and operate in. But experiences on earth are not all there is. There also is a transcendent, timeless realm of "ideas" or "forms."

With his "theory of forms," Plato claimed that ultimate reality is not found in objects and concepts on earth. Instead, true reality exists with forms or ideas that transcend our physical world and exist in another dimension. These forms operate as perfect universal templates for everything in the world. For example, all horses on earth are imperfect replicas of the universal perfect "horse" or "horseness" that exists in another realm. Next, there is a material sensory realm that changes. This is a lesser form of reality.[5] The goal of the person is to escape the transitory physical realm to

---

3   Middleton, *A New Heaven and a New Earth*, 31.

4   Diogenes Allen calls for balance on this point: "Plato's view is by no means that of Genesis, but it is not the total rejection of the world by the Gnostics and Manichaeans. We should not confuse Plato's attitude to the physical universe, however much he stresses the need to transcend it and the body, with views which totally reject it, as superficial Christian writers so often do." Diogenes Allen, *Philosophy for Understanding Theology* (Atlanta: John Knox, 1985), 9.

5   Middleton, 31.

the higher non-physical form of reality.[6] Plato's ideas led to the belief that people become stars in the astral realm after death.[7]

ANTHROPOLOGICAL DUALISM

Before Plato, the Greeks viewed existence after death as tragic. Life in the present, on earth, was perceived as most real and where glory and honor were found. Death, however, leads to a lesser, shadowy existence in Hades. In Homer's, *Odyssey*, the slain Achilles declared from the underworld, "I would rather serve as a laborer to a serf, to a landless man who has no great livelihood, than rule all the perished dead."[8]

This is where Plato became significant, particularly concerning the great importance of the soul. Plato was "influenced by Orphic myths of the soul's preexistence among the stars and subsequent entombment on earth."[9] He also held that the human person was composed of two parts: an immortal soul, which was the true self, and a changing, corruptible body.[10] This was a negative view of the physical body. For Plato, the human body is like a prison and tomb for the soul.[11] Plato's statement, "*Soma sema*," which means "a body, a tomb," exemplified this idea. This reveals a strong anthropological dualism. The immaterial soul is good, but it is trapped in the inferior body. The goal is release of one's soul from the body so the soul can live in the realm of spiritual, immaterial realities.

With Plato's account of Socrates' trial, the great philosopher, Socrates, refused to escape from a death sentence. Why? The true philosopher should seek the soul's release from the body. For Socrates (and Plato) physical death was good since one's soul could be freed from the body.

---

6   Ibid.

7   Ibid., 32.

8   See Caroline Alexander, "How the Greeks Changed the Idea of the Afterlife," https://www.national-geographic.com/magazine/2016/07/greek-gods-ancient-greece-afterlife/. Accessed 9/4/2019.

9   Middleton, 31.

10   Ibid.

11   See, "Phaedo," in *Classics of Western Philosophy*, ed. Steven M. Cahn (Indianapolis, IN: Hackett Publishing, 2002), 49–81. Phaedo 65–68; 91–94.

Gary Habermas observes that Plato's concept of forms, along with his cosmology and views on the immortality of the soul, "probably has the greatest influence in the philosophy of religion."[12] Plato's ideas would influence others. According to Middleton, what Plato bequeathed to later ages "involved the radically new assumption of an immortal, immaterial soul and the aspiration to transcend this present world of matter, sensation, and change in order to attain to a higher, divine reality."[13] This included the purification of the inner person from contamination that comes from contact with the body. These ideas impacted how many would view existence after death. Poythress notes that:

> the influence of Platonism and the focus of some people on hope for the intermediate state has encouraged thinking about the future that is otherwise one-sided. As we turn in our minds to our hopes for the future, we may picture a kind of ethereal existence, of vaporous souls playing harps on clouds.[14]

Plato's ideas influenced Christian theologians such as Clement, Origen and Augustine. Plato's impact on Augustine will be particularly significant since Augustine will influence both Roman Catholic and Protestant theologies in the direction of the Spiritual Vision Model.

PHILO

Plato's philosophy carried over to Judaism in the writings of the Jew— Philo of Alexandria (20 BC –AD 50).[15] Philo harmonized the Jewish scriptures with Greek philosophy, abandoning a literal interpretive method for understanding the Old Testament. He was a bridge for merging Moses with Plato.

---

12   Gary R. Habermas, "Plato, Platonism," *Evangelical Dictionary of Theology*, ed. Walter A. Elwell (Grand Rapids: Baker, 1984), 859.

13   Middleton, 31.

14   Poythress, "Currents within Amillennialism," 23.

15   Habermas, 859–60.

Attempting to make the Old Testament more attractive to the Greeks, Philo allegorized Old Testament passages he thought were too crass and unworthy of God. Statements about God's wrath or God changing His mind needed to be allegorized. According to Burge, "Philo is inspired by his desire to adapt Judaism to Hellenistic thought and he does this by allegorizing his Bible."[16] This had Spiritual Vision Model implications. For Philo, this meant, "The land is reinterpreted as the knowledge of God and wisdom."[17] Also, "Philo does not see a *literal* ingathering of exiled Israel to a literal Promised Land."[18] For Philo, as Burge observes, Judaism's land theology "has been entirely redefined. And it will be a redefinition that will deeply influence the formation of Christian thinking in the New Testament."[19]

Philo's allegorization and spiritualization of the Hebrew Scriptures influenced many Christian theologians. He contributed to a Spiritual Vision Model approach in the church.

NEOPLATONISM

Centuries after Plato, Platonism influenced its religious counterpart, Neoplatonism.[20] Neoplatonism was a complex system for understanding reality linked with the Roman philosopher, Plotinus (AD 204–70). The Egyptian-born Plotinus adopted several key ideas of Plato such as:

1.   An immaterial reality exists apart from the physical world.

2.   A strong value distinction exists between the immaterial soul and the physical body.

3.   The immortal soul finds its ultimate fulfillment as it becomes one with an eternal, transcendent realm.

---

16   Gary M. Burge, *Jesus and the Land*, 22.

17   Ibid.

18   Ibid., 22. Emphasis in original.

19   Ibid., 24.

20   "Neo-Platonism" was not identified specifically as such until the nineteenth century.

Plotinus cast these ideas into a more religious form. The basis of all reality is an immaterial and indescribable reality called "the One" or "the Good." Several levels of reality emanate from this One like ripples in a pond. The second level is Mind or Intellect (*nous*). Mind results from the One's reflection upon itself. The level below Mind is Soul. Soul operates in time and space and is the creator of time and space. Soul looks in two directions—upward to Mind and downward to Nature, which created the physical world. For Plotinus, the lowest level of reality is matter.[21] Thus, a strong dualism exists between mind and matter. Plotinus held such disgust for physical things he even despised his own body and neglected his hygiene.

Plotinus viewed earthly delights as distractions from what people should focus on—contemplation of true beauty that only could be found "in the transcendent world of eternal, immaterial ideas."[22] McDannell and Lang note that for Plotinus the purpose of philosophy, "was to loosen the soul from the body, to strengthen its spiritual power, and to prepare it for its eventual heavenly ascent after the death of the body."[23] Also, this pursuit was an individual matter. It is "through solitary concentration on the divine" that the soul could seek to "ascend to its true home."[24]

Plotinus heavily influenced Christian theologians. Middleton notes that Plotinus, "renovated Plato's conceptual framework...to promulgate a vision of reality that deeply influenced Christian theologians from Augustine to Pseudo-Dionysius and beyond. Known today as Neoplatonism, Plotinus's vision was regarded for centuries simply as an articulation of Plato's own views."[25]

Particularly significant will be the influence of Plotinus and Neo-Platonism on Augustine. Augustine embraced many of their main ideas

---

21   See Christopher Kirwan, "Plotinus," in *The Oxford Companion to Philosophy*, ed. Ted Honderich (New York, NY: Oxford University Press, 1995), 689–90.

22   McDannell and Lang, *Heaven*, 56.

23   Ibid., 56–57.

24   Ibid., 57.

25   Middleton, 33.

and incorporated them into his understanding of the Christian hope—what could be called a Christo-platonism hope.

NON-CHRISTIAN SPIRITUAL VISION MODEL WORLDVIEW

Below is a summary of the non-Christian Spiritual Vision Model worldview:

<u>Cosmic Dualism</u>: Spirit is good; matter is bad/evil/lesser; body is a tomb for the soul.

<u>Anthropological Dualism</u>: The soul of a person is good/divine; the body of a person is bad.

<u>The Problem</u>: Material things, physical bodies, and desires are bad; the material world is an illusion that deceives people.

<u>The Solution</u>: The soul needs escape from the material world and the physical body to union with the spiritual absolute.

<u>Ultimate Experience</u>: A spiritual existence in a spiritual realm with no taint of anything physical.

GNOSTICISM AND MARCION

GNOSTICISM

Gnosticism became influential in the second century AD. Gnosticism was not a formal religion, but it merged key ideas of Platonism with Christian doctrine. It was the most serious threat to Christianity at that time.

Like Platonism, Gnosticism affirmed a dualistic cosmology in which spirit is good and matter is bad. This stemmed from a theistic dualism in which there is a true spirit God and then a lesser, nefarious deity that created the physical world. The true spirit God does not create anything physical, but spiritual emanations flow from this God.

This includes Sophia (which means "wisdom"). From Sophia came the Demiurge also known as Yahweh. This Demiurge is a rebel deity that created the world and people. He also selfishly demands worship from his creatures. When people worship the Demiurge they are deceived and worship a corrupt deity.

Even though people have corrupted physical bodies, they still have souls that contain sparks of divinity. But this divine spark in the soul is suffocated by the physical body and interactions with the physical world. If a person dies in this state his soul will be tossed back into the physical realm in a way similar to Eastern reincarnation. This negative cycle can be broken only through secret knowledge. (Gnosticism comes from *gnosis* which means "knowing"). Salvation from the physical realm to union with the true spirit-God comes through knowledge, not faith in Yahweh.

This is where Jesus enters. Jesus was just a man, not born of a virgin. At Jesus' baptism Sophia possessed him and Jesus became the Christ. The canonical gospels contain some truths about Jesus, but saving knowledge comes from secret truths he revealed to the apostles in the Upper Room before his death. Jesus also gave secret knowledge to Paul before Paul began his public ministry. When Jesus was on the cross Sophia left him and the man Jesus awoke to the agony of his situation. Thus, Jesus was used and then discarded by Sophia.[26]

Gnosticism threatened the early church with its anti-material and heretical views concerning Jesus. As an offshoot of Gnosticism, Docetism asserted that the human body was bad. The Greek term, *dokeō*, means "to appear" and Docetics believed Jesus only appeared to be human. Since the world and human body were bad, Jesus could not take on physical human form. Essential to Christianity, though, is the view that Jesus became human to save humans. As John 1:14a states, "And the Word became flesh and dwelt among us." If Jesus' humanity is denied there is no salvation for humans. Fortunately, theologians in the early church, especially Irenaeus,

---

26   While secret knowledge comes through secret oral tradition, the secret teachings of Jesus are found in the Nag Hammadi, a collection of gnostic writings discovered in Egypt in 1945.

fought Gnosticism. Gnosticism threatened creational realities and the person and work of Christ. It was a major Spiritual Vision Model threat to Christianity.

MARCION

Marcion (c. AD 85–c. 160) promoted key gnostic ideas. He was heavily influenced by Cerdo, a gnostic Christian. Followers of Marcion, known as Marcionites, were considered the most dangerous of the gnostic groups by early Christians. Followers of Marcion could have outnumbered orthodox Christians in some places.[27]

Marcion held to a theistic dualism between the inferior god of the Old Testament and the superior God of Jesus and Paul. The Old Testament god is involved with lesser matters like creation, law, judgment, and Israel. On the other hand, the God of the New Testament is a good spirit being who does not create. He is a God of love, grace, and mercy. This God sent Jesus Christ to deliver people from the creator-god of the Old Testament to the God of grace of the New Testament. Marcion made a strong dualism between the stories of the Old and New testaments. As Tyson notes, "Our ancient sources agree that Marcion made a total separation between the religion that Jesus and Paul espoused and that of the Hebrew Scriptures."[28]

Marcion crafted a Bible canon that included only parts of Luke's gospel and ten of Paul's epistles. Marcion intentionally excluded the Hebrew Scriptures and the Bible's Jewish elements. He believed the Old Testament revealed literal, accurate truths at times, and even predicted the coming of a Messiah. Tyson notes that, "Marcion evidently believed in the authority of the Hebrew Scriptures and accepted Isaiah and the other prophets as trustworthy predictors of the future."[29] But he also held that the Hebrew Scriptures presented the lesser creator-god. And

---

27   Joseph B. Tyson, "Anti-Judaism in Marcion and His Opponents," *Studies in Christian-Jewish Relations*, 1 (2005-06): 198.

28   Ibid., 200.

29   Ibid., 201.

like the Gnostics, Marcion did not believe the god of law, judgment, and Israel in the Hebrew Scriptures could be the God of grace and mercy found in the New Testament. Also, the quality of the New Testament is so much better than the Old, that Marcion could not include the Old Testament in his canon. Marcion rejected the Old Testament because it was of lesser quality and was irrelevant to what the New Testament God was doing in Jesus.

Christianity rightly rejected Marcion's canon and recognized the Hebrew Scriptures—a victory against the Spiritual Vision Model. But three key ideas of Marcion, stemming from gnostic assumptions, have manifested themselves in Christian history. The first is that the Hebrew Scriptures, while being accurate, are qualitatively less than the New Testament writings and do not have continuing relevance on their own. Tyson notes, "He [Marcion] certainly is the first known to us to propose a simple if draconian solution to the problems: to regard the Hebrew Scriptures as valid, accurate, authoritative, and divinely inspired but irrelevant for Christian faith."[30]

While few Christians after Marcion explicitly called the Old Testament irrelevant, the Hebrew Scriptures were largely ignored and treated as lesser than the New Testament by many Christians. Even today many view the Old Testament as a vast landscape of inferior types and shadows and hold that its contents are not relevant in a literal manner. This was not the perspective of Jesus who said all things in the Old Testament must be accomplished (see Matt. 5:17–18). Paul also said his message involved "stating nothing but what the Prophets and Moses said was going to take place" (Acts 26:22).

Also carrying over from Marcion was the assumption that the storyline of the Old Testament is inferior to and discontinuous with that of the New Testament. Marcion believed the Old Testament was about law, judgment, and physical things like land, temples, and Israel. But the New Testament was concerned with more important spiritual truths. So

---

30   Ibid., 207.

instead of seeing the story of the Old Testament continuing into the New Testament, the Old Testament was not viewed as consistent with the New Testament story. This idea, too, remains with many in Christianity today and allows for a connection with the Spiritual Vision Model.

Another issue involves Israel. Marcion's theology "completely separated the God of Jesus from the God of Israel."[31] For Marcion, the lesser creator-god of the Old Testament was inseparably tied to Israel. But the God of Jesus was not concerned about Israel. So, a third implication from Marcion was that ethnic/national Israel lost its theological significance. Israel may exist, but it is no longer relevant or a significant part of God's plans. This is a strong replacement theology position that would become popular in church history.

In April 2020, the Danish Bible Society released a new edition of the Bible called "Bible 2020." Stunningly, this edition removed all references to "Israel" in the New Testament, except for one.[32] Marcion would have been pleased.

Both Gnosticism and Marcion's heretical canon were formally rejected by the church. However, their ideas have never lost influence in the church. Whenever a highly spiritualized view of Christianity is present or a downplaying of the Hebrew Scriptures, physical blessings, or Israel occurs, echoes of those two heresies can be detected.

---

31   Ibid., 198.

32   Of the 73 references to "Israel" only 1 remained in this translation. The term is replaced with "Jews," "land of the Jews," or no alternative at all. See, Adam Eliyahu Berkowitz, "Lutherans Publish New Version of Bible Without the Word 'Israel' In It." https://www.breakingisraelnews.com/148885/lutherans-publish-new-version-of-bible-without-the-word-israel-in-it/. April 20, 2020. Accessed April 24, 2020.

SPIRITUAL VISION MODEL
WORLDVIEW OF GNOSTICISM
AND MARCION

Below is a summary of the Spiritual Vision Model worldview of Gnosticism and Marcion:

Cosmic Dualism:

+ Spirit is good/better
+ Matter is bad/evil/lesser

Theistic Dualism:

+ The god of the Old Testament is the lesser creator god known as the Demiurge/Yahweh; he is a rebel and selfish emanation (via Sophia) of the true spirit-god
+ The true God is the spirit, non-creating God of Jesus and Paul

Anthropological Dualism:

+ The soul of a person is good/divine
+ The body of a person is bad/lesser

The Problem: Souls are trapped in the physical world. The material world is a rebellious act from the creator-god of the Old Testament; the divine souls of persons are trapped in physical bodies and the world; death in this life leads to reincarnation into the physical world again

Jesus: Before his baptism Jesus is just a man. Jesus was possessed by Sophia from his baptism through his crucifixion. Jesus reveals secret truths to achieve union with the spirit-God; the true spirit-God sent Jesus

The Solution: Secret oral knowledge from Jesus allows for escape from the material world and physical body to union with the spiritual absolute; the ideal is fleshless souls

<u>Ultimate Experience</u>: A purely spiritual existence and union with the spirit-God with no taint of anything physical

<u>Bible</u>: Stark value contrast between the Old and New Testaments:

- The Old Testament is accurate but inferior revelation concerning the lesser deity (Demiurge/Yahweh) and matters like Israel, earth, and physical entities

- Marcion believed only parts of Luke's Gospel and ten of Paul's epistles were Scripture

- Gnosticism held that only secret knowledge can give the knowledge necessary to escape the physical world and bodies

14

THE MODELS IN THE
EARLY CHURCH

◆

T his chapter begins a survey of the New Creation and Spiritual Vision
models in church history. This is not an exhaustive study. Other
books like, *Heaven: A History*, by Colleen McDannell and Bernhard Lang
offer more details on this topic. But here we highlight important persons
and events related to the two models in church history.

In short, the New Creation Model was well-represented in the New
Testament era and the early church. But with the influence of Origen, the
Christianization of the Roman Empire under Constantine, and Augustine,
the Spiritual Vision Model took root and became dominant in the Middle
Ages. The reformers would bring a mix between the two models, but trends
coming from the Reformation allowed a serious challenge to the Spiritual
Vision Model. After the Reformation, a battle between Spiritual Vision
and New Creation perspectives continues even until today. But first, we
start with the early church.

NEW CREATIONISM IN THE
FIRST TWO CENTURIES

The church of the first two centuries largely affirmed a New Creation
Model understanding. It taught a coming earthly kingdom of Jesus involving Israel, agricultural prosperity, celebrations, social interactions, and harmony in the animal kingdom. Gabriel told Mary that her Son, Jesus, would
sit on David's throne and rule over Israel forever (see Luke 1:32–33). Jesus
said the humble would inherit the land/earth (see Matt. 5:5). He also said

that a coming renewal of the earth would involve restoration of the twelve tribes of Israel and rewards such as houses, farms, and relationships (see Matt. 19:28–30). Jesus spoke of eating and celebrating in the kingdom of God (Matt. 8:11; Luke 22:30). The disciples and Jesus affirmed a coming restoration of the kingdom to national Israel (see Acts 1:6–7). Paul stated that Jesus' death brings a reconciliation of all things material and immaterial (see Col. 1:15–20). Paul also said creation would be restored in connection with resurrection of the body (see Rom. 8:19–23). John spoke of a coming kingdom reign over the earth (Rev. 5:10) and a time when nations and kings would bring their cultural contributions into the New Jerusalem (see Rev. 21:1–2, 24, 26). These are new creationist ideas.

The New Creation Model was the primary approach of the church immediately after the apostolic era. Christopher Rowland notes that "Early Christians looked forward to the reordering of the world and its institutions."[1] He also explains that Christian writers in "the later part of the Christian century ... include explicit evocations of a this-worldly kingdom of God."[2] For example, Papias (AD 60–130) was Bishop of Hierapolis in Phrygia, Asia Minor. He was a contemporary of Polycarp, who was a disciple of the Apostle John. He affirmed a coming earthly kingdom of Jesus. According to Martin Erdman, Papias "represented a chiliastic [premillennial] tradition which had its antecedents in Palestine."[3]

In the second century, Irenaeus (AD 130–202) set forth new creationist expectations. He believed the world was created good by God and that good things in it should be enjoyed. Irenaeus also believed Jesus' kingdom was a future earthly reign in which creation would be restored and Christians would enjoy relationships, houses, food and drink, etc. He spoke of great prosperity in "the times of the kingdom." At this time food will be in abundance:

---

1 Christopher Rowland, "The Eschatology of the New Testament Church," in *The Oxford Handbook of Eschatology*, ed. Jerry L. Walls (New York: Oxford University Press, 2008), 57.

2 Ibid., 59.

3 Martin Erdmann, *The Millennial Controversy in the Early Church* (Eugene, OR: Wipf and Stock Publishers, 2005), 107.

the righteous shall bear rule upon their rising from the dead; when also the creation, having been renovated and set free, shall fructify with an abundance of all kinds of food, from the dew of heaven, and from the fertility of the earth; as the elders who saw John, the disciple of the Lord related....[4]

Irenaeus further described great agricultural prosperity in the kingdom:

The days will come in which vines shall grow each having ten thousand branches, and in each branch ten thousand twigs, and in each twig ten thousand shoots, and in each of the shoots, ten thousand clusters, and on every grape when pressed will give five and twenty measures of wine. And when any one of the saints will lay hold of a cluster, another shall cry out: "I am a better cluster, take me; bless the Lord through me."[5]

Concerning the coming restoration of animals, Irenaeus said, "all animals feeding [only] on the productions of the earth, should [in those days] become peaceful and harmonious among each other, and be in perfect subjection to man."[6] Irenaeus noted that these beliefs were held by Papias: "And these things are borne witness to in writing by Papias, the hearer of John, and a companion of Polycarp."[7]

Regarding Jesus' promise in Matthew 19:29 that His followers will receive relationships, houses, and farms, Irenaeus says, "These are [to take place] in the times of the kingdom."[8] Summarizing Irenaeus's new creation views, Erdmann states:

The blessing of Isaac will be a time when creation, having been made new and released from the captivity of sin, will bring forth an abundance of all kinds of food. This abundance will simply come from the

---

4   Irenaeus, *Against Heresies*, 5.33.3.

5   Ibid.

6   Ibid.

7   Ibid., 5.33.4.

8   Ibid., 5.33.2.

dew of heaven and the fertility of the earth. Irenaeus relates further that the animals in those days, obtaining their food solely from the produce of the earth, will live in peaceful harmony with each other and mankind.[9]

Also commenting on Irenaeus's earth-oriented eschatological views, Rowland observes that this was the earliest view of the church: "This type of belief was the earliest phase of the Christian doctrine of hope in which an earthly kingdom of God was earnestly expected."[10] He also ties Irenaeus's belief with Jesus' Lord's Prayer and the final chapters of Revelation:

> [Irenaeus's belief] echoing the Matthean version of the Lord's prayer where there is an earnest longing for God's kingdom to "come on earth as in heaven." It is exactly this view that is set out in the final chapters of the Book of Revelation, where the new Jerusalem descends from heaven to a restored earth.[11]

Brian Daley's summary of Irenaeus's theology sounds much like a summary of the New Creation Model:

> Irenaeus's theology is essentially a plea for the religious relevance of ordinary things: of the material world, as the place of God's creation and redemption; of Israel's whole biblical narrative, interpreted and "summed up" in Christ; of the reality of Christ's human flesh, as the instrument by which he revealed in the world the life-giving glory of God; of the coming historical fulfillment of faith in a literal millennium of blessedness for the righteous and a bodily resurrection—both of which Irenaeus sees as the final stage of humanity's long growth to maturity, from sin and alienation toward union with God and an unimaginable "new creation."[12]

---

9   Erdmann, 112.

10   Rowland, 68–69.

11   Ibid., 69.

12   Brian Daley, "Eschatology in the Early Church Fathers," in *The Oxford Handbook of Eschatology*, 95.

Erdmann also discussed Asiatic Christians who were influenced by the apostle John in Asia Minor. In addition to believing in a future earthly kingdom of Jesus (Premillennialism), they believed in normal human activities like eating food: "They embraced, for example, the Jewish idea that the righteous, even after their resurrection, will have to eat food."[13]

There also were expectations concerning a coming earthly kingdom of Jesus, the restoration of Israel, and Jerusalem. Justin Martyr (AD 100–165), for example, said:

> And what the people of the Jews shall say and do, when they see Him coming in glory, has been thus predicted by Zechariah the prophet: "I will command the four winds to gather the scattered children; I will command the north wind to bring them, and the south wind, that it keep not back. And then in Jerusalem there shall be great lamentation, not the lamentation of mouths or of lips, but the lamentation of the heart; and they shall rend not their garments, but their hearts. Tribe by tribe they shall mourn, and then they shall look on Him whom they have pierced; and they shall say, 'Why, O Lord, hast Thou made us to err from Thy way? The glory which our fathers blessed, has for us been turned into shame.'"[14]

Justin Martyr also believed in a coming thousand-year kingdom in Jerusalem in connection with the Old Testament prophets:

> I and others, who are right-minded Christians on all points, are assured that there will be a resurrection of the dead, and a thousand years in Jerusalem, which will then be built, adorned, and enlarged, the prophets Ezekiel and Isaiah and others declare.[15]

Methodius (c. 260–311), bishop of Olympus and Patara, promoted several New Creation Model ideas. He opposed the idea that the earth would be annihilated by fire. Instead, the earth would be purified and renewed by

---

13   Erdmann, 114.

14   Justin, *First Apology*, 52.

15   Justin Martyr, *Dialogue with Trypho*, 80.

fire so that the world would exist and continue. This fate means that God's work with creation was not in vain:

> But it is not satisfactory to say that the universe will be utterly destroyed, and sea and air and sky will be no longer. For the whole world will be deluged with fire from heaven, and burnt for the purpose of purification and renewal; it will not, however, come to complete ruin and corruption. For if it were better for the world not to be than to be, why did God, in making the world, take the worse course? But God did not work in vain, or do that which was worst. God therefore ordered the creation with a view to its existence and continuance ...[16]

Methodius also opposed Origen's use of allegory and Origen's belief that the resurrection body is not the same body a person possesses in this life. He also was a premillennialist, linking Jesus' coming earthly kingdom with the Feast of Tabernacles.[17]

In sum, the earliest Christians viewed the kingdom of God primarily as a future earthly hope. Commenting on this Snyder notes that the kingdom "pointed beyond this life to something more ultimate and complete—not mere spiritual survival only but a final cosmic reconciliation."[18] This future kingdom was viewed as "final cosmic reconciliation itself or as a millennial reign preceding the ultimate summation of all things."[19] The coming of this anticipated future earthly kingdom was "a cosmic reconciliation" and "a final settling of the score regarding all evils and injustices of history."[20] The eschatology of the early church involved a "new creation" and something "greater or more glorious than the state of the cosmos before the

---

16   Methodius, *From the Discourse on Revelation*, 1.8.

17   See Matthew Ervin, "The Premillennialism of Methodius," https://appleeye.org/2015/01/17/the-premillennialism-of-methodius/, January 17, 2015 (accessed March 18, 2023). In line with the Spiritual Vision Model Methodius believed the saints would enter Heaven as their final home.

18   Snyder, *Models of the Kingdom*, 25.

19   Ibid.

20   Ibid., 26.

Fall."[21] This eschatology was also pessimistic about this fallen and ruined world that could only be redeemed by the second coming of Christ.[22]

The early church was not always consistent with New Creation Model ideas.[23] But overall, New Creationism was often taught. Sadly, though, the tangible hope in the early church would soon change. As Rowland notes, "Early Christian hope differs quite markedly from how it appeared in later Christian tradition."[24] But why? The answer is largely found with Platonism's influence on the church.

PLATONISM'S INFLUENCE ON THE EARLY CHURCH

The new creation perspective of the early church soon changed. According to Viviano, as the Gospel spread throughout the Roman Empire the hope of Christian eschatology changed from cosmic renewal to a verticalist view that emphasized the individual in Heaven:

> The main loss was of the apocalyptic dimension of Christian hope. The dual hope of the Christian, the kingdom of God and resurrection of the dead, (or at least of the saints), was reduced to the resurrection of the individual to eternal life in heaven. The social and the this worldly historical dimensions of hope were lost.[25]

This loss of a tangible hope was largely due to a "Hellenistic philosophical mind" that "was primarily interested in the universal, the necessary, the eternal" and "Plato's mathematical bias."[26] As a result, a specific purpose for history was undermined. Spiritual Vision ideas took root.

---

21   Ibid.

22   Ibid.

23   *The Epistle of Barnabas* used allegory, and Justin Martyr was the first to spiritualize Israel to mean the church.

24   Rowland, 70.

25   Benedict T. Viviano, O.P. *The Kingdom of God in History* (Eugene, OR: Wipf and Stock, 1988), 38.

26   Ibid.

The early church promoted a new creationist approach. So what happened? Middleton asks two important questions: In light of "the Bible's holistic vision of the redemption of earthly creation ... How did it come about that so many in the church today seem unaware of God's intent to redeem this world? How did the idea of an otherworldly destiny in Heaven displace the biblical teaching of the renewal of the earth and end up dominating Christian eschatology?"[27]

The transition to a Spiritual Vision understanding coincided with the influence of Platonism in the church which led to non-literal interpretations of the Bible and the spiritualization of Jesus' kingdom. In the late second century Plato's ideas began to infiltrate Christianity. Randy Alcorn explains that biblical eschatology became largely replaced by "Christoplatonism," which is a merger of Christianity and the ideas of Plato.[28]

The anti-material views of Platonism and Neo-Platonism were contrary to the biblical worldview which affirmed the goodness of God's creation (see Gen. 1:31) and the belief that man's destiny involves the earth (Rev. 5:10; 21:1). One might assume that Christians would instinctively resist Plato's ideas since Plato is a pagan source. But many early Christians embraced Plato. Diogenes Allen notes that Plato "astounded the Apologists and the early Church Fathers."[29] For instance, when early Christians encountered Plato's creation story in his *Timaeus*, some believed he had read Moses or received his insights from divine revelation.[30] The alleged similarity of Plato's ideas with Christianity was viewed as evidence why pagans should be open to Christianity.[31]

---

27   Middleton, *A New Heaven and a New Earth*, 283.

28   See Alcorn, *Heaven*. Alcorn devotes an Appendix to the topic, "Christoplatonism's False Assumptions," 475–82.

29   Allen, *Philosophy for Understanding Theology*, 15.

30   See Allen, 15. Christians denied Plato's view of the use of preexisting materials for creation. Christians asserted 'creation out of nothing.'

31   Ibid.

CLEMENT OF ALEXANDRIA (AD 150–215)

Platonism influenced significant Christian theologians. This was true for the Eastern church, particularly those associated with Alexandria, Egypt, and the Alexandrian tradition such as Clement of Alexandria and Origen. As Jeffrey Burton Russell states, "The great Greek fathers of Alexandria, Clement and Origen, firmly grounded in Scripture, were also influenced by Platonism and Stoicism."[32]

Alexandrian theologians highly valued Greek philosophy and believed Christianity was consistent with the best of Greek philosophical thought. Viviano notes that Clement of Alexandria followed his predecessor, Philo, by adopting a "preference for an allegorical meaning of history which turns out, upon closer acquaintance, to transform much biblical history into general moral truths of a philosophical cast."[33] Clement believed God used philosophy to prepare the Greeks for Christ just as God used the law of Moses to prepare the Hebrews for Christ. Clement held both Socrates and Plato in high regard. In line with Greek philosophy, Clement viewed the body and matter as lesser in nature than the spirit (although he did not view the body as evil).

ORIGEN OF ALEXANDRIA (C. AD 185–254)

Origen of Alexandria was significant in the transition to a Spiritual Vision approach as he merged Platonism with Christianity. McGrath observes that Origen "was a highly creative theologian with a strongly Platonist bent."[34] Ilaria Ramelli observes, "Origen can be described as a Christian Platonist."[35]

---

32   Jeffrey Burton Russell, *A History of Heaven: The Singing Silence* (Princeton, NJ: Princeton University Press, 1997), 69.

33   Viviano, 39.

34   Alister E. McGrath, *A Brief History of Heaven* (Malden, MA: Blackwell, 2003), 33.

35   Ilaria L.E. Ramelli, "Origen and the Platonic Tradition," *Religions* 8, 21 (February 2017): 1. www.mdpi.com/journal/religions.

Origen was influential in systematizing and promoting allegorical interpretation of the Bible. He viewed 2 Corinthians 3:6 as sanctioning an allegorical method since Paul mentioned both "letter" and "Spirit." But, in reality, Paul did not refer to allegorical interpretation here. He contrasted the Mosaic Law ("letter") with the New Covenant ("Spirit") in this verse. Origen wrongly understood the "letter"-"spirit" relationship to mean there are literal and spiritual interpretations of Scripture with the spiritual being better. The influence of allegorization would be great in removing a new creationist understanding of God's purposes. As Snyder notes:

> The point is that the allegorical interpretation uprooted and supplanted the more literal, plain-sense, historical interpretation, giving biblical history a different, more 'spiritual,' theological meaning. The interpretation and the worldview were more Platonic than Hebraic— thus further distancing earth from heaven.[36]

Origen also linked his views of "letter" and "spirit" with the Platonic tripartite (threefold) view of the human person—body, soul, and spirit. The "letter" of Scripture relates to the body and the literal interpretation of a passage. Then the "Spirit" of 2 Corinthians 3:6 involves the two immaterial parts of the person—soul and spirit. The soul relates to moral issues; the spirit is related to allegory. Origen's views concerning allegory were followed by later Patristic writers, including Augustine, and then many Medieval scholars. Origen's ideas would become closely related to the fourfold sense of Scripture (i.e., *quadriga*) that dominated the hermeneutics of the Middle Ages.[37] This led to inventing meanings that did not exist and neglecting corporate and tangible realities. An accurate understanding of matters like Israel, land, nations, temples, etc., are forgotten when allegory thrives. Viviano states that Origen "wrought some bold changes

---

36   Snyder, *Salvation Means Creation Healed*, 23.

37   See Keith D. Stanglin, *The Letter and Spirit of Biblical Interpretation: From the Early Church to Modern Practice* (Grand Rapids: Baker, 2018), Kindle Locations 1332.

in Christian eschatology."[38] This would occur particularly with Origen's spiritualization of the kingdom of God.

Positively, the early church embraced two major beliefs as support against encroaching Platonism: (1) the resurrection of the body, and (2) a future earthly millennial kingdom (i.e., Premillennialism).[39] The first affirms the goodness of the human body since it is headed for restoration. The second—an earthly millennial kingdom—affirms that God's kingdom involves planet earth and the restoration of God's "very good" creation (Gen. 1:31). Irenaeus, for example, used Premillennialism as a weapon against Gnosticism.

Origen, though, was weak on the resurrection of the body and he opposed an earthly millennial kingdom. He "dissolved the Christian expectation of the resurrection of the body into the immortality of the soul, since Christian perfection consists, on this Platonizing view, in a progressive dematerialization."[40] And Origen even asserted that "the resurrection body was purely spiritual."[41] Origen also scorned the idea of a coming millennial kingdom of Jesus (i.e., Premillennialism). As Middleton observes:

> While several Christian writers of the second and third centuries affirm the millennium and grant it an important role in their eschatology, it is rejected with great scorn both by Origen (in the third century) as a Jewish and overly literal interpretation of Scripture and by Eusebius (in the fourth century) in his renowned *Ecclesiastical History* as "materialistic."[42]

Origen disapproved of Premillennialism's emphasis on physical realities. "Origen's Platonism led him to critique the earthly, physicalistic elements

---

38   Viviano, 39.

39   Middleton, 284.

40   Viviano, 39-40.

41   McGrath, 34.

42   Middleton, 286.

of the millennial hope" because "the kingdom of God is progressively established within the believer's soul...."[43]

Together, Clement and Origen contributed strongly to a Spiritual
Vision approach. Erdmann notes, "Origen and Clement of Alexandria
held sway over the minds of bishops and catechumens in the Egyptian
metropolis, using mainly the philosophical categories of Platonism to
interpret the Bible."[44]

EUSEBIUS OF CAESAREA (AD C. 260–340)

Blaising notes that the Spiritual Vision Model eventually became "the
dominant view of eternal life from roughly the third century to the early
modern period."[45] Another contributor to the Spiritual Vision Model was
Eusebius. Eusebius (c. 260–340) was a theologian, historian, and close
associate of the emperor, Constantine, during a strategic time when the
Roman Empire embraced Christianity. Christianity went from being a persecuted minority to being the religion of the empire. This Constantinian
merger of church and state had a major impact on the church's eschatological views. With the political empire as an ally of the church, hope for a
coming earthly kingdom of Jesus subsided. Why look for a future earthly
kingdom when Constantine's empire could be viewed as Jesus' kingdom?

Eusebius was antagonistic to Premillennialism. He criticized Papias
for holding to a coming earthly kingdom of Jesus after the resurrection.
For Eusebius, Papias was too literal about Jesus' kingdom when he should
have been understanding the kingdom "mystically":

> To these belong his [Papias'] statement that there will be a period
> of some thousand years after the resurrection of the dead, and that
> the kingdom of Christ will be set up in material form on this very
> earth. I suppose he got these ideas through a misunderstanding of the

---

43   Ibid. Origen also understood kingdom texts in the Bible "in a purely spiritual, interior, private and
     realized sense." Viviano, 41.

44   Erdmann, xviii.

45   Blaising, "Premillennialism" in *Three Views on the Millennium and Beyond*, 164.

apostolic accounts, not perceiving that the things said by them were spoken mystically in figures.[46]

Eusebius said Papias "appears to have been of very limited understanding" on this issue and led many other Church Fathers like Irenaeus astray concerning a literal earthly kingdom of Jesus.[47] He also viewed Constantine's reign as the messianic banquet associated with the kingdom of God. Middleton notes, "Eusebius based his rejection of the millennium on his reinterpretation of the kingdom, seeing it not as an eschatological future cosmic event but rather as the church's providential growth in the Roman Empire that was occurring under Constantine."[48] Eusebius and his understanding of Constantine's reign functioned as a bridge from the long held premillennial understanding to the newly developing view of Amillennialism. This is where the influence of Augustine is significant, to whom we now turn.

---

46   Eusebius, *Ecclesiastical History*, Book 3, 39:12.

47   Ibid., 39:13.

48   Middleton, 286. Snyder also notes, "Since Constantine, things spiritual have increasingly been seen as sacred and otherworldly, while the material world and its affairs are secular and 'worldly'—not really expected to operate by the ethics of Jesus" (Snyder, 19).

15

AUGUSTINE AND THE SPIRITUAL VISION MODEL

◆

A ugustine of Hippo (AD 354–430) was the most famous of the Latin church fathers and one of the most influential theologians in church history. He heavily influenced the Roman Catholic Church of the Middle Ages and beyond. He also influenced Protestantism, including the great reformers—Martin Luther and John Calvin.

Augustine greatly contributed to a strong Spiritual Vision approach in Christianity that continues to this day. His ideas led to a significant change in how the Bible's storyline was understood. In short, Augustine did three things. He: (1) merged Platonist ideas with Christianity (i.e., "Christoplatonism"); (2) presented a Neoplatonist understanding of Heaven; and (3) fathered a millennial view in which Jesus' kingdom was understood as a spiritual kingdom in this present age. Snyder notes that "it was Augustine of Hippo (354-430) who reshaped the storyline."[1] Below we survey Augustine's impact, especially as it relates to the Spiritual Vision Model. Note that Augustine's writings are incredibly vast and complex. Augustine was not a systematic theologian who neatly compartmentalized all his views. Sometimes his writings seem to contradict. Also, some of Augustine's views evolved over time.

---

1   Snyder, *Salvation Means Creation Healed*, 13.

AUGUSTINE'S BENT TOWARDS
THE SPIRITUAL

Augustine had a strong bent toward spiritual and mystical experiences. In his *Confessions*, Augustine admitted that his pre-conversion years were filled with carnal lusts and interest in things of this world. He was attracted to theatre and had relationships with various women.

He also was intellectually curious. Augustine was drawn to pagan philosophy and eventually Manichaeism with its strong cosmic dualism between flesh and spirit. Augustine also had mystical experiences before and after his conversion to Christianity. Thomas Williams notes that a consensus exists that "Augustine had various mystical experiences of a roughly Plotinian sort before his conversion to Christianity."[2]

With the encouragement of his mother, Monica, Augustine converted to Christianity in 387. In *Confessions*, Augustine relates how he and Monica overlooked a garden in Ostia where they had a mystical encounter together.[3] This involved escaping this world to the joy of a transcendent spiritual realm. Monica died soon after this experience but the impact of it remained with Augustine. Scholars debate how similar Augustine's pre-Christian and post-Christian mystical experiences are, but such experiences were important to him. McDannell and Lang note, "The heaven of which Augustine had a foretaste in the garden of Ostia was the hereafter of platonizing Greek philosophy."[4]

SPIRITUAL INFLUENCES
ON AUGUSTINE

Platonism and Neoplatonism strongly influenced Augustine. Diogenes Allen identifies Augustine as "one of the great Christian Platonists."[5]

---

2   Thomas Williams, "Augustine vs. Plotinus: The Uniqueness of the Vision at Ostia," http://shell.cas. usf.edu/~thomasw/ascent.pdf. (Accessed June 8, 2020).

3   See Augustine, *Confessions*, Book IX, Chapter 10.

4   McDannell and Lang, *Heaven*, 56.

5   Allen, *Philosophy for Understanding Theology*, 82.

McDannell and Lang note that Augustine "adopted ... a blend of Platonism and Christianity."[6] Augustine's mentor, Ambrose of Milan (c. 339–97), taught Plato's ideas to Augustine. Alister McGrath observes that Ambrose "drew upon the ideas of the Jewish Platonist writer, Philo of Alexandria" in promoting "a Platonic world of ideas and values, rather than a physical or geographical entity."[7] According to Gary Habermas, Plato's influence on Augustine would have a big impact for the next thousand years: "In particular, Augustine's interpretation of Plato dominated Christian thought for the next thousand years after his death in the fifth century."[8]

Augustine also studied and adopted the ideas of Plotinus (205–70) and Neoplatonism.[9] Viviano notes that "Augustine was strongly influenced by neo-Platonic philosophy," a philosophy "that was highly spiritual and other-worldly, centered on the one and the eternal, treating the material and the historically contingent as inferior stages in the ascent of the soul to union with the one."[10]

Of course, Augustine was a Christian and he used the Bible. Yet his findings often were consistent with his Neoplatonism assumptions. Blaising notes this and connects Augustine's ideas and visions with the Spiritual Vision Model:

> The spiritual vision model of eternal life he [Augustine] contemplated through spiritual interpretation was, he believed, confirmed in his own typically Neo-Platonic mystical visions. After he became a bishop, his writings affirmed the spiritual vision model, and his homilies and commentaries promoted the practice of allegorical interpretation.[11]

---

6   McDannell and Lang, 57.

7   McGrath, *A Brief History of Heaven*, 51.

8   Gary R. Habermas, "Plato, Platonism," *Evangelical Dictionary of Theology*, ed. Walter A. Elwell (Grand Rapids: Baker, 1984), 860. Allen states, "The Greek Fathers and Augustine drew most extensively on the philosophy of Plato and the Platonists." Allen, *Philosophy for Understanding Theology*, 91.

9   "Augustine and many of his contemporaries venerated the work of Plotinus (205-70)." McDannell and Lang, 56.

10   Viviano, O.P. *The Kingdom of God in History*, 52.

11   Blaising, "Premillennialism," in *Three Views on the Millennium and Beyond*, 168.

HEAVEN AS THE MYSTICAL,
ASCETIC IDEAL

McDannell and Lang observe that Augustine's views on Heaven can be placed into two categories—"early Augustine" and "older Augustine."[12] The early Augustine's views on Heaven were much in line with a Spiritual Vision Model approach. He promoted a strong Neoplatonist bent which included the ideals of spirit over matter, mysticism, and asceticism. Augustine's ideas also connected with a monastic lifestyle: "Along with this mysticism, Augustine adopted the ascetic lifestyle recommended by Neoplatonism and firmly established in monasticism."[13] McDannell and Lang call the early Augustine view on Heaven, "The Ascetic Promise: A Heaven for Souls."

Consistent with Neoplatonism, Augustine believed the ultimate experience was the soul's mystical contemplation of the divine in a spiritual realm after death apart from the physical world. It was mental and spiritual union with God: "He decided that a mental, spiritual union with God meant the ultimate human happiness—a decision of momentous consequence for Christian history."[14] Augustine's heaven was an escape of the soul from the physical world to individual communion with God in a spiritual realm.

Whereas Irenaeus' heaven involved rewards on a restored earth, the early Augustine's heaven "was the continuation of an ascetic retired life. It was a world of immaterial, fleshless souls finding rest and pleasure in God."[15] This understanding was the ultimate ascetic dream. While the older Augustine clearly taught resurrection of the body, the early Augustine was not as clear.[16]

---

12   McDannell and Lang, 54–68.

13   Ibid., 57.

14   Ibid., 57.

15   Ibid., 59.

16   Whether the earlier Augustine did so or not, the older Augustine made clear that eternity involved resurrection of the body.

This highly spiritualized and ascetic emphasis of Augustine fit the era in which he lived. In the fourth century, Christianity was adopted by the political empire because of Constantine and the Edict of Milan. Persecution and martyrdom no longer were threats. Denial of worldly comforts and the delights of society became the new way to show one's commitment to God. For Augustine, asceticism was the path to take, and Heaven would be the realization of the ascetic ideal.

Below we will discuss Augustine's views of the millennial kingdom. But for Augustine, eternal life is a forever spiritual experience. As Viviano states, "Indeed, ultimately for Augustine, the kingdom of God consists in eternal life with God in heaven. That is the *civitas dei*, the city of God, as opposed to the *civitas terrena*."[17] This is consistent with the Spiritual Vision Model ideal.

THE SPIRITUALIZATION OF JESUS' MILLENNIAL KINGDOM

Revelation 20 tells of a thousand-year reign of Jesus and the saints after His second coming that is then followed by the Eternal State (see Revelation 21–22). This thousand-year reign of Revelation 20 is often called "the Millennium," which in Latin means "thousand years." How did Augustine view the millennial kingdom of Revelation 20? As will be shown, he promoted a Spiritual Vision Model view of Jesus' millennial kingdom.

In Book 20 of *The City of God*, Augustine presented his views on the Millennium. He once believed Jesus' millennial kingdom was a future earthly kingdom like most theologians before him. But Augustine came to reject this premillennial view. He criticized "Chiliasts" who believed the Millennium involved "the most unrestrained material feasts, in which there will be so much to eat and drink."[18] Reacting against what he considered carnal excesses of this view, Augustine rejected Premillennialism. Origen and Eusebius before him did so as well. But Augustine did more than

---

17   Viviano, 52–53.

18   Augustine, *The City of God*, Book 20, ch. 7.

reject Premillennialism—he introduced an alternative millennial view. Augustine posited that Jesus' millennial kingdom was already occurring spiritually in the present age between Jesus' two comings. The kingdom, for Augustine, is not future and earthly, but present and spiritual. Jesus rules now and Satan is bound, not personally in a prison, but from deceiving the nations. Explaining Augustine's transition from Premillennialism to Amillennialism, Middleton notes that Augustine, "disassociated himself from the millennial views of a future reign of Christ on earth and claimed that 'the church even now is the kingdom of Christ, and the kingdom of heaven.'"[19] This separation of Jesus' kingdom from earth was a move towards the Spiritual Vision Model. Middleton notes how Augustine's millennium is "acosmic" and "atemporal":

> Admittedly, Augustine's understanding of the reign of Christ with the saints unfolding throughout the history of the church (a view that in the twentieth century came to be called "amillennialism") might suggest a positive valuation of historical reality. Yet this affirmation of the historical process stands in significant discontinuity with his view that the ultimate goal of earthly history is a heavenly realm beyond history. Final redemption, for Augustine, was fundamentally acosmic and atemporal.[20]

McDannell and Lang also observe that Augustine's embrace of asceticism contributed to negative views of a coming earthly kingdom: "In an environment dominated by ascetic ideals, traditional images of a this-worldly millennium were too materialistic, too carnal, to be compatible with the new spirit."[21] So Augustine's move to Amillennialism was linked with Spiritual Vision Model assumptions. An earthly kingdom of Jesus was not spiritual enough for Augustine. Middleton notes that Augustine's millennial kingdom view operated under a "Neoplatonic framework":

---

19   Middleton, *A New Heaven and a New Earth*, 292.

20   Ibid., 292–93.

21   McDannell and Lang, 54.

By interpreting the millennium as equivalent to the entire history of the church, Augustine not only extended the vision of Eusebius, but he also, significantly assimilated a Neoplatonic framework for theology, first through the preaching of Bishop Ambrose of Milan (who linked Plotinian philosophy to the Logos teaching of the Gospel of John) and then through his reading of Plotinus's *Enneads* in Marius Victorinus's Latin translation.[22]

In later years, Augustine moved from some of his earlier Neoplatonist ideas and affirmed a coming renewed earth in eternity after the Millennium.[23] He also taught a tangible resurrected body and communion among the redeemed in Heaven. But Augustine introduced a major Spiritual Vision Model move to the church when he asserted that the kingdom of Jesus, the Millennium, was only a spiritual kingdom.

AUGUSTINE'S VERTICALIST ESCHATOLOGY

In his comparison of Augustinian Amillennialism and modern Amillennialism, Michael Williams notes the concept of "verticalist eschatology." This refers to a heavy emphasis on the individual soul's pursuit of Heaven to the exclusion of other broader areas related to eschatology. Williams identifies Augustine with "verticalist eschatology" and notes how Augustine has influenced Reformed eschatology towards this approach:

He [Augustine] brought a Neoplatonic worldview to the consideration of eschatology, a worldview that has had long-lasting and unfortunate

---

22   Middleton, 291.

23   Augustine, *City of God*, Book 20, ch. 16: "then shall the figure of this world pass away in a conflagration of universal fire, as once before the world was flooded with a deluge of universal water. And by this universal conflagration the qualities of the corruptible elements which suited our corruptible bodies shall utterly perish, and our substance shall receive such qualities as shall, by a wonderful transmutation, harmonize with our immortal bodies, so that, as the world itself is renewed to some better thing, it is fitly accommodated to men, themselves renewed in their flesh to some better thing."

implications for Christian theology as a whole. Reformed eschatology
has tended to follow Augustine in his verticalist eschatology.[24]

So consistent with a Christian Spiritual Vision understanding, Augustine
emphasized individual eschatology, not cosmic eschatology.[25] For him,
eschatology is primarily private, individual, and man's goal is Heaven, not
earth. Augustine "thus replaces cosmic eschatology or merely renders it
superfluous, by individual eschatology. The Christian realizes the *eschaton*
upon entering heaven at death."[26]

This was different from the early church that believed the coming
kingdom of God would restore all creation. But, as Williams observes,
"Augustine was scandalized by any thought of grace as restorational."[27]
Williams observes that Augustine removed the kingdom of God from history and the physical realm: "Ultimately for Augustine, the kingdom of
God stands above history and phenomenal reality."[28] And with Augustine,
the earthly aspect of man's destiny is removed: "Human destiny, then, is
fulfilled only in a heavenly dimension beyond space and time."[29]

The New Testament term for "regeneration" is *paliggenesia* and is used
twice. It first occurs in Matthew 19:28 concerning cosmic regeneration
and the renewal of the earth when the tribes of Israel are restored in the
kingdom of God. The second is Titus 3:5 concerning personal regeneration. Both dimensions of regeneration are true—personal and cosmic. But
as Williams notes, for Augustine, "The cosmic aspect of regeneration is
eclipsed by the personalistic."[30]

---

24   Michael Williams, "A Restorational Alternative to Augustinian Verticalist Eschatology," *Pro Rege* 20,
      11. By "verticalist" Williams refers to the idea that salvation is primarily about the individual going to
      Heaven forever, with no serious consideration of life on the new earth.

25   In *The City of God* Augustine does address issues like the Antichrist, the Day of the Lord and other
      issues. But his emphasis was not on cosmic eschatology.

26   Williams, 13. Emphasis in the original.

27   Ibid., 13.

28   Ibid., 12.

29   Ibid.

30   Ibid., 14.

Also, like Neoplatonism, Augustine viewed redemption as a movement from history: "Augustine understood redemption as a rescue of the soul from the world. Redemption takes place in history, but its movement is always away from history."[31] In giving a title to this view, Williams notes that Augustine was an "eschatological personalist," and the goal for the individual person was "beatific rest in heaven."[32]

Below is a summary of Augustine's Spiritual Vision ideas:

+ A strong dualism exists between spirit and matter

+ The ultimate experience is the soul's escape from the world to a spiritual heaven

+ The kingdom of God is beyond history and the physical realm

+ Jesus' millennial kingdom is only a spiritual kingdom

+ Eschatology primarily is individual—the soul's pursuit of Heaven

AUGUSTINE'S USE OF ALLEGORICAL INTERPRETATION

Augustine's Spiritual Vision influence was not just theological—it also was hermeneutical. Augustine applied allegorical interpretation at times to Scripture, particularly the Old Testament. At Milan, he was taught allegorical interpretation from his mentor, Ambrose, who introduced Augustine to the great allegorists Philo and Origen.[33] Augustine interpreted Genesis 1 allegorically. His most famous use of allegory concerns the Parable of the Good Samaritan in Luke 10:25–37.

---

31   Ibid., 13.

32   Ibid., 14.

33   "At Milan he underwent the influence of Bishop Ambrose (339–397), who taught him the allegorical method of Scriptural exegesis, and of some Neoplatonically inclined Christians ...""Saint Augustine," *Stanford Encyclopedia of Philosophy*; https://plato.stanford.edu/entries/augustine/Sept 25, 2019. (accessed June 9, 2020).

Viviano observes that Augustine's spiritual interpretation was similar to that of the great allegorist, Origen: "Thus Augustine was attracted to the spiritual interpretation of the kingdom we have already seen in Origen."[34] Augustine's criteria for using allegorical interpretation involved matters not relating to morals or faith. He said, "Anything in the divine discourse that cannot be related either to good morals or to the true faith should be taken as figurative."[35] Augustine also believed there were four senses of Scripture, one of which was "the way of allegory."[36] A fourfold sense of Scripture (*Quadriga*) became a major part of interpretation for the Roman Catholic Church of the Middle Ages. Augustine's use of allegory also extended to the Book of Revelation. Eamon notes, "According to Augustine, the Book of Revelation was to be understood as a spiritual allegory, and the millennium, begun in the Church. In 431 the Council of Ephesus condemned belief in the millennium as a superstitious aberration."[37]

Augustine did not abandon all historical context. He called for understanding the authorial intent of Old Testament writers, although "another meaning" also could be grasped.[38] In addition, Augustine did not believe all Bible passages have multiple allegorical meanings. He said, "it is equally rash to maintain that every single statement in those books is a complex of allegorical meanings."[39] But he did commend those who found extra spiritual meanings from every event in narratives:

---

34   Viviano, *The Kingdom of God in History*, 52.

35   Augustine, *On Christian Teaching*, 3.10.14.

36   "Four ways of expounding the law have been laid down by some scripture commentators, which can be named in words derived from the Greek, while they need further definition and explanation in plain Latin; they are the way of history, the way of allegory, the way of analogy, the way of aetiology." *Unfinished Literal Commentary on Genesis*, 116.

37   William C. Eamon, "Kingdom and Church in New England: Puritan Eschatology from John Cotton to Jonathan Edwards," (1970) Graduate Student Theses, Dissertations, & Professional Papers, 7.

38   Augustine said, "The person examining the divine utterances must of course do his best to arrive at the intention of the writer through whom the Holy Spirit produced that part of scripture; he may reach that meaning or carve out from the words *another meaning* which does not run counter to the faith, using the evidence of any other passage of the divine utterances. Perhaps the author too saw that very meaning in the words which we are trying to understand." *On Christian Teaching*, 3.27.38. Emphasis not in original.

39   *City of God*, 17.4.

In spite of that, I do not censure those who have succeeded in carving out a spiritual meaning from each and every event in the narrative, always provided that they have maintained its original basis of historical truth.[40]

AUGUSTINE'S CONTINUING INFLUENCE

Augustine's "verticalist eschatology" and Spiritual Vision Model ideas would be accepted and assumed throughout the Middle Ages and beyond. Viviano observes, "Augustine's view [of the kingdom] would dominate and become the normal Roman Catholic view down to our own times."[41] Frank James points out that "until the 17th century virtually every orthodox leader in Christendom held to an Augustinian view of the millennium. And today, numerous postmillennialists and amillennialists still look to Augustine as their forebear."[42]

The title "Augustinianism" is closely associated with a Christian Spiritual Vision Model approach. While not originating this model, Augustine solidified and furthered it.

---

40   Augustine, *City of God*, 17.4.

41   Viviano, 54. Daley points out that near the turn of the sixth century Aeneas of Gaza wrote the "first Christian work to challenge long-accepted Platonic assumptions ..." Brian E. Daley, S. J. *The Hope of the Early Church* (New York, NY: Cambridge University Press, 1991), 191. The Platonist doctrines that were challenged included reincarnation, the eternity of creation, and the preexistence of souls before their bodily existence. Daley points out that these views were "considered favorably as possibilities by Origen and Evagrius."

42   Frank A. James III, "Augustine's Millennial Views," https://christianhistoryinstitute.org/magazine/article/augustines-millenial-views

16

THE MODELS IN
THE MIDDLE AGES

◆

Augustine is a connecting link in the transition from the early church era to the Middle Ages. The Roman Catholic Church of the Middle Ages adopted Augustine's version of Amillennialism and a spiritualized eschatology. These were dominant during this era.[1] The earlier new creation expectation of a coming earthly kingdom was lost. The disappearance of Premillennialism and a New Creation Model worldview led to a dominant Spiritual Vision Model. Blaising notes:

> Ancient Christian premillennialism weakened to the point of disappearance when *the spiritual vision model of eternity* became dominant in the church. A future kingdom on earth simply did not fit well in an eschatology that stressed personal ascent to a spiritual realm.[2]

Christopher Rowland notes that as time progressed in the church "there was a diminution in the hope of the establishment of God's kingdom on earth and a greater emphasis on the transcendent realm as the goal of the Christian soul."[3]

---

1   As McDermott notes, "Augustinian amillennialism dominated the medieval period." Gerald R. McDermott, "A History of Christian Zionism," in *The New Christian Zionism: Fresh Perspectives on Israel and the Land*, ed. Gerald R. McDermott (Downers Grove, IL: InterVarsity Press, 2016), 74.

2   Blaising, "Premillennialism," in *Three Views on the Millennium and Beyond*, 170. Emphases added.

3   Rowland, "The Eschatology of the New Testament Church," in *The Oxford Handbook of Eschatology*, 69.

THE SHIFT FROM STORY TO CREED

Story is a major part of the biblical worldview. On multiple occasions in Scripture the story of God's actions in history are told and retold. Joshua recounted God's actions in bringing Israel into the land (see Joshua 24). In Acts 7, Stephen explained the activities of Abraham, Isaac, Jacob, Jacob's sons (especially Joseph), Moses, Aaron, Joshua, Pharoah, David, Solomon, and the prophets. Stephen also discussed life in Mesopotamia, Haran, Canaan, Egypt, the wilderness, and Mount Sinai. He also detailed Israel's disobedience and idolatry in the land of Israel. Story also is a major part of the sermons in Acts 2–3 and Acts 26. The earliest Christians discussed God's actions in the past, present, and future by way of narrative.

Yet after the acceptance of Christianity in the Roman Empire, a shift occurred from story to creed. The fourth and fifth centuries were the era of creeds: Nicene (325); Nicaea-Constantinopolitan (381); Chalcedonian (451); and Athanasian (500). These were succinct encapsulations of Christian truth, especially concerning Christ and the Trinity.

The creeds are important to Christianity and their format is helpful. They summarize essential Christian truth and refute serious doctrinal errors. Yet the era of creeds coincided with less emphasis on the grand story of Scripture. Creed replaced story to a large degree. Howard Snyder notes that the church of this era was "shifting away from a comprehensive narrative toward abbreviated doctrinal formulations. The theological focus began to shift from story to creed."[4]

Creeds capture parts of the Bible's story, yet they also can leave out essential parts of the story. Snyder notes, "On the one hand, these [creeds] served (and continue to serve) as extremely important anchors of the Great Tradition of Christian belief. On the other hand, such a focus on the creeds began to eclipse the church's larger story of redemption and mission and tended to shift the church toward an over-reliance on formal doctrine itself."[5]

---

4   Snyder, *Salvation Means Creation Healed*, 7.

5   Ibid., 8.

The creeds also leave out a major player in the Bible's storyline—Israel. If one compares the great emphasis Scripture devotes to Israel with what the creeds say about Israel, the contrast is striking. After noting that the creeds "are precious gifts to the Church,"[6] McDermott notes the absence of Israel in them: "But the role of Israel as the essential vehicle for the world's salvation is missing from them. Israel is not even mentioned in the Apostles' and Nicene Creeds. They lead us from creation directly to redemption."[7] This reality contributed to structural supersessionism in which Israel is excluded from being a major player in the Bible's story.

In principle, both creed and story should function together like two wings of an airplane. Yet, unfortunately, creed eclipsed story and key parts of the Bible's narrative. Interest in matters such as earth, land, Israel, the Day of the Lord, and a restored creation largely disappeared. When these important areas of Scripture are ignored or overlooked in the story, Spiritual Vision Model ideas can ensue.

THE SCHOLASTICS

As the Middle Ages commenced, the eschatological views of Augustine were prominent in the church. This included Augustine's amillennial perspective. As William C. Watson observes: "While the early Church was premillennial, expecting the millennium in the future, by the fifth century the dominant view had become amillennial, a belief that the millennium was now in effect in the rule of Christ's vicar on earth, the pope. This was mostly due to the influence of Augustine and the growth of papal power...."[8] Thus, there was little to no discussion of the importance of the earth, earthly kingdom, Israel, and nations.

---

6   McDermott, *Israel Matters*, 111.

7   Ibid.

8   William C. Watson, *Dispensationalism Before Darby: Seventeenth-Century and Eighteenth-Century English Apocalypticism* (Silverton, OR: Lampion Press, 2015), 224.

But the scholars of the Middle Ages did not just maintain the Spiritual Vision eschatology of Augustine. They furthered it. These scholars included Peter Abelard, Peter Lombard, and especially Thomas Aquinas. In reference to these three theologians, Alcorn says they "ultimately took hostage the doctrine of Heaven."[9] They "embraced a Heaven entirely intangible, immaterial, and hence ... more spiritual."[10]

Augustine spiritualized Jesus' millennial kingdom. But he still held to the physicality of the Eternal State beyond the Millennium. Yet Augustine was not much concerned with the geographical locale of Heaven. As McDannell and Lang note, "Augustine made no attempt to explain the spatial dimension of eternal life or to localize heaven within the structure of the universe. All of this was theologically irrelevant."[11]

The scholastics of the twelfth and thirteenth centuries were interested in the locale of Heaven, although their findings were not based in the Bible. With the rediscovery of Aristotle, the scholastics agreed with the Greek philosophers that the universe consisted of concentric spheres and levels starting with the inner earth and moving upwards through the cosmic bodies and then Heaven and finally God Himself. The quality and luminosity of the spheres and levels increased the higher one went.[12] The inner earth was the lowest level. It is coarse and unrefined. But the movement upwards through the moon, sun, stars, and planets brought increasing quality, lightness, and light. Beyond the edge of the universe was the empyrean or light-filled heaven where the souls of saints and angels resided. Just beyond or at the center of the empyrean was the "heaven of the heavens" where only the Trinity resided. That was the cosmology of this era. Thomas Aquinas took this understanding and furthered a Spiritual Vision Model idea of Heaven.

---

9   Alcorn, *Heaven*, 485.

10   Ibid.

11   McDannell and Lang, *Heaven*, 81.

12   See Ibid., 82.

THOMAS AQUINAS AND THE EMPYREAN HEAVEN

The most significant philosopher and theologian of the Middle Ages, Thomas Aquinas (1225–74), promoted a strong form of the Spiritual Vision Model. Arguably, his views of eternity could be the most Spiritual Vision Model-like within the history of Christianity. This is particularly seen with his understanding of the empyrean heaven. After death and the Last Judgment, Aquinas believed saints would ascend to a light-filled empyrean heaven beyond the physical universe.[13] The empyrean heaven exists outside the universe and transcends space and time. The saints surround God, basking in His glory and presence in what some have called, "the soul dazzled by light." The key aspects of Aquinas's empyrean heaven are knowledge and light. The empyrean experience involves a "vision of God" or "beatific vision" in which the saint focuses solely upon God in His glory which brings ultimate bliss. More will be said about the Beatific Vision in a later chapter.

Aquinas's empyrean heaven is a radically different experience from the present life—a total divorce of Heaven and earth. First, the empyrean heaven exists beyond earth and the universe. It is devoid of any of the natural elements—earth, fire, water, and air. Light transcends these.

Second, there is no motion, or change in the empyrean. This must be the case for Aquinas since motion and change imply lack of perfection. Things are in motion because they are *en route* to a better state or situation, or something negative has caused an object to be in motion. These conditions cannot occur in the empyrean since the empyrean is perfection. Thus, the empyrean heaven is a static changeless state. "In heaven,

---

13   In addition to Aquinas, theologians who accepted the empyrean heaven idea around this time included William of Auvergne, Alexander of Hales, Albertus Magnus, Saint Bonaventure, Duns Scotus, Richard of Middleton. See Edward Grant, *Planets, Stars, and Orbs: The Medieval Cosmos, 1200–1687* (Cambridge University Press, 1994), 372. For Aquinas, the empyrean heaven can be accessed after death in this age but after the Last Judgment the saint will receive a resurrected body that adds to the experience in heaven.

according to Aquinas, there will be no more active life; only contemplation will continue."[14]

Third, there is no time in the empyrean heaven since time is also related to imperfection. The common idea that Heaven is devoid of time is related to Aquinas's empyrean heaven idea.

Fourth, there are no animals or plants in the empyrean since these existed to help man. Once man is in his perfect state, no need exists for animals and plants. For Aquinas, animals and plants have instrumental value as they help and serve mankind. But they do not have inherent value. Once man reaches his perfect state in the empyrean animals and plants have no purpose.

Fifth, there will be no social interactions among the saints in the empyrean heaven. Any social or cultural situations would detract from the person's contemplation of God.

Sixth, the universe below the empyrean is not annihilated but it is brought to a standstill. It is frozen with no movement. The universe is not inhabited, perhaps except for the inner part of the earth where hell exists for the damned. The static universe will be filled with God's light. The earth will have a shiny surface, like glass, and will be semi-transparent. Water will be crystal and solid.[15] The universe, including the cosmic bodies, will not have any motion. It will be perfectly still since movement is connected with decay and imperfection.[16]

Thomas Aquinas promoted one of the strongest Spiritual Vision Model versions of eternal life to date. He surpassed Augustine who held a more tangible view of eternity. Yet Aquinas's views still are better than those in the eastern religions like Hinduism and Buddhism. Unlike those religions, Aquinas believed the individual person exists in eternity and has self-consciousness and the ability to reason. While not communicating with other saints in the empyrean Aquinas thought it was possible for saints to be aware of other saints there. Aquinas also affirmed resurrection of the

---

14   McDannell and Lang, 89.

15   See Ibid., 84–85.

16   For more on this idea see McDannell and Lang, 84.

body which contributed to the experience of God in eternity. Aquinas did not believe this body would eat, drink, socialize, or be active, but the saints would possess a body. This is consistent with the New Creation Model. Thus, even extreme Christian versions of the Spiritual Vision Model, as found with Aquinas and the scholastics, contained significant differences from non-Christian versions of the Spiritual Vision Model.

DANTE AND *THE DIVINE COMEDY*

The empyrean heaven of Aquinas and the scholastics was depicted in the third and final part of Dante's *Divine Comedy* called *Paradiso*. *Paradiso* is an allegory of the soul's ascent to God in the realm of light. After visiting several spheres of Heaven, Dante is escorted to the empyrean by his guide, Beatrice, where he is engulfed in light and sees three circles representing the Trinity. With a flash of understanding that could not be stated in words, Dante experienced union with God. His writing abruptly ended.[17] Nothing more could be stated after this experience. For Dante, reaching the heavenly empyrean is the ultimate and final destiny for the saint. Snyder observes, "Dante viewed the highest, ultimate reality as pure nonmaterial light" and that the ultimate experience is the soul being dazzled by light.[18]

Dante's *Divine Comedy*, written early in the fourteenth century, offered a strong Christian Spiritual Vision Model concept of Heaven. Its ideas of Heaven and eternity became entrenched in Christianity even with the coming demise of medieval cosmology. Even today, many cultural depictions of Heaven follow the heavily spiritualized empyrean heaven idea of Aquinas and Dante. Earlier, in the introduction to this book, I mentioned that my then Catholic mother described Heaven as being engulfed in pure light forever. Her depiction was consistent with Aquinas's and Dante's Heaven. Yet this empyrean heaven idea is unbiblical. It is based more on Platonism and logical connections. It does not present the new earth

---

17   Also, part of Dante's experience in *Paradiso* was meeting Thomas Aquinas in the fourth sphere of Heaven—the sun.

18   Snyder, 24. "…Dante viewed the highest, ultimate reality as pure nonmaterial light; 'for him the ultimate truth is that the soul is dazzled by light.'"

situation of the prophets and the Book of Revelation, which reveal social and cultural interactions among ethnic groups and nations in the Eternal State. Writing about the long-lasting damage done by the scholastics concerning the empyrean heaven, Alcorn observes:

> The loss was incalculable. The church to this day has never recovered from the unearthly—and anti-earthly—theology of Heaven constructed by well-meaning but misguided scholastic theologians. These men interpreted biblical revelation not in a straightforward manner, but in light of the intellectually seductive notions of Platonism, Stoicism, and Gnosticism.[19]

SUMMARY OF SPIRITUAL VISION MODEL EXPECTATIONS IN THE MIDDLE AGES

Expectations concerning Heaven and eternity took a dramatic turn to the Spiritual Vision Model in the Middle Ages. As Carolyn Walker Bynum notes, the expectations of the earliest Christians differed from those in the Middle Ages: "Early Christians expected the body to rise in a restored earthly paradise, whose arrival was imminent. Most late medieval Christians thought resurrection and the coming of the kingdom waited afar off in another space and time."[20] As a result, "eschatological yearning was increasingly focused on heaven, to which the soul might go while the bones still reposed underground."[21] Middleton observes that, "Indeed, the redemption of the cosmos entirely fades from view in the Middle Ages."[22]

So with the Middle Ages, Spiritual Vision assumptions were assumed. They were the entrenched preunderstandings with no alternative. As

---

19 Alcorn, 485.

20 Carolyn Walker Bynum, *The Resurrection of the Body in Western Christianity, 200-1336* (New York: Columbia University Press, 1995), 14.

21 Ibid., 13.

22 Middleton, *A New Heaven and a New Earth*, 293.

Snyder notes, "By about 800, ideal Christian spirituality had come to mean an ascent to the realm of the spirit, a journey to the spirit world; enjoying a timeless 'beatific vision' that was seen as the essence of eternal life."[23] The coming Protestant Reformation will challenge the Spiritual Vision Model idea of Heaven of the Middle Ages, but the battle with Medieval concept of Heaven will continue to the present.

---

23   Snyder, 14–15.

17

THE MODELS IN
THE REFORMATION
AND BEYOND

◆

MARTIN LUTHER AND JOHN CALVIN

The Protestant Reformation of the sixteenth century was a theological and political earthquake for the western world. Martin Luther and John Calvin were its dominating figures. Their theological contributions are lasting and many. But where do they fit concerning the models? The answer is in the middle. McDannell and Lang believe Luther and Calvin aligned more with the theocentric (Spiritual Vision) model. Our view is that Luther and Calvin are in the middle, holding to significant parts of both models. Luther and Calvin were an improvement over the Roman Catholic scholastics of the Middle Ages who promoted a strong Spiritual Vision Model. Yet they still retained significant Spiritual Vision Model beliefs.

Some qualifying statements are necessary. Luther, Calvin, and other early reformers focused on salvation issues, justification, the sacraments, the church, and the authority of the Bible. Understandably, eschatology and the earth were not major concerns for them. The reformers did not focus on areas associated with the New Creation Model. One can be wrong on the new earth and be saved, but one cannot be wrong on the nature of the Gospel. As a result, Roman Catholic eschatology was largely maintained. Major breaks with Catholic eschatology would not occur until the seventeenth and eighteenth centuries.

Concerning Luther, Calvin, and the Reformation, McDannell and Lang note, "God the Savior, rather than God the Creator, served as the focus of devotional literature and spirituality."[1] When the reformers created the Augsburg Confession of 1530, "it included no discussion of heaven."[2] One can sympathize since the doctrines of salvation and the church were most essential at this time. Not every movement or system must address every doctrinal issue with equal emphasis. Nevertheless, eschatology and New Creation Model issues were not strengths of Luther, Calvin, and the early Reformation tradition.

Concerning Bible interpretation, like Augustine, Luther tied his future expectations with allegorical interpretation. This is somewhat surprising since Luther condemned allegorical interpretation. But he still fell prey to its use. Winfried Vogel notes, "What also rather typically belongs to Luther's eschatology is his allegorical application to the present era of certain well-known end-time expressions of Scripture."[3] The Spiritual Vision influences of Augustine and allegorical interpretation coincided with Luther's spiritualization of Jesus' millennial kingdom to this present age:

> Naturally, he [Luther] took over some of Augustine's teachings in this respect—so, for example, the latter's allegorizing of last-day events and the belief that the millennium of Rev 20 was already being fulfilled in the present age (commonly called the "amillennial view").[4]

Calvin also viewed Jesus' millennial kingdom as a spiritual kingdom only. As David Engelsma summarizes:

> For Calvin, "the kingdom of a thousand years (of Rev. 20 . . .) is then the spiritual rule of Christ over individual souls in their earthly life

---

1   McDannell and Lang, *Heaven*, 168.

2   Ibid., 150.

3   Winfried Vogel, "The Eschatological Theology of Martin Luther Part I: Luther's Basic Concepts," *Andrews University Seminary Studies*, 24.3 (Autumn 1986): 255.

4   Ibid., 255–56. The spelling "amillenial" is in the original.

until the completion of their course in death and the general resurrection." That Calvin taught that the rule of Christ in present history is solely spiritual through the gospel....[5]

According to Calvin, there would be no political rule of the saints over an earthly kingdom. Engelsma notes, "With all the Reformers, Calvin explicitly repudiated the millennial dream of an earthly kingdom in which the saints exercise political power."[6] So, when it came to the spiritualization of Jesus' millennial kingdom, as found with Amillennialism, Luther and Calvin were firmly in the Spiritual Vision Model camp.

Yet, both Luther and Calvin held to some New Creation Model elements, including the future renovation of creation. McDannell and Lang observe that Luther held to the "renovation" of the universe: "Rather than predicting the elimination of the universe, Luther imagined its renovation."[7] For example, Luther said, "The flowers, leaves, and grass will be as beautiful, pleasant, and delightful as an emerald, and all creatures most beautiful."[8] Concerning whether there will be animals in paradise, Luther stated, "You must not think that heaven and earth will be made of nothing but air and sand, but there will be whatever belongs to it— sheep, oxen, beasts, fish, without which the earth and sky or air cannot be."[9] Luther believed ants, bugs and "stinking creatures" will be delightful and give off a wonderful fragrance. Even the Elbe river and the skies will be restored.[10] Luther's assertions are significantly different from those of Aquinas who did not believe animals would exist in the eternal heaven.

---

5   David Engelsma, "Amillennialism," http://www.onthewing.org/user/Esc_Amillennialism%20-%20 Engelsma.pdf., 31. Accessed July 3, 2020.

6   Engelsma, 31.

7   McDannell and Lang, 152.

8   Cited in Karen L. Bloomquist and John R. Stumme, eds. *The Promise of Lutheran Ethics* (Minneapolis, MN: Fortress Press, 1998), 139.

9   McDannell and Lang, 152–53.

10   Ibid., 153.

Calvin also believed in a "renovated" earth and the restoration of all things.[11] Concerning 2 Peter 3:10 he said, "Of the elements of the world I shall only say this one thing, that they are to be consumed, only that they may be renovated, their substance still remaining the same, as it may be easily gathered from Romans 8:21 and from other passages."[12] Summarizing Luther and Calvin's views concerning a renewed earth, McDannell and Lang state: "Both Luther and Calvin argued that God would renew the earth and purify the universe. Animals and plants would continue for eternity in their newly perfected state."[13]

Yet while Luther and Calvin affirmed a renewed earth, they did not believe the saints would be engaged with this earth: "For Luther, the saints might visit the new earth, but it would not be their home."[14] Also, for Calvin the new earth was not a major concern: "For Calvin, they [the saints] would not even desire to know the new world. God rehabilitated the world only to make it a part of the vision of the divine."[15] The new earth was for contemplation, not use.[16] Summarizing Luther and Calvin's views on the saints in eternity, McDannell and Lang note: "Although there would be a new earth, the reformers refused to allow that the blessed would live an earthly life in it."[17] The idea that saints would not be active on the new earth is contrary to Revelation 21–22 and is consistent with the Spiritual Vision Model.

Another key idea of the Spiritual Vision Model is that Heaven is solely about experiencing God and not fellowship with other saints. This seemed to be the approach of both Luther and Calvin: "In keeping with

---

11   For more on this see Matthew J. Tuininga, *Calvin's Political Theology and the Public Engagement of the Church* (New York, NY: Cambridge University Press, 2017), 112ff.

12   John Calvin, *Commentary on 2 Peter 3:10*; CO 55:476.

13   McDannell and Lang, 154.

14   Ibid.

15   Ibid.

16   "In keeping with scholastic thought, Calvin did not predict that the blessed would live on the renewed earth. There would be a certain distance of the saints from the new earth. The new earth's purpose was for contemplation, not for use." McDannell and Lang, 154.

17   Ibid.

their theocentric outlook, the reformers saw eternal life primarily as the individual's unsurpassed communion with God."[18] Discussing the idea of social reunions, Calvin said that the saints will not interact with each other because they focus solely on God:

> Should they here rejoin that they have it in their power to do the same thing, if (as we believe) they are with God in paradise, I answer, that to be in paradise, and live with God, is not to speak to each other, and be heard by each other, but is only to enjoy God, to feel his good will, and rest in him.[19]

On this issue Calvin was similar to Aquinas who saw no social interactions among the redeemed in eternity.

In sum, Luther and Calvin's views on eternity were largely consistent with the empyrean heaven of Aquinas and the scholastics. But one difference is that Luther and Calvin allowed for the presence of animals and plants on the new earth, while Aquinas did not.

Still another Spiritual Vision Model element of Luther and Calvin involved their belief in the removal of all functional distinctions in Heaven:

> According to Luther, although the blessed will retain their gender, they will lose their identities of rank and profession. Luther and Calvin agreed that there will be no princes or peasants, magistrates or preachers, for all will be equal.[20]

Luther and Calvin also did not believe government or laws would exist in the future Heaven.[21] This is refuted by Revelation 21:24, 26 which tells of nations and kings on the new earth.

McDannell and Lang summarize Luther and Calvin's mixed views on eternity:

---

18   Ibid., 148.

19   John Calvin, *Psychopannychia; or, The Soul's Imaginary Sleep* https://www.monergism.com/theth-reshold/sdg/calvin_psychopannychia.html. See also McDannell and Lang, 155.

20   McDannell and Lang, 154.

21   See Ibid.

The early Reformation view of eternal life combined the features of a renewed world with the absolute rule of God. Luther and Calvin continued the scholastic perspective on the heavenly empyrean, but they softened it by introducing animals and plants into a perfected earth.... Their concern lay not with the end of history but with the individual's heavenly life after his or her death.[22]

Yet, the trajectory coming from the reformers was positive. They adopted a more literal understanding of Scripture, and at least in principle, challenged allegorical interpretation. This resulted in more new creationist thinking. As Blaising notes, "Although the reformers themselves did not directly challenge the spiritual vision model, they did unleash powerful currents of thought that led to both the reemergence of new creation eschatology and the consideration of millennialism."[23]

THE PURITANS

The English Puritans carried the Reformation tradition into the seventeenth century and beyond with mixed implications for the two models. Concerning Jesus' millennial kingdom, as described in Revelation 20, the Puritans took a more tangible and earth-oriented view of the Millennium than did Luther and Calvin. Thus, the Puritans believed in a more New Creation Model-like understanding of Jesus' kingdom. Yet concerning the final Heaven or eternity, they were much in line with Aquinas and the scholastics of the Middle Ages. And in some cases they went beyond Aquinas on the Spiritual Vision Model side.

We noted that Luther and Calvin believed in Augustinian Amillennialism. Some Puritans were amillennialists too. But other Puritans were postmillennialists, believing that Jesus' millennial kingdom would begin on earth in this age with "the conversion of the Jews and will flower rather quickly thereafter, prevailing over the earth for a literal

---

22   Ibid., 156. They also say, "Because of their appreciation of the world, the reformers tempered their theocentric heaven with an eternal life that recognized the importance of the earth." 152.

23   Blaising, "Premillennialism," in *Three View of the Millennium and Beyond*, 174.

thousand years."[24] The kingdom of Jesus will not only involve the spiritual salvation of many, but it will also transform the world in the social, political, cultural, and economic realms. For postmillennialists, Jesus' kingdom has tangible results on the earth. This transformation of the world, for the Puritan postmillennialists, must occur before Jesus' second coming. Jesus, who reigns from Heaven in this age, will return to a world won over by the Gospel.

Such an earth-oriented understanding of Jesus' millennial kingdom is consistent with the New Creation Model. So Puritan postmillennialists were closer to the New Creation Model concerning Jesus' millennial kingdom than were amillennialists who spiritualized Jesus' kingdom. Citing Donald Bloesch, Kenneth Gentry lists six "guiding lights" of Postmillennialism from the seventeenth and eighteenth centuries: "Samuel Rutherford (1600–1661), John Owen (1616–1683), Philip Spener (1635–1705), Daniel Whitby (1638–1726), Isaac Watts (1674–1748), the Wesley brothers (1700s), and Jonathan Edwards (1703–1758)."[25]

Yet some Puritans adopted Premillennialism and its view that an earthly kingdom of Jesus follows Jesus' second coming. Significant seventeenth century premillennial Puritans included Thomas Brightman (1562–1607) and Joseph Mede (1586–1639). William Hooke (1600–77), an English Puritan pastor in New Haven, also was a premillennialist.[26] Noting that some were advocating an amillennial view, Hooke expressed a new creationist approach concerning an earthly, political kingdom of Christ:

> Yet concerning this his *second coming*, to set up his Kingdom on earth,
> some acknowledge no kingdom of Christ on earth, but spiritual and
> invisible in the hearts of the elect … But there is another, a Political
> Kingdom of Christ to be set up in the last times, foretold by Dan. in

---

24   Kenneth L. Gentry, Jr., "Reformed Postmillennialism," https://postmillennialworldview.com/2019/12/03/reformation-postmillennialism/ December 3, 2019. Accessed December 12, 2022.

25   Ibid. One error here is that Isaac Watts was a premillennialist.

26   Watson, *Dispensationalism Before Darby*, 188–89.

Chap. 2... and the Angel Gabriel to the Virgin Mary, Luke 1.32, 33.
And by the Apostle John, in Rev. 19 and 20.[27]

For Hooke, Jesus' kingdom was more than a spiritual, invisible kingdom; it was an earthly kingdom. The influence of Premillennialism at this time was significant. William Eamon notes that, "Puritan eschatology during the seventeenth century, and in fact well into the eighteenth century, was characteristically pre-millennial."[28]

Iain Murray notes the New Creation Model hope of some Puritans who held to a future earthly kingdom of Jesus that involved Israel based on Old Testament prophecies and Revelation 20:

> The attention drawn by such writers as Mede and Alsted to the millennium of Revelation 20, and to the Old Testament prophecies which appear to speak of a general conversion of the nations, led to a revived expectation of a pre-millennial appearing of Christ, when Israel would be converted and Christ's kingdom established in the earth for at least a thousand years before the day of judgment.[29]

Murray also notes that "this belief commanded the support of some of the Westminster divines (notably, William Twisse, Thomas Goodwin, William Bridge and Jeremiah Burroughs)."[30]

Postmillennial and premillennial Puritans adopted a New Creation Model view of Jesus' millennial kingdom, more so than did Luther, Calvin, or amillennial Puritans. Yet concerning the Eternal State, the Puritans adopted a purely spiritual Heaven with no room for the earth. McDannell and Lang note:

---

27 W[illiam] H[ooke], "An Epistle to the Reader" preface to Increase Mather, *The Mystery of Israel's Salvation* (n.p. [Boston], 1669), no pagination. As cited in Watson, *Dispensationalism before Darby*, 189.

28 William C. Eamon, "Kingdom and Church in New England: Puritan Eschatology from John Cotton to Jonathan Edwards," (1970) Graduate Student Theses, Dissertations, & Professional Papers, 136.

29 Iain H. Murray, *The Puritan Hope: Revival and the Interpretation of Prophecy* (Carlisle, PA: Banner of Truth Trust, 1991), 52.

30 Ibid., 53.

Whereas Luther allowed a purified earth to provide a playful diversion for the saints, the Puritans denied the earth an everlasting existence. There may be a this-worldly millennial kingdom of Christ, but they held that when the final time arrived, the earth along with all worldly affairs would vanish.[31]

The devout meditations of Puritans and other ascetic reformers anticipated a spiritual rather than a material heavenly reality. Heaven for the pious could never be a replica of the existing world. The old Reformation doctrine about the renewed world as a place of life everlasting was abandoned. Even those who predicted a fruitful earth during the millennium returned the righteous to their proper heavenly existence after the end of time.[32]

Such a spiritual view of the eternal Heaven might seem surprising since the Puritans believed Jesus' kingdom would transform society. And the Puritans appreciated earthly matters like human fellowship, culture, and work. Also, their contributions to society were many. Yet, their hope for the future Heaven after the Millennium was predominately spiritual. When it came to the Millennium, the Puritans largely embraced a New Creation Model understanding. Jesus' millennial kingdom would transform the earth and society. Yet concerning the Eternal Kingdom, they went full Spiritual Vision Model. The earth will be done away for a purely heavenly existence.

RICHARD BAXTER

The Puritan church leader and theologian, Richard Baxter (1615–91), presented a spiritual view of the future Heaven. In his work, *The Saints' Everlasting Rest*, Baxter offered an encouraging message that the glory of Heaven far exceeds the trials we face in this age. But Baxter presented a spiritual view of eternity that does not take place on a restored earth.

---

31 McDannell and Lang, 177.

32 Ibid., 172.

Chapter 10 is titled, "The Saint's Rest is not to be expected on Earth."[33] The common idea that Heaven will be a heavenly choir in the sky is linked with Baxter who "rediscovered the Augustinian emphasis on everlasting praise."[34] Singing praises to God prepared one for an eternal destiny of standing before God and praising Him forever in Heaven. Baxter does mention that believers will have real physical bodies in Heaven with physical senses that work. And the saints will know each other, also a New Creation Model idea. But the idea that believers will escape earth to worship God in Heaven forever was emphasized by Baxter.

JONATHAN EDWARDS

Jonathan Edwards (1703–58), a postmillennialist, believed the millennial kingdom would transform this world before Jesus' second coming. As Eamon states, "His [Edwards'] millennium was an earthly paradise, brought on neither by the personal appearance of Christ nor a cataclysm, but as the culminating stage in the progressive march of history."[35] Edwards also believed in a coming salvation and restoration of Israel, a new creationist idea.[36]

---

33   Richard Baxter, *The Saint's Everlasting Rest*, 170.

34   Ibid., McDannell and Lang, 173.

35   Eamon, 147.

36   "Nothing is more certainly foretold than this national conversion of the Jews in the eleventh chapter of Romans. And there are also many passages of the Old Testament that can't be interpreted any other sense, that I can't now stand to mention. Besides the prophecies of the calling of the Jews, we have a remarkable seal of the fulfillment of this great event in providence by a thing that is a kind of continual miracle, viz. the preserving them a distinct [nation] when in such a dispersed condition for above sixteen hundred years. The world affords nothing else like it—a remarkable hand of providence. When they shall be called, then shall the ancient people that were alone God's people for so long a time be called God's people again, never to be rejected more, one fold with the Gentiles; and then shall also the remains of the ten tribes wherever they are, and though they have been rejected much longer than [the Jews], be brought in with their brethren, the Jews. The prophecies of Hosea especially seem to hold this forth, and that in the future glorious times of the church both Judah and Ephraim, or Judah and the ten tribes, shall be brought in together, and shall be untied as one people as they formerly were under David and Solomon (Hos.1:1), and so in the last chapter of Hosea, and other parts of his prophecy." Jonathan Edwards, *Works, A History of the Works of Redemption*, vol. 9, ed. John F. Wilson (New Haven: Yale University Press, 1989), 469–70.

Yet, Edwards possessed strong Spiritual Vision Model beliefs concerning the final Heaven in eternity, views that could be even more extreme than those of Thomas Aquinas. For Edwards, after Jesus' second coming to earth and the final judgment, Jesus and His church will travel to Heaven where they will live forever:

> so will Christ return in triumph to heaven, all his armies following him, and shall there deliver up his delegated authority to the Father. As Christ returned to heaven after his first victory, after the resurrection of his natural body, so he will return thither again after his second victory, after the resurrection of his mystical body.[37]

Edwards's Spiritual Vision Model views of Heaven also are expressed in His section, "The Last Judgment" in *The History of the Work of Redemption*.[38] Edwards believed that at the Last Judgment all people of all time, believers and the wicked, would be gathered on earth for resurrection and judgment. Then the saints will be whisked to Heaven, apart from earth, forever:

> the whole Church will be completely and forever delivered from this present evil world. She will take her everlasting leave of the earth where she was a stranger....[39]

> After that [the final judgment], Christ and all his saints, and all the holy angels ministering to them, will leave the lower world and ascend upwards to the highest heavens.[40]

> That is how Christ's Church will leave this accursed world forever, and enter the highest heavens, the paradise of God, the kingdom prepared for them from the foundation of the world.[41]

---

37   *The Works of Jonathan Edwards*, Vols. 2-4, Revised, ed. Anthony Uyl (Carlisle, PA: The Banner of Truth Trust, 2019), 279. Section 743.

38   Jonathan Edwards, "The History of the Work of Redemption," in https://www.preachershelp.net/wp-content/uploads/2014/11/redemption-edwards-481.pdf. (Accessed March 12, 2023).

39   Ibid., 174.

40   Ibid., 176.

41   Ibid., 177.

> All the glory of the Church on earth is only a faint shadow of this, her glorious consummation in heaven.[42]

With the saints in Heaven, the earth then becomes the scene for the fiery eternal punishment of the wicked:

> When they have gone, the world will be set on fire. All the enemies of Christ and his Church will find themselves in a great furnace where they will be tormented forever and ever.[43]

> This world, that used to be the place of his [Satan's] kingdom, and where he set himself up as God, will now be the place of his punishment full of everlasting torment.[44]

Thus, for Edwards, not only is the earth not the home of the saints forever it becomes the place of fiery destruction of the wicked forever. These two ideas of: (1) the saints being taken to Heaven forever; and (2) the earth becoming the place of everlasting fiery torment are summarized by Edwards:

> At the same time, the entire Church will enter with Christ their glorious Lord into the highest heavens, and there they will come into their highest and eternal blessedness and glory. While the lower world, which they left under their feet, is seized with the fire of God's vengeance, with flames kindling upon it, and the wicked entering into everlasting fire, the whole Church will enter heaven full of joy with their glorious Head with all the holy angels attending, coming to the eternal paradise of God, the palace of the great Jehovah their heavenly Father.[45]

Going against the New Creation Model view of the earth as an eternal dwelling for the saints, Edwards explicitly rejected the idea of a

---

42   Ibid., 178
43   Ibid., 177.
44   Ibid.
45   Ibid.

purified, refined earth as the residence for Jesus and His people: "The place of God's eternal residence and the place of the everlasting residence and reign of Christ, and his church, will be heaven, and not this lower world, purified and refined."[46]

According to Willem van Vlastuin, Edwards once held to a material new earth but then changed his mind:

> It appears that, as a young tutor, he believed in a material new earth but later, during his ministry, he became convinced that the new heaven and new earth had to be interpreted spiritually. So, in Edwards's view, there is no expectation of a re-creation of earth. The future of the risen saints will not be on a new earth, but in heaven. But Edwards speaks about the destruction of the old heaven, and the renewal of heaven.[47]

While Revelation 5:10 declares the saints will "reign upon the earth," Edwards believed the reign of the saints would be over Heaven. As Caldwell notes concerning Edwards, "In him [Jesus], they inherit all things and sit on the throne with Christ to reign over heaven."[48]

For Edwards, Jesus and the saints would enter Heaven forever while the universe would be incinerated: "After God's just judgment, Christ, the saints, and the elect angels enter heaven leaving the lower world along with its reprobate inhabitants, whereupon God in his wrath shall turn 'the visible universe ... into a great furnace.'"[49] On this issue Edwards went even further than Aquinas and the medieval scholastics who believed the physical earth would exist into eternity even if not inhabited.

In the early nineteenth century, postmillennialist, David Bogue, could not fathom how anyone could believe that saints could live on

---

46   Jonathan Edwards, *The Works of Jonathan Edwards, Vols. 2-4, Revised,* 275. Section 743.

47   Willem van Vlastuin, "One of the most difficult points in the bible: An analysis of the development of Jonathan Edwards' understanding of the new heaven and new earth," *Church History and Religious Culture* 98:2 (July 2018): 225.

48   Robert Caldwell, "A Brief History of Heaven in the Writings of Jonathan Edwards," in *Calvin Theological Journal* 46 (2011): 70.

49   Ibid., 66. Edwards, "Miscellanies" No. 952, in *WJE,* 20:218.

earth again after their souls resided in Heaven: "How wise and pious men could ever suppose that the saints, whose souls are now in heaven, should, after the resurrection of the body from the grave, descend to live on earth again."[50]

So with Puritan Postmillennialism, a New Creation Model approach to the Millennium existed. This involved a restored earth and salvation for ethnic Israel. Yet concerning the Eternal State, Puritan Postmillennialism promoted an anti-earth view consistent with the Spiritual Vision Model. McDannell and Lang sum up the predominant Spiritual Vision Model assumptions of this era:

> If we eliminate the diverse and unique elements which mark the heaven of Luther, Calvin, Polti, de sales, Nicole, and Baxter, and concentrate on what they share in common, a theocentric model emerges. According to this model, heaven is for God, and the eternal life of the saints revolves around a divine center. The saints may be involved in an everlasting liturgy of praise, they may mediate in solitude, or they may be caught up in an intimate relation with the divine. Worldly activities earn no place in heaven. At the end of time the earth either is destroyed or plays a minor role in everlasting life. Heaven is fundamentally a religious place—a center of worship, of divine revelation, and pious conversations with sacred characters.[51]

THE MODERN ERA

The Modern Era, starting in the seventeenth century, is known for its emphasis on empirical studies and skepticism of traditional philosophical and religious views. This included beliefs on Heaven and the nature of eternal life. McDannell and Lang note, "Since the philosophy of René Descartes (1596–1650), critical thinkers have shied away from making statements about heavenly life."[52] Immanuel Kant (1724–1804), for

---

50   David Bogue, *Discourses on the Millennium* (London: Hamilton, 1818), 17.

51   McDannell and Lang, 178.

52   Ibid., 323.

instance, did not deny immortality of the soul or eternal life, but he held that knowledge on these topics could not be discerned by reason. At best we can speculate on Heaven and eternity, but we cannot have real knowledge on these matters. Theological ideas were unknowable.

The father of Protestant liberalism, Friedrich Schleiermacher (1768–1834), was skeptical about life after death. In a consolation letter to a widow who also lost her son, he did not offer any hope of life after death or reunion with her son.[53] Protestant Liberal theologians continued Schleiermacher's skepticism about eternal life, claiming we can have no sure knowledge of it, or turning it into a purely symbolic matter. Paul Tillich (1886–1965) was skeptical about whether eternal life even existed. "Paul Tillich could not accept any of the standard Christian views on heaven, life after death, or immortality. For him, there was no beatific vision, meeting family members, hugging Jesus, or angelic choir of eternal praise."[54]

CONCLUSION

Church history reveals a battle between the Spiritual Vision and New Creation models. Yet the Spiritual Vision approach has been dominant. It gained strength in the third century and became dominant in the fourth century, largely because of the Constantinian merger of church and state and the theology of Augustine. The Spiritual Vision Model was embraced in the Middle Ages and found its fullest expression in the teachings of Thomas Aquinas. The early Reformation Period continued Spiritual Vision Model ideas since its focus was mostly on individual human salvation. But eventually the Reformation would lead to more New Creation Model thinking.

The Spiritual Vision Model has been challenged but still remains dominant. As Steven James points out, "Still, there is widespread consensus that the history of the church has been dominated by conceptions that

---

53   See Ibid., 324.
54   Ibid., 330.

could be categorized within Blaising's first model, the spiritual vision, and that the emphases of the new creation model generally have been ignored or rejected."[55]

---

55   James, *New Creation Eschatology and the Land*, 2.

18

THE BEATIFIC VISION
AND THE MODELS

◆

T he New Creation and Spiritual Vision models intersect with what
often is called the Beatific Vision. This concerns the believer's vision
and experience of God and what this means. There are two main understandings of the Beatific Vision—the *traditional* understanding, which is
closely linked with the Spiritual Vision Model, and a *new creationist* version. Although the traditional understanding has been dominant in church
history, a new creationist view is most accurate.

BEATIFIC VISION DEFINED

The Beatific Vision concerns direct eternal contemplation of God as the
ultimate goal and experience of man. According to J. Van Engen, "the
beatific vision (*visio Dei*) refers to the direct, intuitive knowledge of the
triune God that perfected souls will enjoy by means of their intellect; that
is, the final fruition of the Christian life, in which they will see God as he
is in himself."[1] Monsignor Edward A. Pace, in the *Catholic Encyclopedia*
(1907), defined the Beatific Vision as:

> The immediate knowledge of God which the angelic spirits and the
> souls of the just enjoy in Heaven. It is called "vision" to distinguish
> it from the mediate knowledge of God which the human mind may

---

1   J. Van Engen, "Beatific Vision," in *Evangelical Theological Dictionary of Theology*, ed. Walter A. Elwell
    (Grand Rapids: Baker Academic, 2001), 146.

attain in the present life. And since in beholding God face to face the created intelligence finds perfect happiness, the vision is termed "beatific."[2]

Thus, the Beatific Vision involves the direct, immediate knowledge of God and seeing His face that results in perfect happiness. This vision does not occur in this life, in which we have indirect and mediated knowledge of God. It awaits the next life.

Three elements of a Beatific Vision idea have scriptural support. First, God is holy and inapproachable to man in his fallen state. First Timothy 6:15b–16a states: "He [God] who is the blessed and only Sovereign, the King of kings and Lord of lords, who alone possesses immortality and dwells in unapproachable light, whom no man has seen or can see." Also, with Exodus 33:20 God told Moses: "You cannot see My face, for no man can see Me and live!"

Second, the greatest happiness is seeing God and being in His presence. As David declared, "One thing I have asked from the Lord, that I shall seek: That I may dwell in the house of the Lord all the days of my life, To behold the beauty of the Lord ... ."

Third, seeing God is a future hope. Note the following:

"Blessed are the pure in heart, for they shall see God" (Matt. 5:8).

For now we see in a mirror dimly, but then face to face; now I know in part, but then I will know fully just as I also have been fully known (1 Cor. 13:12).

We know that when He appears, we will be like Him, because we will see Him just as He is (1 John 3:2b).

They will see His face, and His name will be on their foreheads (Rev. 22:4).

---

2   Edward Pace, "Beatific Vision." *The Catholic Encyclopedia*. Vol. 2. (New York: Robert Appleton Company, 1907; 5 Jan. 2011).

So there is a seeing of God in the future that is not possible now. The believer's hope involves being with God and seeing Him. This is the ultimate experience. What it means to see God who is spirit is difficult to explain. But it will happen. So, various passages teach a vision of God concept. Most Christians affirm some form of a "Beatific Vision."

But there are differences concerning how and when this Vision occurs. From the third century onward the Beatific Vision became highly spiritualized, individual, and divorced from creation and social interactions. It was viewed as individual, contemplative, static, and occurring beyond the universe. This traditional understanding does not include an earthly or physical component. It occurs at death when a believer's soul goes directly into God's presence in Heaven and then escalates further after the last judgment.

PAGAN CONNECTIONS

Christians who affirm the traditional Beatific Vision usually think it is taught in the Bible. But the traditional view borrowed from pagan ideas. As Andrew Louth observes, "The Christian traditions of the beatific vision owe something to pagan antecedents, not least the pagan tradition."[3] The "soul dazzled by light" in another realm idea is consistent with the eschatology of Platonism. As a proponent of the traditional view, Boersma admits the connection to Platonism: "In particular, the Platonic tradition has been influential on the development of the doctrine of the beatific vision."[4] He also connects the long-standing Christian Beatific Vision idea with "Christian Platonism":

> Time and again theologians would turn to Plato and Plotinus for inspiration on how to articulate the biblical truth that we long to see God face-to-face. In fact, it is probably fair to suggest that it is Christian

---

3   Andrew Louth, "Foreword," in Hans Boersma, *Seeing God: The Beatific Vision in Christian Tradition* (Grand Rapids: Eerdmans, 2018), xiii.

4   Hans Boersma, *Seeing God: The Beatific Vision in Christian Tradition* (Grand Rapids: Eerdmans, 2018), 45.

Platonism that sustained the biblical teaching of the beatific vision in Christian doctrine and spirituality throughout the centuries.[5]

Thus, the traditional Beatific Vision has connections with the Spiritual Vision Model through its relationship to Platonism.

THOMAS AQUINAS

The traditional Beatific Vision understanding was most clearly expressed with Thomas Aquinas in the thirteenth century. He promoted an extreme spiritual approach to the Beatific Vision. He linked the image of God with the intellect and rational component of man and thus made the Beatific Vision about mental contemplation of God. Jerry Walls explains:

> An extreme version of this view, and one that is highly significant and influential in the history of theology, is Aquinas's account of the beatific vision. Since we are rational creatures, our happiness consists in activity of the intellect, and since knowledge of God is the final end of our intellectual quest, our perfect happiness consists in contemplation of God. Although he affirmed that the body contributed to our individual happiness, he was reluctant to admit that human fellowship contributed anything essential to heavenly happiness. So strongly did Aquinas believe that God alone is the source of our eternal happiness, that he even saw human society as a possible distraction from our true beatitude.[6]

As stated earlier in this book, Aquinas's view of Heaven was depicted in Dante's *Paradiso* in *The Divine Comedy*. Here, the empyrean (fiery-light) heaven is the final, ultimate, and indescribable experience of basking in God's light and presence. This understanding of the Beatific Vision is strongly associated with the Spiritual Vision Model. It removes creational, physical, and social components from the Vision since those allegedly would be distractions from the ultimate experience of God. But as we will

---

5   Ibid., 47.

6   Jerry L. Walls, "Heaven," in *The Oxford Handbook of Eschatology*, ed. Jerry L. Walls (New York: Oxford University Press, 2008), 402.

argue below, there is a better view of the Beatific Vision—a New Creation Model perspective.

THE BEATIFIC VISION AND THE NEW CREATION MODEL

A new creation perspective takes a holistic approach to the vision of God. And it is not a threat to believers seeing God's face. As Blaising notes, "The new creation model should not be understood as denying the hope that the saved will see God."[7] The best part of eternity will involve being in God's presence and seeing His face. But the real vision of God experience is not beyond the universe, space, and time. The true Beatific Vision is not the empyrean heaven of Aquinas and Dante. It is not a static absorbing of light rays in another dimension divorced from earth. It involves a new earth, space, and time. It includes social interactions with other believers.

Scripture must inform the Beatific Vision experience, not what theologians and philosophers think it should be. The biblical Beatific Vision is described in Revelation 21:1–22:5 with a tangible New Jerusalem that resides on a new earth as nations of the earth serve God and interact socially and culturally with each other.

Knowing the correct vision of God experience means understanding the context for it. First, God will dwell among His people or literally "peoples" (see Rev. 21:3) and they shall see His face (see Rev. 22:4). And there also will be many blessings and gifts on the new earth. None of these gifts will be enjoyed apart from a relationship with the Gift-giver. "Every good thing given and every perfect gift" comes from God (see James 1:17). As one participates with the delights of the new earth God is pleased. As one enjoys fellowship with other believers, God is honored. And as one enjoys the beauty of the new earth, this brings glory to God. Contrary to the traditional view, participating in activities and interacting with people does not mean idolatry. Enjoying good gifts from God is not a threat to God. This is the point of 1 Timothy 4. In reference to those forbidding marriage and the

---

7   Blaising, "Premillennialism," in *Three Views on the Millennium and Beyond*, 163.

enjoyment of food, Paul stated, "For everything created by God is good, and nothing is to be rejected if it is received with gratitude" (1 Tim. 4:4a).

Second, the Beatific Vision occurs in the context of a "new heaven and a new earth." And it involves a New Jerusalem (see Rev. 21:1–3). Just as the first heavens and earth of Genesis 1:1 were tangible, so too are the new heaven and new earth. Thus, there is a tangible earthly platform for the Vision. It is not spaceless or in a non-material Heaven.

This is where protology (first things) helps us with eschatology (last things). The first person to experience a vision of God was Adam. Adam walked with God in the garden. Yet Adam's experience before the Fall was not apart from earth, space, and time. Adam was created last on the sixth day into the context of a beautiful world. And the first blessings and commands given to him were to fill, rule, and subdue the earth (see Gen. 1:26–28). All these were to occur in connection with Adam's relationship with God. God did not view creation as a threat to Adam's experience of Him.

Third, the Beatific Vision experience is societal. The word "they" appears five times in Revelation 21:1–22:5. This experience includes "peoples" (see Rev. 21:3), and "nations" that bring cultural contributions (see Rev. 21:24, 26). Worship of God will not only be individual; it will be corporate as well. The true Beatific Vision will have social interactions among God's people. Being in God's presence and enjoying Him is not contrary to God's people enjoying fellowship with each other. God wants social interactions to occur! Love of neighbor is the second greatest command and exists with the first greatest command—to love God with one's whole being. Living out these two greatest commandments will take place in eternity.

Fourth, the Beatific Vision happens for those in resurrected bodies (see Rev. 20:4). All people on the new earth will be resurrected. The physical component of man must be part of the Beatific Vision. Thus, the Vision is not just mental contemplation apart from a body; it must include the whole person. The saved will perceive and interact with Jesus in His physical, resurrection body.[8]

---

8   We acknowledge that most who hold to the traditional Beatific Vision view also assert belief in the resurrection of the body.

Fifth, the Beatific Vision involves the function of reigning over the earth. The last statement of the Eternal State in Scripture says, "They will reign forever and ever" (Rev. 22:5b).

The New Creation and its components are not threats to the vision of God. In the same sermon, Jesus said, "the pure in heart ... shall see God" (Matt. 5:8) and "the gentle ... shall inherit the earth" (Matt. 5:5). Jesus also said that all who follow Him will be rewarded with houses and farms (see Matt. 19:28–30). Seeing God and inheriting the earth are not mutually exclusive experiences.

CRITICISM OF THE NEW CREATIONIST BEATIFIC VISION

Not all agree with the new creationist understanding of the Beatific Vision. In his book, *Seeing God: The Beatific Vision in Christian Tradition*, Hans Boersma promotes a traditional spiritual Beatific view and expresses disdain for the new creationist understanding. He criticizes Herman Bavinck and others who believe the Eternal State includes cultural and social activities. Even though Bavinck states that believers will have a beatific experience with God, Boersma was not impressed. He said, "Bavinck was simply too much interested in the hustle and bustle of human activity in the hereafter to give any real thought to a positive articulation of the beatific vision."[9] The disdain in his statement is hard to miss. Boersma is skeptical of any who hold to a renewal of the earth view. For him, this cannot coincide with a true Beatific Vision experience. Neo-Calvinists, like Bavinck, according to Boersma, have "typically disregarded, and at times explicitly rejected, the traditional doctrine of the beatific vision."[10] This is because they believe there is continuity between "this life and the next":

> Indeed, neo-Calvinists are not shy about simply abandoning the doctrine of the beatific vision and highlighting instead the continuity

9   Boersma, 40.

10   Ibid., 33.

between this life and the next, so as to extend the priority of the active life from this world into the next.[11]

Michael Allen, too, criticizes those like Bavinck and Kuyper who link the Beatific Vision with earth and social activities. Concerning the climax of redemptive history, Allen complains that "neo-Calvinists have often turned from focus upon communion with Christ, the presence of God, or the beatific vision (the classical image for the eschatological spiritual presence of the Almighty) to focus instead upon the resurrected body, the shalom of the city, and the renewal of the earth."[12] Allen also calls for "the need to return to a theocentric focus upon the beatific vision of God to our eschatology, over against the dominance of earthly aspects in recent neo-Calvinist theology."[13]

The writings of Boersma and Allen offer an opportunity to consider and evaluate criticisms against a more earth-oriented Beatific Vision. But, in our estimation, their claims lack substance. Their concerns are not based on what new creationists are actually saying but on what they think are the implications of the new creationist view. The argument of Boersma and Allen seems to be—If you believe that eternal life involves interactions with people and culture on a new earth, then you are just wanting the next life to be like our present life. You also are removing focus on God and the need for spiritual disciplines and suffering for Christ in this age.

But this is a false argument. New creationists believe God is the most important object of worship. They believe in the importance of spiritual disciplines. And they believe this age involves suffering and forsaking all for Jesus. Believing these things is not contrary to a New Creation Model view of eternal life. Boersma and Allen seem to project what they think will happen if one does not accept the traditional Beatific Vision view. But they do not prove their claim. If God has determined that our experience

---

11   Hans Boersma, "Blessing and Glory: Abraham Kuyper on the Beatific Vision," in *Calvin Theological Journal* 52:2 (2017): 206.

12   Michael Allen, *Grounded in Heaven: Recentering Christian Hope and Life in God* (Grand Rapids: Eerdmans, 2018), 8.

13   Ibid., 18.

of Him will occur on a renewed earth with resurrected bodies within a societal context—we should accept this. We creatures do not get to determine what the vision of God experience will be like. God does. While many want the Beatific Vision to be only heavenly, individual, and intellectual, that is not what Scripture teaches. We should not be more spiritual than God on this matter.

In the end, Boersma and Allen make no compelling argument why the traditional Beatific Vision view is more biblical than the new creationist understanding. They appeal to passages that state God is light, believers will see God, and the need for spiritual disciplines. But new creationists believe those things too. What was needed was an argument showing that the Bible passages that seem to teach a social and cultural aspect to eternity, do not actually teach these things. But this argument is not made.

PART FOUR

MILLENNIAL VIEWS AND THE MODELS

19

THE MILLENNIUM, THE ETERNAL KINGDOM, AND THE NEW CREATION MODEL

◆

This section begins discussion of how the Millennium and millennial views relate to the New Creation and Spiritual Vision models. The following chapters will then delve into how the various millennial views connect with the two models. But in this chapter we want to address why the Millennium, mentioned in Revelation 20, is important to the models. And we want to look at its relationship to the Eternal Kingdom of Revelation 21–22. Before starting we realize that the Millennium is one of the most debated issues in Christian theology and that many excellent Christians disagree on this issue. With that in mind, we proceed with why we think understanding Jesus' millennial kingdom is important for a proper New Creation Model understanding of the Bible's storyline.

TWO KINGDOM PHASES

Both the Old and New Testaments state much concerning the Messiah's kingdom. And although there is significant debate on the nature and timing of the Millennium mentioned in Revelation 20, most theologians agree that the Millennium is related to the Messiah's kingdom. And since Messiah's kingdom is such an important theme in Scripture, we want to discuss how the New Creation Model relates to Jesus' messianic/millennial kingdom. We also want to address how this model relates to the Eternal Kingdom which follows the Millennium.

To start, the Bible presents two future phases to the kingdom of God: (1) the Millennium and (2) the Eternal Kingdom (or Eternal State).[1] The former is explicitly mentioned in Revelation 20 while the latter is specifically addressed in Revelation 21:1–22:5.

These two phases are important for understanding God's kingdom program. The Millennium is the period in history when Jesus fulfills God's mediatorial kingdom mandate for man to rule from and over the earth for the glory of God. Then the Eternal Kingdom is the perfect aftermath and reward of this successful kingdom. It too occurs on earth. What distinguishes these two kingdoms are: (1) the purposes for each and (2) the thrones that are at the center of each. But both occur on earth, and both involve social and cultural interactions among the redeemed.

MILLENNIAL KINGDOM

First, the Millennium is the direct messianic reign of Jesus the Messiah from and over the earth for one thousand years. It is the period when man (via Jesus) fulfills the kingdom mandate of Genesis 1:26, 28 to successfully rule and subdue the earth and its creatures for God's glory. This rule involves reigning over geo-political nations and defeating God's enemies. It *must* happen. As 1 Corinthians 15:25 states, "For He [Jesus] *must reign* until He has put all His enemies under His feet."[2] When describing Jesus' second coming, Revelation 19:15 declares, "From His mouth comes a sharp sword, so that with it He may strike down the nations, and He will rule them with a rod of iron."[3]

---

1   We acknowledge there are present realities for this age related to the Kingdom of God. Revelation 5:10 depicts believers as already being a "kingdom" positionally. But the actual coming of the kingdom reign of the Messiah awaits the future.

2   Emphases added.

3   In the Old Testament prophets, Olivet Discourse, and Book of Revelation, the kingdom reign of the Messiah follows an intense time of global tribulation, often known as the Day of the Lord. In each of these sections there is: (1) a time of tribulation concerning Israel and the nations. This is followed by (2) a coming of the Lord to earth. This is followed by (3) a subsequent kingdom reign of the Messiah over the earth.

While Revelation 20 explicitly refers to this kingdom and reveals it will last for one thousand years, Revelation 20 is not the only Bible passage that concerns this messianic/millennial kingdom. Many kingdom passages refer to an earthly kingdom of the Messiah—Gen. 1:26, 28; 5:28–29; 49:8–12; Lev. 26:40–45; Psalms 2; 72; 89; 110; Isaiah 2; 9; 11; 25; 35; 49; 65; Jeremiah 30–33; Hosea 2:14–23; Zechariah 14; Matthew 5:5; 19:28–30; Acts 1:6; 3:20–21; Rev. 5:10.

These passages, together, present a composite picture in which the Messiah will reign over Israel and the nations from Jerusalem, defeat His enemies, bring international harmony, remove disease, and restore the earth to Eden-like conditions. Every area is affected for good at this time. This kingdom is a time for building houses and planting vineyards in the context of joy and fairness (see Isa. 65:17–25). It is a time of abundant agricultural prosperity (Gen. 49:8–12; Amos 9:13–15). The animal kingdom is restored (see Isa. 11:6–10). It is a time for houses, farms, and relationships (see Matt. 19:28–30). Disease is wiped out on a global scale (see Isaiah 35). Resurrected saints live and reign on a restored earth (Rev. 5:10; 20:4). Satan will be imprisoned with no access to the earth (Rev. 20:1–3).

Thus, many passages address the kingdom of the Messiah. What Revelation 20 adds is how long it will last—one thousand years—before the Eternal Kingdom begins. The claim that the Millennium is only found in Revelation 20 is not entirely true. There are three elements that make the Millennium what it is: (1) an earthly kingdom in which (2) the Messiah reigns over the earth and nations (3) for one-thousand years. Thus there are three elements: (1) earthly kingdom; (2) direct reign of the Messiah; and (3) a kingdom of one thousand years. While only Revelation 20 mentions "one thousand years" other passages address an earthly kingdom of the Messiah. Without Revelation 20 we still could anticipate an earthly kingdom of the Messiah, but we would not know how long it would last before the Eternal Kingdom started.

Also, Messiah's kingdom includes but involves much more than individual salvation from sin. Being saved is necessary to participate in this kingdom, but this kingdom is global, comprehensive, holistic, and multidimensional. It includes earth, land, earth's creatures, nations, ethnicities,

Israel, physical blessings, and spiritual blessings. Attempts to make Jesus' kingdom only a spiritual kingdom or only about salvation from sin, do not do justice to all dimensions of Jesus' kingdom.

PURPOSES OF THE MILLENNIUM

The messianic/millennial kingdom of Jesus fulfills certain purposes that demand a New Creation Model understanding. First, it is the period when the spotlight is specifically on Jesus the Messiah concerning His role as reigning King on the earth. The Jesus who was rejected by the world at His first coming is recognized and honored as reigning King on earth with His second advent. At Jesus' first coming, "He came unto His own but His own received Him not" (John 1:11). While fulfilling the significant Suffering Servant role of bringing atonement for sin, Jesus was rejected on earth at His first coming. But in the Millennium Jesus will have a sustained visible reign and be vindicated in the realm of His previous rejection.[4] Also, this will be a time when God's saints are vindicated in the realm of their persecution (see Rev. 2:26–27; 6:9–11; 20:4).

When Jesus reigns in this messianic/millennial kingdom everyone knows it. It is not a secret or hidden kingdom. As Zechariah 14:9 states, "And the Lord will be king over all the earth; in that day the Lord will be the only one, and His name the only one." Then there will be no competing religions or philosophies. Everyone acknowledges Jesus as King. This is a comprehensive kingdom reign of Jesus the Messiah from sea to sea (see Zech. 9:10). With Psalm 2:8 God promised that He would give the Messiah the nations as His inheritance and the very ends of the earth as His possession. And with Psalm 110:2 the Father will stretch forth the Messiah's kingdom reign from Zion, thus ruling in the realm where the rebellion from nations once occurred. The Millennium sees these things happening. In sum, the Millennium is the unique period in history when the Messiah has a sustained reign on earth where the spotlight is on Him.

---

4   We understand that Jesus' resurrection and ascension include elements of vindication as well.

Second, Jesus' millennial kingdom fulfills the kingdom mandate of Genesis 1:26, 28 for man to rule and subdue the earth for God's glory. This mediatorial kingdom reign of man is the primary purpose of the Millennium. The first Adam was tasked to rule and subdue the earth for God's glory. He failed. All mankind after Adam, including Israel in the Old Testament, failed. But Jesus, the Last Adam (1 Cor. 15:45), will succeed from and over the earth where Adam failed. When Adam sinned God did not give up on His expectation for a successful mediatorial kingdom reign on earth, as passages like Psalm 8 and Hebrews 2:5–8 reveal.

Third, Jesus' millennial kingdom also is the period when all dimensions of the covenants of promise—Abrahamic, Davidic, and New—come together in all their dimensions—spiritual, physical, national (Israel), and international (all nations and ethnicities). These covenants together contain dozens of promises and blessings, some of which have been inaugurated in Old Testament history and with the first coming of Jesus. Yet not all elements of these covenants have been fulfilled yet; they await future fulfillment with the coming of Jesus and His kingdom. As Mark Yarbrough rightly states, "While all covenants are completed in Jesus, Jesus has yet to complete all the covenants. That is why we await the second advent of Christ, when he will return and finish what has been started."[5]

Some promises that await future fulfillment include the restoration of national Israel; the permanent possession of the promised land boundaries of Israel; the Davidic King ruling over the restored twelve tribes of Israel; the reign of the Davidic King on earth from sea to sea over all nations; agricultural prosperity on earth; international harmony; and Gentile nations being blessed in their lands. These elements of the covenants and more will be fulfilled in Jesus' coming messianic/millennial kingdom. Yet it must be grasped that the blessings of these covenants will extend into the Eternal Kingdom. When we say these covenants will be fulfilled in the Millennium, we are not implying that they disappear in the Eternal Kingdom. The Eternal Kingdom is the aftermath and perhaps

---

5   Mark Yarbrough, "Israel and the Story of the Bible," in *Israel the Church and the Middle East*, eds. Darrell L. Bock and Mitch Glaser (Grand Rapids: Kregel, 2018), 60–61.

reward of Messiah's successful millennial kingdom reign. Nevertheless, the Millennium is the time when all aspects of the covenants of promise come together in all their dimensions for the first time in history.

THRONES

The issue of "thrones" for both the Millennium and Eternal Kingdom is important and demands a New Creation Model understanding for each. Each kingdom phase is characterized by a different throne situation related to earth. First, *the Millennium is the direct reign of Jesus the Messiah from David's throne.* The throne of David refers to the kingdom authority of David's descendants from Jerusalem (see Jer. 17:25), with a view of a reign from David's ultimate descendant—the Messiah (see Ps. 132:11). With Luke 1:32–33, Gabriel told Mary that Jesus would sit upon the throne of His father David, and rule over Israel (Luke 1:32–33): "He will be great and will be called the Son of the Most High; and the Lord God will give Him the throne of His father David; and He will reign over the house of Jacob forever, and His kingdom will have no end."

In Matthew 25:31–32a, Jesus said that when He returns to earth He then will sit on His glorious [Davidic] throne and judge the nations: "But when the Son of Man comes in His glory, and all the angels with Him, then He will sit on His glorious throne. All the nations will be gathered before Him." Those who are the sheep will then "inherit the kingdom" (25:34). Significantly, Jesus states that His second coming to earth is when He assumes His glorious Davidic throne.

Also, with Matthew 19:28 Jesus links His throne with the renewal of earth ("regeneration") and the restoration of the twelve tribes of Israel: "And Jesus said to them, 'Truly I say to you, that you who have followed Me, in the regeneration when the Son of Man will sit on His glorious throne, you also shall sit upon twelve thrones, judging the twelve tribes of Israel.'" Again, Jesus' assumption of His Davidic throne occurs with second coming events.

Then with Revelation 3:21 Jesus distinguished His throne from the Father's throne—"He who overcomes, I will grant to him to sit down with Me on My throne, as I also overcame and sat down with My Father on His throne." Jesus distinguishes His throne from the Father's throne, showing the Davidic throne is uniquely the throne of the Messiah. So on multiple occasions Jesus states that at His return to earth He will assume the Davidic throne to reign in His kingdom. This Davidic throne reign of the Messiah is the direct reign of the Last Adam and Messiah who fulfills the kingdom mandate. Thus, the kingdom mandate of Genesis 1:26, 28 and the Davidic/messianic/millennial reign of the Messiah are directly related.

But in the Eternal Kingdom a transition occurs. Jesus will share a throne with the Father. Revelation 22:3 refers to "the throne of God and of the Lamb" in the New Jerusalem. In the Millennium Jesus reigns from His own throne—the Davidic throne. But in eternity, He shares one throne with the Father. This shows the direct nature of Jesus' kingdom reign in the Millennium. Jesus must successfully reign as Messiah before the transition to the Eternal Kingdom can occur. That is why prophecies about Messiah's kingdom must be fulfilled in the Millennium. According to 1 Corinthians 15:24 when Jesus completes His successful kingdom reign as Last Adam and Messiah, He hands His kingdom over to the Father—"then comes the end, when He hands over the kingdom to the God and Father, when He has abolished all rule and all authority and power."

Jesus does not stop reigning. He must reign forever (see Rev. 11:15). But in the transition from Jesus' messianic/millennial kingdom to the Eternal Kingdom, the Father and the Son assume the same throne. Perhaps it is the merger of the Universal Kingdom throne of the Father with the Davidic throne of Jesus the Messiah.

Understanding this helps reveal why Jesus' millennial kingdom must be an earthly kingdom. The Messiah must have a successful earthly kingdom reign. The Millennium is that kingdom reign. It is here where Jesus fulfills God's expectations for a mediatorial kingdom of man on earth. This expectation must happen and is reaffirmed in Psalm 8 and Hebrews 2:5–8.

Some theologians like Anthony Hoekema think that the fulfillment of physical promises can be fulfilled in the Eternal Kingdom, while the Millennium is a spiritual kingdom. But there is a problem with this. *The Eternal Kingdom cannot be the time for the fulfillment of physical promises and covenants since this would put fulfillment of what must happen outside of the direct reign of the Messiah.* Jesus has to fulfill the mediatorial kingdom mandate of Genesis 1:26, 28 in order for the Eternal Kingdom to arrive. Again, that is why Paul said Jesus "must reign" before He hands the kingdom over to the Father (see 1 Cor. 15:24–28). A spiritual kingdom of the Messiah does not fulfill the kingdom mandate, nor can it bring in the Eternal Kingdom.

The Eternal Kingdom is the perfect aftermath of Messiah's successful reign, but this phase of the kingdom is not the direct messianic reign of Jesus. To rebut Hoekema's understanding that Isaiah 2:1–4 can be fulfilled in the Eternal Kingdom but not the Millennium, Saucy aptly observes:

> This interpretation does not acknowledge that this clearly places such portraits of peace among nations beyond the pale of the Messiah's redemptive work and his messianic administration of God's kingdom. If this is correct, his "messianic reign" is one of present spiritual redemption climaxing with the destruction of his enemies and their judgment. His "messianic reign" will never include a reign of manifest glory in which he takes over the government of the world to rule for God as his Anointed One in righteousness and peace in fulfillment of the historical purpose for mankind.[6]

The "Millennium" is not an incidental or unimportant doctrine. It is strategic to the Bible's storyline since it addresses when and how God's kingdom purposes from Genesis 1 will be fulfilled. And it concerns the timing and nature of Jesus' kingdom. To claim that the Millennium is not an important doctrine is to say that the kingdom mandate of Genesis 1 is not important and that the timing and nature of Jesus' messianic kingdom are not important. But they are.

In sum, the millennial kingdom of Jesus will be an earthly kingdom that transforms all creation. It is a time when the spotlight is on Jesus the Messiah as He fulfills God's kingdom mandate for man to rule from and over the earth successfully for God's glory. This is a New Creation

---

6   Saucy, *The Case for Progressive Dispensationalism*, 284, n. 52.

Model understanding. What happens after this is discussed next with the Eternal Kingdom.

ETERNAL KINGDOM

When Jesus has reigned successfully over the earth, nations, and enemies, He then hands the kingdom over to God the Father. According to 1 Corinthians 15:28 this occurs so God can be "all in all." Jesus, thus, functions as a bridge from the Millennium to the Eternal Kingdom. Alva McClain notes that the millennial kingdom of Jesus "will constitute the glorious consummating era of the first order of things and will serve as the divine *bridge* between the temporal order and the eternal order."[7]

The Eternal Kingdom comes after the Millennium (see Revelation 20–21). There is a new heaven and new earth, and a new Jerusalem as the capital city of the new earth (Rev. 21:1–2). The Eternal Kingdom is an escalation from the millennial kingdom era, perhaps the reward or aftermath of Jesus' successful kingdom. Perfection happens during this time that was absent before. The Millennium had a coercive aspect to it. Jesus ruled with a "rod of iron" over nations and enemies (Rev. 19:15). Nations could be punished for not acting as they should (see Zech. 14:17–18). And although rare, sin and death could occur (see Isa. 65:20). But in the Eternal Kingdom no sin or anything negative occurs. The curse is removed and all tears are wiped away (Rev. 21:3–4). The leaves of the tree of life maintain harmony among the nations (see Rev. 22:2). Nations and kings of nations will bring their cultural contributions into the New Jerusalem (see Rev. 21:24, 26).

There also is an escalation of God's presence in the Eternal Kingdom. During the Millennium Jesus was physically present. But during the Eternal Kingdom both God the Father and God the Son share the same throne in the New Jerusalem and dwell among their people(s).

Dramatic change happens with this transition from the Millennium to the Eternal Kingdom. But the change is not an absolute break to

---

7   McClain, *The Greatness of the Kingdom*, 513. Emphases in original.

another dimension. As McClain notes, "The changed conditions in this final Kingdom will be very wonderful and far-reaching. But, in general, it should be observed that there is no *absolute* break with the former world, as in the Platonic postulate."[8] Both kingdom phases involve the earth along with social and cultural interactions.

There is some debate concerning whether the new earth of the Eternal Kingdom will be a replacement of the current earth or a restored/renovated earth that has continuity with the present planet. We discuss this in other parts of this book. The restored/renovated earth view is more consistent with the New Creation Model ideal, and that is the view we hold. But an entirely new planet could still be tangible and consistent with this model. Many who believe the present earth will be annihilated also hold that a tangible earth will replace it. That is not our view, but it does believe in a tangible planet earth that God's people will inhabit for eternity. So the main thing is that the new earth of Revelation 21–22 is a tangible earth with real human and cultural activities on it. It is not a spiritual realm of existence or just figurative of individual salvation truths.

The New Creation Model understanding of the Millennium and Eternal Kingdom differs from what some theological systems and theologians have taught. Augustine eventually believed in a tangible Eternal Kingdom but spiritualized the Millennium (as do many amillennialists). Thomas Aquinas spiritualized both the millennial kingdom and the Eternal Kingdom. Jonathan Edwards and some Puritans believed in a tangible and earthly millennial kingdom of Jesus, but then spiritualized the Eternal Kingdom. Some earlier dispensationalists held to a tangible, earthly millennial kingdom but then spiritualized the Eternal Kingdom. Most Revised and all Progressive Dispensationalists assert that both the Millennium and Eternal State are tangible and occur on earth with social and cultural interactions. This is consistent with the New Creation Model. But the main point is that both the Millennium and the Eternal Kingdom are tangible expressions of the kingdom, and both are related to earth.

---

8   Ibid. Emphases in original.

FOUR PERSPECTIVES CONCERNING THE MILLENNIUM AND THE ETERNAL KINGDOM

1. Spiritual Millennium and Spiritual Eternal Kingdom (Thomas Aquinas; medieval scholastics)

2. Earthly Millennium and Spiritual Eternal Kingdom (Jonathan Edwards; some Puritans)

3. Spiritual Millennium and Earthly Eternal Kingdom (New Earth Amillennialists; Hoekema, Poythress)

4. Earthly Millennium and Earthly Eternal Kingdom (Revised and Progressive Dispensationalists; Historic Premillennialists)

PREMILLENNIALISM
AND THE MODELS

◆

We now shift to examining how the various millennial views relate to the New Creation and Spiritual Vision models. This is not a full discussion of each millennial view, but a survey of how these millennial positions relate specifically to the two models.

WHAT PREMILLENNIALISM IS

The first millennial view we survey is the oldest—Premillennialism. Premillennialism asserts that the thousand-year reign of Jesus and His saints, as explained in Revelation 20, will be an earthly kingdom that involves a reign of Jesus and His saints over the nations. It will occur after Jesus' second coming to earth but before the Eternal State described in Revelation 21:1–22:5. This perspective sees the Millennium as future and taking place on earth.

The rationale for Premillennialism goes back to Genesis 1 and God's original creation and kingdom purposes. God created a "very good" heavens and earth. With Genesis 1:26–28, man is told to fill, rule, and subdue the earth and all its creatures. Adam, as the first and representative man, was given the blessing and mandate to rule the earth and its creatures as God's mediator. Thus, man's mission is both creational and kingdom-oriented. Man was to successfully rule *from* and *over* the earth.

When Adam sinned he broke his relationship with God and the ensuing curse upon the ground meant that mankind could not fulfill the earthly kingdom mandate. While man is separated from God he cannot

fulfill the role God gave him. Israel and Israel's kings also failed the kingdom mandate when Israel functioned as a theocracy before their captivi-
ties. To this day, a successful kingdom reign of man over the earth remains
unfulfilled, which is stated in Hebrews 2:8—"But now we do not yet see
all things subjected to him [man]."

But this failure does not remain forever. Premillennialism asserts
that Jesus, and those in union with Him, will succeed where Adam
failed. At His second coming, Jesus will rule over the earth and the
nations (see Rev. 19:15). His saints will participate in this reign (see Rev.
2:26–27; 5:10).

This successful mediatorial reign of man cannot be accomplished
with a reign from Heaven, or over Heaven, as other millennial views claim.
It must occur *from* and *over* the earth. *Thus, the rationale of Premillennialism
is that there must be a successful reign of man from and over the earth for God's
glory. This has not occurred in history yet. But Jesus, the Last Adam, will make
this happen when He returns to earth and reigns over His kingdom.* When
this is completed, Jesus will hand the kingdom over to God the Father and
the Eternal Kingdom will commence (see 1 Cor. 15:24, 28). All history
points to the summing up of all things in Jesus and the kingdom He brings
(see Eph. 1:10).

A second rationale for Premillennialism concerns the vindication of
Jesus and the saints in the realm (earth) of their persecution and rejection. John 1:11 states that Jesus came to His own, but His own did not
receive Him. And those who belong to God also suffer. But according to
Premillennialism, Jesus must have a sustained, successful kingdom reign in
the realm of His rejection. Likewise, the saints of God who are persecuted
in this evil present age will be vindicated as they reign upon the earth with
Jesus in His successful kingdom reign (see Rev. 5:10; Dan. 7:22). For both
Jesus and His people, there will be vindication and reigning in the realm
where both were rejected and persecuted.

Premillennialism is linked with many elements consistent with a
New Creation Model:

+ Jesus must succeed in the realm (earth) where the first Adam
  failed.

+ Messiah's (Jesus') kingdom is an earthly kingdom.

+ Jesus will have a tangible governmental rule over the earth.

+ Saints will rule the earth under Jesus' authority.

+ Jesus will reign over geo-political nations.

+ This kingdom involves Jerusalem and Israel as the headquarters of this kingdom.[1]

+ The coming kingdom brings bodily resurrection and health, including the widespread removal of diseases.

+ Agricultural prosperity will exist on the earth.

+ Animals will exist and be in harmony with humans and other animals.

+ People will be building and living in houses.

+ Nations and peoples will be doing real work, play, and cultural activities.

+ Social interactions among the redeemed will occur.

+ Celebrations with eating and drinking will happen.

The premillennial view is consistent with the New Creation Model since it envisions Jesus' kingdom reign as involving the earth and all creation realities such as nature, animals, birds, sea creatures, nations, etc. It also includes ethnicities and geo-political nations. Charles Ryrie notes the multi-dimensional nature of Premillennialism:

> In premillennial eschatology much is made of what the Millennium will mean to the world, to Jerusalem, to Palestine, to Israel, to the

---

1   This is particularly true for Dispensational Premillennialism.

nations, etc., and rightly so, for it will affect many changes for good in the entire earth.[2]

Premillennialism believes there are spiritual characteristics to this kingdom. One must be born again to enter it (see John 3:3) and it is linked with repentance (see Matt. 3:2; 4:17). And this kingdom evidences justice, righteousness, and fairness (see Psalm 72). Yet while spiritual characteristics such as righteousness, peace, and joy are most important (see Rom. 14:17), the millennial kingdom takes place in the physical realm and includes material entities. The ideal conditions concerning agriculture, houses, and animals mentioned in the new earth passage of Isaiah 65:17–25 should be taken literally. Houses will be built, agriculture will exist, and animals will reside on the new earth. And all of these occur in the context of fairness and joy.

As we mentioned earlier, some non-premillennialists might hold a transformation of physical realities in the Eternal State after the Millennium. But Premillennialism believes Jesus' direct kingdom before the Eternal State involves the transformation of all things. His millennial kingdom includes spiritual salvation and spiritual realities, but it also affects more than that. Creation in all dimensions is restored.

PREMILLENNIALISM IN HISTORY

Concerning its place in history, Premillennialism was widely held in the early church, as Philip Schaff has noted:

> The most striking point in the eschatology of the ante-Nicene age is the prominent chiliasm, or millenarianism, that is the belief of a visible reign of Christ in glory on earth with the risen saints for a thousand years, before the general resurrection and judgment. It was indeed not the doctrine of the church embodied in any creed or form of devotion, but a widely current opinion of distinguished teachers, such as

---

2   Charles C. Ryrie, *Basic Theology* (Wheaton, IL: Victor Books, 1986), 511.

Barnabas, Papias, Justin Martyr, Irenaeus, Tertullian, Methodius, and Lactantius.[3]

Justin Martyr (AD 100–165) believed in a coming thousand-year kingdom in a rebuilt Jerusalem in connection with what the Old Testament prophets predicted:

> I and others, who are right-minded Christians on all points, are assured that there will be a resurrection of the dead, and a thousand years in Jerusalem, which will then be built, adorned, and enlarged, the prophets Ezekiel and Isaiah and others declare.[4]

Irenaeus taught a strong new creationist understanding of Premillennialism as McDannell and Lang note: "Irenaeus of Lyons in second-century France focused his attention" on "a thousand-year period when the saints will inhabit the renewed earth. During the millennium, the martyrs will be compensated for whatever was denied them in their earlier life. An existence unmolested by enemies, enjoying the goodness of God's creation and producing numerous children throughout a long life...."[5]

PREMILLENNIALISM AS A WEAPON AGAINST GNOSTICISM

Premillennialism had practical results in church history. It was important in the church's fight against a major early heresy rooted in Spiritual Vision Model beliefs—Gnosticism. Donald Fairbairn asserts that "premillennialism was part of the polemic against Gnosticism."[6]

---

3 Philip Schaff, *History of the Christian Church* (Grand Rapids: Eerdmans Publishing Company, 1973), 2:614.

4 Justin Martyr, *Dialogue with Trypho*, 80, *ANF*, 1:239.

5 McDannell and Lang, *Heaven*, 355.

6 Donald Fairbairn, "Contemporary Millennial/Tribulational Debates," in *A Case for Historic Premillennialism: An Alternative to "Left Behind" Eschatology*, ed. Craig L. Blomberg and Sung Wook Chung (Grand Rapids: Baker, 2009), 129.

Gnosticism promoted an unbiblical dualism between the spiritual and the physical—emphasizing the former and denigrating the latter. Gnostic dualism had four important implications:

1. The material world is evil and unredeemable and salvation only applies to the soul, not the body.

2. History is downplayed; if the physical world is unredeemable then the panorama of history played out in the physical world is of little consequence.

3. There is a distinction in gods—the lesser material god of the Old Testament and the higher spiritual God of the New Testament.

4. It led to a docetic view of Christ in which Christ only appears to be human and have flesh.[7]

The church's battle with Gnosticism occurred in the second and third centuries. But Fairbairn points out that, "the church fathers who led this battle—Irenaeus and Tertullian—used their premillennialism as a primary weapon."[8]

In battling Gnosticism, Irenaeus (130–202) strove to demonstrate the unity of Scripture and show that the Old and New Testaments worked in harmony. This "is what drives him into the details of Daniel and Revelation."[9] Fairbairn notes that "behind Irenaeus's treatment of an earthly kingdom lies the concern to refute the gnostic denigration of the material world."[10] This involved belief in a restored earth.

In Irenaeus's mind, "nothing could be more appropriate for the God who created the world and redeemed humanity through early history than

---

7   Ibid.

8   Ibid.

9   Ibid.

10   Ibid.

to conclude his work with an earthly kingdom as a transition to an Eternal Kingdom that will also be on a refurbished earth."[11] Irenaeus believed that denying an earthly kingdom meant denying the goodness of God who created the physical universe.[12]

A. Skevington Wood also affirmed that Premillennialism was a tool used by Irenaeus against the Gnostics who were anti-material:

> It ought also to be borne in mind that the strong emphasis of Irenaeus on the literal fulfillment of the prophecies concerning the Millennium were no doubt conditioned to some degree by the fact that he was contending against the gnostic heretics, who denied the redeemability of the material. The millennial teaching of Irenaeus must not be isolated from the rest of his theology. It is all of a piece with it, and Irenaeus was the first to formulate (however embryonically) a millennial—indeed premillennial—system of interpretation.[13]

For Irenaeus, the significance of eschatology was not just about the details of future events. Instead, "eschatology's significance lies in the way it testifies to the unity of Scripture, the unity of God's purposes, and ultimately the unity and goodness of the God we worship."[14] Also, for Irenaeus and most of the early church an earthly kingdom was a central truth of Christianity, as Fairbairn notes:

> an earthly kingdom following the return of Christ is not merely what Revelation 20 teaches. It is also a central tenet of the faith because it functions to reinforce the central truths of Christianity—that there is one God who in love has created this world for us and us for it, who has personally entered this world in order to redeem us for a future

---

11   Ibid., 129–30.

12   Ibid., 130.

13   A. Skevington Wood, "The Eschatology of Irenaeus," *Evangelical Quarterly* 40 (1968): 36.

14   Fairbairn, 130.

in this world, and who will ultimately triumph in this world over the forces that are arrayed against him.[15]

Fairbairn laments that the battle against Gnosticism and over-spiritualization tendencies have never been totally won. This is because the church does not properly draw upon the truths of a biblical, new creationist eschatology:

> Perhaps part of the reason we have not won it is that we have forfeited the use of one of the greatest biblical/theological weapons in this battle—eschatology. Have we overspiritualized the hope held out to Christians and thus essentially conceded to the Gnostics among us that the material world is not ultimately important?[16]

Premillennialism, thus, refuted attempts to create an unbiblical dualism between the spiritual and the material. It is part of the New Creation Model battle against the Spiritual Vision Model. Sometimes eschatology is viewed as a not-so-important doctrine. But premillennial eschatology was a major weapon in the fight against the greatest early threat to Christianity.

FORMS OF PREMILLENNIALISM

While all forms of Premillennialism affirm a future earthly kingdom of God, not all forms of the premillennial view are exactly the same or equally consistent with the New Creation Model. Below we discuss three major forms of Premillennialism. The first two concern forms of Historic Premillennialism, while the third involves Dispensational Premillennialism.

LADDIAN HISTORIC PREMILLENNIALISM

George Ladd (1911–82) was one of the most influential evangelical theologians of the twentieth century. His views on eschatology remain

---

15   Ibid.
16   Ibid., 131.

well-accepted. Many who hold to Historic Premillennialism at the academic and seminary levels today adopt a version of Premillennialism similar to Ladd's.

Ladd believed the Millennium of Revelation 20 would be a future earthly kingdom of Jesus after Jesus' second coming. Thus, he was thoroughly premillennial. But he also held that Revelation 20 is the sole passage for a Millennium. He did not link the Millennium with Old Testament prophetic passages.[17] For him, there is not much biblical support for a Millennium outside of Revelation 20. Also, while Ladd believed many Jews would be saved in the future, as Romans 11:26 states, he did not believe in a restoration of national Israel. He did not see much of a Jewish element to the millennial kingdom.[18] Ladd also took a supersessionist view concerning Israel and the church: "I do not see how it is possible to avoid the conclusion that the New Testament applies Old Testament prophecies to the New Testament church and in doing so identifies the church as spiritual Israel."[19]

With these points, Ladd separates himself from Dispensational Premillennialism which links Premillennialism with many Old Testament texts and a coming restoration of national Israel.

At times, Ladd presented beliefs consistent with a New Creation Model. He believed the Millennium of Revelation 20 will be an earthly kingdom after Jesus' second coming but before the Eternal State. Second, he also held that the Eternal State would be earthly, and that human destiny was related to this earth. Ladd said, "humanity's ultimate destiny is an earthly one. Human beings are creatures, and God created the earth to be the scene of their creaturely existence."[20] Also, since there is a resurrection of the body for God's people, "so the redemption of the very physical creation

---

17　See George Eldon Ladd, "Historic Premillennialism," in *The Meaning of the Millennium: Four Views* (Downers Grove, IL: InterVarsity Press, 1977), 32.

18　Ibid., 28.

19　Ibid., 23.

20　George Eldon Ladd, *A Theology of the New Testament* (Grand Rapids: Eerdmans, 1993), 682.

requires a renewed earth as the scene of their perfected existence."[21] For Ladd, resurrected believers with real bodies will inhabit a tangible earth for eternity. This is consistent with the New Creation Model.

Middleton, a new creationist, credits Ladd with stirring his thinking in the right direction:

> It was especially the writings of New Testament scholar George Eldon Ladd who most helpfully clarified for me the interconnectedness of what the Bible taught on the redemption of creation, and he explicitly contrasted this teaching with the unbiblical idea of being taken out of this world to heaven.[22]

Ladd, though, had some Spiritual Vision Model tendencies. He admitted that Old Testament prophetic passages predicted a restored earth,[23] but he believed that the New Testament could reinterpret Old Testament promises, at times, so that physical blessings become spiritual blessings:

> The Old Testament must be interpreted by the New Testament. In principle it is quite possible that the prophecies addressed originally to literal Israel describing physical blessings have their fulfillment exclusively in the spiritual blessings enjoyed by the church. It is also possible that the Old Testament expectation of a kingdom on earth could be reinterpreted by the New Testament altogether of blessings in the spiritual realm.[24]

This statement speaks of the *reinterpretation* of physical blessings into spiritual blessings. It means storyline change and aligns with a Spiritual Vision perspective that sanctions the spiritualizing of physical blessings. Ladd also said, "The fact is that the New Testament frequently interprets

---

21   Ibid.

22   J. Richard Middleton, "The Bible's Best Kept Secret," https://jrichardmiddleton.wordpress.com/author/jrichardmiddleton/page/53/ October 29, 2014. Accessed 2/12/2020.

23   Ladd, *A Theology of the New Testament*, 682.

24   George E. Ladd, "Revelation 20 and the Millennium," *Review and Expositor* 57 (1960): 167. Ladd believed some Old Testament prophecies could still have some relevance to Israel. See Ladd, "Historic Premillennialism," in *The Meaning of the Millennium*, 28–29.

Old Testament prophecies in a way *not suggested by the Old Testament context.*"[25] So he believed in strong discontinuity between the testaments. The New Testament changed the storyline of the Old Testament, which is a Spiritual Vision Model belief.

Also, consistent with Spiritual Vision Model thinking, Ladd said that Old Testament prophecies could be radically reinterpreted from their original context. Concerning Peter's understanding of Jesus' ascension in Acts 2, Ladd said: "This involves a rather *radical reinterpretation* of the Old Testament prophecies, but no more so than the entire reinterpretation of God's redemptive plan by the early church."[26] Such language escalates matters toward the Spiritual Vision Model by claiming that both Old Testament prophecies and God's redemptive plan are subject to "radical reinterpretation." It sounds like Ladd is saying the entire storyline from the Old Testament is being radically reinterpreted by the New Testament.

EVALUATION OF LADDIAN HISTORIC PREMILLENNIALISM

Ladd's beliefs on Premillennialism, resurrection of the body, and eternity on a tangible restored earth are commendable and consistent with the New Creation Model. But Ladd's emphasis on Old Testament physical promises being spiritualized and God's redemptive plan being radically reinterpreted are consistent with a Spiritual Vision approach. So, too, are his supersessionist views on Israel and the church. We disagree with George Ladd when he states that the "nationalistic elements in the Jewish concept of the kingdom" are done away with "to lay stress on the spiritual elements."[27] In reality, there is no contradiction between the kingdom involving Jewish and spiritual elements. Both can exist.

Ladd's concept of reinterpretation of the Old Testament also is concerning. Not only does this abruptly change the Bible's storyline, but

---

25   Ladd, "Historic Premillennialism," 20. Emphasis in original.

26   Ladd, *A Theology of the New Testament*, 373. Emphasis mine.

27   George E. Ladd, *The Presence of the Future* (Grand Rapids: Eerdmans, 1974), 110–11.

it also casts doubt on the integrity of the Old Testament. In response to George Ladd's declaration that the New Testament reinterprets the Old Testament, Paul Feinberg asks some relevant questions: "If Ladd is correct that the NT reinterprets the OT, his hermeneutic does raise some serious questions. How can the integrity of the OT text be maintained? In what sense can the OT really be called a *revelation* in its original meaning?"[28]

In sum, Ladd's version of Historic Premillennialism is a mix of the Spiritual Vision Model and the New Creation Model. As we will now discuss, there are two other forms of Premillennialism more consistent with New Creationism.

NON-LADDIAN HISTORIC PREMILLENNIALISM

Another variation of Historic Premillennialism exists, one that does not reinterpret the Old Testament or exclude national Israel and Israel's land from the Bible's storyline. This version of Historic Premillennialism is found with some premillennialists prior to the twentieth century. As Barry Horner observes:

> George Ladd is often upheld today as the quintessential historic premillennialist, although I seriously question his representative status in this regard. I would maintain that earlier premillennialists being more Judeo-centric, better qualify as being characteristic of historic premillennialism. They would include Joseph A. Seiss, David Barton, Adolph Safir, B. W. Newton, H. Grattan Guinness, J. C. Ryle, C. H. Spurgeon, George Peters, Nathaniel West, and Horatius Bonar. As such, they were far more historic in the accepted sense of that term when their lineage is traced back at least to the millennial awakening originating in Protestant England and Europe.[29]

28 Paul Feinberg, "Hermeneutics of Discontinuity," in *Continuity and Discontinuity: Perspectives on the Relationship Between the Old and New Testaments*, ed. John S. Feinberg (Wheaton, IL: Crossway, 1988), 116. Emphases in original.

29 Barry E. Horner, *Future Israel*, 180.

Horner himself is a premillennialist in the line of Ryle, Spurgeon, Peters, West, and the others mentioned above. He is a modern historic premillennialist who disagrees with Laddian Historic Premillennialism on key areas.

It is hard to label this form of Historic Premillennialism, but we can call it "Non-Laddian Historic Premillennialism." A non-Laddian form of Historic Premillennialism is different from Laddian Historic Premillennialism in two main ways:

1. it does not reinterpret or spiritualize Old Testament promises and prophecies but interprets them literally.

2. it affirms the significance of ethnic/national Israel and Israel's land in God's purposes.

A full discussion of non-Laddian Historic Premillennialism is beyond our purposes here. I recommend Horner's Book, *Future Israel*, for more on this topic. But we note a few examples of people who held this form of Premillennialism.

The Reformed English preacher, J. C. Ryle (1816–1900), was a historic premillennialist who affirmed a literal restoration of national Israel to the land by taking Old Testament prophecies at face value. Ryle said:

> Time would fail me, if I attempted to quote all the passages of Scripture in which the future history of Israel is revealed. Isaiah, Jeremiah, Ezekiel, Hosea, Joel, Amos, Obadiah, Micah, Zephaniah, Zechariah all declare the same thing. All predict, with more or less particularity, that in the end of this dispensation the Jews are to be restored to their own land and to the favor of God. I lay no claim to infallibility in the interpretation of Scripture in this matter. I am well aware that many excellent Christians cannot see the subject as I do. I can only say, that to my eyes, the future *salvation* of Israel as a people, their *return* to Palestine and their national conversion

to God, appear as clearly and plainly revealed as any prophecy in God's Word.[30]

Significantly, Ryle viewed the salvation of Israel and Israel's restoration to the land as being as clear and plain as anything revealed in the Bible. He also said:

> I believe that the Jews shall ultimately be gathered again as a separate nation, restored to their own land, and converted to the faith of Christ, after going through great tribulation (Jer. 30:10–11; 31:10; Rom. 11:25–26; Dan. 12:1; Zech. 13:8–9).[31]

Charles Spurgeon was also a historic premillennialist who included the significance of national Israel on the earth. This belief is seen in his 1864 sermon, "The Restoration and Conversion of the Jews":

> There will be a native government again; there will again be the form of a body politic; a state shall be incorporated, and a king shall reign. Israel has now become alienated from her own land.... If there be anything clear and plain, the literal sense and meaning of this passage [Ezekiel 37:1–10]—a meaning not to be spirited or spiritualized away—must be evident that both the two and the ten tribes of Israel are to be restored to their own land, and that a king is to rule over them.[32]

Spurgeon also spoke on the nature and extent of Jesus' millennial reign on earth according to Psalm 72:8:

> Wide spread shall be the rule of Messiah; only Land's End shall end his territory: to the Ultima Thule shall his scepter be extended. From Pacific to Atlantic, and from Atlantic to Pacific, he shall be Lord, and

---

30 J. C. Ryle, *Are You Ready For The End Of Time?* (Fearn, Scotland: Christian Focus, 2001), 152–54.; reprint of *Coming Events and Present Duties.* Ryle's views on a new earth in eternity are currently unclear.

31 Ibid., 9.

32 Charles H. Spurgeon, "The Restoration and Conversion of the Jews," in *The Metropolitan Tabernacle Pulpit,* 10:426.

the oceans which surround each pole shall be beneath his sway. All other power shall be subordinate to his; no rival nor antagonist shall he know. ... As Solomon's realm embraced all the land of promise, and left no unconquered margin; so shall the Son of David rule all lands given him in the better covenant, and leave no nation to pine beneath the tyranny of the prince of darkness. We are encouraged by such a passage as this to look for the Saviour's universal reign; whether before or after his personal advent we leave for the discussion of others. In this Psalm, at least, we see a personal monarch, and he is the central figure, the focus of all glory; not his servant, but himself do we see possessing the dominion and dispensing the government. [33]

Spurgeon's concept of Jesus' kingdom is New Creation Model-like since he spoke of Jesus' reign involving territories between the Pacific and Atlantic oceans. As an expert on the eschatology of Spurgeon, Dennis Swanson observes, "He [Spurgeon] believed that nations would exist in the millennium with their own kings and leaders, but that all would be subject to Christ and His government in Jerusalem."[34]

EVALUATION OF NON-LADDIAN HISTORIC PREMILLENNIALISM

Non-Laddian Historic Premillennialism ranks high on the New Creation Model scale. This is based on its beliefs in Premillennialism, a literal view of Old Testament prophecy, and an accurate view of national Israel and Israel's land in the Bible's storyline. While non-Laddian historic premillennialists are not as clear on the nature of eternity, it appears that they lean towards a tangible new earth in the Eternal State.

---

33 Charles H. Spurgeon, *The Treasury of David: An Expositional and Devotional Commentary on the Psalms*, 7 vols. (reprint of 1870–1884 Passmore and Alabaster ed., Grand Rapids: Baker, 1977), 3:319.

34 Dennis Swanson, "The Millennial Position of Spurgeon," *The Master's Seminary Journal* 7.2 (Fall 1996): 197.

DISPENSATIONAL PREMILLENNIALISM

Dispensational Premillennialism is a form of Premillennialism that began in the mid-nineteenth century. Premillennialism was taught in the first century, and important elements of Dispensational Premillennialism existed in the early church. But as a system it came together in the mid-nineteenth century.

Dispensational Premillennialism is a holistic theological approach that sees multiple purposes in God's creation, kingdom, and covenantal plans. God's purposes include but go beyond the salvation of individual humans. They include the earth, land, earth's creatures, nations, Israel, etc. God's purposes also involve strategic events such as a future seventieth week of Daniel, the Day of the Lord, the return of Jesus to earth, and an earthly kingdom reign of the Messiah.

This perspective also accounts for the multiple dimensions of the biblical covenants—Noahic, Abrahamic, Mosaic, Davidic, and New. These covenants include blessings for individuals, the nation Israel, and Gentile nations. The covenants also involve spiritual and material blessings. Dispensational Premillennialism emphasizes "kingdom" as a primary theme of Scripture. God has destined man to rule and subdue the earth and its creatures for God's glory. This kingdom theme connects Genesis 1–2 with Revelation 20–22.

Dispensational Premillennialism is well known for its view that corporate, national Israel remains significant in God's purposes. This involves a coming salvation and restoration of Israel with spiritual, physical, and land blessings in the coming millennial kingdom of Jesus. It also holds to a distinction between Israel and the church and a New Testament origin of Jesus' church. Dispensational Premillennialism also rejects any forms of replacement theology or supersessionism which see the church as the new or true Israel that makes national Israel's theological significance void.

Thus, the scope of Dispensationalism is broad and multi-dimensional. As Blaising states, "Dispensationalism is known for its recognition of multiple purposes in divine redemption. These include earthly, national, political, social, and spiritual purposes."[35]

Concerning the timing and nature of the Millennium of Revelation 20, Dispensational Premillennialism affirms the following:

1. The Millennium of Revelation 20 will be fulfilled after the second coming of Jesus but before the Eternal Kingdom of Revelation 21–22. (Thus, Jesus' coming is "pre" or "before" the Millennium).

2. The Millennium is an earthly kingdom of the Messiah and His saints.

3. The Millennium involves a reign of the Messiah (Jesus) *from* and *over* the earth and the nations; this fulfills the kingdom mandate for man to rule and subdue the earth (see Gen. 1:26, 28).

4. The Millennium involves a transformation of the earth, the animal realm, society, and culture.

5. Ethnic/national Israel has a geographical and functional role to the nations during Messiah's reign.

6. The Millennium fulfills all the spiritual/physical/land/ earth dimensions of the covenants of promise (i.e., Abrahamic, Davidic, New).

7. The Eternal State, after the Millennium, involves a real, tangible planet, whether a restoration of the current earth or an entirely new planet.

Concerning Bible interpretation, Dispensational Premillennialism believes in consistent literal-grammatical-historical interpretation to

---

35 Craig A. Blaising and Darrell L. Bock, *Progressive Dispensationalism* (Grand Rapids: Bridgepoint Books, 1993), 46.

all passages of Scripture. This includes Old Testament prophetic passages about Israel. Since curses for disobedience literally happened to national Israel, promises of future blessings for Israel must occur someday. Dispensational Premillennialism believes that Old Testament prophecies about the restoration of national Israel will be fulfilled in their entirety in the coming millennial kingdom of Jesus. Thus, this view believes in continuity concerning Old Testament expectations and New Testament fulfillments.

Leading dispensationalists include John Walvoord, Charles Ryrie, Dwight Pentecost, Alva J. McClain, Robert Saucy, Craig Blaising, and Darrell Bock.

EVALUATION OF DISPENSATIONAL PREMILLENNIALISM

Dispensational Premillennialism is consistent with the New Creation Model. It affirms that Jesus' kingdom must be an earthly kingdom over nations. His kingdom transforms all aspects of society and culture, along with earth and all its creatures. Dispensational Premillennialism also embraces the significance of ethnic/national Israel in God's purposes and the blessings this brings to other geo-political nations. It avoids the spiritualization of Israel. Jesus' role as the ideal Israelite and Son means the salvation and restoration of national Israel, not its non-significance. Dispensational Premillennialism also affirms a tangible new earth with real culture and social interactions among God's people.

More will be discussed concerning Dispensationalism in our section on theological systems.

OBJECTIONS AGAINST PREMILLENNIALISM

Premillennialism often has been accused of being a one-text view. Allegedly, if not for Revelation 20 there is no support for Premillennialism. But as we discuss elsewhere in this book, the heart of Premillennialism is the belief that there will be a coming kingdom reign of the Messiah from and over the earth after Jesus' return. This is taught in several passages (see Isaiah 24; Zechariah 14; Matthew 24). What is new in Revelation 20 is the specific mention of a thousand years concerning this kingdom reign. Without Revelation 20 we would still know from the Bible that there will be a coming kingdom reign of Jesus on the earth. What we would not know is how long this kingdom lasts before the Eternal Kingdom starts. Floyd Hamilton was a critic of Premillennialism. But he acknowledged that a literal hermeneutic applied to Old Testament prophecies results in Premillennialism:

> Now we must frankly admit that a literal interpretation of the Old Testament prophecies gives us just such a picture of an earthly reign of the Messiah as the premillennialist pictures. That was the kind of Messianic kingdom that the Jews of the time of Christ were looking for, on the basis of a literal interpretation of the Old Testament promises.[36]

Premillennialism sometimes is criticized for not being spiritual enough. Previously a premillennialist, Augustine came to believe that the premillennial view was too carnal with its focus on earthly realities and matters like food and drink. Even today, some believe Jesus' kingdom can only be a spiritual kingdom. Kim Riddlebarger states, "The kingdom of God, therefore, is not a place of locality in this world...."[37] He also says, "What we do find in the Gospel accounts was Jesus' proclamation that *a spiritual and nonnationalistic kingdom* had drawn near because he had come."[38]

These criticisms are based on Spiritual Vision Model assumptions with an anti-material bias. If God's purposes are creational, then why wouldn't Jesus' kingdom impact creation? Passages like Isaiah 2, 11, and 65 discuss the physicality of Messiah's kingdom. Jesus himself spoke of

---

36   Floyd E. Hamilton, *The Basis of Millennial Faith* (Grand Rapids: Eerdmans, 1942), 38.

37   Kim Riddlebarger, *A Case for Amillennialism: Understanding the End Times* (Grand Rapids: Baker, 2003), 110.

38   Ibid., 107. Emphases not in original.

banquets associated with the kingdom of Heaven (see Matt. 8:11). An earthly kingdom can contain spiritual characteristics like peace, joy, and righteousness. The claim that Premillennialism cannot be true because it is too carnal or physical is not impressive.

SUMMARY COMMENTS ON PREMILLENNIALISM

Premillennialism is compatible with a New Creation Model approach. It is consistent with God's creational and kingdom purposes stemming from Genesis 1. The earth is man's destiny. God tasked the first man, Adam, with a mandate to rule and subdue the world (see Gen. 1:26–28). This involves a mediatorial rule of man *from* and *over* the earth. Premillennialism asserts that Adam failed this mission, but Jesus, the Last Adam, will succeed where the first Adam failed. The successful kingdom of Jesus the Messiah is not just a spiritual kingdom. It is a tangible earthly kingdom that affects all realms of God's creation.

Premillennialism's emphasis on a future earthly kingdom of Jesus links God's creational purposes with the restoration of all things. It also sees the transformation of earth as taking place directly under the reign of the Messiah in history before the final Eternal State.

21

AMILLENNIALISM
AND THE MODELS

◆

O ur purpose in this chapter is to evaluate how the millennial view of Amillennialism relates to the New Creation and Spiritual Vision models.

Amillennialism believes Jesus' millennial kingdom is *spiritual in nature* and *now concerning its timing.* The reign of Jesus is a spiritual kingdom in this age between His first and second advents. Jesus currently reigns in His messianic/millennial kingdom from the right hand of God in Heaven, which also is associated with David's throne. And Satan is bound, not with imprisonment, but from deceiving the nations in this age. The earliest amillennialists believed the "thousand years" of Revelation 20 to be close to a literal thousand years. More recent amillennialists view the thousand years as figurative for a long period of time.

Whether by reigning over the church, the hearts of His people, deceased souls in Heaven, or a combination of these, amillennialists view Jesus as reigning over a spiritual kingdom from Heaven. When Jesus returns to earth this Millennium will end. Then there will be a general judgment and resurrection of all people followed by the Eternal Kingdom.

The following beliefs of Amillennialism are relevant to the two models:

+ Jesus currently reigns in His messianic/millennial kingdom from Heaven; the place of His rule is Heaven.

+ Jesus' millennial kingdom is a spiritual kingdom between His two comings—it is not an earthly kingdom.

    ✦ Jesus' second coming brings an end to His millennial kingdom and ushers in the Eternal State.

AN EXAMPLE OF THE DEBATE

Examining Amillennialism's connections to the New Creation and Spiritual Vision models is complex. This topic was debated by Craig Blaising (premillennialist) and Robert Strimple (amillennialist) in the debate book, *Three Views on the Millennium and Beyond*.[1] Russell Moore also tackled this issue of Amillennialism and the two models in his book, *The Kingdom of Christ*.[2] Blaising claims Amillennialism is reliant on Spiritual Vision Model assumptions which led to a rejection of Premillennialism and the spiritualization of Jesus' millennial kingdom:

> Ancient Christian premillennialism weakened to the point of disappearance when the spiritual vision model of eternity became dominant in the church. A future kingdom on earth simply did not fit well in an eschatology that stressed personal ascent to a spiritual realm.[3]

Blaising claims Spiritual Vision Model assumptions were behind Augustine's turn from Premillennialism to Amillennialism and his view that the Millennium of Revelation 20:1–10 is being fulfilled spiritually in this age with the church.[4] Blaising also asserts that Premillennialism thrives in an environment when New Creation Model thinking and a more literal approach to Scripture are emphasized. With Premillennialism, kingdom promises are taken more literally and physical dimensions of the kingdom are considered. When critiquing the amillennialist, Robert Strimple, Blaising referred to Strimple's "vacillation between these two eschatological models...."[5]

---

1   Blaising, "Premillennialism" in *Three Views on the Millennium and Beyond*, 170–74.

2   Russell L. Moore, *The Kingdom of Christ* (Wheaton, IL: Crossway, 2004).

3   Blaising, 170.

4   Ibid., 172–74.

5   Blaising, "A Premillennial Response to Robert B. Strimple," in *Three Views on the Millennium and Beyond*, 144.

Strimple countered Blaising's claim that Amillennialism is tied to the Spiritual Vision Model by asking, "What evidence does he [Blaising] offer, for example, to support the alleged link between early amillennial thought and Greek philosophical dualism?"[6] Strimple said "no evidence is offered to support the idea that such a bias is present in *modern* amillennialism."[7] In addition, "When we read modern amillennialists themselves, do we find them expressing a purely 'spiritual' (i.e. nonphysical) eschatological hope? Not at all."[8] He then listed amillennial theologians with a "more earth-oriented vision" of eschatology including Herman Bavinck, Geerhardus Vos, Anthony Hoekema, and Greg K. Beale.[9]

Strimple also argued that dispensationalists are inconsistent on this issue. Earlier dispensational premillennialists like Darby, Scofield, and Chafer drew upon Spiritual Vision Model ideas at times, as even Blaising admits. Thus, according to Strimple, "the fact remains that historically the link between the new creation model and premillennialism has not been as clear and strong as his [Blaising's] thesis implies."[10]

Strimple's rebuttal to Blaising focused on three points. First, early amillennial thought was not linked to Greek dualism. Second, recent amillennial theologians believe in a coming tangible new earth after the Millennium in the Eternal State. Third, dispensational premillennialists also have used Spiritual Vision Model ideas.

As this interaction between Blaising and Strimple shows, debate exists concerning Amillennialism's relationship to the New Creation and Spiritual Vision models. Considering what Blaising and Strimple have asserted, I now offer my own observations.

---

6   Robert L. Strimple, "An Amillennial Response to Craig A. Blaising," in *Three Views on the Millennium and Beyond*, 257.

7   Ibid., 258–59. Emphasis in original.

8   Ibid., 259.

9   Ibid., 259–60.

10   Ibid., 261.

AMILLENNIALISM'S CONNECTIONS
WITH THE SPIRITUAL VISION MODEL

Amillennialism has connections with both models, and yet sides with key aspects of the Spiritual Vision Model.

INFLUENCE OF PLATONISM AND
ALLEGORICAL HERMENEUTICS

Premillennialism was the dominant millennial view of the first two centuries of church history. Growing skepticism of Premillennialism from those like Origen and Eusebius eventually led to Amillennialism as a specific alternative view in the later fourth century.

The influence of Platonism and the use of allegorical interpretation in the third and fourth centuries contributed to the rise of Amillennialism. Origen, with his Platonist views, criticized Premillennialism's emphasis on physical realities with Jesus' millennial kingdom and he opted for a more spiritual and individual view. As Middleton notes: "Origen's Platonism led him to critique the earthly, physicalistic elements of the millennial hope" because "the kingdom of God is progressively established within the believer's soul. ..."[11] Eusebius, too, was significant:

> While several Christian writers of the second and third centuries affirm the millennium and grant it an important role in their eschatology, it is rejected with great scorn both by Origen (in the third century) as a Jewish and overly literal interpretation of Scripture and by Eusebius (in the fourth century) in his renowned *Ecclesiastical History* as "materialistic."[12]

---

11   Middleton, *A New Heaven and a New Earth*, 286. Origen also understood kingdom texts in the Bible "in a purely spiritual, interior, private and realized sense." Benedict T. Viviano, O.P. *The Kingdom of God in History*, 41.

12   Middleton, 286.

Augustine, who popularized Amillennialism,[13] was influenced by Neoplatonism. B. B. Warfield observed, "It was as a Neoplatonist thinker that Augustine became a Christian; and he carried his Neoplatonic conceptions over into Christianity with him."[14] Explicitly linking Augustine's eschatology with the Spiritual Vision Model, Moore says, "'spiritual vision' eschatology is firmly anchored in Augustine's role as 'the father of Reformed eschatology.'"[15] Viviano also links Augustine's spiritual views of the kingdom of God with Origen's spiritual interpretation:

> Thus Augustine was attracted to the spiritual interpretation of the kingdom we have already seen in Origen. Indeed, ultimately for Augustine, the kingdom of God consists in eternal life with God in heaven. That is the *civitas dei*, the city of God, as opposed to the *civitas terrena*.[16]

Returning to the disagreement between Blaising and Strimple, Blaising is correct that Amillennialism is linked with Spiritual Vision Model thinking. Acceptance of Neoplatonism and allegorical hermeneutics set the stage for Amillennialism. Strimple is right that modern Amillennialism is more consistent with the New Creation Model than earlier Amillennialism. But Amillennialism's origins were linked with Spiritual Vision Model ideas.

JESUS' SPIRITUAL KINGDOM

Amillennialism asserts that Jesus' millennial kingdom is a spiritual kingdom—a spiritual reign over a spiritual realm. The influential amillennialist, Louis Berkhof, for example, stated, "The spiritual kingship of Christ is His royal rule over the *regnum gratiae*, that is over His people or the

---

13 "Augustine is usually, and rightly, identified as the father of the amillennialist interpretation of Revelation 20." Michael Williams, "A Restorational Alternative to Augustinian Verticalist Eschatology," 11.

14 Benjamin Breckinridge Warfield, *Calvin and Augustine* (Presbyterian & Reformed, 1974), 369.

15 Moore, *The Kingdom of Christ*, 51. Moore agrees with Poythress and Michael Williams.

16 Viviano, *The Kingdom of God in History*, 52–53.

Church. It is a spiritual kingship, because it relates to a spiritual realm."[17] It also is a rule over hearts: "It is the mediatorial rule as it is established in the hearts and lives of believers."[18]

This heavily spiritual view of Jesus' kingdom is detected by Moore who says Berkhof "emphasized the present kingship of Christ, and articulated this reign in decidedly spiritual and soteriological terms."[19] Noting a point of philosophical similarity between Berkhof and Plato, McClain claims, "If Plato were living today, giving a series of lectures on the millennial question, he might very well employ the same language as Berkhof ...."[20]

A similar spiritual understanding of the kingdom more recently occurs with Kim Riddlebarger, in his book, *A Case for Amillennialism*:

> The kingdom of God is a real, though *nonspatial*, rule of God.[21]

> Jesus spoke of a *different kingdom*, where God would bring deliverance from humanity's true enemy, the guilt and power of sin. Because Jesus *did not offer the economic, political, and nationalistic kingdom* so many in Israel longed for, he was put to death.[22]

> What we do find in the Gospel accounts was Jesus' proclamation that *a spiritual and nonnationalistic kingdom* had drawn near because he had come.[23]

> Jesus' kingdom was *a spiritual kingdom, completely unlike the nationalistic kingdom which Israel expected.* This should also be a caution to

---

17   Berkhof, *Systematic Theology*, 406.

18   Ibid.

19   Moore, 45. Moore notes Berkhof's significance as "arguably the most influential American Reformed theologian of the twentieth century" (97).

20   McClain, *The Greatness of the Kingdom*, 523. McClain acknowledges "that Dr. Berkhof is not basically a Platonist in his philosophy" overall, but on the issue of the nature of the millennial kingdom of Jesus his similarity to the Greek philosopher is notable (524).

21   Kim Riddlebarger, *A Case for Amillennialism: Understanding the End Times* (Grand Rapids: Baker, 2003), 104. Emphases not in original.

22   Ibid., 106. Emphases not in original.

23   Ibid., 107. Emphases not in original.

those who would see Jesus' kingdom in terms of nationalism or secular progress in economics, politics, and culture.[24]

The kingdom of God, therefore, is *not a place of locality in this world* …[25]

Put together, Riddlebarger claims that the Kingdom of God: (1) is non-spatial; (2) does not include economic, political, and nationalistic elements; (3) is spiritual; and (4) does not involve progress in economics, politics, and culture. These assertions are consistent with a Spiritual Vision approach. Riddlebarger does affirm a coming future consummation of the kingdom. But like Berkhof, his discussion of what this concerns is scant. In his section, "The Future Consummation of the Kingdom," Riddlebarger does not mention any physical aspects of the kingdom.[26] His overwhelming emphasis concerns the spiritual nature of God's kingdom.

Bruce Waltke also describes the kingdom of God in a spiritualized way that could have hints of Neoplatonism:

> With the transformation of Christ's body from an earthly physical body to a heavenly spiritual body, and with his ascension from the earthly realism to the heavenly Jerusalem with its heavenly throne and the outpouring of his Holy Spirit, the earthly material symbols were done away and the spiritual reality portrayed by the symbols superseded the shadows.[27]

Waltke also says, "the kingdom's character is 'heavenly' and 'spiritual,' not 'earthly' and "political."[28] These comments coincide with the Spiritual Vision Model.

---

24   Ibid., 109. Emphases not in original.

25   Ibid., 110. Emphases not in original.

26   Ibid., 111.

27   Bruce Waltke, "Kingdom Promises as Spiritual," in *Continuity and Discontinuity*, 282. Waltke says, "…the land promise will be consummated in the future new heaven and new earth (168)." Bruce K. Waltke, *An Old Testament Theology: An Exegetical, Canonical, and Thematic Approach* (Grand Rapids: Zondervan Academic, 2007), 168.

28   Waltke, "Kingdom Promises as Spiritual," 270.

Amillennialism's spiritual view of Jesus' kingdom is hard to harmonize with the many passages that link Messiah's kingdom with the transformation of earth (see Psalm 72; Isaiah 11; Zechariah 14; Matthew 19:28). With Messiah's kingdom the earth and nations are restored. The curse on creation is removed. The animal kingdom is healed. Disease is wiped out. Those are powerful aspects of Messiah's kingdom that exist alongside the spiritual salvation of people. These are missing in the amillennial understanding of Jesus' messianic kingdom. Yes, some modern amillennialists believe in a coming restored earth after the Millennium, but that is not the point here. The issue is the nature and scope of Jesus' millennial kingdom in which He rules directly. Amillennialism stands alone among millennial views in seeing Jesus' messianic/millennial kingdom as only spiritual when the Bible presents it as much more than that. On this point, Amillennialism is connected with the Spiritual Vision Model.

HERMENEUTIC OF SPIRITUALIZATION

The New Creation Model is against the spiritualizing of tangible realities. But spiritualization of tangible entities often occurs with Amillennialism. Concerning Old Testament prophecies, Louis Berkhof stated that, "the books of the [OT] prophets themselves already contain indications that point to a spiritual fulfillment."[29] Kim Riddlebarger claims the New Testament can "spiritualize" Old Testament passages: "If the New Testament writers *spiritualize* Old Testament prophecies by *applying them in a nonliteral sense*, then the Old Testament passage must be seen in light of that New Testament interpretation, not vice versa."[30] Waltke acknowledges that amillennialists rely upon spiritual interpretation: "Amillennialists differ from dispensational premillennialists in their hermeneutics by calling for a spiritual interpretation of kingdom promises over against 'literalistic'...interpretation of them."[31]

---

29   Berkhof, *Systematic Theology*, 713.

30   Riddlebarger, *A Case for Amillennialism*, 37. Emphases not in original.

31   Waltke, "Kingdom Promises as Spiritual," 272.

Benjamin Merkle, states that "earthly" and "physical" kingdom matters can be transcended and not taken literally: "At times, the prophets are forced to picture the future kingdom in terms that *transcend* the earthly or physical. Therefore, we must not interpret their earthly, physical descriptions in a literal manner."[32] He even appeals to "metaphorical language" for earthly matters: "Prophecy concerning the end of time or the coming of God's kingdom is often written using *metaphorical language*. The prophets often employed earthly imagery to describe a heavenly reality."[33] Merkle also argues for "symbolic interpretation": "There are abundant examples where New Testament authors offer a symbolic interpretation of Old Testament prophecies concerning the nation of Israel."[34]

Even some amillennial theologians who make New Creation Model-like statements sometimes lurch back to a non-literal hermeneutic that leads to Spiritual Vision Model conclusions. Hoekema, for instance, asserted that while "many Old Testament prophecies are indeed to be interpreted literally, many others are to be interpreted in a nonliteral way."[35] This is confusing. Hoekema says we should be literal with some Old Testament prophecies but then says we should be nonliteral with others. This seems arbitrary and inconsistent.

Storms also makes a similar problematic claim. He rightly notes that the Old Testament prophetic hope was both *nationalistic* (involving Israel) and *earthly*:

> The Old Testament prophetic hope was both *nationalistic* (because focused in Israel, the physical descendants of Abraham, Isaac, and Jacob) and *earthly* (because realized in Canaan, the land of promise).[36]

---

32 Merkle, "Old Testament Restoration Prophecies Regarding the Nation of Israel: Literal or Symbolic?" 22. Emphases added.

33 Ibid., 16. See also Alan S. Bandy and Benjamin L. Merkle, *Understanding Prophecy: A Biblical-Theological Approach* (Grand Rapids: Kregel, 2015), 113. Emphases added.

34 Merkle, 23.

35 Anthony A. Hoekema, "Amillennialism," in *The Meaning of the Millennium: Four Views*, ed. R. G. Clouse (Downers Grove, IL: InterVarsity, 1977), 172.

36 Sam Storms, *Kingdom Come: The Amillennial Alternative* (Mentor: Scotland, 2013), 344. Emphases in original.

But while affirming that "earthly" aspects of the Old Testament hope remain, Storms says, "it seems the 'nationalistic' element has disappeared."[37] For Storms the "earthly" part of the Old Testament hope remains but the "nationalistic" element involving Israel does not. Again, this is inconsistent and differs from a New Creation Model approach that affirms the continuing significance of both earthly and nationalistic elements. Passages like Matthew 19:28; Luke 22:30; Acts 1:6; Rom. 11:12, 15, 26–27; and Rev. 7:4–8 reaffirm the significance of Israel as an ethnic/national entity. We have not seen a compelling argument from amillennialists that Old Testament passages about the earth should be taken literally, but passages about Israel should not be understood in a literal way.

In sum, the spiritualizing of tangible realities often seen with Amillennialism is consistent with the Spiritual Vision Model.

EARTHY AMILLENNIALISTS

Not all amillennialists spiritualize physical Old Testament promises to the church or this age. Some have explicitly emphasized fulfillment with a coming, tangible new earth after the Millennium. For example, Herman Bavinck (1854–1921) expressed belief in a coming renewed earth:

> The renewal of creation follows the final judgment. According to Scripture the present world will neither continue forever nor will it be destroyed and replaced by a totally new one. Instead it will be cleansed of sin and re-created, reborn, renewed, made whole.[38]

For Bavinck, this will involve earthly blessings in the future in a way consistent with the New Creation Model:

> Elsewhere he [Jesus] expressly states that the meek will inherit the earth (Matt. 5:5), He pictures future blessedness as a meal at which the guests sit down with Abraham, Isaac, and Jacob (8:11), enjoy

---

37   Ibid., 347. He thinks Ephesians 2 and Galatians 3 support this idea.

38   Herman Bavinck, *Reformed Dogmatics: Holy Spirit, Church, and New Creation*, 4:715.

food and drink (Luke 22:30), eat of the new and perfect Passover (Luke 22:16), and drink of the fruit of the new vine (Matt. 26:29).[39]

Recent decades also have witnessed the rise of amillennialists who believe in a more literal understanding of Old Testament prophetic passages and a literal new earth with physical blessings in eternity. These are "earthy amillennialists," as coined by Vern Poythress. In addition to Poythress, this group of earthy amillennialists includes theologians like Anthony Hoekema and Sam Storms. Concerning a more "earthy" approach to Bible prophecy, Vern Poythress notes that, "amillennialist thinking in particular has experienced some significant developments in the twentieth century."[40] This involves emphasizing prophecies about the earth: "I may make the same point by calling myself 'an earthy amillennialist.' I am 'earthy' in the sense of emphasizing the hope for a new earth that is a renewal of this earth."[41]

Moore notes that amillennialists like Hoekema and Poythress have a connection with the New Creation Model and Dispensationalism as they view the traditional amillennial view of prophetic promises as "bankrupt":

> Hoekema and other modified covenantalists place the future consummation within a "new creation" model of fulfillment in the new earth. In this, they agree not only with progressive dispensationalists but also with classical dispensationalists in finding the older amillennial view of prophetic promises to be biblically bankrupt.[42]

Anthony Hoekema, in particular, brought a fresh perspective to Amillennialism when he affirmed a coming tangible new earth with real culture and activity. In addition to criticizing the usual over-spiritualization

---

39   Ibid., 719. Hans Boersma notes that Abraham Kuyper also held to a coming renewed earth that even included animals: "Kuyper pays careful attention to the future life of animals and of plants and maintains that they, too, will have a place on the new earth." "Blessing and Glory: Abraham Kuyper on the Beatific Vision," in *Calvin Theological Journal* 52:2 (2017): 210.

40   Ibid., 21.

41   Ibid., 23.

42   Moore, *The Kingdom of Christ*, 51.

within traditional Amillennialism, Hoekema offered New Creation Model ideas in his books, *The Bible and the Future* and *Created in His Image*. Hoekema not only affirmed a restored planet earth, but he linked a restored earth with a literal fulfillment of some Old Testament prophecies. For instance, Isaiah 2:1–4 predicts a coming time when nations would live in harmony without war. While amillennialists often have spiritualized Isaiah 2 and see it being fulfilled with the church in this age, Hoekema said: "Only on the new earth will this part of Isaiah's prophecy be completely fulfilled."[43] This is different than the spiritualized view of Strimple who claimed that the Isaiah 2:2–4 prophecy "is being fulfilled *now* as men and women of every tribe on the face of the earth call upon the name of Zion's King and become citizens of 'the Jerusalem that is above....'"[44]

Hoekema also affirmed that Revelation 21 and 22 foretell a coming new earth with real nations and human culture:

> From chapter 22 [of Revelation] we learn that on the new earth the nations will live together in peace...[45]

> Is it too much to say that, according to these verses [Rev 21:24, 26], the unique contributions of each nation to the life of the present earth will enrich the life of the new earth?[46]

The contributions of nations include "the best products of culture and art which this earth has produced."[47] Also, after mentioning realms like "cultural, scientific, educational, and political endeavors," and "technological achievement," Hoekema says, "God will then [on the new earth] be magnified by our culture in ways that will surpass our most fantastic dreams."[48]

---

43   Hoekema, *The Bible and the Future*, 205.

44   Robert B. Strimple, "Amillennialism," in *Three Views on the Millennium and Beyond*, 93. Emphases is in the original.

45   Hoekema, *The Bible and the Future*, 286.

46   Ibid.

47   Ibid.

48   Hoekema, *Created in God's Image*, 95.

With these types of New Creation Model statements, Moore speaks of "Hoekema's adoption of a new creation model."[49]

Poythress, like Hoekema, argues for a renewed earth with a reign over nations that includes peace and prosperity. He also notes the similarity to Premillennialism on this:

> Hope for a new earth thus gives us a picture that is startlingly similar to premillennialism. I believe that Jesus will return bodily to the world, that all people will be judged, and that the earth itself will be renewed. Jesus will reign over the nations and usher in an era of great peace and prosperity.[50]

Poythress is even open to a future for Israel with land implications in a way rarely seen with amillennialists, yet in common with dispensationalists:

> Sympathetic listening between dispensationalists and nondispensationalists may have also opened up room for exploration concerning the future of the Jewish people. As I indicate in the revised edition of my *Understanding Dispensationalists*, I think that earthy amillennialists should find no problem in affirming that all faithful Jews will join with Abraham in inheriting the land of promise and fully enjoying the blessing of God in the new world. Amillennialism should not be understood as disinheriting Jews, but rather affirming the incorporation of Gentiles into the family of promise through their union with Christ. Hence, Gentiles also will share with Jews as coheirs in Christ (Eph. 3:6; Rom. 8:17).[51]

To be clear, Poythress does not assert a unique functional role for Israel in the future, as dispensationalists do, but his mention of Jews inheriting "the land of promise," is noteworthy. He also said, "Faithful Jews will possess

---

49   Moore, 51.

50   Poythress, "Currents within Amillennialism," 23. I have found Hoekema and Poythress to be the amillennialists most clear on the presence of real nations in eternity.

51   Vern Sheridan Poythress, "Currents within Amillennialism," *Presbyterion*, 23–24.

the land of Palestine, as well as the entirety of the renewed earth."[52] These statements are encouraging and close to the New Creation Model. Sam Storms also expressed belief in a literal fulfillment of the land promise: "Indeed, I would argue that the land promise will yet be fulfilled, *literally* and on the *earth*."[53]

So, several recent amillennialists have offered statements consistent with a New Creation Model. Barry Horner notes this positive move with some amillennialists: "Nevertheless ... it is interesting to consider more recently a number of Reformed amillennialists have upheld a version of Blaising's 'New Creation Model.'"[54] He then says, "I believe this is a step in the right direction."[55] We agree.

EARTHY AMILLENNIALISTS' CRITIQUE OF TRADITIONAL AMILLENNIALISM

As we have noted, belief in the fulfillment of prophecies concerning the earth in the Old Testament have not been emphasized by traditional amillennialists. Earthy amillennialists have been at the fore of pointing out this deficiency. Anthony Hoekema admitted:

> All too often, unfortunately, amillennial exegetes fail to keep biblical teaching on the new earth in mind when interpreting Old Testament prophecy. It is an impoverishment of the meaning of these passages to make them apply only to the church or to heaven.[56]

Hoekema not only disagreed with the traditional amillennial interpretations of Old Testament prophecies, but he also viewed such understandings as "an impoverishment of the meaning of these passages."

---

52   Ibid., 23.

53   Storms, *Kingdom Come*, 346. Emphases in original. We are not saying Storms is affirming a restored national Israel with this land.

54   Horner, *Future Israel*, 215–16.

55   Ibid., 216.

56   Hoekema, *The Bible and the Future*, 205–06.

Vern Poythress agrees with Hoekema's assessment concerning traditional amillennial understandings of biblical prophecies. He said, "amillennial thinking of previous centuries often let the fires of eschatological longing grow dim. Amillennialists sometimes spoke *only* of prophecy being fulfilled in the church, paying little attention to the consummate fulfillment of those prophecies in the new earth."[57] Poythress also notes that the heavy emphasis amillennialists often give to a spiritual kingdom in this age has damaged their ability to argue for any kind of earthly fulfillment:

> This has been particularly bad for amillennialists, because it leaves them with no emphasis at all on a distinctively "earthly" character to fulfillment. Dispensationalists have rightly objected to this kind of "spiritualization."[58]

Poythress is correct. It is difficult for amillennialists to strongly stress a spiritual kingdom of Jesus, and even denigrate the idea of an earthly kingdom of Jesus, and then state there will be a physical Eternal Kingdom.

Storms says that taking Old Testament land promises as figurative leads to an impoverished view:

> It seems that the first option, which views the Old Testament land promise as figurative of purely spiritual blessings is an impoverishment of the Old Testament covenant promises. I prefer to think that a glorious *earthly* consummation of the kingdom rule of Christ is yet to occur in fulfillment of the Old Testament promises.[59]

He says that a change is occurring, though: "This has been the perspective of many amillennialists but is fast giving way to a perspective that takes more seriously the importance of the *earth* in God's redemptive purpose."[60]

In sum, earthy amillennialists have noted that Traditional Amillennialism often spiritualized Old Testament prophecies about the

---

57   Poythress, "Currents within Amillennialism," 21. Emphases in original.

58   Vern S. Poythress, *Understanding Dispensationalists* (Phillipsburg, NJ: P&R Publishing, 1987), 47.

59   Storms, *Kingdom Come*, 346–47.

60   Ibid., 346. Emphases in original.

earth. They encourage traditional amillennialists to follow them in a more "earthy" understanding of Bible prophecies.

CONCLUDING THOUGHTS ABOUT AMILLENNIALISM AND THE MODELS

Amillennialism is complex to evaluate when it comes to the New Creation and Spiritual Vision models. Amillennialism certainly has New Creation Model elements. It believes in the goodness of God's creation and the resurrection of the body. Amillennialists believe that Christians should have a positive impact on society and culture. Many recent amillennialists believe in a coming tangible, restored earth after the Millennium. Yet, Amillennialism sides with the Spiritual Vision Model in several key ways.

First, Amillennialism sprouted from Spiritual Vision Model soil. As we documented, Neoplatonism and allegorical interpretation served as the Spiritual Vision soil from which Amillennialism sprouted and grew. Origen and Eusebius were theologians with Spiritual Vision Model beliefs that heavily influenced Augustine and the early amillennialists. Plus, the rise of Amillennialism was a reaction against the New Creation Model view of Premillennialism.

Second, Amillennialism utilizes a hermeneutic of spiritualization for passages concerning Israel and Israel's land.

Third, Amillennialism does not do justice to the primary functional mandate given to man in Genesis 1. With Genesis 1:26, 28 God gives man a kingdom mandate to rule from and over the earth. The amillennial view of Jesus' kingdom does not fulfill this mandate. Instead, it sees a spiritual kingdom from Heaven over a spiritual realm, but this is not what God intended with Genesis 1. The ramifications of this are significant and reveal a fundamental flaw within Amillennialism. In stressing a spiritual kingdom, Amillennialism changes or removes the primary functional task given to man from Genesis 1, which is to "rule" and "subdue" the earth for God's glory. Amillennialism removes the importance of a sustained reign of man/Jesus in the realm where the first Adam was tasked to rule but failed. It weakens the full scope of Jesus' kingdom by making it a spiritual kingdom only. The first Adam was tasked with completing a successful rule from and over the earth, but Amillennialism places the rule of the Last Adam from Heaven over a spiritual kingdom. This introduces an unwarranted change in the Bible's storyline. It is a serious structural flaw of Amillennialism, a flaw that is avoided by the other millennial views of Premillennialism and Postmillennialism. Those two views also believe there are "spiritual" elements of Jesus' messianic/millennial kingdom, but they also rightly believe that Jesus' kingdom transforms the earth, societies, cultures, nations, etc. Where they disagree concerns when this will happen, whether before Jesus' second coming (Postmillennialism) or after Jesus' second advent (Premillennialism). The kingdom of these two views is much more powerful than the kingdom of Amillennialism.

Claims from amillennialists that Jesus can fulfill physical promises on the new earth after the Millennium miss the point. It is the Millennium in which Jesus rules directly from *His* throne and fulfills the earthly kingdom mandate given to man. According to Psalm 2 and 110 the Father sends the Messiah to rule the earth and the nations, a task Jesus *must* fulfill himself before the Eternal Kingdom can begin (see 1 Cor. 15:24–28). When Jesus does this then He hands the kingdom over to the Father. The Last Adam fulfills His task before the Eternal Kingdom begins.

Also, as Poythress noted, amillennialists often have argued so strongly for a spiritual kingdom of Jesus against Premillennialism that their pivot to affirming a tangible new earth can appear weak. Hoekema and Poythress have come across strong here, but most amillennialists do not.

Fourth, while amillennialists are strong on understanding Jesus' role as Savior, they are weaker on Jesus' role as King. For Amillennialism, Jesus as "King" means Jesus bringing salvation and a spiritual kingdom. But while King Jesus does bring spiritual salvation, He also does much more. Jesus' role as King is much broader and deeper. Jesus also reigns as King over geo-political nations on earth. He transforms creation. Jesus is the transformer of society and culture. By making Jesus as King primarily a spiritual matter, Amillennialism misses out on the multiple dimensions of Jesus' role as King.

On a positive note, we acknowledge that the more recent Earthy Amillennialism of theologians like Hoekema, Poythress, and Storms is

a significant improvement over Traditional Amillennialism. Earthy amillennialists assert that Old Testament passages about the earth should be
taken more literally and they see them as needing to be fulfilled in the
future. This is consistent with the New Creation Model.

Yet Earthy Amillennialism still has three weaknesses. First, like
Traditional Amillennialism, it still spiritualizes Jesus' millennial/messianic
kingdom making it about spiritual salvation in this age when Jesus' kingdom is much more than that. Jesus' direct millennial/messianic kingdom
also involves the transformation of all things including earth, the animal
kingdom, Israel, nations, and other matters. We applaud earthy amillennialists for having a more tangible understanding of the Eternal State, but this
view does not detect everything Jesus' kingdom concerns. Jesus' kingdom is
more than spiritual salvation. So on this issue, Earthy Amillennialism still
lags behind Postmillennialism and especially Premillennialism.

Second, while new earth amillennialists commendably understand
Old Testament passages about the earth more literally, they do not take
Old Testament passages about corporate, national Israel literally, even
when corporate Israel is mentioned in the same passages. Storms accurately observed that many Old Testament prophecies involve both *earthly*
and *nationalistic* (i.e., Israel) elements, but he also argued that earthly elements are still relevant while the nationalistic elements are not.[61] But this
is not consistent or biblical. The Bible (and the New Creation Model) treat
both earthly and nationalistic matters seriously and literally. We do not
understand the argument that Old Testament promises about the earth
will be fulfilled literally but promises concerning national Israel will not.
Also, both earthly and national promises about Israel often are mentioned
in the same context (see Isaiah 11; Matt. 19:28).

---

61   Claims that Israel has now been redefined to be the church because of verses such as Romans 9:6,
     Galatians 6:16, or 1 Peter 2:8–9 are not evidence the church is the new Israel. Romans 9:6 and
     Galatians 6:16 are speaking of Christian Jews. They are not redefining Israel or showing that prom-
     ises to national Israel have been transformed. First Peter 2:8–9 is either addressed to believing Jews
     or is showing how people of God language now applies to believing Jews and Gentiles (see Isa.
     19:24–25).

In his book, *New Creation Eschatology and the Land*, Steven James addresses the issue of theologians who affirm a coming tangible new earth but do not believe in the significance of territorial Israel on this earth. James argues that this is inconsistent:

> In examining the manner in which these texts are utilized by new creationists, a logical inconsistency arises between the new creation conceptions and a metaphorical fulfillment of the promise of the particular territory of Israel. The inconsistency involves the practice of new creationists affirming a new earth that corresponds in identity to the present earth while denying an enduring role for the particular portion of territorial Israel as a part of that earth.[62]

James is right that it is inconsistent to promote a "new creation" concept of earth and then assert a "metaphorical fulfillment" concerning Israel and Israel's land. It is best to apply a new creationist approach to both.

Third, by placing the fulfillment of earthly Old Testament passages in the Eternal State, earthy amillennialists (like all amillennialists) disconnect the need for these prophecies to be fulfilled directly by Jesus in His messianic/millennial kingdom, the kingdom promised to the Son by the Father in Psalm 2 and 110. Earthy Amillennialism does not grasp that Jesus has to fulfill these prophecies so that the Eternal Kingdom can begin. As stated earlier, according to 1 Corinthians 15:24, 28, Jesus only hands His kingdom over to the Father *after* Jesus has completed His successful mediatorial reign. This includes the ruling over and transformation of earth, nature, nations, etc. With Revelation 22:1,3, after the Millennium, Jesus and the Father share the same throne in the New Jerusalem, but this is not the direct reign of the Messiah from His throne (see Rev. 3:21).

Of all the views presented in this book, Traditional Amillennialism is most connected with the Spiritual Vision Model and least tied to the New Creation Model. It sprouted from Spiritual Vision Model soil and promoted an over-spiritualized view of God's purposes to the exclusion of

---

all God is accomplishing through Jesus. It also offers the weakest kingdom of Jesus of all the millennial views. Earthy Amillennialism is considerably better than Traditional Amillennialism but still suffers from significant Spiritual Vision Model weaknesses. Overall, Amillennialism contains too many Spiritual Vision Model elements to be a helpful and comprehensive millennial view.

22

POSTMILLENNIALISM
AND THE MODELS

◆

This chapter will examine how the millennial view known as Postmillennialism relates to the New Creation and Spiritual Vision models. As with the previous chapters on Amillennialism and Premillennialism, the intent is not to thoroughly evaluate Postmillennialism, but to examine how this view relates to the two models.

Postmillennialism asserts that Jesus' millennial kingdom occurs at some point after His first coming but before His second coming. Jesus' second coming is "post-millennial" in the sense that Jesus comes "after" the Millennium. Keith Mathison notes that there is some variance amongst postmillennialists concerning when Jesus' millennial kingdom actually begins: "Until recently, most postmillennialists taught that the Millennium would be the last thousand years of the present age. Today, many postmillennialists teach that the millennial age is the entire period of time between Christ's first and second advents."[1]

According to Postmillennialism, Jesus' millennial kingdom is linked with the spread of the Gospel in this age as Jesus reigns from Heaven and the Holy Spirit is working on earth changing lives and more. As hearts and lives are transformed with salvation this eventually leads to a transformation of society and culture. This will take a long time to occur. Using Jesus' parables in Matthew 13, postmillennialists believe God's kingdom

---

1   Keith Mathison, "The Millennial Maze," https://www.ligonier.org/learn/articles/millennial-maze/ n.d. (accessed February 16, 2010).

starts small and then gradually grows and blooms into a pervasive kingdom throughout the earth. The postmillennial view asserts a mass salvation of people before Jesus returns that also involves a transformation of all
aspects of society. As Loraine Boettner states:

> The Millennium to which the Postmillennialist looks forward is thus
> a golden age of spiritual prosperity during this present dispensation,
> that is, during the Church age, and is to be brought about through
> forces now active in the world. It is an indefinitely long period of
> time, perhaps much longer than a literal one thousand years. The
> changed character of individuals will be reflected in an uplifted
> social, economic, political and cultural life of mankind. The world
> at large will then enjoy a state of righteousness such as at the pres-
> ent time has been seen only in relatively small and isolated groups,
> as for example in some family circles, some local church groups and
> kindred organizations.[2]

As this statement shows, Postmillennialism believes Jesus' millennial kingdom is "spiritual" but also involves "an uplifted social, economic, political and
cultural life of mankind." Like Premillennialism, but unlike Amillennialism,
Postmillennialism believes Jesus' millennial kingdom reign is holistic—it impacts all aspects of God's world. But unlike Premillennialism,
Postmillennialism sees the kingdom reign of Jesus occurring between His
two comings. Thus, there will be worldwide salvation and transformation
even though Jesus is in Heaven apart from the earth.

With Postmillennialism, Jesus currently is reigning spiritually from
Heaven on a spiritualized Davidic throne, but His reign impacts the earth.
Millard Erickson notes that a "distinguishing feature of postmillennialism
is its view that the kingdom of God is a present earthly reality, not a future

---

2   Loraine Boettner, "Postmillennialism: Statement of the Doctrine," Grace Online Library, https://
     graceonlinelibrary.org/eschatology/postmillennialism/postmillennialism-statement-of-the-doc-
     trine-by-loraine-boettner/ n.d. (accessed February 16, 2010).

heavenly reality."³ A reign of Jesus from Heaven results in a kingdom of God on earth.

Postmillennialism asserts that when the world is effectively won for Christ, Jesus will then return to a world conquered in His name. Then there is a general resurrection and judgment and entrance into the Eternal State. Kenneth L. Gentry Jr. explains Postmillennialism this way:

> Postmillennialism expects the proclaiming of the Spirit-blessed gospel of Jesus Christ to win the vast majority of human beings to salvation in the present age. Increasing gospel success will gradually produce a time in history prior to Christ's return in which faith, righteousness, peace, and prosperity will prevail in the affairs of people and of nations. After an extensive era of such conditions the Lord will return visibly, bodily, and in great glory, ending history with the general resurrection and the great judgment of all humankind.⁴

Postmillennialism accounts for creation realties such as the dominion mandate of passages like Genesis 1:26, 28 and Psalm 8. As Gentry explains:

> The postmillennialist holds that God's love for his creation prompts his concern to bring it back to its original purpose of bringing positive glory to him. *Thus, the postmillennialist's hope-filled expectation is rooted in creational reality.*⁵

Postmillennialists also appeal to Old Testament kingdom passages such as Psalm 2 and Isaiah 2 which discuss the kingdom of the Messiah with implications for the earth. Postmillennialism is optimistic that Jesus' kingdom in this age will lead to better conditions on earth.

Also, Postmillennialism historically has believed ethnic Israel will be saved at some point. Some Puritan postmillennialists even believed the Millennium could not start until the Jewish people converted to Christ.

---

3   Millard J. Erickson, *Eschatology: A Basic Guide to Eschatology* (Grand Rapids: Baker, 1998), 66.

4   Kenneth L. Gentry Jr., "Postmillennialism," in *Three Views on the Millennium and Beyond*, 13–14.

5   Ibid., 23. Emphases in original.

Below are some key affirmations of Postmillennialism:

+ The Millennium occurs between the two comings of Jesus.

+ Jesus is reigning from Heaven in this age but this reign impacts the earth in many ways.

+ The Millennium starts small but grows in influence until the world is won to Christ and all areas of society are transformed.

+ Jesus' kingdom includes many who are spiritually saved, but it also involves transformation of the world in every way.

+ The Jewish people as a whole will be saved.

+ Jesus' second coming brings an end to the Millennium and then there is a general judgment and resurrection of all people.

+ The Eternal Kingdom begins after the Millennium.

POSTMILLENNIALISM AND THE ETERNAL KINGDOM

Grasping the postmillennial view of Jesus' millennial kingdom is relatively easy. But the same cannot be said for the postmillennial view of the Eternal State. Discerning the postmillennial view of the Eternal State is challenging. In our earlier section on the Puritans we noted that Puritan postmillennialists like Jonathan Edwards had very strong Spiritual Vision Model views of the final Heaven. Edwards stated: "The place of God's eternal residence and the place of the everlasting residence and reign of Christ, and his church, will be heaven, and not this lower world, purified and refined."[6] We also noted that according to Willem van Vlastuin, Edwards did not believe in a recreation of the earth:

---

6   *The Works of Jonathan Edwards*, Vols. 2-4, Revised, ed. Anthony Uyl (Carlisle, PA: The Banner of Truth Trust, 2019), 275. Section 743.

It appears that, as a young tutor, he [Edwards] believed in a material new earth but later, during his ministry, he became convinced that the new heaven and new earth had to be interpreted spiritually. So, in Edwards's view, there is no expectation of a re-creation of earth. The future of the risen saints will not be on a new earth, but in heaven. But Edwards speaks about the destruction of the old heaven, and the renewal of heaven.[7]

With their evaluation of the Puritans, which contained many postmillennialists, McDannell and Lang state that the Puritans were looking for a spiritual heaven, not a material earth:

> The devout meditations of Puritans and other ascetic reformers anticipated a spiritual rather than a material heavenly reality. Heaven for the pious could never be a replica of the existing world. The old Reformation doctrine about the renewed world as a place of life everlasting was abandoned. Even those who predicted a fruitful earth during the millennium returned the righteous to their proper heavenly existence after the end of time. The other life, either immediately after death or after the millennium, freed the saints from the world; it did not continue their existence there.[8]

What do contemporary postmillennialists believe about the Eternal State? There are different understandings. Spiritual Vision Model thinking could exist with Kenneth Gentry's statement we mentioned above that the Lord's return means "ending history."[9] This led Craig Blaising to state that Gentry was holding to the Spiritual Vision Model: "Gentry adheres to

---

7 Willem van Vlastuin, "One of the most difficult points in the bible: An analysis of the development of Jonathan Edwards' understanding of the new heaven and new earth," *Church History and Religious Culture* 98:2 (July 2018): 225.

8 McDannell and Lang, *Heaven*, 172. We acknowledge this statement was not directed solely at postmillennial Puritans.

9 Gentry, 14.

the spiritual vision model of the eternal state."[10] Blaising also said, "Gentry postulates that the Second Advent will bring about the end of history. In his view, the eternal state is so radically different from present conditions that promises of a messianic kingdom could have no fulfillment there."[11]

Gentry also does not believe Revelation 21–22 offers details about eternity beyond the millennial age. He sees the new creation situation of chapters 21–22 as having "a first-century setting."[12] And then declares, "The coming of the new Jerusalem down from heaven (chaps. 21–22) logically should follow soon upon the destruction of the old Jerusalem on the earth (Rev. 6–11, 14–19), rather than waiting thousands of years."[13] When addressing the question, "But what of all the majestic expressions in Revelation 21–22?" Gentry states, "…John is expressing, by means of elevated poetic imagery, the glory of salvation."[14] Significantly, Gentry does not believe Revelation 21–22 offers information about the Eternal State; it is describing our current salvation! Gentry offers no discussion of what eternity after the Millennium will be like. This leaves great questions about the postmillennial view of the Eternal Kingdom and seems to have the postmillennial view swimming in Spiritual Vision Model waters.

But another contemporary postmillennialist believes Revelation 21–22 describes a tangible future for God's people. In reference to these chapters that follow Revelation 20, Keith Mathison states, "Here there is little controversy among Christian interpreters. All agree that this is a vision of the judgment that is to occur at the end of the present age after the second advent of Christ."[15] Concerning Revelation 21:1, Mathison

10   Craig A. Blaising, "A Premillennial Response to Kenneth L. Gentry Jr." in *Three Views on the Millennium and Beyond*, 72.

11   Ibid., 72.

12   Kenneth L. Gentry, Jr., "A Preterist View of Revelation," in *Four Views on the Book of Revelation*, ed. C. Marvin Pate (Grand Rapids: Zondervan, 1998), 87.

13   Ibid.

14   Ibid., 89.

15   Keith A. Mathison, *From Age to Age: The Unfolding of Biblical Eschatology* (Phillipsburg, NJ: P&R Publishing, 2009), 691.

declares, "It is the restoration of the original creation."[16] And concerning Revelation 21:10–11 he says, "Here John sees the fulfillment of God's original goal for creation, the establishment of his kingdom on earth."[17] Mathison's explanation of Revelation 21–22 reveals a more new creationist understanding of eternity than what is seen with other postmillennialists.

It seems that some postmillennialists view Revelation 21–22 as a poetic description of current salvation, while others view these chapters as referring to a future earthly kingdom situation. The latter view is more consistent with the New Creation Model.

POSTMILLENNIALISM AND THE MODELS

How does Postmillennialism relate to the models? Postmillennialism contains both New Creation Model and Spiritual Vision Model elements. In addition to affirming a coming resurrection of the body, Postmillennialism sides with the New Creation Model in asserting that Jesus' millennial kingdom reign involves more than individual salvation and will transform all aspects of the world. This is a holistic approach to Jesus' kingdom since the reign of Jesus impacts all aspects of earth, culture, and society. On this point, Postmillennialism is similar to Premillennialism which also affirms that Jesus' millennial kingdom transforms everything. Whether Postmillennialism is right that this holistic transformation will occur while Jesus is not on earth is another matter. But Postmillennialism believes in a transformation of all aspects of creation, including society and culture as a result of Jesus' kingdom. Also, belief in the future conversion of the Jewish people is a New Creation Model idea found within Postmillennialism. Jonathan Edwards was strong on this point, as are other postmillennialists.

However, Postmillennialism also has Spiritual Vision Model characteristics. The issue of David's throne is one example. The Bible presents the throne of David as an earthly throne in Jerusalem (see Jer. 17:25).

---

16   Ibid., 692.
17   Ibid., 693.

Jesus himself said He would assume David's throne at His second coming to earth when the earth is renewed, the tribes of Israel are restored, and the Gentile nations are judged (see Matt. 19:28; 25:31; Luke 1:32). Postmillennialism, though, spiritualizes the Davidic throne and places it in Heaven in this age, instead of seeing it as related to Jerusalem on earth as the Old Testament and Jesus presented it. Gentry says, "the center of theocratic rule has been transferred to heaven, where Christ presently rules over his kingdom (John 18:36; Rev. 1:5)."[18]

Also, in connection with a spiritualized throne of David, Postmillennialism believes Jesus' Davidic throne *reign* is happening from Heaven in this age. Although Jesus' kingdom affects earth, the locale for this reign allegedly is Heaven. This belief of a kingdom reign from Heaven is more in line with the Spiritual Vision Model since it transfers the place of Messiah's reign from earth to Heaven. Adam's original task was to rule from and over the earth, but Postmillennialism views Jesus' reign as occurring from Heaven. This leads to an awkward, asymmetrical view concerning the place of Jesus' reign and the realm in which this reign occurs. Allegedly, Jesus reigns from Heaven but the realm of the reign is on earth.

Next, many postmillennialists have rightly affirmed a coming salvation of many Jewish people. But they often have taken a supersessionist view stating that the church is the new/true Israel. And they have denied the significance of national Israel's role in the future. Loraine Boettner, in his presentation of Postmillennialism, declared a strong replacement theology view: "It may seem harsh to say that 'God is done with the Jews.' But the fact of the matter is that He is through with them as a unified national group having anything more to do with the evangelization of the world. That mission has been taken from them and given to the Christian Church (Matt. 21:43)."[19]

Most striking, though, is Postmillennialism's understanding of the Eternal State. Jonathan Edwards held no place for earth in his view of

---

18   Gentry, "Postmillennialism," 35.

19   Loraine Boettner, *The Millennium* (Philadelphia: Presbyterian and Reformed, 1957), 89–90.

eternity. Other postmillennialists like Gentry do not believe Revelation 21–22 addresses a restored earth in the future after the Millennium. Instead it allegedly is a poem about salvation. So at best the Scripture says nothing or almost nothing about eternity. Yet there are some like Keith Mathison who believe earth exists in the Eternal State. This is commendable and more consistent with the New Creation Model than what Edwards or Gentry promote. Recognizing the variances within Postmillennialism, overall, it seems Postmillennialism promotes one of the most Spiritual Vision Model-like views of eternity within orthodox Christianity.

Postmillennialism, thus, contains a mixture of the New Creation and Spiritual Vision models.

23

THOUGHTS ON
MILLENNIAL VIEWS
AND THE MODELS

◆

How do the New Creation and Spiritual Vision models relate to Premillennialism, Amillennialism, and Postmillennialism? In our estimation, Premillennialism is most consistent with the New Creation Model, especially Dispensational Premillennialism of the Revised-Progressive variety. Dispensational Premillennialism understands God's kingdom and covenant purposes are broad and multi-dimensional. They include individual salvation from sin but also encompass creational realities such as the earth, land, earth's creatures, animals, etc. They also include the corporate entities of Israel and Gentile nations. Premillennialism asserts that Jesus will fulfill the task first given to Adam to rule and subdue the earth and its creatures for the glory of God.

Premillennialism also offers the most new creation understanding of the Millennium and Eternal State. All premillennialists believe Jesus' millennial kingdom will be a tangible, earthly kingdom that transforms all aspects of the world, including culture, society, and politics. Premillennialism also grasps the importance of geo-political nations, including Israel, in the millennial kingdom. Amillennialism fails on all these areas, making Jesus' Millennium purely a spiritual kingdom. Postmillennialism is close to Premillennialism by also affirming a tangible, earthly millennial kingdom of Jesus, although it sees this happening before Jesus returns. And it sees Jesus ruling over an earthly kingdom from Heaven, which differs from the

Genesis 1:26, 28 expectation in which man was tasked to rule from the earth, not rule the earth from Heaven.

Others have addressed this issue of millennial views and the models. Although himself a premillennialist, Randy Alcorn does not believe rejecting Christoplatonism must make one a premillennialist. He states, "our beliefs about the Millennium need not affect our view of the New Earth."[20] "Hence, no matter how differently we may view the Millennium, we can still embrace a common theology of the New Earth."[21] Snyder, too, believes that a "Future Kingdom" (or New Creation) model of eschatology is not the sole possession of Premillennialism: "It would be misleading, however, to think of the Future Kingdom model as necessarily implying millennialism, for there can be millennial and non-millennial views of the kingdom as future hope."[22] But Snyder does believe Premillennialism best fits a Future Kingdom model: "Of the various millennial views, however, premillennialism seems best to fit the Future Kingdom model because of its insistence that the kingdom cannot come in fullness until the cataclysmic event of the Second Coming."[23] We agree with this assessment.

Concerning the Eternal Kingdom, Premillennialism again is most consistent with the New Creation Model. Revised/Progressive Dispensationalism affirms a tangible new earth with real cultural, societal, and national activities. Although debate exists whether this new earth is a restored version of the current earth (our view) or a brand-new earth, Dispensationalism affirms a tangible earth in eternity. All forms of Historic Premillennialism also seem to affirm a tangible new earth in eternity.

Traditional Amillennialism often has presented a Spiritual Vision Model view of eternity. The empyrean heaven idea was promoted by Aquinas and the medieval scholastics. But Bavinck and more recent amillennialists like Hoekema and Poythress have offered a New Creation Model understanding of eternity with nations and real cultural activities.

---

20   Alcorn, *Heaven*, 146.

21   Ibid.

22   Snyder, *Models of the Kingdom*, 35.

23   Ibid.

Postmillennialism, as a whole, presents the weakest form of the Eternal State, sometimes denying an earthly existence at all (Edwards) or spiritualizing Revelation 21–22 to refer to current salvation. Mathison is one exception within Postmillennialism as he affirms a tangible new earth in eternity.

To summarize, one can be an amillennialist or postmillennialist and hold to elements of the New Creation Model, yet Premillennialism is most in line with a new creationist approach.

PART FIVE

THEOLOGICAL SYSTEMS AND THE MODELS

DISPENSATIONALISM
AND THE MODELS

◆

INTRODUCTION TO THE
THEOLOGICAL SYSTEMS

We have surveyed how the New Creation and Spiritual Vision models relate to the millennial views. Now we shift to how the models connect with the various evangelical theological systems. This is a bigger task since a theological system is broader than a millennial view. As with the millennial views, our task is not to evaluate these systems in their entirety but to evaluate them as they relate to and connect with the New Creation and Spiritual Vision models.

Sometimes theological systems are evaluated on a "continuity-discontinuity" scale. For example, John Feinberg edited the book, *Continuity and Discontinuity: Perspectives on the Relationship between the Old and New Testaments*.[1] This helpful work, with several contributors, contrasted Dispensationalism and Covenant Theology on how each viewed God's plans across the Old and New Testaments. It involved their views on hermeneutics, law, kingdom, people of God, and salvation. Benjamin Merkle also applied the continuity-discontinuity paradigm to various

---

1   John S. Feinberg, ed., *Continuity and Discontinuity: Perspectives on the Relationship between the Old and New Testaments* (Wheaton, IL: Crossway, 1988).

evangelical systems in his book, *Discontinuity to Continuity: A Survey of Dispensational and Covenantal Theologies.*[2]

The continuity-discontinuity spectrum is helpful for evaluating theological systems. Yet the New Creation and Spiritual Vision models offer another way to evaluate the systems. The systems we now address are Protestant Evangelical systems. They include Dispensationalism, Covenant Theology, Progressive Covenantalism, and the New Christian Zionism. This is not an evaluation of all theological systems within Christendom. We do not cover Roman Catholicism, the Eastern Orthodox Church, Liberal Protestantism, etc. These are heavily infected with Spiritual Vision Model thinking. Roman Catholicism has been the primary promoter of a Spiritual Vision approach since the fifth century. It fully embraced Augustinian Amillennialism and an over-spiritualized view of the Beatific Vision. Roman Catholicism eventually adopted Thomas Aquinas's concept of the empyrean heaven which makes Heaven a purely spiritual experience. The other two forms of Christendom also are heavily influenced by Spiritual Vision Model thinking. Theologians within Liberal Protestantism, at times, denied resurrection of the body.

The systems of Dispensationalism, Covenant Theology, and Progressive Covenantalism all present a more biblical approach to God's purposes than do the non-evangelical systems. While these systems at times contain Spiritual Vision Model characteristics, all possess New Creation Model elements. When we claim that an evangelical theological system is operating from Spiritual Vision Model assumptions at times, this does not mean it is a full Spiritual Vision Model system. Also, these systems are vast so we cannot cover all their beliefs. We will, though, make observations concerning how they relate to the Spiritual Vision and New Creation models. We start with Dispensationalism.

---

2   Benjamin L. Merkle, *Discontinuity to Continuity: A Survey of Dispensational and Covenantal Theologies* (Bellingham, WA: Lexham Press, 2020).

INTRODUCTION TO
DISPENSATIONALISM

Dispensationalism is an evangelical theological system that focuses primarily on God's workings in different dispensations, the kingdom of God, biblical covenants, Israel, nations, the church, and the end times. It also promotes a consistent literal interpretation of all Scripture, including Old Testament prophecies and the Book of Revelation. The key theological belief of Dispensationalism is that national Israel remains relevant in God's purposes, and that Israel will be saved and restored with a role to other nations in the coming millennial kingdom of Jesus. Dispensationalism also believes the church is a New Testament entity distinct from Israel, and the church does not replace Israel in God's plans.

Dispensationalism is not a soteriology or salvation system. While dispensationalists certainly hold soteriological views and their importance, individual human redemption is not Dispensationalism's emphasis like it is with Covenant Theology. Dispensationalism is mostly concerned with broader issues related to creation, the kingdom of God, the church, Israel, covenants, and cosmic eschatology.

Like other evangelical systems, Dispensationalism is a post-Reformation development. Many dispensational ideas are found in the early church, but as a *system* Dispensationalism is linked with the teachings of the Anglo-Irish theologian and Plymouth Brethren minister, John Nelson Darby (1800–82).[3] Darby taught that Israel would experience restoration and earthly blessings in a future dispensation that were different from what the church would experience. He argued for a strong distinction between Israel and the church and for two different peoples with different destinies. Darby believed the church would be raptured or snatched to Heaven just prior to the seventieth week of Daniel.

---

3   For a fair and excellent discussion of the life and teachings of Darby see, Paul R. Wilkinson, *For Zion's Sake: Christian Zionism and the Role of John Nelson Darby*, Studies in Evangelical History and Thought (Eugene, OR: Wipf & Stock, 2008).

Early Dispensationalism began in Britain but soon became popular in the United States. Darby and other Brethren ministers brought Dispensationalism to America. Dispensationalism's popularity arose through Bible conferences, books, study bibles, Bible institutes, Bible colleges, the influence of Dallas Theological Seminary (est. 1924), and dispensational radio and television programs.

There are three forms of Dispensationalism—Classical, Revised, and Progressive. These three share the same essential beliefs of Dispensationalism but at times they have differences. Our goal is to focus on the forms of Dispensationalism as they relate to the New Creation and Spiritual Vision models.

CLASSICAL DISPENSATIONALISM

EARTHLY PEOPLE AND HEAVENLY PEOPLE

The era of Classical Dispensationalism began in the mid-nineteenth century with John Nelson Darby and goes through the release of Lewis Sperry Chafer's *Systematic Theology* in the late 1940s.[4] Classical Dispensationalism asserted that there are two peoples of God with different identities and destinies—Israel/Nations and the church. As Blaising notes concerning Classical Dispensationalism, "God was pursuing *two different purposes*, one related to *heaven* and one related to the *earth*."[5] The church related to Heaven while Israel/Nations related to the earth. For example, Darby stated:

> There are two great subjects which occupy the sphere of millennial prophecy and testimony: the church and its glory in Christ; and the Jews and their glory as a redeemed nation in Christ: the heavenly people and the earthly people; the habitation and scene of the glory of the one being the heavens; of the other, earth.... each has its respective

---

4   Some think the latter part of this era could be called Traditional Dispensationalism.

5   Craig A. Blaising and Darrell L. Bock, *Progressive Dispensationalism* (Grand Rapids: Bridgepoint Books, 1993), 23. Emphases in original.

sphere ... angels, principalities, and powers in the one; the nations of the earth in the other.[6]

According to Classical Dispensationalism, there is an earthly people with an earthly destiny. This earthly people consists of saved Israel and Gentiles at the time of Jesus' second coming to earth. They will enter the millennial kingdom on earth and then live on a tangible new earth after the Millennium. Then, there is a *heavenly people* which consists of all believers who died before Jesus' second coming to earth. And this heavenly people includes the church that will be raptured to Heaven. Both deceased Old Testament saints and the raptured church will live forever in Heaven; they will not live with Israel and the Gentile nations on earth. One difference between deceased saints of old and the living church of this age is that the church knows it is a heavenly people with a heavenly destiny.

Since the church is a heavenly people with a heavenly destiny, it should forsake the mundane concerns of earth and focus only on Heaven and spiritual matters. It should not concern itself with earthly or social-political matters. Emphasis should go to spiritual, heavenly, and individual things. As Blaising notes:

> The heavenly nature of the church's salvation was interpreted by classical dispensationalists in an individualistic manner. Political and social issues were *earthly* matters which did not concern the church. ... Issues in the church were individual, private, spiritual matters, not social, political, earthly matters.[7]

Thus, the church's concerns, by nature, were quite different from those of Israel and Gentile nations, as Blaising observes: "The heavenly, individualistic, and spiritual nature of the church could not be more distinct from the earthly, social, and political nature of Israel and Gentile

---

6   John Nelson Darby, *Divine Mercy*, in the *Collected Writings of J. N. Darby*, ed. William Kelly (Kingston-on-Thames: Stow Hill Bible & Tract Depot, n.d.). 34 vols. Vol. 2. 122–23.

7   Blaising and Bock, 26. Emphasis in original.

nations."[8] On this issue of the church being a heavenly people focused only on spiritual things, Classical Dispensationalism was consistent with the Spiritual Vision Model. Yet its views on Israel and Gentile nations at the time of Jesus' return were in line with the New Creation Model. This dualistic view of a heavenly vs. an earthly people was related to a two-fold hermeneutic, which we now discuss.

TWO-FOLD HERMENEUTIC

Classical Dispensationalism implemented a twofold hermeneutic: (1) literal/grammatical-historical *and* (2) typological/spiritual. First, a literal hermeneutic should be applied to national Israel and restoration prophecies concerning Israel. This reveals that Israel is destined for a kingdom of God on earth. But second, a spiritual/typological hermeneutic should be applied for God's spiritual people, including the church. As Blaising observes, "They believed that if the Old Testament were interpreted literally, then it would reveal God's earthly purpose for the earthly people. However, if it were interpreted spiritually (which they usually termed "typologically"), then it would reveal God's spiritual purposes for a spiritual people."[9] Benjamin Merkle also notes the importance of typology for Classical Dispensationalism in addition to a literal hermeneutic: "A foundational presupposition of dispensationalism is a consistent literal hermeneutic.... But in addition to a literal hermeneutic, classic dispensationalism applied typology as a secondary theological observation."[10] Darby followed this approach: "For Darby, the key was to apply a literal hermeneutic to texts related to Israel, whereas texts related to gentiles or the church could also have a secondary typological or symbolic meaning."[11] For example, Darby stated, "First, in prophecy, when the Jewish church or nation ... we may look for a plain and direct testimony, because earthly things were the

---

8   Ibid., 27.

9   Ibid.

10   Merkle, *Discontinuity to Continuity*, 29.

11   Ibid.

Jews' proper portion." But then, "On the contrary, where the address is to the Gentiles, i.e., when the Gentiles are concerned in it, there we may look for symbol, because earthly things were not their portion, and the system of revelation must to them be symbolical."[12]

Thus, at times, Classical Dispensationalism called for a "symbolical" hermeneutic. In doing so, Classical Dispensationalism borrowed from the Spiritual Vision Model interpretation playbook. This dual hermeneutic would be dropped by later forms of Dispensationalism, but it was part of the era of Classical Dispensationalism.

RAPTURE AS A FOREVER HEAVENLY HOPE

Darby taught a pre-tribulational rapture of the church in which the church would be physically snatched to Heaven to escape God's wrath in the Tribulation Period. In his study of the theme of hope in Dispensationalism, Gary Nebeker documented how Darby expressed a Spiritual Vision Model understanding of the rapture. For Darby, the rapture was not just a rescue of the church from God's wrath on earth; it was the gateway to Heaven forever:

> Darby's hope of heavenly glory was not merely the church's hope for deliverance from future wrath by means of the pretribulational rapture, which was for him a necessary preliminary to the fulfillment of Christian hope. Instead, Christians, he said, are to long for the very intimacy of perfected love with Christ in heaven. The rapture, as blessed as that event will be, is but a corridor to the greater ecstasy and bliss of an infinity of agape. [13]

In contrast to Darby, contemporary dispensationalists view the rapture more consistently with the New Creation Model. The rapture is a rescue of the church from the impending wrath of God of the seven-year

---

12   John Nelson Darby, *The Collected Writings*, ed. William Kelly (Oak Park, IL: Bible Truth Publishers, 1962), 2:35. See Merkle, 30.

13   Gary L. Nebeker, "The Theme of Hope in Dispensationalism," in *Bibliotheca Sacra* 158 (January–March 2001): 6.

Tribulation Period. But when Jesus returns to earth seven years later so too does the church. The church will reign with Jesus on earth, over nations, for a thousand years in fulfillment of texts like Revelation 2:26–27 and 3:21. The heavenly destiny of the church after the rapture is only for a short time, followed by a return to earth for a kingdom reign. Thus, the church's evacuation to Heaven is soon followed by an earthly destiny.

But for Darby the church reached its final destiny in Heaven with the rapture. On this point, Darby's understanding of Heaven as the ultimate destiny of the church was similar to the Augustinian understanding, as Nebeker observes:

> Darby was also following an Augustinian eschatological tradition with his description of heaven as a place of perfect love. In this regard little difference existed between Darby's concept of heaven and the perceptions of heaven by his amillennial predecessors.[14]

So the Classic Dispensational view of the rapture tended towards a Spiritual Vision Model approach. But later dispensationalists adopted a more New Creation Model position.

EVALUATION OF CLASSICAL DISPENSATIONALISM

Classical Dispensationalism contains a mixture of Spiritual Vision and New Creation model ideas. Consistent with the New Creation Model, Classical Dispensationalism asserted that believing Israel and believing Gentile nations, alive at the time of Jesus' return, will inhabit the earth of the Millennium and the new earth of the Eternal State. This coincides with the removal of the curse currently on the earth. As Blaising notes concerning Classical Dispensationalism:

> ... [O]ne of God's purposes in redemption was to release the earth from the curse of corruption and decay, and to restore upon it a humanity free from sin and death. This was the earthly purpose of

---

14   Ibid., 7.

God. God will restore permanently the paradise lost in the Fall, granting immortality to earthly humanity. Some writers envisioned these blessings in quite physical terms, including human reproduction to increase the plentitude of the human race.[15]

Belief in national Israel's restoration to the promised land in an earthly kingdom coincides with the New Creation Model. So too is affirmation that saved Gentile nations will be part of the millennial earth. Thus, regarding Israel and the nations at the time of Jesus' return, and Premillennialism, Classical Dispensationalism was consistent with New Creationism. Also, understanding Old Testament restoration prophecies about Israel literally is consistent with New Creationism.

On the other hand, Classical Dispensationalism's idea that the church is a heavenly people with a forever heavenly destiny is more in line with the Spiritual Vision Model. So also is the idea that the rapture results in a forever existence in Heaven apart from earth.

In sum, Classical Dispensationalism has elements of both the Spiritual Vision and New Creation models. While Dispensationalism as a whole is a New Creation Model system, Classical Dispensationalism is the least new creationist approach within this system. Moore noted that progressive dispensationalists of today view Classical Dispensationalism as too closely related to Platonism in some areas.[16]

REVISED DISPENSATIONALISM

Revised Dispensationalism is a form of Dispensationalism of the 1950s through the 1980s. Leading dispensational theologians of this era were John Walvoord, Dwight Pentecost, Charles Ryrie, Alva J. McClain and theologians associated with Dallas Theological Seminary and Grace Theological Seminary. Revised Dispensationalism is still popular and well-represented today.

---

15   Blaising and Bock, 23.

16   Moore, *The Kingdom of Christ*, 44.

Revised Dispensationalism continued the belief of Classical Dispensationalism that saved and restored Israel will reside on the millennial earth alongside Gentile nations based on a grammatical-historical understanding of Old Testament prophecies. This millennial kingdom will involve a transformed society on earth involving social-political matters. However, Revised Dispensationalism dropped the twofold hermeneutic of Classical Dispensationalism. While keeping the literal-grammatical-historical hermeneutic, it left the spiritual/typological part of the classical view.

Also, Revised Dispensationalism abandoned the dualism between earthly people and heavenly people with different destinies. With Revised Dispensationalism, the church will have the same destiny with both Israel and Gentile nations in the Millennium and Eternal State. Many revised dispensationalists also argue that this shared destiny involves earth, not Heaven. Blaising notes:

> The most important revision introduced by the dispensationalists of the '50s and '60s was their abandonment of the *eternal* dualism of heavenly and earthly peoples. They did not believe that there would be an eternal distinction between one humanity in heaven and another on the new earth. Consequently, they mostly dropped the terms *heavenly* and *earthly* peoples.[17]

But some revised dispensationalists kept elements of a Spiritual Vision perspective. While affirming that Israel, nations, and the church would inhabit the millennial earth, some held Heaven (not earth) was the destiny of these groups after the Millennium. Blaising says there are "two different conceptions of eternity in revised dispensationalism."[18] He explains, "Whereas classical dispensationalists placed the heavenly people in heaven and the earthly people on the new earth, revised dispensationalists either placed all the redeemed in 'heaven' or they placed them all on the

---

17   Blaising and Bock, 31.
18   Ibid., 32.

new earth."[19] McClain, Pentecost, and Hoyt were revised dispensational-ists who did the latter. They "envision eternity as resurrection life on the new earth where the city of God is located. For them the promises of an everlasting kingdom on earth are literally fulfilled on the renewed earth."[20] This is consistent with New Creation Model thinking.

But others promoted a more Spiritual Vision Model approach: "Walvoord and Ryrie, although using the terminology of 'new earth', actu-ally work with a more platonic conception of 'heaven' which bears closer relationship to the 'heaven' of classical dispensationalists."[21] Larry Helyer observes how some revised dispensationalists believed the Eternal State will be in Heaven while others believed it will be on earth:

> Another interesting modification emerged in regard to the eternal state. Some revised dispensationalists, such as John Walvoord and Charles Ryrie, held that in the eternal state all the redeemed, whether Israel or the church, reside in heaven. Others such as Alva J. McClain, J. Dwight Pentecost, and Herman Hoyt, argued persuasively that the redeemed inhabit a new earth.[22]

Blaising explicitly linked the views of McClain and Pentecost on this issue with the New Creation Model. He says their view was important for the soon-to-come Progressive Dispensationalism: "Others, such as Alva J. McClain and Dwight Pentecost, affirmed a new creation model of eternity. Their work paved the way for progressive dispensationalists to develop a consistent holistic premillennialism."[23]

---

19   Ibid.

20   Ibid.

21   Ibid. Blaising: "Ryrie speaks of Israel being taken up into heaven at the end of the Millennium" (33).

22   Larry R. Helyer, *The Witness of Jesus, Paul and John: An Exploration in Biblical Theology* (Downers Grove: IVP Academic, 2008), 110.

23   Craig A. Blaising, "Premillennialism," 189.

EVALUATION OF REVISED DISPENSATIONALISM

Revised Dispensationalism is more consistent with the New Creation Model than Classical Dispensationalism. It called for a consistent grammatical-historical hermeneutic to all Scripture and dropped earlier claims for a typological understanding of the Old Testament. Revised Dispensationalism also viewed the millennial destiny of Israel, nations, and the church as being on earth. There is disagreement, though, concerning the Eternal State. McClain and Pentecost said the Eternal State will be on earth. Others presented eternity as a heavenly destiny. In sum, Revised Dispensationalism moved Dispensationalism even more in the direction of the New Creation Model, and those like McClain and Pentecost were solidly new creationist in their perspective. Today, most revised dispensationalists follow McClain and Pentecost on this issue. Thus, Revised Dispensationalism is a New Creation Model approach. And it set the scene for more new creationist ideas to be found with Progressive Dispensationalism.

PROGRESSIVE DISPENSATIONALISM

Progressive Dispensationalism began in the mid-1980s. Notable scholars of Progressive Dispensationalism are Craig Blaising, Darrell Bock, and Robert Saucy. Some progressive dispensationalists view themselves as revised dispensationalists with a few theological adjustments.

Progressive Dispensationalism holds to fundamental beliefs of Dispensationalism such as a future millennial reign of Jesus over nations; a coming restoration of national Israel; a distinction between Israel and the church; the church began in Acts 2; and rejection of supersessionism. Most progressive dispensationalists also affirm a pretribulational rapture of the church.

This perspective asserts that God's kingdom purposes are unfolding through the progression of dispensations in history, with each dispensation building upon the previous. The various dispensations in history are related to each other with each furthering God's purposes. This involves the unfolding of the biblical covenants of promise—Abrahamic, Davidic, and New covenants—in history. Fulfillments of these covenants occur in stages. There are fulfillments before Christ, fulfillments with Jesus' first coming, and fulfillments associated with the second advent of Christ. In the present church age the covenants of promise are operating in an inaugurated, partial fulfillment way.

Progressive dispensationalists believe the biblical covenants involve a variety of elements—creational, physical, spiritual, national, and international. While the church currently experiences the fulfillment of some spiritual blessings of the covenants, all aspects of the covenants must come to fruition in all their dimensions. Physical and national promises must be fulfilled in the future. Thus, covenant fulfillment is not just about spiritual matters or individual redemption. A holistic view of the covenants is evident with Blaising's statement concerning Abrahamic Covenant promises:

> The blessings promised to Abraham are holistic, that is, they cover the whole of human life and experience: physical, material, social, personal (including mental and emotional), political and cultural, and religious.[24]

Progressive Dispensationalism asserts that the church is the redeemed Messianic community of Jews and Gentiles from Acts 2 onward. The church is not a distinct anthropological group in contrast to Israel and the nations. The church is saved humanity of Jews and Gentiles who have believed in Jesus. Becoming a member of Jesus' church in this age does not mean Christians join a distinct people group in contrast to Israel and Gentiles. A saved person today still keeps his ethnicity both now and in the future. For example, a saved Jewish person becomes part of the church, but he or she still retains his or her Jewishness. The same is true for believers of other ethnicities and nations.

Progressive Dispensationalism claims there are significant "already" fulfillments of the covenants in this age. And there are important "not yet" fulfillments still to come. This is connected with the fact that there are two comings of Jesus. Robert Saucy offers a concise explanation of "already" fulfillment and "not yet" fulfillment:

---

24   Blaising and Bock, *Progressive Dispensationalism*, 131.

That is, progressive dispensationalism sees God's present activity in and through the church as the already of an already-not-yet working out of messianic kingdom salvation. The not yet of messianic salvation will come only with the return of Christ and his righteous reign on earth, when his salvation will encompass all structures of human society and the will of God will be done on earth as it is in heaven.[25]

Progressive Dispensationalism believes in a coming "righteous reign" of Christ "on earth" that "will encompass all structures of human society." This is part of the "not yet" that awaits future fulfillment.

HERMENEUTICS OF PROGRESSIVE DISPENSATIONALISM

GRAMMATICAL-HISTORICAL HERMENEUTICS

The hermeneutical approach of Progressive Dispensationalism is largely the same as that of Revised Dispensationalism. It affirms a consistent literal, grammatical-historical hermeneutic to all areas of Scripture—including Old Testament prophecies and the book of Revelation.[26] As Saucy notes, "Progressive dispensationalism affirms traditional historical-grammatical hermeneutics as its starting point."[27] When this thinking is applied across the entire canon of Scripture, the plain meaning of Old Testament prophecies will be affirmed in the New Testament:

> But progressive dispensationalism believes that, when interpreted on the basis of the principles above, the plain meaning of

---

25   Robert L. Saucy, "The Progressive Dispensational View," in *Perspectives on Israel and the Church: 4 Views*, ed. Chad O. Brand (Nashville, TN: B&H Publishing, 2015), 155.

26   Sometimes Progressive Dispensationalism is linked with the concept of "complementary hermeneutic" in which God may do more than what He promised but He will not do less. This concept has been controversial within Dispensationalism but does not change the fact that Progressive Dispensationalism emphasizes grammatical-historical hermeneutics as the foundation for understanding all Scripture.

27   Saucy, 156.

the Old Testament prophecies is retained in their New Testament fulfillments.[28]

This involves understanding Israel and Old Testament promises literally:

> Israel is to be understood throughout Scripture in its original Old Testament meaning, and its prophesied mission as a special nation in the service of God's salvation program for the world will be fulfilled in accord with the Old Testament prophecies.[29]

And the hermeneutic of literal interpretation, applied to the entire Bible, reveals that Old Testament predictions concerning "cosmic recreation" are maintained and affirmed in the New Testament:

> In short, the Old Testament predictions of the future times of the Messiah on to the total cosmic recreation should be understood as still valid unless the New Testament positively indicates otherwise. Rather than doing so, we will see that the New Testament writers, in broad strokes, give positive evidence of their belief in the continuing validity of the Old Testament predictions.[30]

Thus, the new creation expectation in the Old Testament has continuity with the message in the New Testament: "In fact, the prophecies of the Old Testament extended to the same ultimate goal of God's salvation seen in the New Testament—a new creation including a new heavens and a new earth."[31]

TYPES AND TYPOLOGY

Progressive Dispensationalism believes in types when properly understood. There are several cases where Old Testament realities have historical

---

28   Ibid., 165.

29   Ibid., 156.

30   Ibid., 161.

31   Ibid., 160.

and theological correspondences with New Testament entities.[32] Adam is a type of Jesus (see Rom. 5:12–21). The Mosaic Covenant was a "shadow" of the New Covenant (see Heb. 10:1). In fact, most typological connections concern how the Mosaic Covenant and its elements were shadows of the New Covenant and its realities (see Hebrews 7–10).

But not every correspondence means the New Testament reality dissolves the significance of the Old Testament entity. Progressive dispensationalists perceive typological correspondences between Israel and the church while avoiding the conclusion that the church supersedes Israel in God's purposes. As Saucy explains:

> If a type is understood as a *shadow* pointing forward to the *reality* of its antitype, then Israel is not a type.... On the other hand, if a type is more loosely defined simply as a general historical and theological correspondence, then the many analogies between Old Testament Israel and the New Testament people of God may well be explained by seeing Israel as a type without necessitating its cessation as a nation and the fulfillment of the promises related to its future.[33]

Understanding the significance of types does not lead progressive dispensationalists to adopt "typological interpretation" in which typological connections are the main way to understand the Bible's storyline. Nor do types result in the non-significance of Israel, Israel's land, and physical blessings in the Bible's storyline. Types supplement and support the Bible's storyline known through explicit statements in Scripture. As Darrell Bock notes, "Yes, we do see much biblical typology connected to Christ, finding realization in him, but not always at the expense of groundwork already laid. It comes alongside in complement, not in removal."[34]

---

32   See Ibid., 161.

33   Ibid., 161–62. Emphases in original.

34   Darrell Bock, "A Progressive Dispensational Response," in *Covenantal and Dispensational Theologies*, 227.

PARTIAL FULFILLMENTS

Progressive Dispensationalism believes in partial fulfillments of some Old Testament prophecies. Since there are two comings of Jesus, some prophecies were fulfilled with the first coming of Jesus. But others await fulfillment with Jesus' second coming. If an Old Testament prophecy was not fulfilled with Jesus' first coming, progressive dispensationalists do not spiritualize it to this age. They expect its literal fulfillment in the future. As Saucy summarizes:

> The possibility of a partial fulfillment of many messianic prophecies should be expected, in that the Old Testament prophecies are generally associated simply with the coming of the Messiah, whereas their fulfillment in the New Testament clearly involves two advents.... Progressive dispensationalism thus agrees with many others that a partial fulfillment of the messianic prophecies began with the ministry of Christ at his first coming. But, it insists that the partial fulfillment is a partial fulfillment of the normal meaning of the original prophecy. The future completion of the fulfillment is also understood to be in accord with the original meaning of the prophecy so that ultimately the prophecy is fulfilled according to its original meaning.[35]

JESUS AND FULFILLMENT

Progressive Dispensationalism asserts the central role of Jesus concerning fulfillment of the Old Testament. As Saucy notes, "It is acknowledged at the outset that all of the Old Testament salvation covenants are fulfilled in Christ."[36] But fulfillment in Jesus does not mean Old Testament prophecies are absorbed or dissolved into Jesus in some mystical way: "These truths, however, do not dissolve the meaning of the salvation promises into the person of Christ, nor preclude all other human ministry in salvation

---

35   Saucy, 164.
36   Ibid., 180.

history."[37] For example, literal fulfillment of prophecies with Israel will still occur:

> As the final salvation of Christ is progressively being fulfilled in the case of our individual salvation, so it is progressively fulfilled in salvation history. Thus the fulfillment of the prophecies in Christ does not deny a place or time for Israel's participation in that fulfillment in Christ.[38]

Putting it together, Progressive Dispensationalism affirms the essential elements of Dispensationalism—a future salvation and restoration of national Israel, a distinction between Israel and the church, the church as a New Testament entity, and the importance of grammatical-historical hermeneutics consistently applied to all Scripture.

The main difference from earlier Dispensationalism, though, is the belief that the church is not a distinct anthropological group. Instead, the church is the redeemed humanity of Jews and Gentiles in Christ. Participating in the church does not mean losing one's ethnic identity. An ethnic Israelite does not lose his/her relationship to Israel, nor does a believing Gentile lose his/her relationship to their ethnic group or nation.

Progressive Dispensationalism is consistent with the New Creation Model since it views God's purposes as *holistic*. The following two quotes from Blaising reveal this understanding:

> Consequently, progressive dispensationalism advocates a *holistic and unified* view of eternal salvation. God will save humankind in its ethnic and national plurality. But He will bless it with the same salvation given to all without distinction.[39]

> In progressive dispensationalism, the political-social and spiritual purposes of God complement one another. The spiritual does not replace

---

37   Ibid.

38   Ibid., 180–81.

39   Blaising and Bock, *Progressive Dispensationalism*, 47.

the political nor do the two run independent of each other. They are related in a holistic plan of redemption.[40]

Important also to Progressive Dispensationalism is that the holistic redemption of all things involves Israel and other nations, along with the political and cultural realms:

> Progressive dispensationalists agree with revised (and classical) dispensationalists that God's work with Israel and Gentile nations in the past dispensation looks forward to the redemption of humanity in its political and cultural aspects. Consequently, there is a place for Israel and other nations in the eternal plan of God.[41]

Progressive dispensationalists teach that both the millennial kingdom and the Eternal State will involve a tangible restored earth. Real social, cultural, and political activity will exist, minus the presence and effects of sin and death.

EVALUATION OF PROGRESSIVE DISPENSATIONALISM

Progressive Dispensationalism is consistent with the New Creation Model. Of the systems and views mentioned in this book, it is the most compatible with New Creationism in our estimation.

EVALUATION OF DISPENSATIONALISM

Dispensationalism, particularly Revised and Progressive, fits well with the New Creation Model. It asserts that God's redemptive plans go beyond personal human salvation and involve the earth, earth's creatures, Israel, nations, society, culture and other matters. In doing so, Dispensationalism offers a broad, holistic, and multi-dimensional understanding of God's

---

40   Ibid., 48.

41   Ibid., 47.

purposes. And it does so more than other theological systems. As Blaising notes:

> There are other theological traditions which interpret Bible prophecy almost exclusively in relation to the present ministry of Christ in the church or to a believer's personal experience of salvation. Dispensationalism, however, interpreting these prophecies in a more "literal" manner has always expected God's future blessings to include earthly, national, and political aspects of life. Many of these blessings belong to a future dispensation which will be marked by the return of Christ to earth.[42]

> As a result, the dispensational tradition has offered a broader concept of redemption than found in some other theologies. Redemption extends to political and national levels as well as to individual and spiritual renewal.[43]

A CHALLENGE TO DISPENSATIONALISM

Not all agree that Dispensationalism is a New Creation Model system. While writing this book, I watched a YouTube video that accused Dispensationalism of being consistent with Gnosticism, a bizarre charge considering what we have seen in this chapter.

While not using the language of New Creation and Spiritual Vision models, Howard Snyder argues strongly for a new creationist approach. He is at the forefront of those who espouse that salvation is holistic and includes more than individual human salvation. Yet he is sharply critical of Premillennial Dispensationalism, which he views as bordering on heresy and unorthodoxy. According to Snyder, Premillennial Dispensationalism does not take creation seriously and contributes to the idea of earth and Heaven being divorced:

---

42 Ibid., 18.
43 Ibid.

Darby's theology greatly reinforced the divorce between earth and heaven already afflicting Western theology. In fact, premillennial dispensationalism would very likely not have developed at all had the church from the beginning stayed true to biblical teachings about God's covenant with the earth.[44]

Snyder charges Dispensationalism with not being creational enough. He links this with the pre-tribulational rapture theory and the view that the church is God's heavenly people. He also is critical of the dispensational view that the renewal of creation occurs after the return of Christ. And he dislikes the classical dispensational idea that the world will eventually be destroyed. Note the following two statements from Snyder:

> Premillennial dispensationalism undermines the biblical worldview by locating the renewal of creation exclusively after the return of Jesus Christ. Since the present world is headed for inevitable destruction, any concern with saving it is a distraction from rescuing souls before Jesus returns.[45]

> Premillennial dispensationalism popularized the view that the earth and the whole material creation is destined to be destroyed. This makes creation concerns pointless.[46]

Snyder criticizes Dispensationalism on three points: (1) believing in the pre-tribulation rapture; (2) placing the renewal of creation after the return of Christ; and (3) believing the world is headed for destruction, not renewal.

Are these legitimate claims against Dispensationalism? They are not. At the least, they are not valid concerning contemporary Dispensationalism.

Concerning the first point, Darby did teach that the pre-tribulational rapture snatches the church to Heaven forever. For Darby, the church will not have a relationship to the new earth in the future. We strongly disagree

---

44   Snyder, *Salvation Means Creation Healed*, 57.

45   Ibid., 59.

46   Ibid.

with Darby's view on this issue, and Snyder is correct to be concerned about this perspective. If Dispensationalism still held to Darby's version of the rapture as a forever escape from earth for the church, then Snyder's concern would be correct. But it is not the normative view. Since Snyder published his book criticizing Dispensationalism in 2011 he should have known what Dispensationalism of the last century has been teaching. But he chose to ignore this.

Contemporary Dispensationalism believes the pre-tribulational rapture rescues the church from God's wrath, but when Jesus returns to earth seven years later, the church will return with Jesus and reign with Him *on the earth* (see Rev. 2:26–27; 5:10). The rapture is not an escape to Heaven forever, but an evacuation to Heaven for a short time followed by a kingdom reign on earth. Thus, the argument that Dispensationalism is consistent with a Spiritual Vision model because of its view of the rapture no longer is invalid.

The second charge is the weakest. Dispensationalists believe the renewal of the earth will take place after Jesus' second coming. But that does not make Dispensationalism anti-creational. The heart of New Creationism is belief that creation is important and is headed for full restoration, not that the restoration must occur in this present age before Jesus returns. Two thousand years of church existence has not led to a restored earth and there is no biblical evidence that the earth will be restored before Jesus returns. But it will be restored in the future. Jesus must return to earth for creation to be restored.

Third, what about the claim that Dispensationalism teaches the destruction of creation? Some dispensationalists believe the earth will be annihilated after the Millennium. For them, Snyder's criticism has some validity. But this view is not inherent to Dispensationalism. Many dispensationalists today, including myself, believe the current earth is headed for renewal and restoration, not annihilation. The fiery language mentioned in 2 Peter 3 is for the purging of the earth, not its annihilation. The earth experiences restoration in the coming Millennium and Eternal Kingdom. This is not an anti-creational view.

Snyder's three concerns do not apply to contemporary Dispensationalism. Dispensationalism of today is squarely in the New Creation Model camp.

25

COVENANT THEOLOGY
AND THE MODELS

◆

INTRODUCTION

C ovenant Theology (or Covenantalism) arose in the late sixteenth century in the aftermath of the Protestant Reformation and came to a
mature expression in the middle of the seventeenth century. It is closely
associated with Reformed Theology. Covenant Theologian, Michael
Horton, quotes John Hesselink favorably who says, "Reformed Theology
is simply covenant theology."[1]

Covenant Theology claims to be a comprehensive system for understanding the Bible. Horton states, "Covenant Theology is the architectural design or framework of Scripture itself."[2] Essential components
of this "architectural design" are "Law and Gospel."[3] Law is linked with
commands that kill but gospel is linked with promises that make alive.
This "law-gospel" theme, which allegedly permeates Scripture, manifests
itself in two covenants—the Covenant of Works (law) and the Covenant
of Grace. As Geerhardus Vos declares, "The contrast of law and gospel is

---

1   Michael S. Horton, "Covenant Theology," *Covenantal and Dispensational Theologies: Four Views on
     the Continuity of Scripture*, eds. Brent E. Parker and Richard J. Lucas (Downers Grove, IL: IVP
     Academic, 2022), 36.

2   Ibid.

3   Ibid., 37.

brought to bear on the contrast between the covenant of works and the covenant of grace."[4]

Covenant Theology primarily is a soteriology system. It focuses on individual salvation and redemption. How Christ relates to soteriology is also much emphasized with Covenant Theology. As Richard P. Belcher, Jr. states, "Covenant theology provides a substantive framework for understanding the plan of God's salvation worked out in redemptive history."[5] In his presentation of "Historic Covenant Theology," Robert Reymond stated that Covenant Theology has "three main characteristics." These are: (1) "It stresses the unity and continuity of redemptive history from Gen 3:15 to the farthest reaches of the future"; (2) "It asserts the unity of the covenant of grace and the oneness of God's people in all ages"; (3) "It insists that Old Testament saints were saved precisely the same way that New Testament saints are being saved."[6]

As a human salvation system Covenant Theology focuses much on predestination, calling, atonement, regeneration, justification, sanctification, and other soteriological issues. Willem VanGemeren claims four related concepts define "the essence of Covenant Theology."[7] These are: "the eternal covenant of redemption between the Father and the Son, the federal headship of Adam, the unity of the covenant of grace, and justification by faith."[8]

Three soteriological covenants are at the heart of Covenant Theology—Covenant of Redemption, Covenant of Works, and Covenant of Grace. These concern the roles of God and man concerning the salvation

---

4　　Quoted by Horton, 39. Geerhardus Vos, *Redemptive History and Biblical Interpretation: The Shorter Writings of Geerhardus Vos*, ed. Richard B. Gaffin Jr. (Phillipsburg, NJ: P&R, 2001), 274.

5　　Richard P. Belcher, Jr., *The Fulfillment of the Promises of God: An Explanation of Covenant Theology* (Geanies House, Fearn, Ross-shire: Christian Focus Publications, 2020), 259.

6　　Robert L. Reymond, "The Traditional Covenantal View," in *Perspectives on Israel and the Church: 4 Views*, ed. Chad O. Brand (Nashville: B&H Academic, 2015), 17.

7　　Willem VanGemeren, "Systems of Continuity," in *Continuity and Discontinuity: Perspectives on the Relationship Between the Old and New Testaments* (Wheaton, IL: Crossway, 1988), 43. He refers to the work of Paul Helm in making this claim.

8　　Ibid., 44.

of the elect. First, the Covenant of Redemption is a pre-time covenant in which the Father and Son covenanted together concerning their roles for saving the elect. Louis Berkhof states, "The covenant of redemption may be defined as the agreement between the Father, giving the Son as Head and Redeemer of the elect, and the Son, voluntarily taking the place of those whom the Father had given Him."[9] Horton says the Covenant of Redemption is "an eternal pact between the persons of the Trinity for the salvation of the elect from the mass of condemned humanity."[10] This Covenant of Redemption is foundational to Covenant Theology since the other two covenants (works and grace) will stem from this covenant. And it shows that the starting point for Covenant Theology is salvation of the elect.

Next, is the Covenant of Works. According to the Westminster Confession of Faith, "The first covenant made with man was a covenant of works, wherein life was promised to Adam; and in him to his posterity, upon condition of perfect and personal obedience."[11] This Covenant of Works is a covenant between God and man in which eternal life is based on perfect obedience to God. Man is to work or merit his way unto eternal life. Adam, as representative of mankind, was created in a state of innocence but not merited righteousness. He needed to obey perfectly to earn eternal life. This involved not eating from the tree of the knowledge of good and evil (see Gen. 2:15–17) and doing what God commanded in Genesis 1:26–28. Failure to obey God perfectly on Adam's part meant death, while perfect obedience would earn eternal life.

For Covenant Theology, eternal life, in principle, is based on works. Adam failed this Covenant of Works. But the Covenant of Works is still required for all of Adam's descendants. It still applies to each person. But after Adam no one can perfectly obey God unto eternal life. The one exception is Jesus, the Last Adam, who fulfills the Covenant of Works with His perfect law-keeping. He then imputes perfect law-keeping to the elect so

---

9   Berkhof, *Berkhof's Systematic Theology*, Revised. (Ontario: Devoted Publishing, 2019), 206.

10   Horton, 41.

11   "The Westminster Confession of Faith," 7.2.

that the Covenant of Works is fulfilled on their behalf by Jesus. In sum, the Covenant of Works is a soteriological covenant since it deals with what man must do to earn eternal life. Eternal life ultimately is merit-oriented; it is based on perfect works.

The third covenant is the Covenant of Grace. The Westminster Confession explains:

> Man by his fall having made himself incapable of life by that covenant, the Lord was pleased to make a second, commonly called the covenant of grace: wherein He freely offered unto sinners life and salvation by Jesus Christ, requiring of them faith in Him, that they may be saved, and promising to give unto all those that are ordained unto life, His Holy Spirit, to make them willing and able to believe.[12]

So after Adam's fall no person could earn eternal life by their own works. So grace is needed to be saved. God initiates the Covenant of Grace whereby eternal life is given to the elect by grace through faith in Jesus. Allegedly, the Covenant of Grace is expressed via the explicit biblical covenants—Noahic, Abrahamic, Mosaic, Davidic, and New. The explicitly mentioned covenants in Scripture are believed to be outworkings of this Covenant of Grace. Like the first two covenants of Covenant Theology, the Covenant of Grace also is a soteriological covenant since it addresses redemption for the elect by grace in Christ.[13]

But the main thing to note here is that *the foundational covenants of Covenant Theology are primarily soteriological covenants. They concern the salvation/redemption of the elect.* They do not address broader creation and kingdom purposes of God. This does not mean covenant theologians will never make statements on other matters. They do. But at its heart, Covenant Theology is a salvation/redemption of the elect system.

12　Ibid., 7.3.

13　Most covenantalists affirm all three alleged covenants, but some do not believe in the Covenant of Redemption or the Covenant of Works. All seem to affirm the Covenant of Grace. There also is significant debate within this system concerning the Mosaic Covenant, particularly whether it is part of the Covenant of Works, Covenant of Grace, or a mixture of both. So, there is some diverse thinking on covenants within Covenant Theology.

RELATIONSHIP TO THE MODELS

Our focus now turns to Covenant Theology's relationship to the New Creation and Spiritual Vision models. As will be shown, Covenant Theology's relationship to the models is complex, evidencing elements of both models.

PRIMARILY A SALVATION OF THE ELECT SYSTEM

As shown, Covenant Theology is a soteriology/redemption system that mostly focuses on the salvation of elect individuals in Christ.[14] This is shown with the three covenants of Covenant Theology. The pre-time Covenant of Redemption concerns the Trinity's pact to save elect people. It does not focus on broader creation issues of Genesis 1–2 but focuses on Genesis 3 and man's need for redemption. So redemption of elect individuals is the emphasis. Next, the Covenant of Works concerns soteriology since it asserts that eternal life must be merited by works/obedience. Then, the Covenant of Grace concerns salvation of the elect after Adam's sin through faith in Christ.

Covenant Theology, therefore, emphasizes individual salvation of the elect, not broader creation issues or cosmic eschatology that will be found with other theological systems. Even the explicit biblical covenants—Noahic, Abrahamic, Mosaic, Davidic, and New—will be viewed as extensions of the soteriological covenants of Redemption, Works, and Grace. The material and national elements of the explicit biblical covenants are not emphasized in Covenant Theology.

In the book, *Covenant Theology: Biblical, Theological, and Historical Perspectives*, Kevin DeYoung wrote an Afterword titled, "Why Covenant Theology?"[15] It briefly summarized what Covenant Theology is about. To help people understand "what does covenant theology look like?" he

---

14   The role of Jesus to these doctrines and God's glory are central, too.

15   Kevin DeYoung, "Afterword: Why Covenant Theology?" in *Covenant Theology: Biblical, Theological, and Historical Perspectives*, eds. Guy Prentiss Waters, J. Nicholas Reid, and John R. Muether (Wheaton, IL: Crossway, 2020), 589–98.

said, "we need to understand three different covenants, one covenant of grace, and two ways of existing in this one covenant."[16] He then explained the Covenant Theology view of the "Covenant of Works," the "Covenant of Grace," and the "Covenant of Redemption." Next, he proceeded to show how the Covenant of Grace "stretches across the Bible from cover to cover."[17] Then he explained that there are "Two Ways of Existing in This One Covenant."[18] This means "We belong to the covenant community externally by family but belong internally by faith."[19] In concluding the chapter DeYoung states, "...covenant theology helps us see the grand sweep of salvation history."[20] In addition to being a helpful and clarifying insight into Covenant Theology from an excellent proponent of this system, this chapter reveals how Covenant Theology focuses on individual redemption and how the covenants of Covenant Theology relate to salvation from sin.

The heavy emphasis on soteriology within Covenant Theology has been noted by others. Paul Helm observes that "the development of covenant theology...was the outworking, in theological detail, of the basic Reformed principle: the glory of God in the salvation of sinners."[21] Commenting on covenant theologian, Francis Turretin (1623–87), VanGemeren explains that Turretin "did more than any other seventeenth-century theologian in defining 'the system' of Covenant Theology, emphasizing the soteriological elements of Calvinism: the decrees of God, predestination, reprobation and salvation."[22] Howard Snyder notes that "key covenant theologians such as Johannes Cocceius largely ignored God's covenant with the earth itself (Gen 9:8–17; Jer 33:20, 25).... the focus was

---

16   Ibid., 590.

17   Ibid., 593.

18   Ibid., 596.

19   Ibid., 598.

20   Ibid.

21   Paul Helm, "Calvin and the Covenant: Unity and Continuity," *Evangelical Quarterly* 55 (1983), 81.

22   VanGemeren, "Systems of Continuity," 46.

solely on the covenant between God and humans."[23] This emphasis on individual spiritual salvation in Covenant Theology also has been detected by Moore:

> The Reformed tradition tended to emphasize the Kingdom of Christ in almost entirely present, spiritual terms, much to the chagrin of their premillennialist interlocutors. Covenant theologian Louis Berkhof argued that this present spiritual reality of Christ's reign is precisely what made the future-oriented Kingdom of premillennialism so untenable.[24]

Moore also notes that Berkhof, "emphasized the present kingship of Christ, and articulated this reign in decidedly spiritual and soteriological terms."[25]

Covenantalists certainly address other issues beyond salvation. A survey of systematic theologies written by covenantalists reveals sections on creation, eschatology and other issues. And covenantalists, at times, make statements consistent with the New Creation Model. In his systematic theology book, Michael Horton notes that the Christian worldview differs from Platonism by affirming "resurrection of the body and the complete renewal of creation."[26] Yet the main emphasis of Covenant Theology is salvation of the elect. Works that summarize this system focus almost exclusively on human redemption in Christ.

---

23 Snyder, *Salvation Means Creation Healed*, 31. Snyder also says, "Johannes Cocceius (1603-69), despite his concern to be biblical, focused almost exclusively on the relationship between God and humanity, with little or no reference to the earth and God's relationship with the earth—understandable given the nature of the debates at the time."

24 Moore, *The Kingdom of Christ*, 45.

25 Ibid. Our study of Berkhof affirms this. Berkhof devotes one page to the final state of the righteous and even this page is vague. (*Systematic Theology*, 736–37). In a book with 710 pages of body content one page is devoted to the eternal state and the discussion here is vague.

26 Michael Horton, *The Christian Faith: A Systematic Theology for Pilgrims on the Way*, 940. Yet, on the other hand, Horton seems to spiritualize the transformation of nature predicted in some Old Testament passages like Isaiah 11:6–9 and Isaiah 65:25. These speak of various animals in a state of harmony with people and other animals. Horton, though, says, "Wolves and lambs, serpents and doves, routinely describe the violent and peaceful conditions of nations" (942).

AMILLENNIALISM AND
SPIRITUALIZING THE KINGDOM

Covenant Theology often is linked with spiritualizing the kingdom of God. For example, covenant theologian, Mark Karlberg says, "In the eschatological age of the Spirit the kingdom of God is a spiritual reality unencumbered by the shadowy earthly forms (types) characteristic of the ancient theocracy."[27] Kim Riddlebarger states, "If the New Testament writers *spiritualize* Old Testament prophecies by *applying them in a nonliteral sense*, then the Old Testament passage must be seen in light of that New Testament interpretation, not vice versa."[28] Beale says, "Perhaps one of the most striking features of Jesus' kingdom is that it appears not to be the kind of kingdom prophesied in the OT and expected by Judaism."[29] These statements are consistent with the Spiritual Vision Model since they involve spiritualizing the kingdom of God so it is not an earthly kingdom. Moore also asserts that Reformed covenantalists often missed the material aspects of Jesus' kingdom: "The seemingly material aspects of the coming Kingdom spoken of even in the Passover meal of Jesus with His disciples (Luke 22:15–16), were often neglected by earlier generations of Reformed theologians."[30]

Spiritualizing the kingdom of God could be linked with Covenant Theology's close relationship to Amillennialism. When it comes to millennial views most covenantalists are amillennialists. Some are postmillennialists. A few are premillennialists. Thus, Covenant Theology is not tied to one millennial view. But Amillennialism is the dominant millennial view with implications for the system.

---

27   Mark Karlberg, "The Significance of Israel in Biblical Typology," *Journal of the Evangelical Theological Society* 31/3 (September 1988): 268.

28   Kim Riddlebarger, *A Case for Amillennialism*, 37. Emphases not in original.

29   G. K. Beale. *A New Testament Biblical Theology: The Unfolding of the Old Testament in the New* (Grand Rapids: Baker Academic, 2011), 431.

30   Moore, 62.

Moore observes that "amillennialism was most often articulated within the parameters of confessional, Reformed covenant theology."[31] Mark Karlberg believes Amillennialism only is consistent with Covenant Theology: "Among the various schools of prophetic interpretation within the Reformed tradition only amillennialism is fully compatible with covenant theology—specifically covenant typology."[32]

Amillennialism spiritualizes the messianic, millennial reign of Jesus, making it a spiritual kingdom in this age. But Amillennialism does not account for the holistic and multi-dimensional aspects of Jesus' messianic kingdom, which transforms earth, land, nations, the animal realm, society, culture, etc. Jesus' kingdom involves salvation, but it also includes much more. Thus, Covenant Theology's embrace of Amillennialism ties it more closely to the Spiritual Vision Model. Covenant theologians who are postmillennial or premillennial would be relatively closer to the New Creation Model.

THE USE OF TYPOLOGICAL INTERPRETATION

Covenant Theology's reliance on typological interpretation also links it with the Spiritual Vision Model. With typological interpretation national and physical promises of the Old Testament are viewed as "typological" of alleged greater spiritual realities. Covenant theologians often stress that national Israel and the land of Israel are inferior types that are transcended in light of Jesus and New Testament realities.[33] As Mark Karlberg, writes:

> If one grants that national Israel in OT revelation was truly a type of the eternal kingdom of Christ, then it seems that, according to the canons of Biblical typology, national Israel can no longer retain any independent status whatever.[34]

---

31   Ibid., 45. Moore points out this is particularly true within American evangelical discussions.

32   Karlberg, "The Significance of Israel in Biblical Typology," 269, n. 33.

33   "Typology plays a prominent part in the hermeneutical approach of covenant theology." Benjamin L. Merkle, *Discontinuity to Continuity*, 143.

34   Karlberg, 259.

But genuine typological interpretation rules out any additional literal fulfillment of the land promise in a future restoration of national Israel subsequent to or alongside the messianic fulfillment.[35]

O. Palmer Robertson uses typological interpretation to replace the literal meaning of Old Testament prophecies about Israel:

Some might insist that "literal" fulfillment of new covenant prophecy requires the return of ethnic Israel to a geographically located Palestine. Yet the replacement of the typological with the actual as a principle of biblical interpretation points to another kind of "literal" fulfillment.[36]

The heavy emphasis on typology and typological interpretation by many covenantalists leads to Spiritual Vision Model conclusions since Israel and Israel's land are removed from having theological significance.

SUPERSESSIONISM

Denial of the continuing importance of national Israel in God's purposes is part of the Spiritual Vision Model. And we see this often with Covenant Theology of the last century. New Creationism embraces the importance of nations, including Israel, in God's purposes. Not all covenant theologians are supersessionists, but covenant theologians often deny the continuing theological significance of national Israel. For example, Horton states, "Israel no longer is identified with a nation or ethnic people but with Christ as the head with his body...."[37] He also claims that "temporal nationhood, land ... are rendered obsolete by Christ's redeeming work."[38] And, "Yes, the

---

35   Mark W. Karlberg, *Covenant Theology in the Reformed Perspective: Collected Essays and Book Reviews in Historical, Biblical, and Systematic Theology* (Eugene, OR: Wipf & Stock, 2000), 195.

36   O. Palmer Robertson, *The Christ of the Covenants* (Phillipsburg, NJ: Presbyterian and Reformed, 1980), 300.

37   Horton, "Covenant Theology," in *Covenantal and Dispensational Theologies*, 71.

38   Ibid.

national election of Israel has come to an end with the exile."[39] These statements are consistent with supersessionism and a Spiritual Vision Model approach. In his presentation and defense of Covenant Theology, Robert L. Reymond explicitly promoted "replacement theology" and the idea that national Israel's standing would be transferred to the church[40]:

> Here is a biblical "replacement theology," and it is Jesus himself who enunciated it: National Israel, except for its elect remnant, would be judged, and the special standing that it had enjoyed during the old dispensation would be transferred to the already existing and growing international church of Jesus Christ (whose roots go back to Abraham, indeed, to the divine promise of Gen 3:15) made up of both the elect Jewish remnant and elect Gentiles.[41]

Herman Bavinck also taught a strong replacement theology view concerning Israel:

> The salvation rejected by Israel is shared by the Gentiles, and the community of Christ-believers has in all respects *replaced* national Israel.[42]

---

39 Ibid., 69.

40 Covenant theologians today often dispute the claim they teach "replacement theology" and some resist the title, "supersessionism." We affirm that no one should be called something they do not accept or like. Yet the concepts behind these titles are often taught with Covenant Theology. Concepts, not titles, are the real issue. At the heart of replacement theology or supersessionism is the idea that corporate, national Israel no longer is theologically significant as a corporate entity because the church in Jesus is the new and/or true Israel. Allegedly, a redefinition of the people of God has occurred and Jesus fulfills Israel in such a way that the corporate, national entity ceases to be significant in the Bible' storyline. The corporate entity that received curses and dispersion will not see the blessings and restoration also promised to it. Thus, the main concepts behind what can be called replacement theology or supersessionism are taught by many today. And sometimes covenant theologians have used "replacement" language. Yet we also acknowledge that some covenantalists of previous generations did not teach replacement theology/supersessionism. The claim that "fulfillment theology" exists but not "replacement theology," commits the fallacy of "distinction without difference" in which a distinction is claimed but no distinction actually exists.

41 Robert L. Reymond, "The Traditional Covenantal View," in *Perspectives on Israel and the Church: 4 Views*, ed. Chad O. Brand (Nashville, TN: B&H Academic, 2015), 49.

42 Bavinck, *Reformed Dogmatics*, vol. 4:664. Emphases not in original.

The community of believers has in all respects *replaced* carnal, national Israel.[43]

Likewise, Bruce Waltke asserts national Israel's replacement with the church: "Jesus taught in several places that the true people of God are not to be found in national Israel but in the Christian community that replaced it."[44] Karlberg speaks of Israel's kingdom dissolving into the church: "In that day the typological phenomenon of the ancient Israelite theocracy would be dissolved into the antitypical reality of the Church as the New Israel."[45]

EMPHASIS ON FIRST-COMING FULFILLMENT

Covenant Theology often emphasizes first-coming-of-Jesus fulfillment over second-coming fulfillment when it comes to Old Testament prophecies. This often has led to spiritualizing prophecies that were not literally fulfilled with Jesus' first advent. Matters such as earth, land, nations, Israel, and physical blessings often are spiritualized and linked with Jesus' first coming. Sensing the weakness of this "first-coming" approach, Vern Poythress recommends that fellow amillennialists give more attention to second coming fulfillments:

> Amillennialists today must try to be increasingly faithful to the biblical accent, and speak not only of a first stage of fulfillment in the life of Christ, the New Testament age and the church, but also of a second, consummate stage in the new heavens and the new earth.[46]

In a similar way Anthony Hoekema called on amillennialists to stop spiritualizing passages like Isaiah 2 to today:

---

43   Ibid., 667. Emphases added.

44   Bruce K. Waltke, "Kingdom Promises as Spiritual," in *Continuity and Discontinuity,"* 279.

45   Karlberg, "The Significance of Israel in Biblical Typology," 267.

46   Poythress, "Currents within Amillennialism," 21–22.

All too often, unfortunately, amillennial exegetes fail to keep biblical teaching on the new earth in mind when interpreting Old Testament prophecy. It is an impoverishment of the meaning of these passages to make them apply only to the church or to heaven.[47]

Some covenant theologians have begun to emphasize second coming fulfillment. As Moore notes:"the amillennial covenant tradition ... has undergone a reconsideration of its 'already/not yet' eschatology."[48] Hopefully, more covenantalists will follow Poythress and Hoekema on this issue.

VARIATIONS WITHIN COVENANT THEOLOGY

TRADITIONAL COVENANTALISM

Three variations exist within Covenant Theology that are relevant in this discussion. The first and most dominant form is Traditional Covenant Theology. This form is Augustinian concerning eschatology reaching back to the late fourth century. Its primary focus concerns individual salvation of the elect. It also spiritualizes many Old Testament prophecies and is supersessionist concerning Israel and the church. Traditional Covenantalism does not stress cosmic eschatology and issues like national Israel, geo-political nations, the Day of the Lord, and Messiah's coming earthly kingdom. Most attention goes to the Law-Gospel contrast and the covenants of redemption, works, and grace—issues that are primarily soteriological. Traditional Covenantalism often is amillennial, viewing Jesus' messianic/millennial kingdom as a spiritual kingdom relating to salvation in this age.

---

47   Hoekema, *The Bible and the Future*, 205–06.

48   Moore, *The Kingdom of Christ*, 44.

MODIFIED COVENANTALISM

A second form of Covenantalism is Modified Covenantalism. Modified Covenantalism shares most beliefs with Traditional Covenantalism but it also addresses issues beyond individual human redemption. It is more cosmic and earth-oriented, believing that some Old Testament prophecies concerning the earth, animal realm, nations and other areas will be fulfilled literally in the coming Eternal State. Modified covenantalists include Herman Bavinck, Abraham Kuyper, and more recently Anthony Hoekema, and Vern Poythress. Moore uses Poythress to show that modified covenantalists break with the "spiritual vision of eternity" found with Traditional Covenantalism:

> Poythress argues that modified covenantalists are ready to concede many of the most contentious premillennial objections to the typical eschatological formulations of Reformed evangelicals. The spiritual vision of eternity was less informed by the biblical vision of the Kingdom of Christ than by an ethereal, if not almost Platonic, hope for a temporal, heavenly existence.[49]

Moore notes that some Reformed evangelicals (i.e., covenantalists) often were closer to Platonism than the Bible on the kingdom and eternity. But modified covenantalists adopt a more tangible understanding of God's kingdom purposes. This was documented in our earlier section on Amillennialism where we saw Poythress and Hoekema depart from traditional, Augustinian Amillennialism for a more literal view of earthly promises in the Bible. Moore notes the contrast of Hoekema's groundbreaking "modified covenantalism" with earlier Covenantalism—"distancing himself from the inordinately spiritual emphases of some of his American covenantalist forebears."[50] Moore also observes that Modified Covenantalism corrects the Platonic tendencies of the traditional amillennial view: "For modified covenantalists, Hoekema's 'new earth' model of future

---

49   Moore, 49–50.

50   Ibid., 46.

consummation corrects the crypto-Platonic aspects of the older model of amillennial eschatological hope....["51]

Moore also observes that some in the Reformed tradition are breaking from the Spiritual Vision Model in general: "...Hoekema and those within the Reformed tradition who follow his lead, break decisively with the 'spiritual vision' model of eschatology."[52] For example, Anthony Hoekema stated, "The Bible assures us that God will create a new earth on which we shall live to God's praise in glorified, resurrected bodies."[53] This new earth includes "contributions of each nation to the life of the present earth" and "the best products of culture and art."[54]

The more earth-oriented view of Modified Covenantalism puts this group closer to Premillennialism: "Poythress further argues that the 'new earth' envisioned by Hoekema and other modified covenantalists 'changes the scene entirely' because it is 'very much like the millennial earth as envisioned by premillennialists.'"[55] This also leads to a closer affinity with Dispensationalism against over-spiritualized Augustinianism:

> Modified covenantalists are right to agree with the older dispensationalists in charging traditional covenant theology with holding to an Augustinian "spiritual vision" eschatology, with which it is impossible to reconcile the "earthy" feel of the prophetic promises, not only of the Old Testament but of the New as well.[56]

Yet some inconsistencies exist with modified covenantalists. At times they revert to a spiritualizing hermeneutic consistent with Traditional Covenantalism and the Spiritual Vision Model. Hoekema, for instance, asserts that while "many Old Testament prophecies are indeed to be

---

51   Ibid., 51.

52   Ibid., 50–51.

53   Hoekema, *The Bible and the Future*, 274.

54   Ibid., 286.

55   Moore, 52. Vern S. Poythress, "Response to Paul S. Karleen's Paper 'Understanding Covenant Theologians,'" *Grace Theological Journal* 10 (1989): 148.

56   Moore, 62.

interpreted literally, many others are to be interpreted in a nonliteral way."[57] Also, modified covenantalists hold supersessionist views concerning Israel and the church. Bavinck declared, "The salvation rejected by Israel is shared by the Gentiles, and the community of Christ-believers has in all respects *replaced* national Israel."[58] On these points, Modified Covenantalism is consistent with Traditional Covenantalism and the Spiritual Vision Model.

PREMILLENNIAL NONSUPERSESSIONIST COVENANTALISTS

While very small in number, some covenantalists have been premillennialists who affirm the significance of corporate, national Israel in God's purposes. They also affirm that Old Testament prophecies concerning national Israel will be fulfilled literally with national Israel in a coming earthly millennial kingdom. We call these theologians, "premillennial nonsupersessionist covenantalists." Ligon Duncan notes, "Now, there have been however, some who fall into the category of being Covenant Theologians who are premillennial. Horatius Bonar, Robert Murry McCheyne and some of the other great Scottish Calvinists last century."[59]

This form of Covenantalism even extended to some Westminster Confession theologians. Sung Wook Chung notes, "Several Puritan theologians who participated in the production of the Westminster Confession of Faith also espoused historic premillennialism. One of the representative figures is Thomas Goodwin (1600–1680), a renowned, English Puritan theologian."[60] In his book, *The Puritan Hope*, Iain Murray notes the presence of Premillennialism among "some of the Westminster divines":

---

57   Hoekema, "Amillennialism," in *The Meaning of the Millennium: Four Views*, 172.

58   Bavinck, *Reformed Dogmatics*, 4:664. Emphases added.

59   J. Ligon Duncan, III, "Covenant Theology: Dispensationalism A Reformed Evaluation," Thirdmill. org Covenant Theology Dispensationalism
 A Reformed Evaluation (HTML) (thirdmill.org)

60   Sung Wook Chung and David Mathewson, *Models of Premillennialism* (Eugene, OR: Cascade Books, 2018), 17.

The attention drawn by such writers as Mede and Alsted to the millennium of Revelation 20, and to the Old Testament prophecies which appear to speak of a general conversion of the nations, led to a revised expectation of a pre-millennial appearing of Christ, when Israel would be converted and Christ's kingdom established in the earth for at least a thousand years.... Stated in its more moderate form this belief commanded the support of some of the Westminster divines (notably, William Twisse, Thomas Goodwin, William Bridge and Jeremiah Burroughs).[61]

In his study of pro-Israel theologians of the seventeenth century, William Watson observed the significance of Westminster Assembly Divines who were premillennial and philo-Semites: "The Westminster Assembly chosen by the British Parliament to restructure the Church of England in 1643 may have been overwhelmingly Calvinist, but it included many premillennial philo-Semites."[62] Watson says this included William Bridge, Jeremiah Burroughs, Joseph Caryl, John Dury, Thomas Goodwin, William Gouge, Herbert Palmer, Peter Sterry, William Twisse, James Usher, and George Walker.[63] Thomas Goodwin (1600–80), a member of the Westminster Assembly, believed the Saints would rule on earth: "We shall raign on earth ... We shall have a hand in guiding the affairs of the earth."[64]

Horatius Bonar (1808–1889), in his *Political Landmarks*, spoke of a coming salvation and restoration of Israel to the land based on a literal understanding of Old Testament prophecies.[65] Concerning theologians like himself he says, "They believe that Israel will be converted, and they rejoice in this as the glorious issue towards which the prophets point. But

---

61   Murray, *The Puritan Hope*, 52–53.

62   Watson, *Dispensationalism Before Darby*, 23.

63   Ibid., 24.

64   Thomas Goodwin, *A Sermon of the Fifth Monarchy. Proving by Invincible Arguments That the Saints shall have a Kingdom here on Earth* (London, 1654), title page. See Watson, *Dispensationalism before Darby*, 89.

65   See "Israel," chapter 13 in Horatius Bonar, *Prophetical Landmarks: Containing data for helping to determine the question of Christ's premillennial advent* (1847).

they believe more; they believe not only that they will be converted, but they will be restored to their own land."[66] *Political Landmarks*, thus, presents a clear presentation and defense of Premillennialism and the role of national Israel in God's purposes. Bonar taught that passages like Isaiah 11:6–10 teach a literal restoration of the animal kingdom and all nature—a return to Eden-like conditions.

Like Bonar, J. C. Ryle (1816–1900), a Reformed English preacher, expressed belief of the restoration of Israel as a nation to the land: "I believe that the Jews shall ultimately be gathered again as a separate nation, restored to their own land, and converted to the faith of Christ, after going through great tribulation (Jer. 30:10–11; 31:10; Rom. 11:25–26; Dan. 12:1; Zech. 13:8–9)."[67] Ryle believed the salvation and restoration of national Israel to their land was "as clearly and plainly revealed as any prophecy in God's Word":

> Time would fail me, if I attempted to quote all the passages of Scripture in which the future history of Israel is revealed. Isaiah, Jeremiah, Ezekiel, Hosea, Joel, Amos, Obadiah, Micah, Zephaniah, Zechariah all declare the same thing. All predict, with more or less particularity, that in the end of this dispensation the Jews are to be restored to their own land and to the favor of God. I lay no claim to infallibility in the interpretation of Scripture in this matter. I am well aware that many excellent Christians cannot see the subject as I do. I can only say, that to my eyes, the future *salvation* of Israel as a people, their *return* to Palestine and their national conversion to God, appear as clearly and plainly revealed as any prophecy in God's Word.[68]

In sum, premillennial nonsupersessionist covenantalists went even further than modified covenantalists like Poythress and Hoekema regarding a new creationist approach. Like modified covenantalists, these

---

66   Ibid., 109.

67   J. C. Ryle, *Are You Ready For The End Of Time?* (Fearn, Scotland: Christian Focus, 2001), 9; reprint of *Coming Events and Present Duties.*

68   Ibid., 152–54. Emphases in original.

premillennial nonsupersessionist covenantalists affirmed a literal fulfillment of Old Testament physical promises. And they affirmed the significance of national Israel in God's purposes and an earthly kingdom of Jesus after His second coming. They also avoided the inconsistent view of taking some Old Testament prophecies literally while viewing others spiritually. While very few in number, these premillennial nonsupersessionist covenantalists showed that it is possible to hold to Covenant Theology and still affirm consistent New Creation Model ideas. Unfortunately, though, this form of Covenantalism is rare today and seems more connected with the past than the present or future of Covenant Theology.

EVALUATION OF COVENANT THEOLOGY

Covenant Theology's relationship to the models is complex. There are two main reasons for this. First, Covenant Theology primarily is a human redemption in Christ system. It is not structured to address many issues associated with the New Creation Model such as cosmic eschatology, the holistic dimensions of the biblical covenants, the earthly nature of the kingdom of God, Israel, geo-political nations, physical blessings, and other areas. This does not mean covenantalists never comment on these other areas or even say good things on them. Covenant theologians like Bavinck, Hoekema, and Poythress have addressed some of these broader areas and have made helpful insights. But as a system Covenant Theology focuses mostly on individual human salvation and Christ's role in this. The three covenants of Covenant Theology—Redemption, Works, Grace—focus on God's salvation plans for elect persons, but they do not address broader creation realities.

Second, Covenant Theology is complex to evaluate since covenant theologians have expressed different views on matters like Old Testament prophecies and Israel. As seen above, nonsupersessionist premillennial covenantalists expressed ideas consistent with the New Creation Model. But these covenantalists are rare. Most covenantalists today are traditional covenantalists and espouse ideas more in line with the Spiritual Vision Model. And most covenantalists are amillennialists. Amillennialism is tied to the Spiritual Vision Model. Supersessionism also remains an issue with Covenant Theology today. In his defense of Covenant Theology in 1988, Willem VanGemeren pleaded, "I have asked and am still asking that the exegetical case of Israel in the plan of God be reopened."[69] Yet, in the decades since VanGemeren's statement resistance to the significance of corporate, national Israel within Covenant Theology remains. It seems that covenant theologians of the 1600s–1800s were stronger on the issue of corporate Israel in God's plans than most covenant theologians of today.

Gerald McDermott offers a challenge to Covenant Theology on this issue of Israel that is worth considering. He states, "Pastors who preach covenant theology need to think through the meaning of Israel.... If God will keep his promise to redeem our bodies and the whole earth, what about his promise to keep special the land of Israel? And what about the portrayals of the renewed world in Isaiah 2 and elsewhere that picture Israel at the center of the renewed earth?"[70]

On the issues of resurrection of the body and a tangible earth in eternity, Covenant Theology espouses new creationist elements. But, overall, Covenant Theology is a mix between the Spiritual Vision and New Creation models, with too many Spiritual Vision Model elements. While making contributions in the area of individual redemption in Christ, other systems are more comprehensive and helpful when it comes to God's broader creation, kingdom, and covenant purposes.

---

69   VanGemeren, "Systems of Continuity," 61.

70   McDermott, *Israel Matters*, 115–16.

26

PROGRESSIVE
COVENANTALISM
AND THE MODELS

◆

Progressive Covenantalism is a new theological system but appears to be growing in influence. This system was introduced in 2012 with the book, *Kingdom Through Covenant: A Biblical-Theological Understanding of the Covenants*, written by Peter J. Gentry and Stephen J. Wellum. A second edition of this book came out in 2018. *Progressive Covenantalism: Charting a Course between Dispensational and Covenantal Theologies*, was published in 2016. A presentation and defense of Progressive Covenantalism also occurs in Stephen Wellum's chapter, "Progressive Covenantalism," in the 2022 debate book, *Covenantal and Dispensational Theologies: Four Views on the Continuity of Scripture*. Wellum's chapter here is helpful since it offers a 37-page summary of Progressive Covenantalism in a book that also addresses Covenant Theology and Dispensationalism.

Progressive Covenantalism focuses on the biblical covenants and Jesus' role in fulfilling them for understanding the Bible's storyline. With *Kingdom Through Covenant*, Wellum and Gentry strive to accurately put together the biblical covenants.[1] They believe covenant theologians and dispensationalists offer understandings of the covenants that "are not quite

---

1   Peter J. Gentry and Stephen J. Wellum, *Kingdom through Covenant: A Biblical-Theological Understanding of the Covenants* (Wheaton, IL: Crossway, 2012), 23.

right"[2] and "go awry at a number of points."[3] Covenant theologians are wrong for believing the Abrahamic Covenant is linked with infant baptism. And dispensationalists err in claiming the Abrahamic Covenant still means a coming literal fulfillment of land promises for national Israel.

For progressive covenantalists, the biblical covenants are "the backbone to Scripture's entire storyline...."[4] The canonical narrative of Scripture is structured by the following covenants—Creation, Noahic, Abrahamic, Mosaic, Davidic, and New. While the Davidic Covenant is the culmination of the Old Testament covenants, the New Covenant with Jesus is the "fulfillment" and "terminus" of God's one redemptive plan for His people.[5] So Christians are not under the previous covenants, as Wellum claims:

> The previous covenants are forever part of Scripture, which is for our instruction and growth (2 Tim 3:16–17). Yet now that Christ has come, Christians are no longer under the previous covenants as *covenants* (other than the creation and Noahic until the consummation).[6]

With Progressive Covenantalism, the covenants of the Old Testament predicted much concerning Israel and Israel's land, but a literal fulfillment of these should not be expected. The covenants are fulfilled in Jesus so a literal fulfillment of Old Testament promises will not occur.

Types and typology are important for Progressive Covenantalism. In doing a word search in the book *Progressive Covenantalism*, we found terms related to "typology" or "typological" appearing 155 times. This highlights the heavy emphasis of typology in this system. Typology, for Progressive Covenantalism, is key for how the canonical narrative unfolds from promise to fulfillment.[7] Jesus and the New Covenant bring antitypical

---

2   Ibid.

3   Ibid., 37.

4   Stephen Wellum, "Progressive Covenantalism," in *Covenantal and Dispensational Theologies*, 75.

5   Ibid.

6   Ibid., 87.

7   Craig A. Blaising, "A Critique of Gentry and Wellum's, *Kingdom Through Covenant*: A Hermeneutical-Theological Response," *Master's Seminary Journal* 26.1 (Spring 2015): 115.

fulfillment of the previous covenants.[8] National and land promises are fulfilled antitypically. Thus, one should not expect a literal fulfillment of covenant promises concerning national Israel and Israel's land. Gentry and Wellum state:

> Christ, then, as the antitype of Israel, receives the land promise and fulfills it by his inauguration of a new covenant which is organically linked to the new creation.[9]

> ...we argue that the "land" functions as a type/pattern in the Old Testament context.[10]

> In other words, "land," when placed within the biblical covenants and viewed diachronically, was intended by God to function as a "type" or "pattern" of something greater, i.e. creation, which is precisely how it is understood in light of the coming of Christ and the inauguration of the new covenant.[11]

> In the New Testament, it is our contention that the land promise does not find its fulfilment in the future in terms of a specific piece of real estate given to the ethnic nation of Israel; rather it is fulfilled in Jesus, who is the true Israel and the last Adam, who by his triumphant work wins for us the new creation. That new creation has 'already' arrived in the dawning of the new covenant in individual Christians (2 Cor 5:17; Eph 2:8–10) and the church (Eph 2:11–21) and it will be consummated when Christ returns and ushers in the new creation in its fullness (Revelation 21–22).[12]

In the book, *Progressive Covenantalism*, Oren Martin summarizes the idea that the land is fulfilled in Christ: "First, the land is viewed as a type that

---

8   See Wellum, "Progressive Covenantalism," 84.

9   Gentry and Wellum, *Kingdom Through Covenant*, 122.

10   Ibid., 707.

11   Ibid., 706.

12   Ibid., 607.

reaches its antitypical fulfillment first in Christ who inaugurates a new age, second in believers as God's new covenant people (2 Cor 5:17), and finally in the consummated new creation (Revelation 21–22)."[13]

So Progressive Covenantalism relies heavily upon alleged typological connections. Israel and Israel's land supposedly are types that are fulfilled with Jesus and the New Covenant in a way that makes literal fulfillment of these areas unnecessary. Predictions about Israel and Israel's land should not be taken literally once Jesus arrives. Progressive Covenantalism criticizes Dispensationalism's belief in a literal fulfillment of land promises to Israel:

> In the case of dispensational theology, if they viewed as typological both the land of Israel and the nation itself, then their view, at its core, would no longer be valid. Why? For the reason that the land promise would not require a future, "literal" fulfillment in the millennial age; the land itself is a type and pattern of Eden and thus the entire creation, which reaches its fulfillment in the dawning of a new creation. Christ, then, as the antitype of Israel, receives the land promise and fulfills it by his inauguration of a new covenant which is organically linked to the new creation.[14]

So, for Progressive Covenantalism, accurately grasping the Bible's storyline does not include belief in the literal fulfillment of Old Testament passages about Israel and the land; the answer is found with antitypical fulfillments linked with Jesus and the New Covenant.

Like Covenant Theology, Progressive Covenantalism appeals to fulfillment in Jesus to argue that literal fulfillment of promises to national Israel will not happen. Brent Parker states, "Jesus is the 'true Israel' in

---

13   Oren R. Martin, "The Land Promise Biblically and Theologically Understood," in *Progressive Covenantalism*, eds. Stephen J. Wellum and Brent E. Parker (Nashville, TN: B&H Academic, 2016), 273. Also, "Within the OT itself the land functions as a type of something greater that would recapture God's original design for creation" (268). In addition, "Matthew interprets the eschatological land promises through the lens of the many typological and universalized texts in the OT (Matt 5:5)" (269).

14   Gentry and Wellum, 122.

that he typologically fulfills all that the nation of Israel anticipated and hoped for."[15] Wellum claims, "Jesus is the antitypical fulfillment of Israel and Adam, and in him, *all* of God's promises are fulfilled for his people, including the land promise realized in the new creation (Rom. 4:13; Eph 6:3 ....)"[16]

With belief in typological interpretation and antitypical fulfillments in Christ, Progressive Covenantalism presents strong discontinuity between Old Testament expectations and New Testament fulfillments. This involves "massive change" in the Bible's storyline from Old to New. Wellum and Gentry claim that "precisely because Jesus has fulfilled the Old Testament, there is also *massive change or discontinuity* from what has preceded, which entails that in Christ an incredible epochal shift in redemptive-history has occurred."[17] Also, because of Christ and the New Covenant, "many of the themes that were basic to the Old Testament have now been transposed and transformed."[18] Note the striking discontinuity language concerning the two testaments that they offer:

+ "massive change"
+ "discontinuity"
+ "transposed"
+ "transformed"
+ "incredible epochal shift"

They also quote another author favorably who says, "Eschatology is thereby transformed."[19] Thus, Progressive Covenantalism presents a strong discontinuity approach to the Bible's storyline. The story of the Old is not the same you find in the New, at least not in a literal sense.

Putting it together, Progressive Covenantalism asserts the following: the biblical covenants are the backbone of Scripture. The covenants of the

---

15   Brent E. Parker, "The Israel-Christ-Church Relationship," in *Progressive Covenantalism*, 44–45.

16   Wellum, "Progressive Covenantalism," 76.

17   Gentry and Wellum, *Kingdom Through Covenant*, 598. Emphases added.

18   Ibid.

19   Ibid.

Old Testament offer promises concerning Israel and Israel's land, but these should be understood typologically, not literally. With the interpretive lens of the New Testament and arrival of Christ and the New Covenant, prophecies concerning Israel and the land are fulfilled antitypically, not literally. There will be no literal fulfillment of promises concerning national Israel and Israel's land. Fulfillment comes in the true Israel, Christ, and by extension all who are in Christ—whether Jew or Gentile. Jesus is the true Israel thus Israel now refers to all in Jesus, regardless of ethnicity. This has implications for this age and the coming new earth. In the end, land promises do not find fulfillment with Israel in the land of Israel, but in Jesus now and eventually the new earth. Matthew 5:5 and Romans 4:13 are offered as support for universalization of land promises to Israel in the Old Testament.

ANALYSIS OF PROGRESSIVE COVENANTALISM

Our analysis of Progressive Covenantalism does not concern the entire system but how it intersects with the New Creation and Spiritual Vision models.

Progressive Covenantalism has New Creation Model elements. It affirms resurrection of the body for both Jesus now and believers in the future. Adherents of this view believe Jesus' bodily resurrection is one way in which physical realities of God's purposes apply to this age. Also, progressive covenantalists affirm God is "Creator and triune Lord" who "is the king of the universe."[20] They rightly assert that the Noahic Covenant shows God's commitment to His creation.[21] Also, while their treatment of the Eternal State is scant, Progressive Covenantalists appear to affirm a coming tangible new earth.

Yet Progressive Covenantalism contains several Spiritual Vision Model elements. First, Progressive Covenantalism primarily is a

---

20   Wellum, "Progressive Covenantalism," 88.

21   Ibid., 91

soteriological (i.e. salvation) system. As Wellum begins his presentation in the chapter, "Progressive Covenantalism," he starts with human redemption: "Progressive covenantalism argues that the Bible presents a *plurality* of covenants that *progressively* reveal our triune God's *one* redemptive plan for his *one* people, which reach their fulfillment, *telos*, and terminus in Christ and the new covenant."[22] This is then linked with "how we are to live as God's new covenant people."[23] Thus, this view primarily concerns how the covenants reveal God's one redemptive plan for His one people and what this means for Christian living now. The rest of his chapter does not discuss the restoration of other aspects of creation or the nature of Jesus' messianic/millennial kingdom. The emphasis is on human redemption and its relationship to Christ and the New Covenant in this age. So like Covenant Theology, Progressive Covenantalism focuses mostly on human redemption.

Second, Progressive Covenantalism claims there is "massive change" between Old Testament expectations and New Testament fulfillments. But a massive discontinuity approach is consistent with the Spiritual Vision Model since it removes the significance of key tangible realities in the Bible such as national Israel, land promises, and geo-political nations. However, if such storyline change were really occurring, we probably would see explicit statements in the Bible about it. Yet we do not. As Blaising states, "It is reasonable to assume that if there were to be any change in God's plan, it would be revealed verbally by explicit divine declaration, in like manner as the plan was originally revealed."[24]

Third, Progressive Covenantalism departs from the New Creation Model by emphasizing universal blessings to the negation of particular blessings. This system opts for an either/or approach when a both/and is best. Both particulars and universals work together with the former contributing to the latter. We do not have to choose between the significance

---

22   Ibid., 75.

23   Ibid.

24   Blaising, "A Critique of Gentry and Wellum's, *Kingdom Through Covenant*: A Hermeneutical-Theological Response," 116.

of the particular of Israel and the universal of all nations. We embrace both. Particular promises to Israel include Israel but this leads to the blessing of Gentiles and Gentile nations (see Gen. 12:2–3). Also, the particulars of Israel and the land are part of the means for blessing all nations in their lands. Blaising points out the logical fallacy of progressive covenantalists when they do not include the *particular* in their storyline:

> This argument suffers from a logical fallacy that often appears in Covenantal readings of the story of the Bible. The whole, the universal (in this case, the new creation) replaces the part, the particular (the land promised to Israel). Accordingly, our authors say that the biblical narrative moves from a particular land to the whole of the new earth. While it is certainly true that the narrative moves from an expressed plan for the entire creation to God's specific dealings with Israel in OT narrative and then to gospel proclamation to all nations with a culminating vision of a new creation (also predicted by the prophets of Israel), our authors draw the conclusion that the land of Israel somehow disappears and is replaced by the eschatological reality of the new earth.[25]

We also do not believe the Scripture texts used by progressive covenantalists to emphasize the universal over the particular support their claim. Jesus' statement in Matthew 5:5, that the gentle will inherit the "earth" or "land," does not imply that particular land promises to Israel will not happen or have been universalized to the whole earth to the exclusion of Israel.[26] Israel can experience the fulfillment of land promises in a

---

25   Ibid., 123. Blaising also says, "However, in this movement from the part to the whole, unless the so-called "whole" is a completely different reality (which our authors want to deny) the statement is nonsense. A whole logically includes all of its parts. If a part is removed from a whole, then it is a different "whole" from what it was before. Such a new whole does not replace a part in the old whole, rather, it replaces the whole. However, if the new whole is the old whole renewed, then all the parts of the old whole would be renewed as well. The particular part must be in the whole, renewed along with all the other parts, for the whole to be the whole that it is." Ibid. Emphases in original.

26   For an excellent treatment on how Matthew 5:5 does not negate the particular land promise to national Israel see Nelson Hsieh, "Matthew 5:5 and the Old Testament Land Promises: An Inheritance of the Earth or the Land of Israel?" *Master's Seminary Journal* 28.1 (2017): 41–75.

coming kingdom, while other nations are blessed in their lands (see Isaiah 19:16–25). The claim that inheriting the earth or land must mean that land promises to Israel no longer apply is difficult to accept.

Romans 4:13 teaches that Abraham is heir of the world in the sense of being the father of believing people groups—both believing Jews and believing Gentiles (see Rom. 4:10–12). This text is not addressing land or the earth. A statement that Abraham is the father of all ethnicities who believe in Christ does not imply that land promises to Israel no longer will be fulfilled. One must have a strong bias to see this implication because it does not seem clear or obvious from the context of Romans 4. As David Rudolph states, "Transference theology proponents often consider Romans 4:13 to be the clearest statement in Paul's writings that the particularity of the land promise was voided after the coming of Christ. The case for this, however, is surprisingly weak."[27]

Hebrews 11:10 teaches that Abraham was looking for a permanent city that he did not experience yet, but someday will. This, too, does not universalize Israel's land promise. Matthew 2:15 reveals that Jesus is linked with Israel, but this does not mean that national Israel's significance has been absorbed into Jesus so that the nation no longer has theological significance. Jesus' identity as the true and ultimate Israelite means the restoration of national Israel will occur. So too will Gentile blessings, as Isaiah 49:1–6 reveals.

In their attempt to remove the significance of particulars concerning Israel and Israel's land, progressive covenantalists infer significances from certain Bible texts that are not accurate. Since they do not have explicit or implicit support from the Bible, their view does not hold up well.

Fourth, the attempt to establish the Bible's storyline from typological connections does not work. Yes, types and typological connections exist. But these support the Bible's storyline as revealed in explicit statements of Scripture. Types do not change the Bible's narrative, as Blaising notes:

---

27   David Rudolph, "Zionism in Pauline Literature," in *The New Christian Zionism*, 171.

The critic is right to be suspicious of a claim like this (that types are the means of establishing the divine plan) when the claim is employed to contravene, suppress, or subvert the meaning of explicit covenant promise, and even more so when the NT explicitly repeats and reaffirms the same promise as declared in the covenants of the OT.[28]

Fifth, Progressive Covenantalism departs from the New Creation Model by using the concept of fulfillment in Jesus to propose nonliteral fulfillments of Old Testament promises. But this is not the real meaning of what fulfillment in Jesus means. In Matthew 5:17–18 Jesus links fulfillment of everything in the Old Testament ("Law" and "Prophets") with everything being "accomplished." The correct view of "fulfillment in Jesus" is that Jesus literally fulfills messianic prophecies about himself in detail, and He is the *means* for the literal fulfillment of everything else the Bible promises. This includes predictions and promises about Israel, nations, the Day of the Lord, land, and events in the kingdom of God.

But with Progressive Covenantalism, "fulfillment" in Jesus means that details of Israel and Israel's land promises subsume or morph into Jesus in a mystical manner. Blaising likens this approach to "a vague mysticism" and "a variant of metaphysical Personalism":

> KTC [*Kingdom Through Covenant*], at times, reads the Person of Christ as Himself the mystical consummation of the whole narrative. He personally is the fulfillment of Israel, the land, the nation, the church, the creation. The result is a vague mysticism that looks somewhat like a variant of metaphysical Personalism.[29]

Jesus is central to God's plans, but Jesus does not evaporate specific predictions concerning geographical locations or entities that are not Him. He is the *means* for the fulfillment of God's promises, not the source for the dissolving of the promises even if one calls this "fulfillment." Saucy says

---

28   Blaising, 117.

29   Ibid., 124.

the idea that Israel's land promises are fulfilled in Jesus confuses *Jesus as a person* with *land as a place* where human beings live:

> [T]he idea that the land promise is fulfilled in the person of Christ seems to deny the physical, material nature of the human being. To be sure, all true worship is in Christ, in whom we live, and we can worship him in any place. But as bodied entities, we do worship him in a place. If, as is acknowledged ... the new creation is an actual space where we worship God, then it is surely possible to see Israel restored to the land, and an actual Jerusalem with a temple where peoples come to worship, as the prophecies portray.[30]

Blaising points out that "in Him" in the New Testament can mean "through Him" in the sense that Jesus is the means through which literal fulfillment happens:

> KTC [*Kingdom Through Covenant*] does say that the narrative of Scripture converges on Jesus Christ. He is the central focus of the divine plan. All the covenant promises find their fulfillment in and through Him. Our authors particularly emphasize the fulfillment of promise "in Him." Actually, "in Him" is a thick concept in Scripture that includes "through Him." It includes multiple aspects of the relationship of Christ to the redeemed creation. However, KTC tends to read "in Him" in a reductive, mystical manner rather than in the thick, holistic, political, material, and spiritual interconnectivity that Scripture ascribes to the kingdom of God, the inheritance of Christ.[31]

Blaising also is concerned that Progressive Covenantalism diminishes Christ by dissolving creation realities into Jesus' person:

---

30   Robert L. Saucy, "Response by Robert L. Saucy," in *Perspectives on Israel and the Church*, ed. Chad O. Brand (Nashville, TN: B&H Academic, 2015), 295.

31   Blaising, 124.

While this may seem to exalt the Person of Christ, it actually diminishes Him, because it threatens the integrity of the communion of attributes that gives Him a distinguishable identity within and among His creatures while at the same time affirming His divine transcendence and immanence. It diminishes His Person because it deprives Him of the rich, thick inheritance that Scripture predicts for Him, an inheritance that retains the integrity of its created reality as the earth and the heavens, land and lands, people and peoples as individuals and as nations, including Israel and all the Gentiles, all worshipful of Him and in service to Him, not mystically dissolved into the reality of His person.[32]

Sixth, Progressive Covenantalism is vague concerning key elements of the Bible's storyline. Most attention with this system goes to how the biblical covenants relate to human redemption, particularly the New Covenant. But little is stated concerning the coming restoration of earth and its creatures. Not much is said about nations and ethnicities. Little is said about the Day of the Lord and details of Messiah's kingdom. Significantly, we cannot detect a specific understanding of the Millennium with this view, which means no specific view on the nature and timing of Jesus' messianic kingdom. At the time of this writing, Progressive Covenantalism seems to contain a mix of amillennialists and Laddian historic premillennialists. But Progressive Covenantalism does not address the kingdom of God or Millennium in much depth. God is mentioned to be sovereign over the universe and Jesus is said to be currently reigning somehow. Some discussion of "already/not yet" occurs, yet not much detail is offered concerning Jesus' messianic/millennial kingdom. It is hard for a system to be a compelling, comprehensive theological system when there is little discussion on Jesus' kingdom and what this kingdom means beyond the realm of human redemption.

Seventh, Progressive Covenantalism promotes supersessionism. A redefining of Israel occurs with this system. Corporate Israel loses its

---

32   Ibid.

theological significance because it is allegedly fulfilled in Jesus in some mystical way. Some adherents appear to believe in a coming salvation of many Jews because of Romans 11:26, but there is no significance given to corporate, national Israel now or in the future. Concerning Wellum's supersessionist view, Bock aptly notes, "Wellum's approach results in a similar, problematic loss of elements through a supersessionist and covenantal reading that loses Israel as a nation, questions what God says, and suffers from underestimating God's faithfulness."[33] Commenting on Wellum and Gentry's book, *Kingdom through Covenant (KTC)*, Blaising notes how Progressive Covenantalism falls short of New Creation eschatology because of its deficient views on Israel and the land:

> In the past couple of decades, many theologians have come to embrace what I call New Creation eschatology.... KTC says that it affirms this idea of the new creation. However, it fails to draw the logical consequences of this view for its understanding of the land promised to Israel. And that failure raises questions about the conceptual clarity of the new creation in Progressive Covenantalism.[34]

Mark Snoeberger's observations concerning both Covenant Theology and Progressive Covenantalism are accurate in our view. Snoeberger states that focusing only or mostly on human redemption makes a system insufficient: "In the main, both covenant theology and progressive covenantalism view Scripture as a history of redemption." He then offers four reasons concerning why starting with a "redemptive center" is problematic:

> First, it is "insufficiently comprehensive."

> Second it is "functionally narrow (i.e., giving scant treatment to human civil structures, political and legal structures, advances in art, science, agriculture, etc.)."

---

33 Bock, A Progressive Dispensational Response," in *Covenantal and Dispensational Theologies*, 226.

34 Blaising, "A Critique of Gentry and Wellum's, *Kingdom Through Covenant*: A Hermeneutical-Theological Response," 122.

Third, it is "uncomfortably anthropocentric (homing in on benefits that accrue overwhelmingly to humanity)."

And fourth, such an approach is "relatively ambivalent toward eschatological concerns that make up a substantial portion of the biblical canon."[35]

In sum, while affirming important elements of a New Creation Model, Progressive Covenantalism falls short of this model in significant ways. Progressive Covenantalism, therefore, is not a consistent New Creation Model system.

---

35   Mark Snoeberger, "Traditional Dispensationalism," in *Covenantal and Dispensational Theologies: Four Views on the Continuity of Scripture*, 164.

27

NEW CHRISTIAN
ZIONISM AND
THE MODELS

◆

New Christian Zionism is a relatively recent addition to the theological community. At the forefront of this perspective is Gerald R. McDermott and the book he edited, *The New Christian Zionism: Fresh Perspectives on Israel and the Land*.[1] McDermott has also written, *Israel Matters: Why Christians Must Think Differently about the People and the Land*.[2] As a former supersessionist by his own admission, McDermott admits he once believed the church was the new Israel that superseded Old Testament Israel. He also thought that Jew-Gentile unity in Christ meant corporate Israel was not theologically significant anymore.[3] But as he further investigated these issues he came across "some startling discoveries."[4] "One of the first was that the New Testament never calls the Church the New Israel," he says.[5] Another was that Israel currently is beloved by

---

1   Gerald R. McDermott, *The New Christian Zionism: Fresh Perspectives on Israel and the Land* (Downers Grove, IL: InterVarsity Press, 2016).

2   Gerald R. McDermott, *Israel Matters: Why Christians Must Think Differently about the People and the Land* (Grand Rapids: Brazos Press, 2017).

3   See *Israel Matters*, ix–xvii.

4   Ibid., xii.

5   Ibid.

God and that passages like Matthew 19:28 and Acts 3:21 teach a future for Israel.[6]

With *The New Christian Zionism*, McDermott and other contributors are disturbed by the traditional Christian paradigm that omits Israel and Israel's land from the Bible's storyline. They argue that Israel and Israel's land are strategic to the Bible's narrative. This includes Israel both in the present and in the future. Concerning the purpose of their book, McDermott says:

> The burden of these chapters is to show *theologically* that the people of Israel *continue* to be significant for the history of redemption and that the land of Israel, which is at the heart of the covenantal promises, *continues* to be important to God's providential purposes.[7]

For the New Christian Zionism, the gospel involves more than just individual human salvation. It also includes what God is doing in history, including Israel's history. McDermott says, "the gospel means getting connected to Israel's history, not getting away from it."[8] This is in contrast to supersessionism which "suggests that Israel has been left behind."[9]

Yet this approach does not focus only on the significance of Israel. Israel is important but the story does not stop there. Israel is a particular that leads to the blessing of the universal. McDermott states, "God is on a mission to redeem the world (the universal) through Israel (the particular). It is not a matter of *either* the particular *or* the universal, but the universal *through* the particular."[10]

McDermott notes that New Christian Zionism is not Dispensationalism, and it does not identify with the theological nuances of Dispensationalism. Also, it does not like Dispensationalism's emphasis on discerning end-times events. Yet, New Christian Zionism's belief in the

---

6   See Ibid., xiii–xiv.

7   McDermott, "Introduction," *The New Christian Zionism*, 13. Emphases in original.

8   McDermott, "A History of Supersessionism," in *The New Christian Zionism*, 35.

9   Ibid.

10   McDermott, *Israel Matters*, 47.

theological significance of corporate Israel both now and in the future is similar to Dispensationalism. McDermott's book includes the writings of two progressive dispensationalists, Craig Blaising and Darrell Bock. Thus, the ideas of New Christian Zionism are largely consistent with Progressive Dispensationalism.

Since New Christian Zionism is recent it is difficult to give a full evaluation of it. Also, New Christian Zionism does not cover as many issues as Dispensationalism, Covenant Theology, and Progressive Covenantalism. Its focus mostly is on the significance of corporate Israel in God's plans, a coming future earthly kingdom of Jesus the Messiah, and a proper hermeneutic for understanding the Bible's storyline. Concerning hermeneutics, this perspective offers a robust defense for understanding Old Testament prophecies and the book of Revelation literally.

In addition, New Christian Zionism affirms the significance of nations and the nation Israel. This can be seen with the following statement by McDermott:

> They [theologians] should recall that Ezekiel's vision of dry bones coming to life is a vision not of individuals but of a whole nation coming back to life. Both the prophets and the book of Revelation speak of the nations in the world to come, not simply a swarm of undifferentiated individuals. And at the center of the nations in the world is the nation Israel. Theologians need to come to terms with that.[11]

The authors also assert that Jesus' kingdom involves earth. Concerning the kingdom Jesus preached, McDermott notes, "But what if that kingdom was not simply hidden in the hearts of men and women but was also envisioned by Jesus to be an earthly reality in the future, with territorial Israel at its center?"[12] This mention of "earthly reality" and "territorial Israel" reveals strong New Creation Model elements.

---

11   McDermott, "Implications and Propositions," in *The New Christian Zionism*, 325–36.
12   Ibid., 320.

In sum, the New Christian Zionism offers a robust contextual, literal hermeneutic that is nonsupersessionist and affirms the literal fulfillment of Old Testament prophecies. While not explicitly mentioning the New Creation and Spiritual Vision models, the following statement reveals a new creation understanding:

> In short, the New Christian Zionism hopes to alert scholars and other Christians to beware of the geographical-docetic temptation that anti-Zionism proffers. Supersessionist anti-Zionism proposes theology divorced from embodiment and physicality—a people without a land, a Jesus without his people and land and tradition, and the early church living, as it were, suspended in air above the Palestinian ground.[13]

In his chapter on "Biblical Hermeneutics," in *The New Christian Zionism*, Craig Blaising presents a new creationist hermeneutic and refutes hermeneutical beliefs often associated with a Spiritual Vision approach. He addresses "four key lines" of textual material that are often used by supersessionists to support their idea of a reality shift in the Bible's story-line: (1) "fulfillment" declarations in Matthew; (2) the "spiritual language" of John; (3) typology in Hebrews; and (4) Paul's universalism (as opposed to particularity involving Israel).[14] He then shows that these areas are misunderstood by supersessionists.

Addressing the common structural supersessionism that often leads to missing the significance of Israel in the Bible's storyline, McDermott argues that a proper understanding of Israel should lead to a reexamination of texts often missed or ignored:

> Once translators and readers of the Bible are convinced that Israel is not merely past but also present and future, they might see things in the biblical text that were always there but they somehow missed.

---

13   McDermott, "Introduction," in *The New Christian Zionism*, 29.

14   Craig Blaising, "Biblical Hermeneutics," in *The New Christian Zionism*, 83.

For example, they might be newly struck by the intimate connection between Jewish history and its land.[15]

EVALUATION OF NEW CHRISTIAN ZIONISM

New Christian Zionism affirms a new creationist approach to the Bible's storyline. It seriously seeks the Old Testament and Revelation for information on the Bible's storyline without spiritualizing them. And it affirms a future earthly kingdom of the Messiah, the significance of national Israel, and the presence of nations in an earthly kingdom. It also accurately asserts that God uses particulars to bless the universal in a way that does not make the particular disappear in significance. God uses Israel and Israel's land to bless all nations in their lands. New Christian Zionism also rejects Platonism and Augustinianism; and in doing so, refutes a Spiritual Vision Model hermeneutic.

New Christian Zionism also shows that belief in the significance of national Israel is not just for Dispensationalism. This approach is recent, but we look forward to more contributions from its scholars.

---

15 McDermott, "Implications and Propositions," in *The New Christian Zionism*, 321.

28

SUMMARY THOUGHTS ON MILLENNIAL VIEWS AND THEOLOGICAL SYSTEMS

◆

We have examined how various theological systems and millennial views relate to the New Creation and Spiritual Vision models. Here we want to succinctly categorize our findings. This involves which views are consistent with the New Creation Model, which are a mix of the two models, and which are mostly in line with the Spiritual Vision Model.

NEW CREATION MODEL SYSTEMS

The perspectives most consistent with the New Creation Model are Progressive Dispensationalism, Revised Dispensationalism, Non-Laddian Historic Premillennialism, and the New Christian Zionism. These systems address more than individual human salvation and they affirm a holistic restoration of all things. They assert the importance of earth, earth's creatures, land, physical blessings, national Israel, nations, ethnicities, etc. These perspectives seriously consider the Hebrew Scriptures in their own right, including Old Testament prophetic sections and the Book of Revelation. They also strongly reject supersessionism and affirm the significance of national Israel in God's purposes. They also avoid the error of spiritualizing or typologizing tangible and national entities that were not meant to be spiritualized.

Of the three main evangelical theological systems—Covenant Theology, Dispensationalism, and Progressive Covenantalism— Dispensationalism is most consistent with New Creationism, especially Revised and Progressive Dispensationalism. Interestingly, Classical Dispensationalism does not qualify as a consistent New Creation Model system since it contains too many Spiritual Vision Model elements. Its belief that Old Testament saints and the church are a heavenly people with a forever heavenly destiny apart from earth coincides with a Spiritual Vision approach. Plus, its use of a typological hermeneutic in addition to a grammatical-historical hermeneutic is more in line with the Spiritual Vision Model.

Non-Laddian Historic Premillennialism such as found with J. C. Ryle, Charles Spurgeon, and more recently, Barry Horner, is much in line with the New Creation Model. This view affirms a future earthly kingdom of Jesus, a future for national Israel, and a role for geo-political nations in the future. New Christian Zionism also affirms these beliefs as well.

A MIX OF THE MODELS

COVENANT THEOLOGY

Covenant Theology is difficult to categorize on a Spiritual Vision Model– New Creation Model scale since it is mostly a salvation of the elect system. It focuses on human soteriology and not cosmic eschatology or the holistic dimensions of the kingdom and biblical covenants. The three main covenants of Covenant Theology—Redemption, Works, and Grace—drive the discussion to individual salvation issues. These covenants are also used by covenant theologians to make the biblical covenants only or mostly about spiritual redemption. The multiple dimensions of the biblical covenants are often missed.

Covenant theologians also have different views on matters such as the Millennium, Israel, and how to understand prophetic Bible passages. Covenantalists can be amillennialists, postmillennialists, or premillennialists, although the majority are amillennialists. Traditional amillennial covenant theologians would be least in line with the New Creation Model.

Postmillennial covenantalists would be more so than amillennial covenantalists. But both are less new creationist than premillennial covenantalists. Covenantal premillennialists like Bonar and Ryle were considerably
more new creationist in their thinking than other covenantalists since they
held to a future coming reign of Jesus over the earth and the future significance of corporate, national Israel in God's plans. Plus, they understood
Old Testament prophecies literally.

Also, covenantalists have held differing views on national Israel
throughout the last few centuries. Most covenantalists of the last century
have promoted supersessionism concerning Israel and the church. But
a significant number of covenantalists of the seventeenth through nineteenth centuries expressed belief in the significance of national Israel in
God's plans. While most recent covenantalists are supersessionists some
earlier covenantalists were not. Thus, one cannot say Covenant Theology is
inherently supersessionist. However, many of its adherents have expressed
a supersessionist view, and a supersessionist view is common today.

Many covenantalists view Old Testament eschatological issues
involving Israel and land as types and shadows. And many believe the
Old Testament has been transcended or redefined by the New Testament.
So, Covenant Theology of today has several beliefs consistent with the
Spiritual Vision Model. Yet, covenant theologians believe in resurrection
of the body and often assert belief in a future tangible new earth. These
are New Creation Model ideas. But overall Covenant Theology is a mix
between the two models and contains too many Spiritual Vision Model
elements to be a helpful, comprehensive system for understanding God's
big-picture purposes. Its theological lane is individual redemption in Jesus,
a very important area. But Covenant Theology does not contribute much
to a big-picture understanding of God's purposes in history.

PROGRESSIVE COVENANTALISM

Progressive Covenantalism contains both New Creation and Spiritual
Vision Model elements. It affirms a tangible new earth in the future. It
also teaches resurrection of the body. These are consistent with the New
Creation Model. But like Covenant Theology, Progressive Covenantalism

mostly is a soteriology or salvation of the elect system. It focuses on redemption of the elect through the New Covenant. At times it mentions that the covenants are related to "all creation" but little is said concerning the restoration of all creation or the physical dimensions of the covenants. The focus of the covenants with Progressive Covenantalism goes almost exclusively to salvation from sin and spiritual blessings.

In addition, Progressive Covenantalism's use of typology to redefine Old Testament expectations about Israel and Israel's land also is consistent with the Spiritual Vision Model. This system does not let explicit statements in the Bible determine the Bible's storyline; instead, it looks to alleged typological connections that are questionable or in error. Its emphasis on transformation of strategic Old Testament entities leads to storyline change. Progressive Covenantalism, therefore, holds elements of the New Creation and Spiritual Vision models.

NEW EARTH AMILLENNIALISM

What about Amillennialism and the models? The answer to this question is complex and depends on which form of Amillennialism is being discussed. The newer version of Amillennialism—New Earth Amillennialism—contains real New Creation Model elements. It takes a more literal approach to Old Testament prophecies and expects some literal fulfillment of these on a tangible new earth in the Eternal State. For instance, Hoekema's assertion that there will be real culture and work in the Eternal State is commendable and consistent with the New Creation Model.

Unfortunately, though, New Earth Amillennialism, like Traditional Amillennialism, still misses the tangible and holistic nature of Jesus' messianic/millennial kingdom. It insists that Jesus' millennial/messianic kingdom is a spiritual kingdom only that does not involve tangible entities and a rule over the earth and geo-political nations. Thus, New Earth Amillennialism misses a major part of the Bible's storyline—the truth that Jesus' kingdom includes but is more than spiritual salvation from sin. Jesus' kingdom involves a holistic and tangible restoration of all aspects of creation, including society and culture, and a rule over the earth and nations. In short, New Earth Amillennialism misses the truth that the messianic/

millennial kingdom of Jesus before the Eternal State is the fulfillment of the mediatorial kingdom task given to man in Genesis 1. To its credit, New Earth Amillennialism believes many physical promises will be fulfilled in the Eternal State, but it excludes these matters from Jesus' millennial kingdom.

And while holding that some Old Testament prophecies should be interpreted literally, New Earth Amillennialism still also spiritualizes many Old Testament prophecies, especially those concerning Israel and the land of Israel. And it affirms supersessionism by insisting the church in Christ is the new/true Israel and that national Israel no longer is significant in God's purposes. A system cannot be consistently new creationist if it spiritualizes Israel. Thus, in several areas New Earth Amillennialism is not consistent with the New Creation Model. Overall, it is better than Traditional Amillennialism, but it still falls short of the New Creation Model in key areas. But the improvement of New Earth Amillennialism over traditional Augustinian Amillennialism is noteworthy and commendable.

LADDIAN HISTORIC PREMILLENNIALISM

Laddian Historic Premillennialism, too, is a mix between the New Creation and Spiritual Vision models. Premillennialism, by nature, is new creationist since it affirms a coming earthly kingdom of Jesus after His second coming that transforms creation. Laddian Historic Premillennialism also recognizes a tangible new earth in eternity. These two beliefs are significant and place this form of Premillennialism over several other systems.

But there are two key areas where Laddian Historic Premillennialism is inconsistent with New Creationism. First, Ladd holds that the New Testament spiritualizes and reinterprets Old Testament prophecies and spiritual blessings. And second, Ladd spiritualizes Israel to make the church a new spiritual Israel. He sees little place for national Israel in Jesus' coming kingdom. These ideas are more in line with the Spiritual Vision Model.

POSTMILLENNIALISM

Postmillennialism also contains elements of the New Creation and Spiritual Vision models. Consistent with the Spiritual Vision Model it spiritualizes David's throne to be a heavenly throne at God's right hand in this age. The Bible, however, consistently presents David's throne as being centered in Jerusalem and involving a tangible reign over Israel and the nations of the earth (Jer. 17:25). Jesus affirms this in Matthew 19:28–30 by stating that His sitting upon His throne occurs at the time of the renewal of the earth (*paliggenesia*) when the twelve apostles will judge the restored twelve tribes of Israel. When Postmillennialism transfers the Davidic throne to Heaven it makes a Spiritual Vision Model move. Jesus sits at the right hand of God in Heaven where He shares the Father's throne. But this is different from the Davidic throne that Jesus will sit upon after His return (see Matt. 25:31). The Father's throne and Jesus' throne are distinguished by Jesus himself in Revelation 3:21: "He who overcomes, I will grant to him to sit down with Me on My throne, as I also overcame and sat down with My Father on His throne."

And while often affirming a future salvation of the Jewish people, Postmillennialism is supersessionist since it denies the continuing significance of national Israel in God's plans.

Yet Postmillennialism has New Creation Model beliefs. In addition to belief in resurrection of the body, Postmillennialism believes that Jesus' millennial/messianic kingdom transforms all aspects of society and culture, which is a new creationist concept. Along with Premillennialism, it rightly believes Jesus' kingdom involves more than spiritual salvation. His messianic/millennial reign transforms all creation. On this point Postmillennialism is more new creationist than is Amillennialism.

But there are problems for Postmillennialism concerning the Eternal State. Clarity amongst postmillennialists on this topic is elusive and its views on the Eternal State are varied. As we stated earlier, some postmillennialists like Jonathan Edwards promoted a Spiritual Vision Model view of the Eternal State after the Millennium. For Edwards the Eternal State does not take place on a renewed earth. Not all postmillennialists spiritualize the Eternal State like Edwards did, but little has been offered by postmillennialists on the Eternal State. It appears some believe in a literal Eternal State. But others spiritualize the Eternal State of Revelation 21–22, thinking this passage refers figuratively to our present salvation. This spiritualizes the last two chapters of Scripture. So Postmillennialism has more New Creation Model elements than does Amillennialism, but it has less than Premillennialism. Thus, Postmillennialism has elements of the New Creation and Spiritual Vision models.

MOSTLY SPIRITUAL VISION MODEL

Traditional Amillennialism, associated with Augustine, Roman Catholicism, and many Protestants, can be categorized as "mostly Spiritual Vision Model." It affirms resurrection of the body and often affirms a tangible new earth after the Millennium, which is consistent with the New Creation Model. But it asserts that Jesus' millennial/messianic kingdom is only spiritual and sometimes ridicules the idea that Jesus' kingdom could be an earthly kingdom. It also is supersessionist concerning Israel. In addition, Traditional Amillennialism often uses a spiritualizing and typological hermeneutic to redefine and reinterpret tangible realities into spiritual ones. This leads to storyline change from the Old Testament to the New Testament. These are strong Spiritual Vision Model characteristics. In fact, of all the theological views discussed in this book, Traditional Amillennialism is least consistent with the New Creation Model and has the least to offer concerning God's cosmic and eschatological purposes. There simply are too many elements of the Spiritual Vision Model associated with Traditional Amillennialism for it to be a helpful view.

THE TREND

There appears to be good news. As we documented, the millennial views and systems vary on the New Creation Model–Spiritual Vision Model scale. But the systems, overall, seem to be trending in the direction of the New Creation Model and against the Spiritual Vision Model. Steven James observes, "The growing discontent regarding the tendency toward a spiritual vision eschatology throughout history spans across various denominations and ecclesial traditions."[16]

For example, recent New Earth Amillennialism is an improvement over Traditional Amillennialism. And current traditional amillennialists seem to be more clear on a tangible new earth in the Eternal State than were earlier amillennialists. While postmillennialists say little about the Eternal Kingdom, it seems that some postmillennialists affirm a tangible Eternal Kingdom with a new earth, an improvement over the Postmillennialism of Jonathan Edwards and some Puritans. The more recent forms of Dispensationalism—Revised and Progressive—have more new creation elements than did Classical Dispensationalism. As we mentioned earlier, Covenant Theology is difficult to evaluate. Some covenant theologians seem to be adopting more new creationist ideas concerning the new earth in eternity. Yet supersessionism seems to be more prevalent with Covenant Theology of the last century than it was in the seventeenth through the nineteenth centuries.

While not an evangelical system, even Roman Catholicism appears to be trending in the direction of the New Creation Model. In the book, *Four Views on Heaven*, the Roman Catholic, Peter Kreeft, expressed belief in a coming tangible new earth. This is far removed from Thomas Aquinas's version of eternity in which there is an empyrean heaven beyond the physical universe where God's people reside forever.

---

16   James, "Recent New Creation Conceptions and the Christian Mission," 26, n.7.

CONCLUSION:
THE NEW CREATION
MODEL AND THE
WAY FORWARD

◆

With this book we have argued for the New Creation Model over the Spiritual Vision Model as the biblical paradigm for accurately understanding God's purposes. This model is not imposed on Scripture— it arises from an inductive study of all Scripture. It also is not a new theological system but a perspective that allows one to detect all God is doing in history as revealed in the Bible.

The Bible's storyline centers on creation and a restored creation with a mediatorial kingdom reign of man on God's behalf. Jesus, both in His person and work, is central to God's kingdom and covenant purposes. He is the One who brings all of God's purposes to completion. This occurs through His two comings to earth.

The New Creation Model detects God's original intent for mankind to "rule" and "subdue" the earth and all its creatures. It makes an intrinsic link between the creation of Genesis 1–2 and the new creation of Revelation 20–22. Redemption of humans is an important theme, yet this fits with God's big-picture kingdom purposes. Humans are saved to be in relationship with God and reign over the earth in God's presence for His glory. This is true for both Jesus' messianic/millennial kingdom and the Eternal Kingdom when man reigns over the earth in the full presence of God. Revelation 5:10 predicts that God's people will reign on the earth. In the final scene describing the new earth in Scripture, the saints are pictured as being in the presence of God and reigning forever on the new earth (see Rev. 22:1–5). Relationship with God in His presence is coupled with a functional kingdom reign. Such an understanding is broader and more holistic than the common idea that God's purposes only concern human redemption, as important as that is. Human salvation is very strategic in God's plans but it is a means to greater creation and kingdom purposes. Jesus saves people so they can relate and function as God intended for them.

These ideas are at the heart of the New Creation Model. But what should a New Creation Model approach practically mean for Christians and the church going forward? We offer eight suggestions.

First, it means thinking broadly and deeply about all God is doing. We need a big and comprehensive worldview. We need to detect all dimensions of the Gospel and its implications for all creation. Yes, we still teach passionately and often on the importance of individual salvation from sin and living a godly life. The Gospel must be taken to the lost with great intensity and urgency. Yet also we should study God's big-picture purposes. We seek to grasp all that is happening in the Bible. We must connect the theological dots from Genesis 1–2 (creation) through Revelation 20–22 (new creation). This involves grasping the multiple dimensions of God's kingdom and covenant purposes. We must contemplate the significance of nations, ethnicities, societal, and cultural matters. We should pursue God's purposes for the earth, animals, birds, fish, creeping things, trees, water, and the inanimate creation. In addition, the Day of the Lord, the millennial/ messianic kingdom of Jesus, and the Eternal Kingdom also must be deeply considered. These are part of our hope. Understanding God's big-picture purposes better positions us to understand the church's role in this age, and our role in the Grand Story.

And in addition to grasping Jesus' role as Savior, we also anticipate Jesus' role as ruling King over the world and nations. The Christian storyline has five major parts—Creation, Fall, Promise, First Coming realities (salvation), and Second Coming realities (restoration/kingdom). Learn and teach about all five. This results in a better understanding of the Bible's storyline.

Second, the New Creation and Spiritual Vision models should compel us to examine our preunderstandings to make sure they are biblical. Sometimes unbiblical ideas infiltrate Christian thinking. Randy Alcorn rightly noted that Christians often operate from a mixture of Platonism and Christianity—what he calls "Christoplatonism." But we must shed any remnants of Platonism or eastern religions from our worldview. Is there too much Spiritual Vision Model in your thinking? Strive to make sure your perspective on reality and the future are thoroughly biblical.

Third, study eschatology more. This point goes against current thinking today. Some Christians and churches simply write off eschatology and discussions about the future. They pat themselves on the back for never talking about the rapture, or the Day of the Lord, the Millennium, or the future of Israel or nations. But a new creationist approach embraces the serious study of future events. Things to come matter. They are a major part of our hope. And they force us to think beyond the here and now. Not everyone will agree on all details of eschatology, but that should not stop us from studying what the Bible says about the future. A complete biblical worldview involves a coherent understanding of where history is headed. Bible passages about the restoration of all things should be an encouragement and hope to all Christians.

Fourth, New Creationism should lead to studying all Scripture passages. All of the Bible contributes to God's purposes, including Old Testament prophecies and the Book of Revelation. These reveal important information in their own right. They should be taught, not avoided. If you are in a church that never teaches the Old Testament, prophetic books, or Revelation, ask why not? Respectfully request that the whole counsel of God be taught.

Fifth, consistent New Creationism means rejecting supersessionism. Israel is a major part of the Bible's storyline. But the church has a long history of teaching that corporate Israel no longer is significant in God's purposes. As Romans 9–11 shows, a mostly Gentile church can think God has rejected Israel (see Rom. 11:1). Such a view Paul deems "arrogant" (see Rom. 11:18). Supersessionism hinders a proper understanding of what God is doing by removing Israel's role in being used by God to bless the nations. Israel is not the only part of the Story. Nor is it the most important part of the Story. But Israel is a major part of the Bible's storyline and we should strive to understand this important player in God's purposes. Emphasize

Israel as much as the Bible does. No more and no less. New Creationism, therefore, is non-supersessionist. It affirms the theological significance of ethnic/national Israel in God's purposes. This does not mean everyone must agree on everything concerning Israel. But it does mean embracing Israel's significance in God's plans.

Sixth, *a new creationist approach should lead to more writing and research on God's creational/kingdom purposes.* Steven James' book, *New Creation Eschatology and the Land* is helpful.[1] So too is Andrew Kim's work, *The Multinational Kingdom in Isaiah.*[2] These are explicit promotions of God's purposes from a new creationist perspective. James argues that those who hold to a New Creation Model should also recognize the significance of Israel and the land of Israel. Kim discusses the importance of geo-political nations in Isaiah. More works like these that flesh out a consistent New Creation Model should be pursued. I try to offer a biblical theology of the kingdom of God from a New Creation Model perspective with my book, *He Will Reign Forever: A Biblical Theology of the Kingdom of God.*[3] Randy Alcorn's book, *Heaven,* offers much needed information from a new creationist perspective on the nature of eternal life.[4] While differing with our view on Israel, the works by Snyder, Middleton, and Moo mentioned in this work are helpful for understanding God's multi-dimensional purposes.

Seventh, *a new creationist approach means applying the Christian worldview to every area.* It seriously accounts for all aspects of our environment—including the social, cultural, and political realms. Since all aspects of reality matter to God, we should apply a Christian worldview on all areas. This means having a Christian view of life issues relating to abortion and end of life matters. It involves possessing a Christian view

---

1   James, *New Creation Eschatology and the Land.*

2   Andrew H. Kim, *The Multinational Kingdom in Isaiah: A Study of the Eschatological Kingdom and the Nature of its Consummation* (Wipf & Stock, 2020).

3   Published by Lampion. Eugene, OR, 2017.

4   We are not saying Alcorn explicitly uses the title "New Creation Model." Nor are we saying he agrees with everything in our book.

of ethnicities and nations. It means promoting the Christian perspective of marriage and gender. These areas do not have to be surrendered to the secular culture and the political Left.

While the current social and political structures of this world are deeply evil and will not be rooted out and fixed permanently until Jesus returns, we are still called to be salt and light to a decaying and dark world. We can stand for righteousness and truth in all areas. We can resist evil wherever it is found. Churches should teach Christians to espouse and apply a Christian worldview to everything and every area. Christians should be encouraged to influence the society and culture. We need more Christian influence in the realms of education, science, art, music, theater, technology, medicine, agriculture, architecture, etc.

Eighth, let a new creationist understanding encourage your heart. As our world deteriorates, more and more people are in despair. Many are fearful. Addictions and suicides are at astronomical levels. Outside of Jesus there is no hope. But this is not the case for the Jesus-follower. Be encouraged! Jesus said, "In the world you have tribulation. But take courage; I have overcome the world." Yes, like others in the present age, we experience sufferings and sorrows. Our bodies decay. We lose people we love. It seems the longer we live the more we keep saying "Goodbye." Tears are part of this valley we now walk. But there is another side. We grieve but we do not grieve as those who have no hope (see 1 Thess. 4:13). We suffer loss in this age in many ways. But in the end—nothing is lost! Jesus is coming again to bring the restoration of all things (see Acts 3:20–21). God is making all things new (see Rev. 21:5). He will remove every tear and there will be no crying or pain (Rev. 21:3). Jesus promised that with the renewal of the earth, everything we lose will be multiplied back to us—including relationships, farms, and homes (see Matt. 19:28–30). Truly, nothing is lost!

Everything impacted by sin and death will be restored. The many negative, evil, and tragic events and experiences we face and overwhelm us in this fallen world will one day be past. And not only will they be in the past, but they will also be replaced with what is good and beautiful. Cancer will not exist. Heart disease will cease. No more murders. No more car accidents. No wheelchairs. No more children dying young. No more wars.

Funerals and cemeteries will be forever gone! Loved ones lost through death will be reunited. You will be in the presence of your God and Jesus who died for you. You will enjoy relationships with others who love God. And all of this will take place on a beautiful and spectacular new earth—love in the context of beauty. That is our destiny! Live in light of that hope!

The New Creation Model is practical both now and for the future. With it we better understand God's purposes and our relationship to them. We better understand our part in the Grand Story. It draws out the hope the Bible offers. The kingdom of God and the restoration of all things are exciting parts of the Christian worldview. Let us slice through the fog of the Spiritual Vision Model and embrace the glorious hope Scripture reveals. And let us share this hope with others.

APPENDIX

◆

RESPONSE TO CRITICS OF THE
NEW CREATION MODEL

The New Creation Model believes the focus of eternal life is God and being in His presence. This experience takes place on a new earth with social and cultural interactions among the redeemed. With His Beatitudes Jesus declared that the pure in heart will "see God" (Matt. 5:8). And he also stated that the gentle will "inherit the earth" (Matt. 5:5). Thus, seeing God and inheriting the earth are both true.

This model also upholds and affirms the majesty, transcendence, and glory of God who alone is worthy of all worship and honor. And it also gives people "their due as creatures with independent dignity."[1] But not all support the New Creation Model. In his book, *Seeing God: The Beatific Vision in Christian Tradition*, Hans Boersma asserts that a more earthy concept of eternity does violence to the traditional spiritual approach to communion with God. While Randy Alcorn called on Christians to reject "Christoplatonism," the merger between Christianity and Platonism, Allen notes that Boersma argues "for the need to return to a Christian-Platonist synthesis that is more other-worldly."[2]

A sustained argument against New Creationism occurs with Michael Allen's book, *Grounded in Heaven: Recentering Christian Hope and Life on God*. Allen criticizes the New Creation Model which he pejoratively

---

1   McDannell and Lang, *Heaven*, 142. The authors noted that this is what Renaissance theologians and artists tried to do.

2   Michael Allen, *Grounded in Heaven*, 45.

calls "eschatological naturalism."[3] According to Allen, "eschatological naturalism" places God in a secondary role, more as a means to an end or an
instrument for other things:

> By eschatological naturalism, I refer very specifically to a theological
> approach that speaks of God instrumentally as a means or instigator
> of an end but fails to confess substantively that God's identity as our
> one true end (in whom only any other things are to be enjoyed).[4]

Allen thinks this view also is a threat to communion with God:

> We need to be wary, therefore, of unwittingly falling into an eschato-
> logical naturalism that speaks of God instrumentally (as a means to,
> or instigator of, an end) but fails to confess communion with God as
> our one true end (in whom alone any other things are to be enjoyed).[5]

Allen also believes eschatological naturalism involves "a bent toward
the elevation of the earthy, embodied, and material as that of ultimate
significance."[6] He also thinks a new creationist approach makes secondary
matters primary and leads to the primary (God) being removed altogether:

> In the hands of eschatological naturalism, the secondary is elevated
> to the primary position in terms of Christian hope, and that which
> is in fact primary is relegated (at best) to the fringes, if not outright
> dismissed.[7]

For Allen, this leads to a marginalizing of the presence of God:
"Eschatological naturalism marginalizes the presence of God and regularly
maligns the spiritual hope of earlier Christians."[8] This makes God leave the
stage He created: "Eschatological naturalism presents a particular vision

---

3   Theologians that Allen criticizes include Herman Bavinck, Richard Middleton, and N.T. Wright.

4   Allen, 39.

5   Ibid., 23.

6   Ibid., 129.

7   Ibid., 39–40.

8   Ibid., 41.

of God's kingdom, wherein the triune God sovereignly brings about that kingdom but then seemingly slides off stage-right upon its culmination."[9]

For Allen, eschatological naturalism is linked with idolatry: "The danger of idolatry lurks especially in the realm of eschatology."[10] It also results in the eclipse of "heavenly-mindedness, spiritual-mindedness, self-denial, or any of the terminology that has marked the ascetical tradition (in its patristic or, later, in its Reformed iterations)."[11] Importantly, Allen believes a new creationist approach negatively affects Christian living in the present. It neglects heavenly and spiritual things and compromises the need for self-denial.

Allen also claims eschatological naturalism harms communion with God and the traditional Beatific Vision (vision of God). He says, "the neo-Calvinist emphases upon the new creation and the earthiness of our hope can and have morphed at times from being productive Reformed corrections to the catholic faith to being parasitic to the basic lineaments of the Christian gospel."[12] The last part of this statement is striking since Allen believes a new creationist approach is "parasitic" to the "Christian gospel." This takes the stakes to a serious level. Allen also says, "Eschatological naturalism marginalizes the presence of God and regularly maligns the spiritual hope of earlier Christians."[13]

The solution for Allen is a return to heavenly-mindedness and the ascetic ideal found with Augustine, Thomas Aquinas, the Puritans, and some Reformers. Allen states that "The way forward in dogmatic theology should be Augustinian ..."[14] Allen believes Jesus calls us to "a distinctly evangelical asceticism in the tradition of Calvin and the Puritans and their reception of the patristic ascetical tradition."[15] For him, we need a return to

---

9   Ibid., 47.

10   Ibid., 36.

11   Ibid., 9.

12   Ibid., 8-9.

13   Ibid., 41.

14   Ibid., 47.

15   Ibid., 9.

"the systemic significance of ascetical theology and heavenly-mindedness for classical Christian theology."[16] This even includes the traditional catholic understanding of the Beatific Vision: "[W]e will argue for a refinement of the catholic doctrine of the beatific vision and the Christian practice of ascetic self-denial" that comports with reformational principles.[17] Allen praises Roman Catholic theology in the modern era for continuing "to attend to this classical locus." But he criticizes "Modern Protestant divinity" for not doing so.[18]

Allen's argument seems to be: *If we believe eternity involves a new earth in which God's people have social and cultural interactions, we lose our focus on God. We make God secondary and a means to an end. We lose the importance of the ascetic life and spiritual disciplines. And we also forsake and ridicule the traditional Beatific Vision of the late Patristic Era and Middle Ages.*

THOUGHTS ON CRITICISMS OF THE NEW CREATION MODEL

For New Creation Model adherents it is helpful to listen to critics. While Allen is a critic, we appreciate several things in his writings. Allen rightly notes that God is most important, and that created things should never be sought or emphasized more than the Creator. All glory and worship go to God alone. We also affirm the necessity of the Christian disciplines, self-denial, and the willingness to persevere and forsake all for Jesus in this age. Allen also says much good about the nature of God and living the Christian life.

However, Allen's critique of the New Creation Model or what he calls "eschatological naturalism" fails. First, new creationists also affirm the things mentioned above about worshipping God and the need for self-denial and Christian disciplines in this age. Second, Allen infers things

---

16 Ibid., 18–19.

17 Ibid., 19.

18 See Ibid., 61.

about the New Creation Model that are not true or necessary. He assumes the worst about this view without showing how New Creationism leads to the things he is worried about. Third, Allen does not adequately refute the case for the New Creation Model from the Bible. His response is more emotional than biblical.

Allen's perception of the new creationist perspective or what he calls "eschatological naturalism" is flawed. He thinks that holding to a new creationist approach, as expressed by theologians like Kuyper, Bavinck, and Middleton, takes attention away from God. Allegedly, this model focuses more on created things than the Creator. It makes God a means to and end. It forsakes an ascetic lifestyle and the Christian spiritual disciplines. This model is even "parasitic" to the Gospel. But new creationists do not advocate what Allen suggests. Nor does Allen give any evidence that the new creationist view leads to such extremes. He assumes the worst and presents a slippery slope connection. Allegedly, if you believe eternal life involves specific social and cultural interactions then you are not God-centered enough. Even if you state that worship of God is indeed central, Allen does not accept this. But this is a classic case of strawman argumentation and not presenting your theological opponent accurately.

Next, Allen does not sufficiently refute "eschatological naturalism" from Scripture. He cites Bible verses showing that God is light, we will see God's face, and the need for spiritual disciplines. But that is not evidence against the new creationist perspective. New creationists also believe these things. Allen offers no rebuttal to texts used by new creationists to support the New Creation Model. One wonders if Allen is even aware of the arguments new creationists are making. He does not refute new creationist understandings of Bible passages that discuss social and cultural interactions in the coming kingdom of God. Since he is taking on "eschatological naturalism" Allen needed to show that social and cultural interactions on the coming new earth are unbiblical or that new creationists are overstating their case. Texts like Matthew 19:28–30 teach that there will be houses, farms, and relationships in the kingdom. Revelation 21:24, 26 teaches that nations and kings will exist on the new earth, and they will make cultural contributions. Matthew 5:5–8 reveals that seeing God will occur for saints who also "inherit the earth." The inherited earth is the context for seeing God and being in His presence. Do these passages not teach a new creationist understanding of the future?

God does not view social and cultural interactions among His people as a threat to Him or His glory. He determines these to occur and they please Him. As J. Richard Middleton states in response to Allen,

> I simply do not see why we need to diminish human cultural accomplishments in order to emphasize our giving glory to God. Of course, God is glorified in our verbal praise. But in a more fundamental sense, God is glorified by our living out God's normative purposes in the fullness of our embodied lives. Affirming the latter does not contradict or diminish the former, unless we begin with an a priori assumption to that end.[19]

Probably the most significant argument Allen offers concerns lack of marriage in eternity. Allen argues that since marriage and procreation do not exist in eternity then we should be hesitant about being dogmatic on other social and cultural matters in the future. His point is worth considering but does not negate the many Bible passages that speak specifically about the tangible and social nature of eternal life. It is not good logic to state that if God does not want marriage and procreation to exist into eternity future, then we cannot know anything about social and cultural interactions among His people. If God has deemed that marriage and procreation will not continue in the Eternal State, that reality can exist alongside social and cultural interactions among the redeemed.

Allen often appeals to church history for his traditional view of the Beatific Vision. But while relevant, church history is not the main authority—Scripture is. Allen wants to get back to the traditional Beatific Vision views of Augustine, Aquinas, and certain Reformers and Puritans. But he does not offer why these men had a superior understanding. More than sentiment for old understandings must occur. New creationists have offered

---

19   J. Richard Middleton, "Response to Michael Allen," in *Four Views on Heaven*, Michael E. Wittmer, ed. (Grand Rapids: Zondervan, 2022), 147–48.

specific reasons why theologians like Augustine and Aquinas were not accurate in their understandings. In addition, McDannell and Lang have documented that the church has often fluctuated between the Spiritual Vision Model and New Creation Model. The New Creation Model view also has deep roots in church history. What about Irenaeus in the second century who believed that Jesus' millennial kingdom would involve a real earth with social interactions and cultural matters? Irenaeus believed Jesus would reward back and more everything a person loses for Jesus in this age, including houses and farms. He is part of church history as well. Why not criticize Augustine and Aquinas for abandoning what Irenaeus believed? Why should we uncritically accept what Spiritual Vision Model adherents believed? Why not also seek those in the past who were more in agreement with the New Creation Model?

In 2022, Allen's views were further expressed in his chapter, "A Heaven on Earth Perspective," in the book, *Four Views on Heaven*.[20] Here Allen interacted with three other theologians on the topic of Heaven. This included contributions from new creationist, J. Richard Middleton. So it was an opportunity to see a direct exchange between a new creationist (Middleton) and someone critical of New Creationism (Allen).

Allen's statements in this book were more gracious and less emotional than those in his previous book, which was encouraging. And Allen stated belief in a coming renewed earth, although he cautioned against being sure about the specifics of it. We found less to disagree with from Allen in this book. Perhaps as Allen better understood what Middleton was really saying, his concerns were not as great. Also, Allen's beatific vision understanding, as expressed in this book, is much better than Aquinas's. Unlike Aquinas, Allen does not argue that the universe will be vacated and frozen in light as saints exist motionless in another dimension staring into God's light with no movement whatsoever. Allen's approach certainly contains more caution on what the future looks like, and we respect that. But it appears that Allen is closer to the new

---

20   Michael Allen, "A Heaven on Earth Perspective," in *Four Views on Heaven*.

creationist view of eternity then he is to Aquinas and others he holds highly. In sum, Allen is less sure than new creationists on the specific nature of eternal life, but he does affirm a coming new earth with activities beyond just mental contemplation. Allen is content with a generic, non-detailed eschatology, while new creationists are more concerned about the details of the coming new earth.

Belief that eternal life involves a restored earth with cultural and social activities is not a threat to being God-centered, the necessity of spiritual disciplines, and the importance of living humbly in this present evil age. Revelation 21–22 states that God will dwell with His people(s) and they will see His face. This takes place in the context of a new earth, a New Jerusalem, nations, and cultural activities (see Rev. 21:1–2, 24). Such an understanding was not invented by new creationists. It is found in the Bible.

New Creationism also affirms the centrality and glory of God. The triune God of the Bible is central to everything. God is the hero of history. God alone is worthy of worship. Jesus is at the center of God's kingdom purposes. Jesus is the Last Adam (see 1 Cor. 15:45). He is the ultimate seed of Abraham (see Gal. 3:16). He is the ultimate Israelite (see Isa. 49:3–7). He is the ultimate Son of David. He is the One who establishes the New Covenant. Jesus purchased with His blood people from all tribes, languages, peoples, and nations (see Rev. 5:9). Not only are His people saved because of Him, all creation is restored because of Jesus (see Col. 1:20). When all death is destroyed, all disease is wiped out, all creatures are restored, and every tear wiped away, it will be because of Jesus. The best part about the coming kingdom will be seeing God and enjoying His presence. This will include direct worship of our great God. The Creator will always be the main object of our love and focus. As we anticipate this glorious culmination, we must be serious and heavenly minded. We must pray and employ the spiritual disciplines. We must be willing to give up all for Jesus in this age.

Yet in addition to these great truths, God has designed that our eternal home involves a real place for people with resurrected, physical bodies. We will reside on a restored planet earth where we will fellowship with other saved saints and enjoy the beauties of the new creation, including all of its beauty and cultural delights. As we enjoy God's gifts for us, God is glorified. He delights in this. God determines what brings Him the most glory, not what theologians think should be the case.

SUBJECT/AUTHOR INDEX

◆

SCRIPTURE INDEX

◆

413

Made in the USA
Middletown, DE
09 September 2023